THE DELEGATE FOR AFRICA.

David Ivon Jones, 1883-1924

Portrait of David Ivon Jones, hanging at the Welsh National
Library, Aberystwyth

First published in 1995 by
Core Publications
c/o 13 Talbot Av, London N2 OLS

ISBN 897640 02 1

Typeset by voluntary labour
Printed and bound in Great Britain by UTL, London.

The authors wish to thank the following for their assistance:
Gwyn Jenkins, Keeper of Manuscripts, National Library of Wales, and Colin
Thomas, TeliEsyn.
In addition, Baruch Hirson wishes to thank Brian Willan for information on the
location of the Ivon Jones papers and the following for providing or securing
documents in South Africa, or suggesting references: Dave Everatt, Lou
Haysom and Miriam Basner, David Blake, librarian at the Institute of Commonwealth Studies, for obtaining photographs taken during the general
strike of 1922 and Susan Weissman for providing writings by Victor Serge.
Finally to those who read chapters or assisted in the editing and in the final
printing: Paul Flewer, Paul Trewhela and Dave Bruce.

THE DELEGATE
for
AFRICA

David Ivon Jones,
1883-1924

by

Baruch Hirson
&
Gwyn A Williams

Core Publications

London

Foreword

The celebration of the life of David Ivon Jones, the man from Wales who travelled physically and spiritually across the world before landing in Russia in 1921 did not seem extraordinary when this book was first conceived in the mid-80s. This was an account of a man destined to play an important role, first in galvanizing the socialist movement in South Africa and then in Moscow, surprising those who gathered in the newly formed socialist state that replaced the tyrannical Tsarist empire.

Although Ivon Jones had played a major role in transforming the left in South Africa little was known about his background. References to him in books written by members of the Communist Party of South Africa have been brief and vague. His background was unknown (or concealed) to all but a few until the authors of this book read his diary and the letters he wrote to his friend and mentor in Aberystwyth, George Eyre Evans, all carefully kept and donated to the Welsh National Library. These documents reveal a man whose quest for 'truth' led him to break with the Methodist chapels of his kith and kin and adopt the Unitarian faith. His search was over the universal riddle of creation and being and he battled with the solutions that were on offer.

It is not certain that he would have restricted himself to chapel activities, particularly as so many of his friends leaned towards the newly founded Independent Labour Party. But that will never be known because Ivon (or Dai as he was known to his friends) was found to be suffering from tuberculosis, the scourge of Welsh valleys in general and the Jones family in particular. With the financial assistance of GE Evans and others, Ivon embarked in 1907 on a sea voyage to New Zealand at the age of 24. By a strange twist of fate he met two Russians who had been involved in the recent Russian revolution. His absorbtion in the places he saw and the people he met on the longest of all sea voyages were as nothing compared to the fascinating stories he heard from the two men he encountered.

New Zealand was far from Wales in every respect, although here he did meet some Welsh families — including some who were of the same faith — and felt at ease in their company. Without a penny to his name he went to work, fruit picking, rabbiting, or helping in various capacities in stores. It was a physical rather than an intellectual experience until he met with the Iversens. Although Ivon probably contributed more than he received, he appeared to be more alert than elsewhere in those small and closed communities. But still he wrestled with the 'truth' without changing his religious faith. He knew which direction he was to follow when he announced to his friend in far off Wales that he had become a socialist.

This was the second of his momentous changes of direction although he still had much to learn. He was still beholden to Lloyd George as a politician, that man whom the ILPers in Britain detested because he would take socialist policies and convert them into Tory slogans. There was as yet no indication that Ivon Jones's 'conversion' to socialism went beyond a desire for liberal compassion. Important, but hardly a philosophy that would lead to a changed pattern of life, or have an impact on men of similar suasion in South Africa.

Jones was urged to return to Wales but treasured his new-found independence. Nonetheless he felt the need to move on but was uncertain of his destiny. One brother urged him to come to Canada, others invited him to join them in South Africa. It was the latter that won his assent and in 1910 he departed for South Africa. Still very much the Welshman — and he never lost his love for the valleys he knew — he took with him his pro-Boer sympathies. Lloyd George and General Botha were his guiding stars even when, after a short period in the country he joined the all-white Labour Party. The 'truth' had been added to by Lloyd George and Botha, liberalism and labour, the Unitarian faith and Emerson and Ruskin (the writers he revered).

Joining the South African Labour Party was less momentous than Ivon might have expected. Although the party seemed at the time to be a coming force, its policies were as racist — and perhaps even more racist — than other white political parties. In the society controlled by a white minority the discrimination that was practised by every white person was not challenged. It was obvious to all men and women who came ultimately from Europe that they were superior to the 'natives'. If there was a problem of 'race' in 1910 it was perceived as the conflict between English and Afrikaans speakers, most particularly in the Transvaal.

For Jones the difference between English and Afrikaner took on another dimension. The owners of the gold mines on the Witwatersrand, preeminantly from Britain, were associated with 'mammon'. This biblical term had been used to describe financiers by Labour leaders in Britain, and it was widely used in labour circles in South Africa. Who could be considered more evil than those men of finance, castigated by Hobson in his classical condemnation of international capitalism — or as he named it 'imperialism'? The men who owned the gold mines, and dominated the Witwatersrand, were not only profiteers, they were also responsible for the fatalities on the mines due to silicosis, or phthisis. Alongside his search for the truth Jones had come to abominate deadly evils: and central to these was the ungodly Mammon that he learnt to hate with a passion that was all but consuming.

In a climate of political and social instability leading members of the Labour Party, including Jones, sided with the white miners in their conflict with the all-powerful Chamber of Mines and the government of South Africa. Having done that they could not remain neutral in the struggle on the Witwatersrand, particularly as this involved the miners. So it was that several prominent Labour Party leaders in the Transvaal were radicalised when British troops shot down the unarmed crowds that gathered in Johannesburg during the miners' strike in mid-1913. Two events followed in 1914 that further inflamed Jones and his friends. A strike by railwaymen in January 1914 was crushed by armed force and the illegal deportation of trade unionists and Labour Party officials. Later that year South Africa entered the Great War. This led a small group into a War on War League prior to forming the International Socialist League. In all of this Ivon Jones became a leading figure.

The development of Jones during the war was remarkable. Besides condemning the war (and pamphleteering against the mindless looting of German shops and houses), Jones was the editor of the new group's newspaper and the inspiration behind the formation of the first African trade union. His drafting of a leaflet on the Bolsheviks led to the first trial of communists in the country (although the party of that name was only to be launched two years later), and his report on 'Communism in South Africa', presented to the Communist International, was a succinct summary of all that had been achieved.

The war turned Jones from an activist in South Africa to a man of international stature. He was one of the first to declare that the Second International was dead and to have called for a new International. His understanding of world events also led him to a new appraisal of world politics in which a condemnation of Tsarist Russia (the glorious ally of Britain and France) seemed obvious. It was thus no accident that Jones greeted the first Russian revolution in March 1917, and then the Bolshevik Revolution in November.

For some young readers, who are not acquainted with events in the second decade of the twentieth century, enthusiasm for the revolution in Russia might come as a surprise. The changes wrought by the new rulers of that country, the jubilation of the champions of capitalism, and the retreat into 'free market' rhetoric conceals the feeling of liberation that was felt throughout the world by the success of those who destroyed the old regime. Those were the times when Lenin was greeted as the greatest mind in Europe, and Trotsky was admired as the founder of the Red Army and as an intellectual and political giant. The collapse of the USSR, as an entity and as a symbol of 'socialism' was only one phase in the development of world socialism. Its ignominious collapse is only the end of a false start, and the necessary prelude to another phase which must bring new ideas into play. In 1917 that could not have been foreseen. What was visible to Jones and his comrades was the gigantic step taken by the Russian working class in having taken over the machinery of state of this colossus of a country.

It was a triumphal conclusion to Jones's life that he found his way to Russia in 1921. Rejuvenated, he learnt Russian, read and translated

works by Lenin, became the 'delegate for Africa' on the Executive Committee of the Communist International, and wrote on events inside
Soviet Russia for the British and South African communist press. Yet
even then, despite illness and an ever greater work load, Ivon Jones kept
close contact with the South African communists. In this period he
called for a world congress of Negro toilers and he wrote a remarkable
article on the 1922 General strike on the Witwatersrand. That too is part
of his achievements.

Jones found a resonance with the changes that had to emerge from
the misery of a destructive war. That placed him head and shoulders
over other commentators, not only in South Africa but across the world.
A celebration of Ivon Jones is also a celebration of the most advanced
thinking of the time — and the failure of the left in South Africa to pay
homage to the man is a sad commentary on the political backwardness
of the country.

There were four major changes in the life of Ivon Jones: his passage
to Unitarianism in Wales, his declaration that he was a socialist when he
was in New Zealand, his piloting of the left in South Africa to a radical
non-racialism, and his enthusiastic reporting of events in the Communist
International. This geographical spread of Jones's life has allowed the
authors of this book to produce a biography in four parts. Gwyn Williams in writing a rounded account of Jones's life has concentrated on
events in Wales and New Zealand, Baruch Hirson takes the account
through South Africa and the Soviet Union. Written in co-operation the
contributions are nonetheless different in content and in style. Furthermore, each text was felt to be more complete if some extracts from
Jones's writings were repeated. The authors felt that this overlap would
not detract from the material presented. After a Welsh reader had seen
the manuscript written by Gwyn Williams, the authors were asked if his
portion (the first six chapters) could be published separately for Welsh
readers and Unitarians in particular. Those chapters now appear in a
separate publication under the title, *The Making of A Unitarian*.

Perhaps now, seven decades after his death, the life and times of
David Jones can be celebrated — both because of the achievements in
his lifetime, and also as a foretaste of a socialism, more humane that the
regime that was built in the Soviet Union. That must still emerge and,
when it does, it will be nearer the society that Jones thought he was
witnessing in the revolutionary Russia of 1917-24.

CONTENTS

Abbreviations Used

APO	African Peoples Organisation
ASRHS	Amalgamated Society of Railway and Harbour Servants
CPSA	Communist Party of South Africa
ECCI	Executive Committee of the Communist International
FoT	Federation of Trades
ICU	Industrial and Commercial Workers Union of Africa
ISL	International Socialist League
IWA	International Workers of Africa
IWW	Internationial Workers of the World
MLA	Member of the Legislative Assembly
NAD	Native Affairs Department
NEP	New Economic Policy
OFS	Orange Free State (or Free State)
RILU	Red International of Labour Unions
SAIF	South African Industrial Federation
SALP	South African Labour Party
SAMF	South African Manufacturers' Association
SANP	South African National Party
SANNC	South African Native National Congress
SLP	Socialist Labour Party
TMA	Transvaal Miners Association
VFP	Victoria Falls and Transvaal Power Company
WNLA	Witwatersrand Native Labour Association

1

THE MAKING OF A UNITARIAN

1

A PLACE AND A PEOPLE

David Ivon Jones was born on 18 October 1883, at Aberystwyth, a resort
and market town on the Irish sea, which was also a university town and,
small though it was — 8,000 people in 1901 — the biggest town in the
county of Cardiganshire within Wales. David Jones was born a
Welshman, early in a decade which experienced a 'democratic
revolution' in Wales. To be born Welsh was to be born into a tiny but
distinctive people, with its own language, whose survival over 2,000 years
was itself a minor miracle. This was a highly self-conscious people,
whose sense of nationality was nevertheless impaired and divisive. It felt
itself to be permanently under threat.

The Welsh as the English called them, the *Cymry* (compatriots) as
they called themselves, emerged into history out of the wreck of
Romano-Celtic Britain as heirs of those Britons. For centuries, they
thought of themselves as 'British' rather than 'Welsh'. As the British
language gradually became *Cymraeg* (Welsh) within two western penin-
sulas of Britain inhabited by mixed kindreds developing intensely
localised kingships and a distinctive Celtic form of Christianity, the
slowly-forming 'Welsh' beyond Offa's Dyke fell heir to an already
developed Romano-British culture which acquired new life in their
Heroic Age poetry and romance. Out of this culture emerged the legendary figure of Arthur, in origin a rough, tough, British-Welsh hero,
Christian and half-Roman, waging a crusade against pagan Saxons who
had stolen the Island of Britain.

The language and the culture remained dynamic and complex for
centuries. The multiple, piratical kingdoms, periodically throwing up a
High King, achieved some social coherence, fairly sophisticated codes
of law (hailed by romantic Welsh socialists a millennium later as a very
model of Marx's 'primitive communism'!), shadowy guilds of lawmen,
remembrancers and poets — poets who were 'bards' (*bardd* in Welsh
simply means poet) because they had specific social and political functions and responsibilities (a tradition which persists in Welsh-speaking
Wales and which was still powerful in David Ivon Jones's time). That
institution which was 'remembered' and revived centuries later as the
Eisteddfod — a disciplined competitive festival, uniquely Welsh-national in scope, focusing on the arts with a complicated and difficult poetry
as its prime mystery, served as an embryonic national academy.

But at no stage was this cultural unity translated into political
cohesion. Until the discovery of its mineral resources, the country was
poor, the people often cabbined into pastoral uplands. They were too

few to resist intruders. Their kingdoms dissolved under the Viking assault, fell subject to the Anglo-Saxon crown. The Normans tore away the east and south into a hybrid Welsh March, assimilated the Arthur traditions and transmitted them into Europe. They precipitated in reaction an attempt to create a miniature Welsh feudal state under the first and last native Prince of Wales, whose principality was blotted out by Edward I at the end of the thirteenth century.

In the two centuries of colonialism which ensued, the Welsh were dismissed as contemptible and they were subjected to a bleak and belittling apartheid. Some of the symptoms of a particular mentality which this condition generated have proved long-lasting. Their kings gave way to princes, to lords, to gentry among the elite, as repeated outbreaks of plague after the Black Death disrupted both manorialism and colonialism and merchant capitalism began to penetrate. As the English realm slithered into dynastic conflicts and civil war, the process climaxed in the rebellion of Owain Glyn Dwr (Glendower) in 1400, a twelve-year 'national' struggle which was also a civil war.

After the rebellion, assimilation into English social structure was rapid, particularly after the accession of the Tudors to the English throne, a dynasty part-Welsh in descent and widely regarded as Welsh. The Tudor century witnessed the first of the recurrent Welsh explosions into English society, an administrative rationalisation and integration of Wales into the English shire and gentry system, an enriching of economic and cultural life and the advent of a Welsh Protestant Bible. But as the Welsh colonised the political centre and a new 'British' mythology, their old language stammered before the Renaissance and increasingly fell victim to political and social discrimination.

With the coming of the Stuarts, the country dwindled into a backwater. The upheavals of the revolutionary seventeenth century decimated the lesser gentry of Wales, product of its kindred structure and critical to its separate identity, and integrated landowners into the broad and flexible oligarchy of the eighteenth century, leaving a few strongholds of Puritan Dissent, Independents, Baptists, Presbyterians, inching from the borderlands into the west as nuclei of an alternative society. An ambiguous process of anglicization virtually removed its gentry from the Welsh world. The Welsh language became archaic and threatened to disintegrate, even as it remained a massive presence in popular life. By the early eighteenth century, most Welsh historical and cultural traditions had gone into limbo and a widening gulf opened between elite and common people, soon to be widened still further by religious animosities.

An alternative society was born in the eighteenth century. Merchant capitalism steadily transformed hitherto backward Wales into an export sector of the imperial and Atlantic economy of the new Great Britain. 'Middling and lower orders' multiplied as the gentry went into demographic crisis. Into the cultural vacuum of Welsh life flowed a rising tide of popular literacy in Welsh, product of a major evangelical drive, out of which developed the phenomenon known to Welsh history as the Revival.

This was a complex of often contradictory movements. In what was essentially an enterprise in rescue archaeology, handfuls of dedicated scholars started to resurrect and revivify Welsh history, literature and language. Under the influence of the French Revolution, it was transformed into a movement of national re-assertion, charged with romanticism, which in the rapid growth of an industrial society acquired some popular force. Early in the eighteenth century, Wales produced an independent Methodist movement of its own, dominated by Calvinists, whose evangelical style started to infect an Old Dissent increasingly informed by the rationalist and democratic impulses of the Enlightenment. All was accelerated by the population explosion of the late eighteenth century, the abrupt intrusion of industrial capitalism which planted massive and modern ironworks, serviced by coal pits, on the coalfields to north-east and south-east, the penetration of Lancashire entrepreneurs into the rural cloth trade and the transformation of Welsh hill farming into a capitalist enterprise.

During the generation-long war against the French Revolution and Napoleon, there was a social crisis in rural Wales to the west, an emigration to America strongly nationalist in temper, the brief but potent flowering of a Jacobin democratic movement. This was driven underground by the reaction and the inertly conservative response of Methodists (who quit the Church in 1811 only because they were driven out) and men of similar temper among Dissenters. The more radical of the latter, however, continued to cultivate the styles of a measured Enlightenment and budded out an entirely new denomination, the Unitarians. Denying the divinity of Christ, these were in reality freethinking radicals thinly clad in Christian garb. They had originated in a heretical breakaway from the Carmarthen college of the Independents which found an unexpected lodgement in a strip along the river Teifi in the south-west in the heart of a very Welsh district — Cardiganshire — which was rapidly going over to Calvinistic Methodism. Their settlement achieved permanence in a hostile environment. From their fourteen chapels in what Calvinists denounced as The Black Spot, the teacher-ministers of this small but influential sect fanned out over Wales and found a response among the textile workers of mid-Wales restive in their new factories, in the disturbed rural hinterland of the riotous and distinctly 'sans-culotte' town of Carmarthen and, above all, in the booming iron and coal valleys of the south-east, where they supplied the first-generation leadership to the new working-class movements.

Throughout the first half of the nineteenth century, southern Wales was in turmoil. Starting around 1800, the south-east was convulsed by huge strikes, an armed rising in the iron capital of Merthyr Tydfil in

1831, the short-lived sweep of the Owenite trade union movement and by a Chartism which not only staged a rebellion at Newport in 1839, designed to set off a republican revolt throughout the country, but which persisted as a movement and even experienced something of a rebirth in the 1860s. At the height of the Chartist agitation over 1839-43, south-western Wales was convulsed in turn by a prolonged guerila war of small farmers in the Rebecca Riots. Not until mid-century, as immediate pressures in industry and agriculture eased, as Whigs soothed middle-class pains and Peelites those of the workers, and as Britain settled into the pudding-time of its mid-Victorian imperial prosperity, did south Wales subside, much of it finding a home in the molecular construction of a new Liberalism.

Underlying these times of travail was a change whose speed and scale was to transform the lives of the people. From the late eighteenth century, the growth of Dissent, old and new, accelerated; in the early nineteenth century, it became breakneck. By the first religious census of 1851, some three-quarters of the Welsh who attended Sunday services were Nonconformist. In the next generation, their grip grew stronger still. Many people, of course, remained outside both church and chapel, but they became historically invisible. The chapel came to exercise hegemonic power. 'The Nonconformists of Wales', said one of their spokesmen, 'are the People of Wales.' The first official recognition of the existence of a distinctive Welsh people by the modern British state was the Welsh Sunday Closing Act of 1881 (though they'd been beaten to it by the US Immigration Service!). The major political objective of the 'Welsh Nation' according to its official historiography was the Disestablishment of the Church of England in Wales — *yr hen fradwres* (the old traitress).

In this wholesale shift of a people out of Establishment into Dissent, a 'nation' of some kind was clearly emerging whose spokesmen, like the contemporary Czechs, spoke of it as 're-emerging'. But it was riddled with contradictions. Calvinistic Methodists were the largest single denomination, though they were significantly outnumbered by the total of the others. The great stronghold of the Methodists was western, Welsh-speaking, still largely rural Wales. And although differences in practice and style were dwindling to the vanishing point and the Unitarians themselves were settling into the all-pervasive 'respectability', there remained a striking differentiation in terms of political outlook. This could divide brothers, a recurrent phenomenon; the Methodist would be a pietist preacher, his brother the Independent, a 'politician', more often than not a journalist. The history of late nineteenth century Wales could quite plausibly be written as the history of a new conformist nation entering into its political kingdom.

This pseudo-nation formed along a religious and a language line which was also a class line. Essentially middle-class in character and an instrument of 'modernisation', it was nevertheless strongly populist in spirit and erected the *werin* (people, folk, pueblo) into its symbolic image. In a striking victory over the public mind (and over historical fact!), it was able to pillory the Welsh squirearchy and the Anglican church as alien and 'anti-Welsh'. It found a political home in a multi-faceted Liberalism.

In the late nineteenth century, the Liberal Party could justifiably claim to be the 'party of Wales'. At the critical general election of 1906, not a single Tory MP was returned from the country and public life was utterly dominated by the ambitions and nostrums of Welsh Dissent, even as an industrial south Wales, which by then housed anything from two-thirds to three-quarters of the population, moved into a world entirely alien to them − a painful contradiction between ideology and reality which did not explode until after the First World War.

This hegemonic power, however, had been slow to form. Central to it was a process which has passed into historians' parlance as 'the radicalizing of the Methodists'. In the third quarter of the century, south Wales achieved maturity as an industrial society based on steel, tinplate and coal, with great ports mushrooming along the coast and many of its workers gaining the vote through the Reform Act of 1867. A newly respectable working class, in its multiplying self-help and self-improvement societies, was embraced in Nonconformity and found a subordinate but recognised place within the new liberalism. A similar process affected the industrial north-east, whose growth had stopped. In the booming quarry industry of the north-west, still in the grip of a colonial oligarchy, it was harder.

Hardest of all were the still largely rural districts of the centre and centre-north where the power of Anglican landowners was overwhelming and the politics of deference prevailed, even though the people were virtually all Nonconformists, most of them Methodists. Not until the 1859 election in Merioneth, followed a few years later by others in Cardiganshire, were the gentry challenged. Their response was ferocious. A wave of evictions of tenant-farmers who had voted Liberal broke over both counties, to provoke widespread horror, to power a radical mythology and to precipitate a campaign which helped secure the Ballot Act of 1872. Politically, however, the Nonconformists were defeated and driven back into quiescence. The Liberation Society, a skilled pressure group working for the Disestablishment of the Church, made these districts a target, south Wales radicals in desperation demanded the instant creation there of a middle-class with spirit; not until the Reform Acts of 1884 and 1889, could Dissent and Liberalism make their breakthrough.

What such people did achieve in those years, however, was a campaign for their own educational system which became a central legend in modern Welsh history. By this time, the rural counties to north and west, which had long seen their surplus population creamed off into emigration, were experiencing absolute depopulation and while the education campaign was fought in Welsh-national terms, almost inevitably its core was a rescue operation directed to the (largely Methodist and Welsh-speaking) west and north. A handful of middle-class reformers, with increasing popular support, built up a network of British and Foreign Bible Society schools to challenge the Anglican monopoly and created a celebrated Normal College at Bangor (supplemented by another at Swansea) to service them. This proved vital to a whole generation before the advent of Board Schools after 1870.

Having helped organise the National Eisteddfod, now a great popular festival served by railways, they moved on into a long, heart-breaking struggle to give Wales its own university. There was already one, St David's at Lampeter, founded in 1826 precisely as a bastion of Anglicanism — and dismissed for that reason. They ultimately created a University College of Wales, which (largely by accident moved into a disused railway hotel in Aberystwyth in 1867 and opened in 1872, to prepare students for the examinations of the University of London. It was a desperate struggle. The major patron was David Davies, an aggressive industrial entrepreneur from mid-Wales, a railway builder and coal magnate who created Barry Docks as the hub of an international trade. But what caught people's minds were the 100,000 subscriptions under half-a-crown, the hard-won donations from miners and quarrymen, the University Sundays in the chapels: in those minds, Aberystwyth became the 'people's university' of the Welsh.

Under this pressure, Gladstone, who had become something of a Welsh national hero, appointed the Aberdare Committee to survey education in Wales (a subject which was becoming a Welsh national obsession). During the 1880s, the implementation of its report inaugurated a new age. In the first state-funded secondary school system to be created in Britain, the Welsh by 1914 had established a hundred effective county schools which transformed the lives of talented but starved generations (and offered clever youngsters something other than a career as a Nonconformist minister!). Over 1883-84, the first state-aided university colleges in Britain opened at Cardiff and Bangor.

Aberystwyth was left to wither. The response (wholly unexpected by the resolute rationalists of the Committee) was an extraordinary surge of popular emotion, intensified by a fire which nearly destroyed the old place. By this time, many of its graduates were in influential positions. Government was forced to extend its grant to Aberystwyth. By the time the University of Wales was established in 1893, Aberystwyth had an honoured place in it. So powerful had its myth become that when Wales was granted a National Library in 1907, this great copyright library was sited in Aberystwyth, a place which could perhaps claim the national distinction of being almost equally inaccessible to every corner of the country; the great city of Cardiff, mushrooming at American speed, had to make do with a Museum!

The floodgates opened with the passage of the Reform Act of 1884 and the creation of county councils in 1889. The miner, the tinplater, the steel worker, the quarryman and the rural worker got the vote. The electoral landscape was transformed. Wales was over-represented at Westminster and by a large preponderance of working class single-member constituencies. With the creation of elected county councils, the three-hundred-year reign of the squires came to an abrupt end (though in many places their social prestige did not). Most of the gentry went into a kind of internal exile as they were no less forcibly expelled from the history of their nation which the new men in their new schools and colleges set themselves to write. All over Wales the old bastilles went down before the ballot as the Nonconformist People, in their legal revolution, entered their political kingdom.

The years running from the 1880s to the Great War were a 'golden age' for Liberal, Nonconformist, radical and Welsh-speaking Wales. All the old battles against landlords, the tithe, the Church of England and the Tories were fought and won. The new nation equipped itself as a modern people, fit to take its place as a directive centre of the new imperial democracy of Britain. These were the years of a mushrooming Welsh press, creative generations of academics, preachers and politicians, the time of a nationalist movement *Cymru Fydd* (the Wales-that-is-to-be), of the Welsh Party in the Commons, the great Land Commission and the struggle for the Disestablishment of the Church. It achieved its appropriately ambiguous triumph when its most trenchant spokesman, David Lloyd George, finally reached Downing Street, the first outsider to get there. What carried it, powered it, and ultimately destroyed it, was the great surge of economic power into south Wales. Industrial society there — and its working class with it — were products of an imperial formation located in buoyant export enterprise which gave south Wales a world empire. In 1881, Cardiff raised its merchant palace of a Coal Exchange, one of the mightiest public buildings in the Principality. Cardiff, challenged by Barry, became the greatest coal port in the world; its Bute Street was the jugular vein of that capitalist Wales, to which every other Wales had to adjust. From the 1870s, the marriage rate, even in remote Merioneth, followed the price of coal, the general index of prosperity. By 1913 one in every four Welsh males was a miner. Not only did John Cory's coal bunkers straddle the globe and south Wales coal keep the Royal Navy afloat, the capital, technology, technicians, skilled workers of south Wales acquired world power.

South Wales coal and its servitors distorted the development of Spain, wrenching its heavy industry away from Asturias into the Basque lands where Cardiff power was entrenched in Bilbao. South Wales merchants bought up shipping companies and port capital in French and German harbours; Italy, Argentina, Chile and Brazil worked to the rhythms of south Wales exports. For years, the real economic capital of Chile was Swansea with its waterfront a forest of ocean-going masts. It was south Wales which first launched the iron and steel of the Donets basin in Ukraine and of Pennsylvania in the USA. At home south Wales was nicknamed 'American Wales' as it sucked people in not only from rural Wales but from the rest of Britain, from Italy, Spain and many more far-off places.

During the frenetic expansion of the first decade of the twentieth century, south Wales as a centre of world immigration ranked second in intensity only to the USA itself. With its increasingly cosmopolitan population, it towered over the rest of Wales. The long retreat of the Welsh language accelerated; by the time of the first language census in 1891, barely a half of the Welsh spoke Welsh; over the years it withdrew further and further to west and north. In this Wales, the assumptions and obsessions of Nonconformist Liberal Wales had become irrelevant years before they were formally rejected. The emergence of giant Coal Combines precipitated a working-class response which started the miners on a two-generation struggle which made their militancy a legend. After a fierce battle in 1898, they created their South Wales Miners' Federation, The Fed, a huge union which had to organise a whole people. Five years later the quarrymen of north Wales fought a three-year lockout which almost destroyed the industry. From 1910, there were years of uncompromising struggle which ran through the War to climax in the General Strike of 1926 — the Tonypandy Riots, the *Miners' Next Step*, the Plebs League and Marxist education classes, waves of syndicalism and a change of miners' leadership virtually every five years. The leadership of the Fed passed from Liberal-Labour to Communist in little more than a dozen years.

In the stunning general election of 1906, Wales returned six Labour MPs, including James Keir Hardie, leader of the Independent Labour Party and patron saint of much British socialism. After passing through the cauldron of the War, when the miners' union wrote the abolition of capitalism into its rule-book, it rejected the Liberal hegemony. Liberals, too, withdrew into west and north, and Labour took an easy majority. The landlords, long in retreat and hammered by war taxation, inflation and the artificial post-war boom, finally gave up and in their 'green revolution' Welsh smallholders came temporarily into their own, even as The Fed, organising 200,000 out of the 270,000 miners, confidently braced themselves to take over their own industry. Yet another Welsh people, with Labour inheriting the role of Liberalism, seemed poised to move in turn into their kingdom.

They marched instead into the blizzard of the terrible Depression which killed their Wales stone dead. Out of that Depression, Wales emerged under an entrenched Labour hegemony as total as the Liberals' had been, with Conservatives inching back into anglicised areas and on the margins, a socialist ILP bubbling in frustrated evangelism and a small but influential Communist Party whose performance had made it almost as respectable as an eisteddfod.

David Ivon Jones saw nothing of the Depression; the climax of the Lloyd George years he was to witness from abroad. But he grew up and lived his young manhood through the first breakthrough of Dissent and Liberalism; he had seen the general election of 1906 before he left. He grew up, however, in a corner of Wales where many of the later struggles would have seemed alien, in an Aberystwyth and a Cardiganshire which were the despair of Welsh radicals who denounced their people as servile laggards.

Cardiganshire was one of the most Welsh counties. As late as 1901, of a population of 61,000, nearly a half, 29,000, were monoglot Welsh speakers who knew little if any English, while a mere 3,800 spoke English only. The county had long been distinctive, the birthplace of Wales's patron saint and its native Calvinistic Methodist movement and incongruous home of its Unitarian Black Spot. It was celebrated above all for its emigrants. It had never been able to support its native-born population; some of the earliest London-Welsh had been Cardiganshire people. Waves of migrants, to London and the English south, at first seasonal, had created something of an emigrant tradition, both plebeian and middle class — the London milk trade was a particular colony. As the south-eastern coalfield of Wales expanded, *Cardis* were strongly represented among its colliers and ironstone miners. At home, it was a land of biting land-hunger and inching self-improvement. *Cardis* enjoyed (if that's the word) the reputation which Aberdonians enjoyed in Scotland and Scots the world over.

It was a hard land. There were pockets of fertility and comfort along the river Teifi and the vale of Aeron, small and lively harbours along the coast which experienced a minor shipbuilding and marine expansion in the nineteenth century; the towns were mixed and active, particularly Aberystwyth, which added the attractions of a seaside resort to those of a market town. There were isolated lead-mining settlements in the hills. But most of its people were the farmers, labourers and artisans of hill-country farming, ravaged by the diseases of poverty and dominated by landlords; they lived in communities which were virtually models of organic, deferential politics.

Well into the nineteenth century, the county was in the pocket of its landlords. Some forty-five families, with estates ranging from 1,000 to 3,000 acres and annual incomes from £2,000 upwards, accounted for a third of the county's acreage. Beneath them, occupying another third of that acreage, were 1,800 families with holdings of 500 acres or less and incomes from land of less than £50, ranging from reasonably well-off farmers to poverty-stricken smallholders who had also to work as labourers. About 50 families ran the county and the real powers were three major dynasties, the Earl of Lisburne with 42,000 acres, his rivals, the Pryses of Gogerddan, with 27,000 acres to the north of the county, embracing mineral rights, and the Powells of Nanteos whose 22,000 acres covered both the north and the south-east whose town of Tregaron was a Nanteos fief. The voice of these three families, with their networks of dependent clans, was decisive in all political matters, though there

was an occasional yelp from the southern and more particularly agricultural landowners, the Gwynne family of Aberaeron (4,000 acres) and the
Harfords, an active bunch of former industrialists turned respectable
who owned some 6,000 acres around Lampeter. The few towns of the
county were naturally more mixed and potentially more lively, with well-
off and poor living cheek by jowl in old-regime style, full of merchants,
shopkeepers and solicitors who were determinedly Nonconformist. In
fact they were completely under the gentry's thumb. Even in
Aberystwyth, the largest of them, growing quite rapidly particularly
after the coming of the railway and the only one at this time in which a
distinct 'workingclass' or plebeian quarter was emerging, equipped
moreover with minimal instruments of self-government by the municipal
legislation of the Whigs, nothing could be done without a nod from
Gogerddan (generally Whig) or Nanteos (normally Tory).

This county, overwhelmingly but inertly Nonconformist, had naturally become the target for exasperated liberals and radicals, but the election of 1865 graphically illustrated the realities. The incumbent Tory, a
Powell of Nanteos, announced that he would retire because of ill health.
The hope of the Liberals, who were scarcely organised, lay in another
squire, Sir Thomas D Lloyd of Bronwydd, but when Powell declared
that he had recovered enough to stand again, Lloyd in typical gentry-
politics style said he would not oppose a fellow-gentleman. The discon-
certed Liberals were thereupon confronted with two candidates, both
dramatic: Henry Richard, born in Tregaron within the county, who had
achieved notoriety as an 'extremist' Nonconformist radical, backed by
the tough-minded Liberation Society and David Davies the Methodist
industrialist, loud with promises of railway development. On the eve of
the selection meeting, Powell declared that he would after all retire and
Davies of Bronwydd promptly announced his candidature. This
produced confusion.

Henry Richard withdrew, saying he did not want to split the Liberal
vote. The real reason was that he had failed to win the support of the
house of Gogerddan. Moreover his radicalism had frightened the wits
out of the Nonconformists of the county; even the Unitarians of the
south had succumbed sufficiently to the prevailing atmosphere to make
their 'extremism' a purely intellectual matter. Typically, Henry Richard
was to find his parliamentary home three years later in the steel and iron
town of Merthyr Tydfil, after its workers had been enfranchised by the
Reform Act of 1867. There, Henry Richard, embracing the survivors of
Chartism and standing as a spokesman for 'Wales and the Working
Man', won a legendary triumph and went on to become the first parliamentary hero of the new Wales. His native county wouldn't touch him.

David Davies, however, almost a caricature of the self-made man in
the Commons (Disraeli commented that he obviously loved his Maker!)
went full-steam ahead like the railway king he was. He relied less on his
pork-barrel promises than on his standing as a leading Methodist. But,

though he won support around Lampeter and Tregaron, in this Liberal civil war (no Tory stood) he lost by a small but decisive margin. The defeated attributed their discomfiture to gentry pressure, which had rallied around the most conservative candidate, but the root cause was the failure of Nonconformists, and Methodists in particular, to vote the way they 'ought' to have done.

During the campaign a small group of committed radicals formed in Aberystwyth. After the withdrawal of Henry Richard, they threw themselves into David Davies's campaign. Their leader was Rev James Rhys Jones, known by his pen-name of *Kilsby*. Kilsby was a celebrated Methodist preacher and a lecturer notorious for his radicalism. Closely allied with him were two Aberystwyth men, John Matthews, a prosperous grocer of Princess Street, and another, more intimate friend with whom he had corresponded for many years on matters literary. This man was prominent among a coterie of intellectuals, commercial men, shopkeepers, craftsmen and apprentices who had made the town something of an intellectual centre even before the coming of the University College. He was John Jones, known after 1865 by his own pen-name of *Ivon*. Their defeat confronted then with a hard and inescapable reality. Henry Richard denounced the politics of the county as 'feudal' with 'clans' voting blindly for their 'chieftains'. Even the Aberystwyth radicals were embarrassed when David Davies went ahead anyway — he had not even bothered to consult the Pryses of Gogerddan, whose imprimatur was a *sine qua non* for every Liberal. Even in Aberystwyth, most substantial of the towns, with a quite developed structure, there was no politics without the house of Gogerddan, which claimed to have created the town in the first place.

In the immediate aftermath, both the Liberation Society and David Davies set to, nursing the constituency against the odds. Kilsby tried, and failed, to launch a newspaper in opposition to the town's Tory journal. He tried to set up a Welsh Freehold Society, on the Irish model, to prise tenants free. John Jones, 'Ivon', was a director and its principal agent. This also failed for lack of support. When they went into the critical election of 1868, therefore, they moved very carefully indeed. By mutual arrangement, the seat for the boroughs passed from a Pryse to Davies of Bronwydd and the candidate for the County, E M Richards, a Swansea industrialist who made promises of development in David Davies style, nevertheless took infinite pains to win the support of Gogerddan and to woo majority Nonconformist opinion by vigorously distancing himself from the liberation society's Disestablishment campaign, while supporting such a measure for the Irish Church in good Gladstonian style.

The Tories, who fielded a nephew of the Earl of Lisburne, scarcely bothered to campaign. They resorted to coercion, threatening potential Liberal voters among tenant-farmers with eviction. Richards responded with a defiant call for tenants to vote according to their conscience. The pressures were reflected in the result. Only in Aberystwyth did Richards win a substantial majority. He also did well in the north where freedom to vote meant freedom to vote with Gogerddan. Elsewhere, the margin was very narrow. It was probably those few brave enough to defy the landlords who gave Richards a majority of only 156 in a poll of 4,000. The evictions which ensued, following on those of Merioneth, shocked much Welsh opinion into a campaign and a *Fund y Gorthrymedigion* (Fund for the Oppressed). But they seem to have worked; the Tories recaptured the seat in 1874. The Fund was supported far more strongly outside the county than within it. The one outstanding exception in Aberystwyth was John Jones, 'Ivon', who was active in its service and audacious in his defiance of the men with power.

Though the Liberals recovered the county seat in 1880 and John Gibson set up his *Cambrian News* in Aberystwyth as the mouthpiece of an outspoken Liberalism, it took the 'democratic revolution' of the 1880s to rivet Liberalism on the county. The Reform Acts of 1884-85 added some 6,000 critical new voters to the register and merged the Boroughs into the County. In 1889 Cardiganshire got its county council. The townsmen of Aberystwyth at last achieved some political independence and other areas were soon to be groaning about the arrogance of their shopocracy. The uncharitable might feel that they had gained a power they had done little to win. They were confronted almost at once by another Liberal civil war. In 1885, David Davis the railway king at last won the Cardiganshire seat, backed by a new Liberal Association run by an Aberystwyth solicitor who was also to become the first clerk of the county council. But Davis soon displayed his social conservatism and, when Gladstone introduced his Irish Home Rule Bill in 1886, joined the Liberal Unionists and declared his total opposition to Celtic separatism. This split the county wide open. The Gladstonians fielded W Bowen Rowlands, an Anglican who was shortly to turn Catholic, who spoke little Welsh and who was so committed to the Irish cause that he had Michael Davitt on his platforms at Aberystwyth and Lampeter (described as 'Gladstonian to the core'). Davis could rally the squires and their clientele from both parties and much support from official Methodism. It was a ferocious, indeed poisonous struggle but the unlikely Liberal Bowen Rowlands won by nine votes. David Davis, in characteristic reaction, promptly withdrew his support from the college at Aberystwyth. This verdict, rejecting patronage by a squeak, was decisively ratified at the election of 1892, when Bowen Rowlands won a majority of 2,000 over a Liberal Unionist. Thereafter, however, it was political stagnation for a generation.

This reflected the decline of the county in general. Depopulation, intensified by the agricultural depression, was a central feature of the county's landscape. Its population declined by over nine percent between 1881 and 1891. Over the years from 1871 to 1911, the population dwindled from 73,000 to 59,000. The loss of mainly young men drained the life out of it. A high proportion of its young men were in the coal pits of the Rhondda. Over a fifth of its people were engaged in the most precarious sector of hill farming — the fifth highest proportion in England and Wales. The proportion of females to males was the highest for England and Wales for six successive decennial censuses — 1,274 females for every 1,000 males in 1891. The surplus of unmarried women was grotesque. There was a high prevalence of idiocy and deaf-mutes in the county, a preponderance of the 45-65 and over-65 age groups.

The lead industry withered, leaving ghost towns in the hills. The great estates were hard hit, their owners withdrawing into the home demesne and out of direct control. Almost uniquely among county Tories, those in Cardiganshire came to lack any central great house, even as the old Whig landlords withered away from Liberalism. Life and growth, such as they were, centred on the coastal towns, notably Aberystwyth which the railway turned into a fashionable resort. Society was static and its politics were stagnant. It was Liberal almost by default, the great storms which followed the electoral victory of 1906 seem to have passed it by. Only after the War did life return in another ferocious civil war between Lloyd George and Asquith Liberals, whose consequence, perhaps paradoxically, was a Liberal permanence — apart from a brief Labour interlude, the county has remained Liberal almost to this day.

It could certainly claim to be the most Liberal constituency in Britain. Lloyd George could declare that, if every constituency were a Cardiganshire, there would not be a single Tory in the House of Commons. But it was a slow, inward-looking and complacent Liberalism which ruled in default of opposition over a virtually static society.

David Ivon Jones was three years old at the election of 1886; in the year of total Liberal triumph in Wales in 1906, he was twenty-three. For a young man growing up in Aberystwyth and acquiring a Welsh and radical temper, the political tradition of his native town and county could hardly have been inspiring. There were, of course, a few isolated heroes. Besides Kilby Jones and the combative grocer John Matthews, there was Gwilym Marles, a dauntless minister from the Unitarian Black Spot on the Teifi who fought fiercely against the evictions. When he was himself thrown out of his chapel, radical Wales raised money to build him a new one.

And there was a hero much closer to home. David Ivon Jones was the grandson of that John Jones who called himself 'Ivon' and who seemed to embody the slogan which the Welsh Bards proclaimed at their Eisteddfod — *Y gwir yn erbyn y byd* — Truth against the World. From his grandfather, David Jones evidently inherited a sight more than a penname. For a few years, indeed, he inherited his grandfather's old business. John Jones, 'Ivon', was a Methodist grocer in the Aberystwyth which was beginning to call itself the Athens of the West.

2

A TOWN AND A FAMILY

'Aberystwyth was a theocratic society, ruled by priests and elders', wrote Goronwy Rees, who had spent a childhood there as the son of a Calvinistic Methodist minister, a generation later than David Ivon Jones. 'They formed a sort of unofficial Sanhedrin which exercised an absolute dictatorship over the morals and behaviour of the town.'

Naturally, he exaggerated. There was always a bohemian fringe to Aberystwyth, in the plebeian and unrespectable districts south of the river and behind the harbour, which tended to overflow into the old centre as the railway and the Promenade shifted the place bodily northwards. Some of the strongest Methodist missions prayed, studied and sang in streets around the Town Clock populated after dark by drunken brawlers. The heir to the gentry house of Gogerddan which long controlled the town's politics, used to take his friend the poet Swinburne into well-known pubs to savour the 'Rabelaisian conversation' of even better-known barmaids.

There were other people who managed to wriggle free a little from the grip of determinedly respectable shopkeepers, professional people, hoteliers and aspiring artisans in their now monumental chapels. There was never much of a 'working class' in the town, but it was full of workers. The whole west coast of Wales was alive with a small but lively maritime trade. There was ship building in Aberystwyth, a distinctive community of sea-captains and mariners some of whom flit through the pages of Joseph Conrad. There were other windows on the world. The coming of the University College and its growth from the 1880s energised an already active cultural life, adding a dimension to its experience. The National Library of Wales followed early in the twentieth century. The almost mythical status which Aberystwyth acquired in the Welsh national revival seems to have charged the place with a sense of national responsibility which it did not always bear lightly.

And, of course, after the coming of the railway from mid-century, it became a fashionable resort. The railway drove new streets like boulevards to the splendid sweep of the Promenade and moved the heart of the town northwards into a new centre of often elegant hotels, retail establishments and fashionable houses. Despite some tourist embellishments, the resort tried to serve the quality. Aber was the kind of place where one would not have been too surprised to encounter the Crown Prince of Prussia cycling in knickerbockers down Prom.

Almost despite itself, the town had become a bastion of Nonconformist Liberal politics. It was the home of the influential *Cambrian*

News, run by John Gibson, a Lancashire immigrant who never bothered to learn Welsh, but laid about him with a will in the Good Old Cause. Caustic and fearless, Gibson made many enemies, but made his paper a power in the land . . . 'every public man in the counties of Cardigan and Merioneth lived in fear of being dipped in his inkpot'. Lloyd George paid attention to what Gibson had to say even after he became Chancellor of the Exchequer; in 1915, he knighted him. Aberystwyth, a semi-isolated market town perched in a remote corner at the end of its life-giving 'thin red line' of the railway (an early Labour stronghold) was also the site of Wales's great copyright library, a port in touch with the Atlantic, the home of a national newspaper and of a 'people's university' which had become a legend. As much of Cardiganshire shrivelled in population, Aberystwyth flourished. Its 8,000 population of 1901 was distinctive. In sharp contrast to the rest of the county, a mere 500 or so were monoglot Welsh-speakers; over 2,000 spoke only English.

Yet, in a fundamental sense, Goronwy Rees was correct — and he lived through years more relaxed than any David Ivon Jones knew. There was a kind of schizophrenia in the place. Behind the splendid Georgian and neo-Georgian façades, the baroque towers of the College building rearing up against the spectacular sunsets, behind the imposing frontage of the National Library on its hill, control lay in the grip of a tight, middle and lower-middle class society clamped into Calvinism.

The mildly sophisticated pleasures of the Promenade were characteristically engulfed every evening in season by immensely popular open air communal hymn-singing around the carefully preserved Castle ruins. *Cor Y Castell* (The Castle Choir) could serve as a symbol. However open and cosmopolitan the place might seem, the chapels of the shopkeepers, hotel-keepers, lawyers and doctors, the multiplying artisans of the service trades attended by their dependent crowds of servants, shopassistants, journeymen, had the town stitched up.

The place was a stronghold of Welsh Nonconformity and towering over all, as in western Wales generally, were the peculiarly Welsh Calvinistic Methodists, easily the strongest single denomination. In the democratic revolution of the 1880s, they achieved a real power, which was more than local. They had spent an unconscionable time getting there and, after the upheavals of the 1880s, settled into a complacency which was not broken until Lloyd George precipitated a kind of local civil war hard on the heels of the Great one. This apparent torpor masked a myriad tensions, contradictions and conflicts within the overpowering and often inward-looking, sometimes stifling hegemony of Welsh Nonconformity and its fissiparous Liberalism.

If the ethos of a whole town could ever be summed up in the single phrase 'petty-bourgeois', Aberystwyth would be that town. It was in this town that David Ivon Jones's grandfather made himself something of a local hero. John Jones, 'Ivon', was born in 1820 into a family of small

farmers near Mynydd Bach (The Little Mountain) in southern Cardiganshire. During his childhood in that hill country, its tenant farmers
and artisans, intensely Welsh and Nonconformist, fought a protracted
guerilla war — *Rhyfel y Sais Bach* (the war of the Little Englishman) —
against an intruding English and Anglican gentleman who enclosed
their commons and annulled their 'ancestral' rights in forest and marsh,
bludgeoning them with soldiers and hired goons. Under Dai Jones the
blacksmith, they imposed their own extra-legal Turf Act (which morally
legitimised 'poaching' on their expropriators) and their own secret
society of the *Ceffyl Pren* (the *wooden horse, the cock-horse* of *village
discipline*) to mobilise 600 men, who dressed in women's clothes at the
sound of a hunting horn and, in repeated riot, sabotage and passive
resistance drove out the offender.

They waged their war in precisely the same style as their industrial
cousins (often quite literally their cousins) among the militant and in-
genious colliers of Monmouthshire (Gwent) in their own resistance
movement of the *Scotch Cattle* — terrorist bands wearing women's
clothes and turned coats, each under A Horned Bull *(Tarw Scotch, gelyn
pob dychryndod — the Scotch Bull, enemy to all fear)* It was a style which
was to transfix and bewilder government officials and London
newspapers twenty years later in the Rebecca Riots, a four-year revolt
of small farmers throughout west Wales, which brought into their
country not only redcoats with muskets, but the reforming commissions
of an alarmed Whig administration.

After they had won their little war on Mynydd Bach, his pragmatic
parents packed off fifteen-year-old John Jones to Aberystwyth to serve
his apprenticeship in a grocer's shop. It is impossible to say whether
childhood memories moved him, but in later life, in the cause of poverty-stricken Liberal tenant-farmers ruthlessly evicted by Tory, Anglican
landlords, he was to prove himself in sober reality an enemy to all fear.
His grandson was to inherit that courage.

John Jones worked hard in Aberystwyth, made his first acquaintance
with the printing press, became the manager of his shop and in 1848,
married the daughter of a town mercer and set up on his own in Princess
Street. Twelve years later, he had prospered sufficiently to buy a smallholding at Waun-grug in the southern outskirts of town and to move into
new premises at Commerce House, No 17 in then fashionable Bridge
Street. His brother David, ten years older, was already mighty in the
municipality as manager of the National Provincial Bank — *Dafydd
Jones y Banc*.

Over thirty years, John Jones turned Commerce House into a nest of
singing birds, a port of call for practically every poet, writer and
musician of a Wales in cultural renaissance. Swept into the Temperance
Movement as early as 1836, he with his friends, John Matthews, a tough
radical and later mayor of Aberystwyth, and Edward Edwards, *Pencerdd
Ceredigion* (Master-Singer of Cardigan), took over an old Bridge Street

pub with a thatched roof, *The Shades* and made it the town's first temperance hotel.

It was in fact an adult school, run from *Tabernacl Methodist* chapel, in a quarter turning rough. It taught Welsh literature, the complex rules of Welsh prosody, Welsh grammar and tonic sol-fa, washed down by Mrs Moses's elderberry wine. Jones wrote little poetry himself, but was a master of the rules; no musician, he nevertheless composed, translated and transcribed hymns, carols, songs, and helped Edwards launch a choir which became celebrated. For many years, no literary or cultural society in Aberystwyth could prosper without the services of John Jones. In 1842 he and his friends tried to launch a journal, *Y Cwmwl (The Cloud)*; in 1850 he was central to the creation of an English-language literary society and a Mechanics' Institute, both dominated by the Methodist connexion. Two years later, the death of three of Wales's major poets prompted him to organise a prize competition for an elegy which attracted entries from all over Wales and culminated in a dramatic assembly in the Town Hall.

The late sixties were his great days. In 1865 the National Eisteddfod came to Aberystwyth. John Jones inevitably became its Secretary. By now the focus of correspondence with everyone of note in Welsh cultural life and Liberal politics, it was in this year that he adopted his bardic name of *Ivon*. By that name he was known throughout Wales. And in the years immediately following he was at the heart of the great struggles against political evictions. Those evictions were to become the very stuff of Welsh radical martyrology, which his grandson was to evoke even in South Africa — *Y Gwir yn erbyn Y Byd* (Truth against the World). Among his pusillanimous Liberal colleagues in Cardiganshire, 'Ivon' stands out like a beacon.

His political notoriety did not last (except in the memory of his grandson) though he remained a favourite lecturer among the Aberystwyth Young Radicals at the highly political Temperance Hall which he helped to found. He settled into something of an Aberystwyth institution. His knowledge of Welsh dialects, folklore, local history was legendary. The already vigorous cultural life of the town gained fresh impetus from the establishment of the University College and 'Ivon' became a close collaborator of academics, particularly Silvan Evans, Professor of Welsh; they published an important collection of texts in 1872.

In that same year, 'Ivon' gave up the shop, passing it to his son William. He went on to serve as an effective member of the Poor Law Board. When he retired in 1895, the Board wanted to add ten years to his pension but he rejected the offer. His wife had died three years earlier, and the chest troubles which had afflicted the man throughout his life finally finished him. His retirement lasted three months, plagued by bronchitis. He died in September 1898.

His grandson David, like his brothers, inherited that affliction. He also inherited Ivon's taste for poetry, literature and history. He inherited something else. Everybody who ever wrote about John Jones used the same adjectives. He was *'siriol'* (cheerful) and *'llon'* (happy). David Jones, who spent most of his childhood and early youth with his grandfather, invariably described him as 'merry Ivon'. John Jones, 'Ivon', seems to have been what a majority of his fellow-countrymen of other denominations would have regarded as a contradiction in terms — a Merry Methodist!

But a Welsh Calvinistic Methodist he was, right down to his dogmatic and didactic fingertips. Men like John Jones and his friend, the cultivated teacher David Samuel, could combine (in a chemistry which now eludes us) an attitude to culture and society which was, in some central senses, liberal and even radical with a commitment to a religious creed which quite frequently was neither. It was an exacting and totalising creed. Its adherents, steeped in an earnest study of Biblical texts, were required to master those 'fine points' of doctrine which marked them out from others and were to govern every aspect of their daily lives. It was a religion of the desperately grave and silent Sabbath, of Sunday schools, prayer meetings, of an often warm and companionable chapel society which nevertheless embraced and directed the entire life of a member in general and in particular. It bred a people who were literate, almost incredibly learned in a Biblical sense, alive to a wider culture, provided it was respectable, hard-working, independent towards the outside world and enterprising.

It also bred a people who could be almost incredibly narrow-minded, crabbed, hierarchical and continuously censorious, with hypocrisy their occupational hazard. The harrowing and humiliating public arraignment of backsliders before a full congregation was a disagreeable feature of all the Nonconformist chapels, but none were so dread as those of the Methodists. Ivon's own brother, the awesome David Jones the Bank himself, was once mercilessly pilloried in Shiloh: he had been seen polluting the Sabbath afternoon by strolling down Prom in a flippant manner, with his hands in his pockets.

Methodism has been dubbed a school of democracy and of the labour movement. There is truth in this but only within strict limits. It was more true of the Wesleyans than of the Calvinists, more true still of the older sects, the Independents and Baptists. The chapel democracy of the Calvinistic Methodists was tempered by ingrained deference, the elective tyranny of almighty deacons and by a tightly controlled federal system of Circuits and Sessions directed from a centre, for many years their theological college at Bala. Other sects recoiled from 'The Methodist Pope with his Bulls of Bala'.

This was the world the young David Jones grew up in, more loose-textured perhaps than in earlier days but still powerful, not least in its treatment of its children which, at its worst, could be joyless. His grandfather 'Ivon' was pillar of this establishment, which itself dominated the town.

'Ivon' had been a member of the mother chapel of *Tabernacl* and active in its many missions into the rougher side of town. When *Tabernacl* grew too large, it amicably budded out Shiloh to the north, in the new and more fashionable centre. 'Ivon' and David Samuel moved to the new place, which opened in 1863, took over the mission work and soon challenged *Tabernacl* itself in its prestige. It was one of Wales's 'great chapels'. It was stiff with shopkeepers, but also attracted university lecturers, professional people, better-off craftsmen and some mariners. It was considered 'uncommonly genteel'. In 1870, after seven years, its membership numbered 150 men and 250 women; of the latter, seventy were servants who automatically followed their mistresses. During David Jones's youth, it grew into one of the town's strongest centres.

Under Rev Griffith Parry between 1876 and 1883, however, cold war broke out. Many members rebelled against the minister and his clutch of stony deacons. The origins of the quarrel are obscure. The official history of the chapel indicates delicately that the minister was 'thoughtful and scholarly . . . with perhaps limited appeal'. The Ivon Jones family thought differently. To them, he was a frightful and arrogant snob. They were among the leaders of the resistance and the most intriguing relic of the quarrel is the text of a drama which the Jones family performed at home on 27 April 1882, shortly before David's birth.

This is, in fact, chronologically the very first document in the personal archive of David Ivon Jones. Years later, when he started to keep a spiritual and intellectual journal in a grocer's account book, he carefully copied out the text of the drama in his best handwriting, adding informative footnotes. On the minister's daughters Kate and Annie, David commented, 'They seem to have been somewhat "snobbish"'. They must have been; they were the only characters in the play to speak in English!

'Dear Father, don't be silly, daddy dear
Fight them out, though they are many, daddy dear,
A lot of low and mean shopkeepers,
Coal and tape and leather sellers . . .'
cried Kate, to be echoed by Annie . . .
'I was born a "thorough lady", mamma dear,
I dare not work, to be untidy, mamma dear.
Let the servants work and pay them
Put the Shilohs down and crush them,
Stay at home and pray not for them, mamma dear.'

The Rev Parry and his wife, in Welsh verse replete with nicknames and jeers, revile many leading Shiloh members, singling out David Jones the Bank. They end by shaking the contemptible dust of the chapel from their superior feet. True enough, Mr Parry quit the next year and though he stayed six more years in Aberystwyth, he never preached in Shiloh again.

There was evidently a strong streak of petty-bourgeois populism in the Joneses and this was without doubt a force behind the much more catastrophic schism which ripped open Shiloh four years later, precipitated a ferocious internal struggle which raged for six years and, in 1893, ended in secession. It was, in short, a Chapel Split, almost as characteristic a feature of nineteenth-century Welsh culture as an Eisteddfod Scandal or a Union Breakaway.

In 1887, Shiloh was effectively run by three deacons, stern, authoritarian men who brooked no dissent (two of them were north Walians which was probably another irritant!). They fished throughout Wales for 'great preachers' to fill the pulpit and scorned the local Circuit of the Monthly Meeting. There was no scope for local talent or 'unknowns' (in a Welsh society where the ministry was still the first choice of budding intellectuals). They combined this lust for prestige with an assertion of rigid tradition and impregnable hierarchy. The rebellion was led by the university graduate David Samuel who attempted to install four new deacons. Those in power resisted. They took the case upwards through the Methodist organisation, fighting all the way.

But if this were the origin of the schism, it was soon lost in what was a familiar Welsh descent into a boiling pit of mutual hatreds. Underneath an icy veneer of formality, life in the chapel became intolerable. The Methodist organisation, in ever-widening circles, was drawn in. Meeting followed meeting. No fewer than six successive deputations waited on Shiloh, one led by the Principal of the University College. They gave up in despair — 'A spirit wholly alien to the Spirit of the Cross reigns there . . . ' In the end, the Monthly Meeting had no choice but to recommend that the minority withdraw to a new chapel. They urged the majority in a chapel worth £7,000 to donate £1,000 to the new cause. They refused. The Monthly Meeting begged them at least to give £500 as a gesture, but they would not pay a penny. The dissidents pulled out in 1893 and built their own chapel, Salem. In characteristically Welsh style, these singularly unfraternal Christians now worshipped separately, quite literally (and perhaps appropriately) within a stone's throw of each other!

A local journalist, commenting on the feud, recalled a story from the Middle East about a man who'd rented a donkey. In the midday sun, he took shelter in its shadow, whereupon the owner objected that he'd rented out the donkey, not its shadow. During the prolonged litigation which ensued, the donkey died. There is a standard Welsh tale about a Welshman shipwrecked on a desert island for twenty years. He was ultimately rescued by a frigate, whose captain observed that the Welshman had built himself a small town. This achievement, itself impressive, was dwarfed by two even more impressive buildings which dominated the scene. 'What are those?' asked the captain. 'They are my chapels', replied the Welshman. 'Most praiseworthy', responded the captain, 'but tell me, why two?' 'Ah!' said the Welshman, 'This is my chapel. The other is the chapel I don't go to!'

From 1893, Shiloh was the chapel David Ivon Jones did not go to. He was five when the quarrel started, eleven when he moved with his family to Salem. David was the brightest young sprig in one of the major Welsh Methodist 'dynasties' of Aberystwyth. Not only this, he was the most promising youngster in a particular Methodist cause which had proved itself dedicated, intransigent, combative and demanded loyalty. His subsequent defection was to be all the more shattering. That defection was perhaps imprinted on his unhappy childhood. 'I cannot think of Aberystwyth without picturing a place with muddy streets', he was to write, 'Perhaps the reflection of the character of most of its inhabitants'.

David was born at the Waun-grug smallholding just outside the town, where his parents, John and Mary, were settled. Though they produced eight boys and a girl, those parents are shadowy figures. They died young. The family was scattered, the children farmed out to kinsfolk. Arthur, the eldest boy, was sent off to north Wales. The three youngest, Tom, George and David, were billeted for a few happy years on their grandparents. When Ivon Jones's wife died in 1895, their sister Florrie moved in to look after them. But the death of 'merry Ivon' in 1898 destroyed what was left of family life. 'Sometimes', said David Jones 'I feel I've been a lodger all my life.'

That dispersal became a diaspora, as the children were blown away by the winds of the world. George went to Canada and no fewer than six of them ended up in South Africa; three of them were to die there. South Africa seems to have become something of an obsession in a Cardiganshire where emigration was a way of life. The Joneses went partly to seek a better climate, mainly in search of an Eldorado. Their attitude was ambiguous. Among many Welsh people, particularly those of a more nationalist temper, there was strong sympathy for the Boers, who were seen as a small people struggling for existence against arrogant English imperialists, the bullying of the British Empire and its voracious capitalists. It found vivid expression in Lloyd George's audacious pro-Boer campaign. On the other hand, no region in Britain contributed more volunteers than Wales to the Boer War. An assertive British patriotism embraced ambitions which were more personal. Many Welsh war veterans settled in the country. The Secretary of the Uitlanders before the War, after all, had been Sam Jones of Tredegar, who kept their minutes in Welsh to defeat Kruger's detectives! Such evidence as there is on the Jones brothers suggests that they were motivated largely by the familiar urge to 'better themselves' and to seek a cure for their physical condition. They seem to have felt some sympathy for Afrikaners, which did not long survive the first encounter. As in so much else, David was to prove himself distinctive. When he finally got there, he made a serious effort to understand and work with Afrikaners, despite a personal distaste for many of them. What is certain is that South Africa was a distant but sensed presence throughout his youth. He was twelve when brother Arthur passed through Aberystwyth on his way there, to be followed by William, Eben, James and, after her marriage, by sister Florrie.

After Ivon's death, however, the problem was to find some tolerable life at home — indeed to find a home at all. He moved in with his uncle at the family shop. It was a distressing experience. David was already displaying unusual talents and his uncle William, a crabbed and disagreeable man, was jealous and resentful. Nor was there much comfort outside. He had left school at fourteen and became an assistant in an ironmonger's. He did not much like the work and became depressed and bored by the 'snob pauperdom' of Aberystwyth. He was later to conjure up a youth spent shuffling around its 'muddy streets', identifying with stray dogs and mourning the loss of merry Ivon. His life had been, and still was, encased in Calvinistic Methodism, but the unhappy boy grew restless.

'How anxiously the early Christians awaited the Second Coming of Christ!', he wrote in his journal five years later, 'When I was a mere chick of a child, the mere thought of the Second Advent sent me melancholy. I had an idea, such was the atmosphere I was brought up in, that Judgement Day might happen at any moment.' Many a Sunday was ruined by the terrible hymns they gave out ... 'I can remember now what a dreadful effect the hymn — *Ai marw raid i mi?* (*Must I die?*) — used to have on me. How my soul rebelled at it!'

He described his rebellion as 'unconscious'. It needed a 'gentle leader' to turn the unconscious into conscious rebellion ... 'consequently to strike out on a path of its own'. He used to agonize over 'Eternal Punishment' which he found abhorrent. In one discussion, Dan Rowlands, a butcher's son, replied to his passionate revulsion — *'Leicen ni gredi'r un fath a chi, ond ...'* ('I'd like to think like you, but ... '), going on to list 'the customary platitudes in defence of Damnation'.

'That was my state of mind, my unconscious rebellion with regard to Damnation. As regards the other "points" of belief, Deity of Christ etc, confirmed "orthodox" so far as acceptance of *authority* and tradition went; as far as private research and judgment — nil, indifferent. What I remember with aversion is repeating the line — *"Tragwyddol wae neu hedd dilith* (Eternal woe or endless peace)" ... What a "regrettable necessity" I thought it was!' 'In this stage, about 1900', added David Jones in 1905, 'I came in contact with George Eyre Evans ... The first thing impressed on my memory was his description of the "orthodox" and "heterodox" God: one an immanent homogeneous God, another Tritheistic heterogeneous one. In his words — "The Trinity is a Roly-Poly God!"'

In George Eyre Evans, David Jones found his 'gentle leader' and a home. The older man, then forty-three to David's seventeen, took him into his house and his life, threw open his library and prised open his mind. They were close from the start and the relationship had become quite astonishingly intense by the time David Jones emigrated in 1907. Over the years, as David went on an intellectual odyssey which took him clean out of Eyre Evans's world, they became ideological aliens to each other and the younger man grew prudent in his correspondence. But the correspondence — and the relationship — did not slacken. Wherever he went, New Zealand, South Africa, France, Soviet Russia, affectionate letters flowed endlessly between them.

In Moscow in August 1921, David Jones, then an official of the Communist International, could still write cheerfully to his old mentor and friend . . . 'To me the world has become very small now and a run over to Russia looks no more than a trip to Pontrhydyfendigaid used to be in the old days!! Except that in the former case, you have to watch the police!' Three years later, when he was dying, a dedicated Communist in Yalta sanatorium, David was worried because he had not heard from George . . . 'I often sit here and muse over Ty Tringad — how nice it would be to sit by the fire in that library . . . but I feel there is an estrangement . . . I had not realized that "Communism" had made a vast difference . . . I remember how you once sent me a card — "Follow the gleam, lad, come what may" and I did not think, nor do I now, that you made any reservations . . . '

As soon as he got that letter, the first he'd had for nearly three years, George Eyre Evans burst out in reply 'At last! At last! dear old Dai! . . . you've never been a night out of my thoughts . . . No, Dai, no, be your opinions what they may, no holding of such is to separate me from you. Your gleam you have followed, yes, I told you I made no reservations. I make none now. This door is as open to you today as it ever was . . . ' The letter was returned to Eyre Evans unopened; the day it reached him, he learned that David was dead.

George Eyre Evans was in many ways a remarkable man. To a young Methodist like David, he must have seemed a creature from another planet. A free thinking Unitarian, he was heir to a distinguished Unitarian tradition. His father, David Lewis Evans, a man from the Unitarian Black Spot along the Teifi, had known the legendary Romantic poet Iolo Morganwg in the revolutionary days of early Welsh Unitarianism and was himself a founder of its journal *Yr Ymofynydd* (*Enquirer*). He became professor of Hebrew and Mathematics at Carmarthen College and married the daughter of a naval captain.

Their son George was born in 1857 in Colyton, Devon while David Evans was serving a chapel there; the family moved to Carmarthen where George completed his education under the renowned Gwilym Marles, a Unitarian who fought against political evictions and was evicted himself. At eighteen, young Evans was apprenticed to cotton brokers in Liverpool, to enter the offices of Barings there in 1879. By this time, he was already preaching and lecturing, frequenting the theatre and the opera in London, enrolling in the Junior Reform Club, moving along a Unitarian network into the world of the great and the good. By the time he was thirty, he had several publications to his name and was chairing literary societies.

In 1889, he gave up business and took a Unitarian chapel in Whitchurch, Shropshire. The antiquarian passion which was to be the driving force of his life seized him and he began to publish serious work on Unitarian history and local antiquities. A friend of the Unitarian thinker James Martineau and a subscriber to the *Athenaeum*, he finally gave up preaching, to live on a private income supplemented from a Ministers' Fund and to settle in Aberystwyth in 1898, first at Tan-y-Bryn in fashionable Llanbadarn Road, later at Ty Tringad on the lower slopes of Pen Dinas, an Iron Age hillfort overlooking the town.

He certainly made his mark on the place. His great passions were archaeology and antiquities. He published over a dozen books on such themes and left several more in manuscript. He plunged into local history with his customary enthusiasm, even though his Welsh was inadequate. He seemed to appear everywhere at once. He lectured endlessly on such themes as 'Across American Plains' and 'Ancient Welsh Punishments'. Every Christmas Day he gave readings from Dickens to the patients at the Infirmary. Every research project produced pamphlets which were promptly showered on everyone within reach. He bombarded the local press with reports on his work and comments on every subject under the sun. He served on the town's library committee and on that preparing the new National Library of Wales. A sprightly writer, he buzzed around Aberystwyth like a gadfly.

Utterly respectable himself, he liked to shock the uncommonly proper and used his quizzical Unitarianism as a weapon. For that reason, despite his eminence and his familiarity with people of substance and power, he never quite made the local establishment; the citizens tended to look at him sideways, not least because of his Unitarian rationalism. Characteristically, his closest connection was with the staff of St David's University College at Lampeter, some thirty miles away; this was an Anglican bastion which at times, and understandably, felt somewhat beleaguered!

Much of his historical work, notably on the old Courts Leet of Aberystwyth, the history of Lampeter, editions of Unitarian letters, was of real value. For eighteen years he did research for the Royal Commission on Ancient Monuments in Wales and Monmouthshire; for thirty-three years he served as secretary to the Carmarthenshire Antiquarian Society. His donations of books and papers to the National Library of Wales form a substantial collection. David Jones used to say the only appropriate end for Eyre Evans was for a cromlech to fall on his head!

He had a certain style. He kept several Life Histories and Life Registers in which his own career was carefully documented (and religiously copied by David Jones) in minute detail, from his first tooth to his first opera! Possibly the largest single collection within his personal archive was of photographs of himself. He favoured smoking and hunting jackets, with breeches, and sported a goatee. A caricature of himself — Reader! he greets you on Christmas Day! — he used as a calling card. In his diaries, which were no less minutely precise and written in a somewhat regal third person, entries ranged from '24 December: His dearly beloved Aunt Laura passed on to Higher Service in the Nearer Presence. Eheu! Vale! Vale!' to '31 December: Bathed in the open sea at Clarach at 3.15 pm' and included 'September: His friend George Barker took cramp and drowned while swimming with George Eyre Evans, who found the body.' His donations to the National Library filled his study with formal acknowledgement slips. He carefully bound them into a volume and presented that — which prompted a leading Welsh historian to anoint him 'Bloody Ass of the Decade'!

This was not enough; he wanted to be a mover and shaper, particularly of the rising generation. Typically, he responded to the Boer War by rushing to organise physical fitness classes for young men and he threw himself enthusiastically into the Boy Scout movement. He became County Commissioner for the Carmarthenshire Scouts and ended as Chief Scout, Wales — more photographs for the desk. The abrasive tone and what he considered the un-Welsh vulgarity of Gibson's *Cambrian News* displeased him and he was an active supporter of George Rees's *Welsh Gazette* at its launch in April 1899. It proclaimed itself strongly Liberal and Progressive, but was more measured in tone than Gibson and it was certainly more specifically Welsh than he was; indeed, it declared itself Welsh Nationalist — in the essentially cultural sense then current. From May, Eyre Evans contributed a free article weekly. Many of them were antiquarian but they ranged from *Wayside Notes* to ethical debate. He kept his Unitarianism out of them but he often challenged orthodoxy and while invariably high-minded, he could write lively and often racy prose. He won a loyal readership. For some reason he wrote under the pseudonym Philip Sidney — which must have been the worst-kept secret in the Principality, since he was regularly introduced as such at his endless after-dinner speeches!

Philip Sidney's piece on 28 December 1899 gave voice to what was an obsession of his. It was a passionate plea to save the town's young men from becoming 'a prey to the evening wolves — drink, immorality, impurity, idleness, gambling, lying, cheating . . . they are destined to be the rulers and guiders of the town's tomorrow'. A striking feature of Eyre Evans's life was that everywhere he went, he gathered around himself an intense and active group of bright young men. The process seems to have started in Whitchurch after his return from a month's tour of the USA when he met Oliver Wendell Holmes. His diary entry for October 1889 reads: 'George Eyre Evans threw open his library to all who wished to borrow books.'

That he certainly did in Aberystwyth. In that library, clever if generally poor young men would gather to be fed and entertained, to read, argue, debate and in return to help Eyre Evans with his books. For many it was a liberal education they never forgot. When David Jones entered this little world, he was entranced. To the end of his life, he always cherished the memory of a warm, welcoming house, the charm of Eyre Evans's sister, the humour of Mrs Thomas the housekeeper, the milk and rum of the old cook, Hannah Rhyd-y-Bont. There were the old paintings and furnishings, the mountains of Unitarian mementoes, books, books, books, endless good-natured argument and discussion, the planting of trees and plants in a garden nicknamed Purgatory. It was the nearest thing to a home he ever knew. And there was the intense society of aspiring young men, vying for favour, in competition and companionship, rich in all aspects of such a group life, not excluding jealousies. This Aberystwyth circle is very reminiscent of others, more celebrated, in those years, such as the high-minded socialist fraternity which gathered around Edward Carpenter. Inevitably, some sniff the atmosphere of suppressed homosexuality (in Aberystwyth, it would most certainly have been suppressed!). A niece of David Ivon Jones who wrote an absurd monograph which sought to prove that he had always been a good Methodist boy at heart, nevertheless felt constrained to discuss his sexuality. It seems in fact to have been ambiguous. He was certainly very close to Eyre Evans and throughout his life enjoyed intense relationships with congenial young men. On the other hand, he was evidently attractive to women. He liked to flirt — though usually at a safe distance, as in his correspondence with Eyre Evans's sister Kitty. There was certainly one serious love affair in New Zealand.

And there was one startling story current in Aberystwyth, whose source was none other than James Jones, David's own brother, with whom he lodged for a while in South Africa and, more pertinently, in whose London house he stayed during his dash to Moscow in 1921. When David made a hasty one-day visit to Aberystwyth to say goodbye, according to James Jones, he had in tow 'a Polish countess born in Knightsbridge'! It should perhaps be noted that James Jones, though a good Methodist who detested Ivon's politics, was also a bit of a wag, who seems to have grown more waggish in a relaxed old age in Cardiganshire. On the other hand, the story is so utterly implausible that one has a sneaking suspicion that it must be true!

It is possible that Ivon Jones was constitutionally incapable of establishing a sustained and serious relationship with a woman: the affair in New Zealand failed. Not proven would seem to be the safest verdict. Such matters are not what concerned him in Aberystwyth; what fills his writing is the joyful embrace of intellectual challenge. In 1905, he remembered his reaction to Eyre Evans's jibe that the Trinity was a 'Roly-Poly God' ' It was not that I accepted his doctrine, far from it, I was shocked at the rather vulgar definition of the Trinity — though as a matter of fact I rather enjoyed the joke.' This set the tone of their early relationship. Eyre Evans subjected David Jones to shock after shock; he responded with spirit. He rose like a dolphin to Eyre Evans's books and sparkling talk; he felt the first stirrings of literary ambition. It was the start of an intellectual journey which was to end only with his death.

It is not known when and how Evans and David met. Quite possibly it was at one of the former's physical fitness classes, which were advertised in the *Welsh Gazette* of January 1900. These were decidedly military in style. From the first of them, Alfred Smith graduated to serve his country with the Royal Bucks Hussars in the Transvaal. They worked to the Sandow Method, using clubs and sticks. At a display in the Town Hall in April 1900, Eyre Evans's class staged a 'full assault at arms' before a large audience. Twenty-six of them showed off their skill with dumb-bells, Indian clubs and cutlasses and there were bouts at English single-stick. In the register for the class which started in September 1900, there appears a David Jones, aged 17. This would fit — and a fellow class-member was Tom Phillips who is known to have been Ivon's companion at sports. If this David Jones were in truth David Ivon, then he was certainly very slight, no more than five feet one inch tall, with a chest of 29 inches which expanded to 30. Not that he was frail, far from it. Perhaps to compensate for his lack of stature, David Ivon threw himself into sports of all kinds, running, swimming, cricket. He had a passion for rugby and he was a great walker. He won a walking race from Aberystwyth to Borth, six miles away, and he was to repeat the triumph.

Whether through the Sandow Method or not, David Jones was already Eyre Evans's favourite when he made his first appearance in the latter's diary on 17 March 1901: 'Afternoon walk with Professor Foster Watson and David to Llangowen church.' So it continued. On 4 April Watson, David and Eyre Evans took a train to Tregaron in the south and on Good Friday, walked back to Aberystwyth through the ruined abbey of Strata Florida and the historic site of Ystrad Meurig. Later that month, it was an examination of the first castle site in Aberystwyth. This set the pattern, long, sometimes arduous and always self-improving walks, to look at churches, take brass-rubbings, inspect relics and collect histories and folklore. They talked about his craft with Old Samuel the Weaver at Llanbadarn. And always, said Eyre Evans, 'David is a most intelligent companion.'

These excursions, generally two-day weekend affairs at fortnightly intervals, filled the early summer months and it is clear that Ivon Jones was by then enmeshed in Eyre Evans's own work; he translated a Welsh response to one of Evans's regular antiquarian queries in the *Welsh Gazette*. Late in June, the scholar left for a fortnight in London. The letters David wrote to him then are the earliest we have; they are lively and engaging. The first, on 22 June, from 17 Bridge Street, celebrated his very first publication — two or three inches in the *Gazette* . . . 'On Thursday morning, I was a great deal too big for my boots . . . Your article read well (nearly as good as mine). You would have suffered an eclipse like the *Lleuad* of old.' (*Lleuad* means moon and was the title of an earlier journal.)

A week later, David told Eyre Evans that his letters were 'rather categorising. Have you lost faith in human nature or is it the London fogs?' He'd taken up shorthand again after his holiday on Celtic folklore. He'd gone to look for an old Roman road and found himself on a secret path . . . 'trespassing on fairy roads, with secret meeting places'. David had examined the ancient stone at Llanbadarn and learned from Old Samuel the Weaver there that the technical Welsh word for a shuttle was '*gwennol*' (swallow). He was busy translating an old Welsh dictionary and planned a botanical dictionary in Latin and Welsh. This ambitious project, however, ended on a gloomy note: 'My last half-days are gone. Nothing to look forward to now but three months of monotony.'

He was mistaken. Within a month, he was offered a shop assistant's job in Lampeter. He took it, fell in love with the town at first sight and was to cherish warm memories of it for the rest of his life. It is difficult now to detect the magic. Lampeter was a very small place with some 1,700 people in the town and perhaps 5,000 in the district covered by its petty sessions. The great majority of the townspeople were bilingual; some 300 were monoglot Welsh, while only 140 spoke only English. It was attractively sited on the river Teifi in a district far more fertile and comfortable than much of the county. It had all the features of a small, Nonconformist market town, but there was some distinctiveness. St David's University College was there, the oldest in Wales, an Anglican establishment at the heart of a Wales in which the campaign for the disestablishment of the Church of England in Wales was raging. This may have bred some creative tension! Three generations later, when Lampeter was finally incorporated into the University of Wales, Aberystwyth College would have nothing to do with it — the sponsorship was left to Godless Cardiff! Perhaps more immediately significant, the town had a big Unitarian chapel and to its immediate south-west along the Teifi stretched the Black Spot with its fourteen Unitarian causes. Certainly election organisers knew that the place needed careful handling; it was a radical corner within county Liberalism. For whatever reason, David found it infinitely more open and genial than Aberystwyth.

It was on 16 August that George Eyre Evans entered a sad note in his diary: 'David left Aberystwyth for his new situation at Lampeter, to me personally a great but I hope temporary loss.' Two days later, his young protege was perky . . . 'Tidy little trade here. There is a great fair . . . I listened to a good Methodist sermon, with half a dozen white haired and patriarchal looking deacons in the chapel . . . This is a splendid little town'. For David Ivon Jones, Lampeter spelled escape.

3

BREAK WITH TRADITION

David Ivon Jones wrote his last letter to George Eyre Evans on 25 January 1924. It was a letter stricken with intense, personal grief at the death of Lenin — 'the greatest figure of the present century' — and charged with melancholy reflection on the loss of old friendships. The last words he addressed to his former mentor, from the Communist Party Tuberculosis Institute at Yalta, evoked his own youth.

'Aberystwyth has only painful memories. Lampeter has far more attraction, it is free from the associations of snob pauperdom of one's early life which meet one in ghost form at every corner in Aber. Ah! the beautiful Teifi, the trout, the trees, the jovial people there, the touch of pagan humanism which respectable Aber has not!'

Nineteen years earlier, writing in a grocer's account book he used as an intellectual diary, two years after leaving the little town on the Teifi, he had been more dismissive. 'I went to Lampeter to work, my mind having been opened to receive light from the four winds of heaven. I did not read much there, moulded ideas more than anything from companionships, some indifferent, some excellent, the former having been weeded out towards the end of my first year there. Played rugby more than anything else.'

That he certainly did. He joined a rival team to the town's and revelled in its triumphs, notably against the formidable crew from St David's College. 'We played two men down', he reported to Eyre Evans in December 1902 . . . 'just what I like, to fight against the odds'.' Once again I embrace all-round excellence', he wrote the next month . . . 'I am reading the *Method of Creation* and organising another combination that shall vanquish the doughty St David's College and retrieve the title Invincible to its former holders.' He took up boxing — 'a good influence against the evils of drink', — and on 'so-called' Coronation Day in June 1902, won second prize in a bicycle obstacle race.

This slightly-built young man went swimming as often as he could in a Teifi which was pure, unlike the lead-polluted river of Aberystwyth, and he walked. How he walked! Over the hills around, up and down the valleys, ferreting out anything he could from chapels, churches, old craftsmen, learned ministers, anyone who knew anything of the past, in that passionate Welsh hunt after a lost identity characteristic of the time, which the word 'antiquarianism' only pallidly reflects.

The friends he made were people of like mind. There was John Davies, 'the clogger', an artisan who had built himself into a formidable scholar of popular history, a lively, irascible man, permanently enraged at the *Welsh Gazette* which published hardly any of his innumerable reports. John Davies, who later got a job in the new National Library of Wales, swept up an enthusiastic young Ivon into sustained searches for documents, testimonies, forgotten Welsh journals which, in Jones's own words, turned them into a pair of Robin Hoods. Another companion, Ben Morris, a poet and chronicler of Aberdare, then becoming an ILP stronghold, made such an impression that, when news of his death reached Jones in South Africa, he tried to organise a memorial to his friend.

This small group, like the countryside of south Cardiganshire, was to lodge permanently in Jones's memory. Throughout his life, he was to recall his eighteen months in Lampeter as a kind of idyll. They were an earnest, high-minded, rather puritanical bunch. Jones loudly deplored the trivialising effect of the bioscope and denounced the *Gazette* for its 'facts, fancies and football news'. 'What an enormous amount of fiction is written!', he once cried in some bewilderment. Defending Harry Rees, the local correspondent of the paper, against some strictures from Eyre Evans in October 1901, he called him a 'martyr to the journalistic profession'. He didn't lounge about the square as nearly every other young chap did . . . 'there is ill-feeling against him because of his pieces in the *Welsh Gazette* on their loitering habits and their custom of sitting in doorways or window sills smoking and chewing and making insulting remarks on every passer-by'. These young men were very conscious of being a select few. But they were high-spirited, lively, their minds stretching to new ideas, bubbling with in-jokes.

Jones evidently looked on his after-hours work in Lampeter as a critical training. It had to be part-time. He and two other shopassistants lived in and worked from eight to five, with a half-day Wednesday. He had his own bedroom, with a dusty and unused case of good books, but it was so cold that his fingers froze and he could not write. Writing on the shopcounter (which he often did) carried its own perils. 'I'm sorry I lost your proof', he told Eyre Evans in April 1902, 'I was correcting it on the counter, turned my back and a colleague used the proof as packing paper!'

George Eyre Evans sent him 'giant envelopes' every week. They were packed with the proofs of his book on the history of Aberystwyth followed by his essays on Cardiganshire. Jones was to check the proofs and correct the Welsh. Evans sent the *Welsh Gazette* and many other journals, the occasional book; he sent paper to write on and stamps for the envelopes. And he sent letters expounding his own philosophy, exhorting the young man towards 'all-round excellence', sharing experiences, jokes and some of his intimate feelings . . . 'Follow the gleam, lad, wherever it may lead!'

They were growing close. David from time to time would slump into nostalgia for the Evans home where they used to work together — the study, the 2,000 books, the fireside chats. 'How goes it at the Temple of Peace?', he asked in March 1902, in a letter which vividly conveys the atmosphere of the household. 'Is my thatched hut deserted o'nights now? Has the red light ceased to glow to welcome day-workers who, physically wearied, come for mental exercise?' He conjured up a vision of sustained researches into 'antique lore, modern sciences and arts of all times'. Did the 2,000 books still 'behold a busy amanuensis indexing and composing . . . ardent book lenders coming for renewal and change . . . County Scholars talking on all matters . . . Or are there counter-attractions, Radical Clubs, Literary Societies etc — to whom all honour is due . . . I hope they have a taste of everything . . .'

He was sometimes jealous. Within three weeks of the move, he was asking, 'How is that so-called Will coming along with you? He seems to be filling my chair pretty satisfactorily . . . Do not shock him too soon.' Two months later, he was commenting on Eyre Evans's use of quotations from 'a youthful writer . . . he surpasses me in descriptive talent and also his grammar. I will have to look to my laurels'. By January 1902, he was petulant . . . the latest *Philip Sidney* column showed 'the growing powers of your new pet. You need not look to me for help now that you have University College of Wales and such initials after your notes. You should put those initials at the head of the column not Philip Sidney . . .'

These were aberrations; Ivon Jones was clearly Eyre Evans's star protégé. He worked on Evans's manuscripts and supplied a variety of notes for his column, mainly on place-names and folk customs. His notes and his letters, which were often a running commentary on them, in fact form an engaging and often comic chronicle of a young man who had been encased in a Calvinist way of life moving from his eighteenth into his twentieth year and trying to make himself into a Welsh 'man of letters', through the only real medium available — the *Welsh Gazette*.

He was painfully aware of his limitations. 'I am ignorant as yet of the elementary rules of English grammar', he wrote in January 1902, complaining that Eyre Evans had not answered his requests for advice. He had given up shorthand again after four months. What was he to do? i.e French? Latin? General browsing? Why had Evans not said something? 'I must work in new fields', he resolved on New Year's Eve 1902 'to reveal another page of history, to read the silent witnesses, to bring another atom to add to the mighty sum of human knowledge . . . but I had better acquire an atom of the mighty sum of human knowledge before attempting to add to it, what say you?' In fact, his writing developed steadily through this apprenticeship. And he was certainly no sycophant . . . 'the same, old, docile, peace-loving fellow', as he ironically called himself in South Africa in March 1913 'only uncompromising underneath . . .' He ribbed Eyre Evans mercilessly on his inadequate Welsh. 'Please observe commas in compound abbreviated which makes it more like colloquial Welsh . . . It is a riddle to me what enjoyment you

get in collecting place-names when you cannot understand nor com-
prehend their beauty and appropriateness . . . Yet more errors in your
transcription! . . .' He sometimes took a mock-lordly tone with his mentor . . . 'Your style is improving greatly', he commented on an article Eyre
Evans had placed in the *Gentleman's Magazine*, 'Take this from a Judge.'
When he did some work for Professor Edward Anwyl of Aberystwyth
and got a five shilling postal order for his pains, he became the worldly
academic . . . 'What chance does Prof Anwyl have of the Principalship at
Cardiff? Why is Darlington out of it? (Lteratteurs always stick up for
their patrons!)'.

It is his occasional angers which punctuate his growth into self-con-
fidence. After some weeks in Lampeter spent on Eyre Evans's proofs,
Jones sent him a note on the place-name Bro-nant, only to see it appear
in the *Philip Sidney* column on 19 September 1901. He was shocked to
see his 'letter to a considerate friend exposed to a harsh and criticizing
public, with more errors heaped on!' 'I would very much like to know',
he added, 'who is or where are the "quarters of high knowledge". I wish
you would give "specific information" instead of speaking in riddles . . .'
And since his wages had not been paid, he would like some postage
stamps.

He was still irritated in October, returning Eyre Evans one of his
sheets of writing paper with lines drawn on — 'so don't say this is blank!'
But by the 19th, Evans had remembered his birthday and sent him
photographs of the Celtic Cross at Llanbadarn and the Tregaron communion plate. Warmly responsive, Jones suggested that *Philip Sidney*
start a 'bygones', column in the *Gazette* entitled *Cymru Fu* (The-Wales-
that-Was). The editor welcomed the notion and the new column started
on 12 December. Its first number was written by Ivon Jones.

This was a serious enterprise. Engrossed by a series of fiery speeches
which Lloyd George was making at the time, Jones with John Davies the
clogger, in an access of Welsh patriotism, climbed the Alltgoch iron age
hill-fort two miles north of Lampeter and started serious work on the
early history of the Welsh . . . 'English authors have to translate Chaucer
for the peasants, but Welsh peasants can understand the contemporaries of Chaucer's Welsh originals . . .' After a trip to London, Eyre
Evans walked south Cardiganshire in early December, took tea with the
Principal of St David's College and met David Jones, whom he evidently
encouraged to write a long essay on Alltgoch. The first instalment of
three duly appeared in the *Welsh Gazette* of 12 December, under the
pen-name *A Reader*.

'I would like to know if my name is not good enough to be shown in
the *Welsh Gazette*', wrote Ivon on the 14th. 'Your excuse is not sufficient.
Who knows what door in a literary sense would be thrown open to me
by the insertion of my name? It is true I send notes for the love of the
thing, but why should the editor block up the only avenue from where a

reward can be expected?' Eyre Evans had not even transcribed his article properly. The death of Eyre Evans's much loved aunt Laura in that month seems to have blunted Ivon Jones's resentment and he had a piece on Welsh superstitions in the *Gazette* for 30 January 1902 under the name of *Dafydd o Bont Stephan* (David of Lampeter), but there was a slackening off of his personal work during the spring and this was not the last explosion of injured self-esteem. In January 1903, after having been immersed in Eyre Evans's family papers — 'where every development of little George is described, every new tooth etc' — he sent another rebuke, after one of his notes failed to appear in the *Gazette*. 'I wish you would say frankly that it does not merit insertion, if that is the case, instead of beating about the bush, or is it that you shrink from inserting what looks dangerously like a criticism of an incident in your History of Aberystwyth?'

But in fact Eyre Evans had become central to Ivon Jones's emotional life. During his stay at Lampeter Ivon's sister got married and went abroad, his brother George went back to sea and brother Tom decided to join other members of the family in South Africa. The young man heard of all this only through Eyre Evans. His uncle William in Bridge Street was as unfriendly as ever, even concealing Ivon's *Gazette* pieces from his sister. Jones mourned the break up of the family circle around 'merry Ivon', and at Christmas 1902, decided to stay in Lampeter — 'I feel more homely here.'

Throughout 1902, he was busy on Eyre Evans's material and hunting books and journals to serve his growing obsession with Welsh history, philology and antiquities. Evans lent or gave him books, including Macaulay and Carlyle by whom, after initial difficulty, he was captivated. In the spring, he was signed on as a local correspondent of the *Gazette* to assist Harry Rees. This could in fact be considered his first initiation into a form of 'practical politics', which he would have called 'sordid and vulgar' since he had to cope with the over-sized shopkeeper egos of an under-sized market town. Not the least of them was his own boss, Samuel D Jones, an opinionated man who quarrelled easily. Having alienated the local dynasty of Harford, he won a County Council seat in the autumn after a campaign which was notably abrasive even by local standards. Samuel Jones was hostile to the *Gazette*, which had not supported him, but also tried to use Ivon Jones to push his own interests through the paper. As Jones was to comment in later years in South Africa, his experiences in Lampeter and Aberystwyth were a good training in the difficult art of keeping the contradictory demands of stomach and soul in harmony!

In the autumn, Ivon Jones replaced Harry Rees as the Lampeter stringer for the *Welsh Gazette* and the connection survived his return to Aberystwyth. Trivial and frustrating though the experience often was, it was the only work he did outside the shop. When Ivon Jones left Wales in 1907, the only 'training' he'd had was in local journalism. In that same autumn of 1902 he gave his first public lecture. Siloh Calvinistic Methodist chapel, which he regularly attended, invited him to give a talk to the regional Methodist meeting on the state of the Jewish people, political and religious, under Solomon (a characteristic subject for what could have been a critical Bible-bound audience). In something of a panic, he begged Eyre Evans for books on the Oriental monarchies and the looming ordeal haunted his letters. In the event, the paper passed off splendidly; the young minister pronounced it the best he'd heard and he was asked to repeat it . . . 'I was not loud enough, ,Jones told Eyre Evans, 'but I quite surprised myself with my self-possession. I felt as if I could have done anything.' In later years, he was to claim that he was never a platform man but in fact he followed up this initial venture with a series of effective addresses to the Aberystwyth Unitarians and he turned their minute-book and magazine into his own personal journal. These years in obscurity proved to be something of an apprenticeship to an as yet totally unforeseen career.

His membership of the Siloh Methodists, however, was now coming under strain . . . 'What I am at my wits-end to solve is the Deity of Christ', he wrote to George Eyre Evans on 11 May 1902. 'I sway to and fro with conflicting evidences, or, bar that, I am a Unitarian now. But the fact is that all intelligent Calvinists do not believe or have thrown overboard the old notions about predestination etc. I am now reading Channing's essays . . .'

The immediate occasion for this confession was a lecture by a celebrated Unitarian minister, Copeland Bowie, on the text 'Come unto me' to an audience of some 500 of the orthodox denominations in Lampeter Town Hall in April. It clearly impressed Ivon. The lecture's theme, in effect, was 'What is a Unitarian?' and what surprised and delighted the disturbed young Methodist was the Unitarian's 'reverence for Christ and his sufferings, his unbounded admiration for the Lover of Man, the man of sorrows'. It was precisely the Unitarians' denial of the divinity of Christ which made them outcasts to the orthodox majority who often regarded them as a species of infidel Anti-Christ, a worse plague even than the Catholics, who were at least 'Christian'. The transformation of Christ into a human being, however noble, overthrew most received doctrines. Coupled with it was an openness to every current of thought, an endless questioning, all designed to tap whatever of the 'divine' (of a God conceived essentially as an ethical and energising principle) there was in humanity. The denial of the divinity of Christ was probably the toughest obstacle for any youngster steeped in Calvinism who was edging out of it into a new and breathtakingly wide universe of discourse. Copeland Bowie's reverence for a nevertheless human Christ seems to have taken Jones's mind by storm. Why, the lecture even ended with the hugely popular Crucifixion hymn *O Fryniau Caersalem* (*From the Hills of Jerusalem*). David Jones sent a detailed account of the meeting to Eyre Evans.

It promptly appeared in the *Gazette*. 'By the tone of it', commented the young man, 'it might have been written by a Unitarian. It seemed as it was written by a Unitarian or no-arian at all. The fact is, I am at the dangerous parting of the ways where I don't know what to believe . . .' It was in that April that Eyre Evans started the Unitarian cause in Aberystwyth, holding services in his own library. 'How does Aber take it?', asked a fascinated Ivon Jones, 'Are they startled or do they slumber along in contempt?' About this time, too, David found a friend, a young man who was a pupil teacher in a Board school, a Unitarian of his own age. They became inseparable, walking the hills and the Teifi valley, arguing out everything on earth − and perhaps more immediately relevant, in heaven . . . 'He very often says that I am not a Calvinistic Methodist at all, he doesn't know what I am . . .' It was from this point that Ivon Jones got John Davies the clogger to hunt up copies of the *Ymofynydd* (*Enquirer*) the Welsh Unitarian journal and that his letters echo to the challenge of the 'Unitarian fiend'.

The turmoil must have got worse in early October, when Eyre Evans took the youngster with him as a companion on a week's jaunt to London. While the scholar worked on Nonconformist records at Somerset House, Ivon Jones enjoyed himself on his first (and almost his only) visit to the capital. Not that there was much self-indulgence! On 12 October they went in the morning to the Little Portland Street chapel for the Rev Stopford Brooke, in the afternoon to St Paul's for the Bishop of Stepney and in the evening to Jewin Street Welsh Methodist chapel for a 'hearty service'. On their return, Eyre Evans presented David with a copy of the *Mabinogion*, the fabulous collection of medieval Welsh stories, which entranced him.

There was, no doubt, another lurch out of orthodoxy. In February 1903, Jones read in the *Ymofynydd* a scathing attack on an address by a celebrated preacher Cynddylan Jones on the theology of Methodism and wrote to Evans . . . 'Between you all, I read more Unitarian literature than the average Unitarian. It is a wonder I have not been converted a hundred times over. Somehow I take an interest in everything Unitarian. I admire their men and follow their movements and I know more of Unitarianism than of Methodism, which is very strange, but the fact is, there is nothing to know of Unitarianism except that it leaves one to know whatever it likes, whereas in Methodism there are the "fine points" to tackle if one is to be a thorough Methodist.'

Writing in recollection two years later, he stated baldly in his day-book diary, 'I left Lampeter a confirmed Unitarian though still a faithful member of Siloh Calvinistic Methodist chapel there.' This is the self-deceiving hindsight of a recent convert. It was a harder struggle than that. Over and above all dogma, there was the strong emotional pull of the traditional services, the power of the hymns, which he never ceased to love, the drive of sermons which were often as complex as they were eloquent; above all there was the intense Welshness of a religion which had come to express the aspirations of a small people in the throes of a national revival. Nine years later, writing from South Africa as a confirmed Unitarian, though one about to transfer an almost religious commitment to the Labour Party and Socialism, he told Eyre Evans: 'I am a Unitarian — but something more. For I should not consider the foreswearing of National ideals and an aloofness from Welsh life and thought warranted by the embracing of views on religion which do not agree with those of the chapel ... Were I to come home, I should most certainly vary my attendance at the [Unitarian] meeting house with frequent visits to the scenes of former days, to hear again the mysterious charm of Welsh oratory, of that Welsh hymnology which from childhood days and through ancestral veins, throbs with the throbbing of our hearts. We leave the ancient valley of tradition, thinking to see it never more, but unwittingly the path up the mount of truth takes a turn again and we view the old altars and holy groves in a wider prospect but with undiminished love.'

This rather remarkable testimony stressed the necessity for intellectual dissenters not to cut themselves off from what he called the Common March of the Welsh people. David Jones was in fact a 'Welsh nationalist' in the non-exclusive and open style of the time, which was the style of a national-popular liberation and one of the 'progressive' movements of the age. It was a style which infused the early socialist movements in Wales and even some of their communist successors and challengers. The peculiar historical development of Wales had made Nonconformist (though, *pace* David Jones, not especially Calvinistic Methodist) religion into a vehicle for such a movement, had made it almost as much of a 'national church' of a resurgent people as Catholicism had become to the Irish. This sense that no 'vanguard' (for such the Unitarians considered themselves intellectually to be), should ever cut itself off from the 'common march', remained strong in Jones throughout his later political career. In a more specific sense, too, he used sometimes to offer the example of the Welsh national movement to both Afrikaners and blacks in South Africa.

Overriding all else was the necessity of total commitment. It was not the indifferent and the inert who would break from obscurantism into religious liberalism and intellectual freedom. Again writing later from South Africa, he voiced his views in an argument, abruptly and perhaps significantly yoked to a discussion of the dignity of labour which, in contrast to New Zealand, he found degraded in South Africa, which has a curiously, and perhaps prophetically, *dialectical* ring ... 'Kaffirs do all the work here. And who can rise into that glow of high thinking or high feeling, without the proud consciousness of an arduous job well done and tingling from the exertion of doing it. Strange thought it may seem, advanced religious ideas can only be imbibed by such bigoted Methodists as those of Wales, who recoil from the expression of heresy. People who are indifferent to all strivings about the deeper meaning of life are incapable of becoming religious liberals. They must first be *religious*.'

Whatever light that remark may throw on his state of mind on the eve of his commitment to socialism, it certainly reflects his real predicament at the end of his stay in Lampeter. He was still a man struggling out of Methodist bigotry in highly religious dedication, still essentially a 'no-arian at all'. It took the return to Aberystwyth to force the break.

Circumstance forced that return. By October 1902, his uncle William, 'in the same moods as usual' and disgruntled at the threatened departure to South Africa of brother Tom, who evidently helped out in the Bridge Street shop, announced that he would be giving up the business in the spring. Ivon Jones was himself beginning to feel restless — 'I feel I must go somewhere from here, however much I like the place, to get more experience in the trade, for it is evident that I shall never get very "superfluous" wages.' By January 1903, his Lampeter boss Samuel Jones was in trouble. Drink and speculation had multiplied his debts and, in the aftermath of the county council election, the Harfords were threatening the lease of his *Emporium*; they vowed that Councillor Sam would not tenant a pigsty on their estate. Samuel Jones swore he would close the shop before the expiry of the lease in September and the foreman was already looking for a place. By March, the boss seemed to have got out of his difficulties but rented a house in town and talked of retiring. Back in Aberystwyth, uncle William forced the issue by dying.

Once again, Eyre Evans intervened to decisive effect. On a working trip in south Cardiganshire in February, he saw David and floated the idea that he and his brother Tom take over the Bridge Street grocery. He seems to have talked Tom out of going to South Africa and personally arranged a bank advance of £80. April was full of preparations for the move, with much discussion of zinc-proofing the warehouse and ordering stocks. David Jones may well have become conscious that he was in fact inheriting a business started by his celebrated grandfather Ivon in 1839, for it was at this point that he started working on the old radical's papers. On 11 June, the *Gazette* printed his edited version of an Ivon letter of 1843 announcing his launch of the Aberystwyth journal *Y Cwmwl* (*The Cloud*). The move apart, it was 'philology', which was now filling the young man's mind. He had several notes published under the name of *Dafydd o Bont Stephan* and in April a long essay in three parts on 'Dialectical Baby-Talk', discussing the dialect of south Cardiganshire with an Italian study as an example.

He had very mixed feelings about the move . . . 'The day of the "wondrous return" is fast drawing nigh, not without many misgivings as

to the future and regrettings for the pleasant past at Lampeter which
will be left behind only to be longed for . . . The "wanderer" also feels
that no place can suit his dreamy and unconventional spirit so well as
Lampeter, the free and homely Lampeter . . . yet he welcomes the return
to the region of learning, to the atmosphere of knowledge and the abode
of books, to a Templum Pacis! . . . The wanderer leaves the field of his
favourite study — dialects — for a place where there is no dialect,
therefore no study, which he deplores. He leaves the musical speech of
the Teifi Vale for a Welsh-English jargon . . . Yet he is promoted to higher
responsibility . . . ', at which point Ivon Jones was interrupted by the
auction of the *Emporium*. He was back in Aberystwyth by 28 April,
when he and Eyre Evans went on one of their long and self-improving
walks, taking tea with antiquarian vicars. It was on 30 April 1903 that he
started business on his own account, carrying on his grandfather's old
place at 17 Bridge Street under the style of D and T Jones. And at that
point, direct, personal testimony from David Jones dries up.

For seventeen months, all we know of him we learn from entries in
Eyre Evans's diary and the pages of the *Welsh Gazette*. He did not find
a grocer's shop congenial, unless he could turn it into a seminar on
language, history and ethics with his customers, as he often seems to
have done! He was to describe himself in a later reminiscence as an
'uncouth grocer'. His relations with Eyre Evans were close, but not yet
as intense as they became. In the October, he was helping post off the
latter's study of Cardiganshire, in regular parts, as he did with his study
of Shropshire parish registers which succeeded it. They went on several
walks, one of sixteen miles. On his twentieth birthday in October, Ivon
was presented with Eyre Evans's silver watch and the next month, was
closeted with Evans and Professor Anwyl in the latter's study at the
university college. David submitted an essay on the place-names of
Lampeter for a local Eisteddfod at Christmas and initiated what was to
become for them an arduous seasonal tradition by setting off by bicycle
for the Teifi from Eyre Evans's house on Christmas Day, returning there
for a Boxing Day supper. Jones was frequently in and around Lampeter,
in fact, while Eyre Evans's diary is full of the new Unitarian venture
which during the year moved to a small room in the New Market Hall in
the heart of town. There is no record that Ivon Jones was involved.

There was one breakthrough; in July the young man got his own
weekly column in the *Welsh Gazette*, often signed *Ivonfab* (Ivon's son) It
was a Welsh-language column entitled *Lloffion* (Gleanings). And from
July 1903 to March 1904 that is precisely what they were. It was a hodge-
podge of a column or to be more charitable, a miscellany without much
rhyme or reason, more a compilation than a composition. There were
extracts from Welsh and Welsh-American poetry, stories, stray comments, some occasional high-minded gossip, the spirit aptly caught by
the title of an occasional column in English he ran alongside — *Leisure*

Hours. Only twice did he put some bite into it, though hindsight makes those occasions seem prophetic: he wrote an intelligent essay on comparative vital statistics and, in March 1904, a rare but biting political comment on Liberal absentees from the Commons during the debate on the import of Chinese labourers into the Transvaal. He peppered his column with quotations from notable writers. These were not developed, but if they are an indication of his own reading, it was impressive — Pascal, Ruskin, Huxley, Nietszche, Manzini, Carlyle, Macaulay and the Unitarian thinker James Martineau.

In his day-book a few months later, Ivon Jones said that in Aberystwyth the practice he had adopted in Lampeter continued . . . 'After coming up here, did a double game, a sort of half and half allegiance to Salem Calvinistic Methodists and Market Hall Unitarians, the latter gaining ground . . .' Certainly, in early 1904, his relations with Eyre Evans become visibly closer. Regularly, twice a week at least, the latter's diaries record . . . 'David came in the evening . . . David and I read much proof . . . David and I worked at night . . .' Eyre Evans was now working on a history of Lampeter, was frequently in the area and just as frequently met David Jones there. There were more long walks, from minister to minister. Ben Morris and other friends came up. From June, David Jones often spent the night at Eyre Evans's 'Temple of Peace', when interesting guests were present. Whether because of this or not, from March, David's *Lloffion* column suddenly became more coherent. It now concentrated on Welsh literary history and on sympathetic though critical exposition. There seems to have been some shift in June. Eyre Evans was in Lampeter at the end of the month and on the 29th there were a series of meetings there of like-minded men 'over the *Welsh Gazette*'. David Jones was present at all of them and from that moment his column in the *Gazette* not only got much longer, it focused more and more on intellectual radicals and heretics in both Welsh and English writing. From July Eyre Evans's diary starts to record that 'David and I worked as usual', on Sunday evenings and over hours — five to ten — which seem to have straddled the Unitarian services. David took to staying on at Eyre Evans's for long discussions with visiting Unitarian ministers. It seems a reasonable inference that he was attending those services and the discussion groups which formed around them. By November 1904, it is obvious that the young man is on track for crisis and decision. From early November, in an abrupt change, each *Lloffion* column in the *Gazette* is devoted to the analysis of a single writer — Lowell, Tolstoy, Victor Hugo, Emerson, Thoreau and Carlyle. On 12 November he starts a day-book to record his own intellectual and spiritual development. And on 4 December he takes his first service with the Unitarians.

The day-book he started on 12 November is a remarkable, indeed unique, document. It was an ordinary shop account book, the right-hand pages filled with weekly transactions. The left-hand pages, the margins, sometimes the spaces between the lines of price-lists, this 'uncouth grocer' filled with verse, aphorisms, long accounts of arguments with his authors and with himself. It constitutes a prolonged interior dialogue in which he records his own intellectual and spiritual development over a critical year of his life. 'Man's greatness lies in the field of his obscure ideas', he quotes from Immanuel Kant in the January of 1905 at an intensely lonely moment of isolation from his family and former friends. 'I had often contemplated on the fact', he adds, 'that every individual mind had a mould or set of ideas and even ideals, which when put into the poor language of time and place, look gallingly plain and commonplace.' Kant had called these ideas 'obscure' . . . 'Even amongst the closest of friends, all are barricaded from divulging their own obscure ideas', which were known only to themselves and God . . . 'then comes the necessity of God and a belief in His existence very obvious . . . I even see the necessity of a God for the poor cur who, harried by men and fellow beast, trots his lonely way through the rain in silent contemplation . . . The failure of men to reveal their "obscure ideas" is the source of all religious dissensions of Christendom.'

After a brief, practical note that his bank overdraft had fallen to £50, Ivon Jones plunged into his 'obscure ideas'. The day-book opens with an explosion of poetry, Welsh verse translations of English classics and several Welsh poems of his own. This was an impulse which stayed with him. He wrote verse in South Africa, entered a Welsh eisteddfod there and his sense of poetry was to inform even some of his toughest writings as a Communist. These early poems, in Welsh, were in fact hymns and it is clear that, however firm his hard-won grasp of Jesus Christ as a human being, David Jones at this moment was still wedded to the conception of an intensely personal and benign God and a belief in the immortality of the human soul, which became increasingly difficult to reconcile with his growing Unitarian rationalism. He quotes with approval from the American poet James Russell Lowell who was a major influence on him at the time . . .

Perhaps the longing to be so
Helps make the soul immortal.

and many of the aphorisms he cites in that November celebrate the supremacy of the Ideal . . . 'A loveless power could not fashion the human heart (Crossley) . . . The things that are seen are temporal, but the things that are not seen are eternal (St Paul) . . . Thoughts rule the world (Emerson).' Ivon Jones's God and his Ideal, however, were both of a high radical temper.

Think you truth a farthing rushlight to be pinched out when you will?
With your deft official fingers and your politician's skill?

Is your God a wooden fetish to be hidden out of sight
That His black eyes may not see you do the thing that is not right?

He quoted from Lowell in a religious invocation whose corollary was social action in the cause of justice,

Where empires towered that were not just,
Lo! the skulking wild fox scratches in a little heap of dust.

The most striking illustration of the radical spirit in which Jones set about ordering his 'obscure ideas' was the verse he chose as the very motto of his day-book, pasting it into the cover and translating it into Welsh. It was *God Save The People* by the Corn Law Rhymer Ebenezer Elliott, poet and hero of the working-class and Chartist movements of the early nineteenth century:

When wilt Thou save the people?
O God of mercy, when?
Not kings and lords, but nations!
Not thrones and crowns but men!
Shall crime bring crime for ever,
Strength aiding still the strong?
Is it Thy will, O Father
That men shall toil for wrong?

It was in this spirit that Ivon Jones presented Victor Hugo, Emerson, Thoreau and Carlyle to Welsh-speaking readers of the *Gazette* and, the day after he translated *God Save The People*, addressed the Market Hall Unitarians on 4 December on the theme of 'Encouragement and Hope' — an address Eyre Evans found admirable and of which they may have been in some need.

It was at Christmas that he took the irrevocable step. On Christmas Day he and Eyre Evans set out on an epic sixty-mile walk through south Cardiganshire. It took them three days, in brilliant winter sunshine over wild country, moving from one Unitarian minister to another. It was evidently an exhilarating experience, which Eyre Evans wrote up for the *Gazette*. During the first fortnight of the New Year, David Jones was in Eyre Evans's house every evening, working, talking and walking. Some time in the first week of January 1905, he deliberately retrained from sending in his annual contribution to Salem Calvinistic Methodist, leaving a blank opposite his name in the chapel Report.

This brought Dr David Lloyd, one of the elders, to his door. He demanded, in tones of utter incredulity, whether this, the brightest sprig of one of their notable Methodist dynasties, seriously intended to make his home with the unspeakable Unitarians. David said he did, adding that it was purely from the dictates of conscience that he did so. Surely, snorted Dr Lloyd, it was worthwhile ignoring the dictates of conscience for the sake of believing in the Deity of Jesus Christ! David Jones was adamant . . . 'I gave him consent to erase my name from the books.' A Calvinist retribution inexorably followed.

It is perhaps difficult for anyone today fully to appreciate the enor-
mity of this twenty-one-year old's offence, at a time and in a place where
ethical, social and political values were wholly encased in Christian
theology and denominational loyalties were fierce, even tribal.
Unitarianism was the very last of the Nonconformist creeds to be
granted toleration by the British state. The dominant Methodism of
Aberystwyth was less tolerant. Unitarianism as a system of belief, if the
term can be applied to so open a doctrine, cherished by 'Atheist Christians and Christian Atheists', was loathsome. Even socially prominent
Unitarians like Eyre Evans were viewed with deep suspicion, at best as
eccentrics, at worst as subversives, not least by Dissenters who were
politically Liberal. In Aberystwyth at the time the word 'Unitarian', carried the same stigma as the word 'Communist', in later years. In fact, to
this day, there are kinsfolk of David Ivon Jones in Aberystwyth who find
it easier to forgive his conversion to Communism than his conversion to
Unitarianism. The fact that he was 'merry Ivon's', grandson hugely compounded his offence. In making his decision, the young man condemned
himself to the loss of family, friends, esteem and the comforts of a homely tradition.

His brother Tom seems to have become virtually hysterical, half-
weeping and excommunicating David for ingratitude, betrayal and
heresy. His brother George, shortly to join the Salvation Army and become a 'ten horse-power advocate of Salvation', broke off all relations
and did not write to him for seven years. Brother John was at that
moment creating an exclusive, mystical and yet evangelical sect of his
own; his reaction may be imagined. His sister was appalled at the
'betrayal' of his family. Wave after wave of the orthodox came at David
Jones, at his counter and in the street, denouncing, haranguing, exhorting, with brother Tom as an ardent fifth columnist within the household.
It must have been a hellish experience. David Jones held his ground and
it is not fanciful to see in the principled and obdurate defiance of this
young man in Aberystwyth the faint future profile of the white man who
stood in the dock in Pietermaritzburg in South Africa fourteen years
later and told a bigoted and bullying white magistrate to his face that the
Lenin of South Africa might well be a black working man without a shirt
to his back.

On 9 January, Mr David Samuel, MA was at the door. This was a
formidable man, a celebrated Welsh scholar, teacher and writer, head-
master of the new Ardwyn County School in Aberystwyth, a product of
the political victory of Welsh Nonconformist Radicalism. He did not
openly chastise David, merely asked whether his decision was irrevocable and how he was to announce it at the *seiat* (chapel meeting)
three days later. But his very presence, emollient in tone, was a rebuke,
keenly felt by brother Tom. Samuel took pains to impress on a distraught
Tom that David was in no sense considered a *gwrthgilwr* (backslider),
that he was leaving without a stain on his character, in no need of a *papur*

aelodaeth. This, a 'membership paper', was a letter of dismissal which a man on the move took to his chosen chapel in his new home. In the mobile world of the Welsh, with people moving along a chapel network, it was in fact a vital testimonial to character, a 'certificate of civism'; without it, a man was suspect. Samuel, in what turned out to be a hypocritical act, assured both brothers that the defector did not need one. David found him surprisingly pleasant, chatting about the Unitarian thinkers Channing and Martineau. Reminded that he himself had often quoted Channing in chapel meetings, Samuel turned huffy and retorted that, in such matters as he had cited, Unitarians were indistinguishable from the orthodox when quoted. He said he would announce David's final withdrawal at the chapel meeting on the following Thursday, 12 January, and advised Tom not to attend . . . 'evidently expecting some unpleasantness about it . . .'

He showed foresight. After he had left, David brooded over the *papur aelodaeth*. He decided he had agreed to its omission too readily; it would have been of little use to his new Unitarian friends and 'more than that, I never imagined that there was the remotest probability of an Ultra-Calvinist church giving a letter of recommendation to a doubter averting to the Unitarian faith'. On second thoughts, however, he came to the conclusion that its withholding would be interpreted as a slur on his character. He therefore, in very careful Welsh, composed a letter to Samuel requesting a letter of dismissal. To his day-book he confided his intention of pushing 'some home truths into their heads in a pleasant way, so that I should not imperil the getting of the letter by bickering of any sort'. In fact, the letter was extraordinarily conciliatory, stressing that his decision had been made solely on grounds of belief and referring to the Unitarians as 'fellow-Christians'.

That evening, in cathartic mood, he walked out to a favourite place, the Castle Rocks, which jutted out to sea from the vicinity of the castle ruins, where communal hymn-singing was a Sunday evening entertainment . . . 'the moon to the west bathing the sea in a flood of silver, stars twinkling as best they could through the moon's rays, the promenade deserted . . . It occurred to me how the Creator could have enveloped our little planet in a perpetual shroud of mist similar to that of Jupiter or Saturn and I considered that the privilege of looking out into an infinity of space meant a corollary privilege of the hope of immortality throbbing in the human breast having a basis of reality too . . .'

He had need of such cosmic consolation. At the Thursday meeting, his letter was not even read, David Lloyd the elder asserting that brother Tom had told him David did not need it. This denial of a character reference, which rankled for a long time, was followed up by a sustained emotional and intellectual assault which made it unsafe for David to walk the streets. W T Price, an elder who had known his grandfather Ivon, came at him 'in fierce, bigoted ignorance', quoting grandfather

Ivon to the effect that 'there was no food to be had with Unitarians'; he contemptuously dismissed the young man as Eyre Evans's puppet and, citing his own brother Tom in support, said David had babbled without knowing what he was taking about: *'Edrychwch 'ma, was, ma rhywun yn ych forco chi!'* (Look here, boy, someone's forcing you!) He asserted that two out of every three suicides in the Unitarian Black Spot in south Cardiganshire were Unitarians — an assertion which rocked David Jones, until Eyre Evans pointed out that Unitarians were far more than two thirds of the population there! A Salem woman stormed into the shop denouncing a Unitarian she had known in the vale of Aeron to the south: *'A hen slwt gas oedd hi!'* (And a nasty old slut she was!) David was driven back on the reflection that if she'd had to walk nine miles to service every Sunday, she'd shown a dedication unknown to a slut. And so it went on, for weeks on end.

These, to any detached and distant observer, petty and absurd persecutions were to the newly fledged Unitarian a torment to the spirit. The early pages of his day-book are full of defensive justifications of Unitarianism, dredging up any and every favourable testimonial he could find. The agony did not last, by the spring it was behind him. But he never henceforth lost the sense of being an outsider in his own homeland — any homeland — a 'permanent dissenter'. So they all felt, the little bunch of intellectual dissidents he had joined; their nickname for their own congregation was the Catacomb. It was clearly with his new fraternity in mind that David Jones quoted his favourite Lowell again:

> Then to side with truth is noble, when we share her wretched crust,
> Ere her cause brings fame and profit and 'tis prosperous to be just.
> Then it is the brave man chooses, while the coward stands aside,
> Doubting in his abject spirit, till his Lord is crucified,
> And the multitude make virtue of the faith they had denied

David Ivon Jones was very conscious in January 1905 that he had made a crucial choice. So he had. Everything he did in the rest of his life stemmed originally from that decision. But he could not have known that his real travail was yet to come. In January 1905, his journey had just begun.

4

A UNITARIAN IN THE MAKING

In October 1912, David Ivon Jones wrote from Germiston near Johannesburg to inform George Eyre Evans that he had joined the South African Labour Party. 'There is no other party in South Africa worthy of the enthusiastic support of anyone who feels strongly the need for a revolution in our social system here . . . The Labour Party, though extreme and narrow in many respects, advocates Liberal principles, though it will not call them so. *Therefore I look upon it as a kind of religion* [my italics] . . . There is no Liberal Party. Labour is the liberal here. The whole country wants a Lloyd George to shake it inside out like a dusty sack.'

Nearly two years later, on 3 August 1914, very eve of World War I, after he had gone through the dramatic strikes and been elected General Secretary of the Labour Party, he was tougher with Eyre Evans. 'I must say that in the course of time one's reading changes and one gets impatient of the purely "palliative" pabulums of the old favourites. The *New Age*, *Labour Leader*, *Clarion*, *New Statesman* and other organs proclaiming revolutionary changes, spiritual and social, for the ills of the times have supplanted many old favourites. In this I fear I have travelled far from your old world conservatism. You cling to the past . . . '

The basic thrust of the argument, however, was unchanged . . . 'I have been swallowed up in the activities of a movement which is more than political, is indeed spiritual in its influence. I came to South Africa without a God in the world. You know what I mean. With frequent spells of depression and pessimism unaccountable. Life a futility. I found South Africa permeated with a spirit of snobbery. The cure for my pessimism and South Africa's snobbery has since been found in the entirely spiritual enthusiasm for a new Heaven and a new Earth, in which the publicans and sinners do share, with which Labour's awakening fires us. For it must be remembered that the Labour movement out here is largely Socialistic. Socialism of the large and glowing kind.' This particular stance, this approach to the workers' movement and to Socialism, which seems remote from the Marxism he was to embrace in a matter of months, in fact reflects an intellectual formation which took shape in him during his three years among the Unitarians in Aberystwyth.

He remembered them with pride and affection. In June 1913, after he had been virtually 'exiled' to Vereeniging for his Labour activities, he could write: 'Do you ever hear of the old comrades Drew and Pugsley?

In my experience, those chaps were connected to the cause in the period of its — not success as the world understands it — but of exaltation. I wonder if they look back to that time with the same sense of having been in an order of knights pursuing a holy greal? . . . Some of the visions fade, even the "Greal" itself. Other "greals" not so glorious but perhaps more to the practical task of King Arthur's knightly heart, who I think was averse to the rash surprise of the Holy Greal — other "greals" come and take possession of us . . . but still none of the new command the pure devotion that the old wrung from us . . . What an inspiration to look back on that time, the time when we were "saved" in a sense which Methody parsons cannot understand . . .'

They were certainly a remarkable crowd in the Aberystwyth Unitarian meeting house in 1905, never more than twenty or thirty, sometimes as few as eight, but all of them intelligent, independent, light of spirit and full of humour, often quirky, sometimes eccentric but genuinely dedicated to the pursuit of Truth as they saw it. Their politics are not very visible. They, and their co-religionists on the Teifi, had lost the militant and aggressively democratic spirit of the embattled Unitarians of a previous generation; they were all immersed in variants of 'Liberalism' of a peculiarly ethical and high-minded temper. But many of them could be radical. They gave money and help to the quarrymen of north Wales during their desperately fought lock-out of 1901-1903 and welcomed a party of south Wales miners on strike into the meeting house — where they greatly improved the congregational singing!

Such political attitudes as they entertained were a by-product of their central obsession — the elaboration of an ethical approach to life and society grounded in a rational understanding of the world which did not eliminate, but on the contrary celebrated, a sense of the spiritual. David Jones felt the impulse immediately. On 11 January 1905, he noted in his day-book: 'To my mind, there is no more effective evidence to the worth of the Unitarian Religion than my own experiences. Day by day, I feel myself, in every contact with customers or others, connecting unconsciously the act I am about to accomplish with the profession I hold as a Unitarian. And these sudden flashes from the Divine check or prompt me, as the case may be, to higher action. Higher, not high action. I am not so egotistical as that, I hope.' He said every grocer should read Thomas à Kempis before he sold as much as a bag of sugar; it would do both his soul and his business some good!

By definition, they had no 'confession of faith'; opinions were infinitely various. Their services were not unlike those of the orthodox, with readings, prayers, a sermon and hymns. George Eyre Evans and some others, notably David Jones, invariably evoked 'God', but it is not clear in what sense they used the word. Most preferred to refer to the 'Divine' and several were outright agnostics and even atheists. 'It is very peculiar in the Unitarian mind', David wrote, after delivering his second talk to the congregation on 5 February on Dr Richard Price, the eighteenth-century Dissenter democrat, 'that principles and not persons are the great object of his worship. Thus, if any appeals to his emotions and says "Trust in God", he will correct the supposed mistake and says "Trust in the Divine". Repugnance for hero-worship, I think, or perhaps an irreverent want of faith in the existence of God. Even the most "rational" of Unitarians is convinced that there is such a thing as the "Divine" in the universe; a great overpowering principle permeating all. But they are not so convincible as to the existence of God. They rely on the intellect. Confronted with a "God", they have to fall back on their much despised emotions or to deny him altogether ... The taunt so often hurled by us − "What did God give you a reason for, but to use it?" − can easily be reverted and hurled back at us "what did God give you emotions for, but to use them?"'

This is what caused Ivon Jones the most anguish. Having wrestled with The Son to reduce him to the human, he was confronted with The Father, whom he found even more difficult to foreswear. What made it worse was that, apart from George Eyre Evans, who remained very God-centred, the closest friends he made were men of distinctly agnostic temper. J D Stephens, 'the staunch J D', became an intimate, in later years Jones's only regular Aberystwyth correspondent apart from Eyre Evans. He had belonged to the Wesleyan Methodists, a more liberal denomination than their Calvinist cousins and one heavily involved with the Labour movement. Stephens had been engaged with the workers' movement in south Wales and was a socialist, though, to David Jones's horror, he was to support the War of 1914. He could not abide the way in which the word God was bandied about the meeting house.

There were two students of the university college, the 'old comrades Drew and Pugsley'. Both were of mature age and unusually talented. F W Drew was a writer of some power. A man of caustic and critical mind, he alienated David Jones at first, but soon registered as a man of intellect and integrity, with the saving grace of humour. Shortly before his third address, on the place of Christ in the Unitarian religion, David was, as usual, out on the Castle Rocks, prising limpets from a rock. 'Looking for inspiration, are you?'. Drew called from his window − to comment after the sermon − 'Now I know why your ideas are so watery!' Drew cultivated an ideal of 'world unity', believing that all religions were inadequate attempts to penetrate to the essentially human truth of life. According to Ivon Jones, Drew in his addresses 'soars into obscure realms of thought far above his audience and cares not who follows'. His relationship to any form of Christianity would seem to have been tangential.

Alfred S Pugsley, on the other hand, who read physics, was a teacher born, with a 'rare power of getting to the heart of an audience'. Firm, gentle, earnest and outspoken, he riveted the attention of his hearers. He had a habit of praying, 'Forgive us not our trespasses as we forgive them that trespass against us', and of defining his ideas about God and prayer 'with many abrupt utterances about the latter which drew a laugh'. The gist of his argument was 'that he considered himself a part of God and therefore the latter was unnecessary'. His creed was 'Do as you would be done by' and he was strong on the 'desirability of getting people to think, remarking that he would rather be an atheist and know why he was one, than a Christian who did not know'. He used to lead the congregation into a closing hymn and prayer to 'the power beyond our comprehension.'

With friends like these, David Jones hardly needed intellectual enemies! For most of 1905, he was obsessed with the problem of a 'personal God'.From the New Year the *Lloffion* column in the *Welsh Gazette* became sporadic and incoherent and soon disappeared; Jones had probably given it up. Eyre Evans's Philip Sidney column finished soon after. Eyre Evans continued on his endless circuit of the great and the good and David worked regularly at his house on the proofs of his *Lampeter*. The latter, obsessed with his own intellectual endeavour, filled his day-book with his reading. After working on the *Mabinogion* and an essay on comparative mythology and going through Dr Richard Price's eighteenth-century prose with a tooth-comb, he was fairly pleased with his performance on 5 February . . . 'My excitability had vastly diminished compared to my previous attempt . . . I could say long passages without looking at my manuscript', though he was too quick.

During February and March, he was wrestling with the life of Savonarola and the difficult texts of St Anselm and Plato . . . 'I do not understand in order to believe, but I believe in order to understand' . . . 'Faith is the assurance of things hoped for and the proving of things not seen . . . ' This was a real tussle for him and what is striking to anyone aware of what he was to become, is his growing alertness, expressed in his day-book throughout 1905, *to a dialectical inter-action of contradictions*. He was getting to grips, too, with the powerful Unitarian writer James Martineau, even as his day-book fills with sweaty definitions of the 'ontological' and the 'teleological'.

On 19 March, after working hard with Eyre Evans, David gave his third address, on Christ . . . 'I spoke in good *hwyl* (a word meaning joyful enthusiasm with a peculiarly Welsh application to sermons) and was not very dependent on my manuscript either. Rather nervous at the start, became homely.' Martineau, he noted, criticised conservatives like the Catholics who cherished the past and scorned private judgement and the progressives who loved 'the oracle of God in the sanctuary of the soul', but who hated and denied the inspirational revelation of the past'. The objective was a synthesis. He and Eyre Evans went for a walk to Clarach, north of Aberystwyth, on 29 March, took samples of stream

water for the Rochdale Boys' Brigade, camping there 300 strong, and
then worked together through a long evening.

He had need of sustenance, for early in April, he seems to have
entered some dark night of the soul over the existence of a personal
God. On 11 April, he wrote into his day-book a long account of the day's
experiences, which had clearly been crucial to him. It was very carefully
composed and corrected, in quite astonishingly pretentious language,
capped by some verse, which is worse. It sadly confirms his earlier cita-
tion of Kant to the effect that men find their 'obscure ideas' incom-
municable. In a manner which is now unassimilable, he tried to convey
what had clearly been for him a transcendental experience.

He had been walking Pen Dinas, a hill-fort just south of town, where
he and Eyre Evans used to read in good weather, and climbed a tough
ridge to win a superb view. But as rabbits skittered away, he was plunged
into misery which the scene could not dispel . . . 'Up I started at last to
mentally brace myself to face this demon in my heart. What was it, asked
I? What spoiled my enjoyment of Nature thus? Was it the ordinary trial
of business, the difficulties of life? No, they seemed sweet and in lovely
accord with these joys. Was it my conscience? Had I sinned in aught
offensive to the moral nemesis who visits upon the immoral the restless-
ness of remorseful conscience?

'No, 'twas not so! For I had of late made a vow to eschew all immoral
contemplations, although I had not wholly succeeded yet my aim had
been upwards of late and as an emanation of it. I had sent a few lines of
prose on the joys of virtue to the *Ymofynydd*. Then what was it that
marred the view of nature? What demon of despair flitted between me
and its bliss? I asked myself and before long, I found, the answer to the
problem.

'I had been striving for some time, in fact since I had embraced
Unitarianism unconditionally, to realize for myself the true existence of
God in the universe and my soul. Yet I had only nurtured the existence
of God from a repellant horror of the other alternative and, as a matter
of policy, as I beheld it to be the better way. This and no burning inward
consciousness were my grounds for Theism. Martineau's discourses on
the subject left me with no solid grounds of belief, except the ardent
hope that it was true and so it was, while enjoying the pleasant scene on
Alltwen Hill. Theoretically, there was a God above it all, but in my heart
I beheld him not and this was the lurking sadness, and obtruding belief
that all was dull and clodded, with no ethereally divine leaven spreading
through.

'On realizing this, peace put to flight the sadness of my mind . . . I now
perceived the soul in it all, nothing was dull or clouded any more . . .' and
under this 'Divine revelation', he constructed some 'poor lines', *Verses
on Alltwen Hill*, which it would be a mercy to reader and writer to omit.

A fortnight later, he confided to his day-book, '. . . even a Diary is not
capable of receiving one's thoughts correctly. I find myself writing about

eternals . . . catch myself attitudinizing to myself very often!' One can only agree with him, but in so far as his Alltwen confession is comprehensible, it seems to mean that he had overcome a grave crisis of doubt and retained his God by dispersing Him through nature, rather in the style of the eighteenth-century Enlightenment.

This was hardly the end of it. During the summer, he was sharply exposed to a Unitarian with strong evangelical leanings on the one hand and an Ethical Society student called Watkins on the other. The latter impressed him, gave him a volume of Ethical hymns which he read with pleasure. Jones had already read Stanton Coit's collection of Ethical scriptures and pronounced him 'the James Martineau of the present age'. Ethical Society people dispensed with God altogether and saw the world as a dialectical conflict between good and evil.

It was while he was wrestling with these problems during the summer and delivering addresses to the meeting house in which he tried to work them out that Ivon Jones encountered his evangelical co-religionists, Hector Waylen and his wife, who had witnessed and been overwhelmed by the tumultuous religious revival of Evan Roberts then sweeping industrial south Wales. Waylen was desperately anxious to rid Unitarians of the 'arid intellectualism' with which they were charged and to infuse their movement with proselytizing passion.

This, the last of the religious revivals, had started with the conversion of young Evan Roberts on the Carmarthen edge of the industrial belt in November 1904. It swept over south Wales and for eighteen months sent people packing into chapels, with spontaneous prayer meetings and Bible classes breaking out everywhere often among scenes of mass enthusiasm. Many ministers were alarmed by the anarchic passion of its evangelism which swept away denominations, challenged authority and asserted a popular identity which made the strange, mystical figure of Evan Roberts briefly a power in the land. The *Welsh Gazette* filled its pages with the Revival which it ran parallel to the Russian Revolution of 1905 and prophesied political consequences. It was correct. Within a year, radicalism swept the Welsh polls. In 1906 not a single Tory MP was returned from Wales; the six who were not Liberal were Labour. Four years after that the south Wales coalfield plunged into the successive, rolling revolts of Socialism, Syndicalism, Marxism in which leadership of the huge South Wales Miners Federation swung from Liberal to communist in a dozen years. Several communist leaders had begun as boy preachers during the Revival. Two collier uncles of the present writer who had been rather tepid Independents and Liberal voters were swept up in it. Their passion did not last, though they remained teetotallers all their lives — and they moved straight from the Revival into the (little less evangelical) socialism of Keir Hardie's ILP.

David Jones saw none of the political consequences (though he ran into the South African sector of the Great Unrest within capitalism on the Rand), but he could scarcely have missed the Revival itself and could not avoid Hector Waylen. Waylen had been amazed at the popular reception of the dualism Christ and Devil, the sheer power radiated by people standing up to proclaim their allegiance to Christ. Unitarians must tap this spirit. He came up with the banal suggestion that Unitarians 'tested' by their preacher stand up not for God, but for Good, even if it meant losing £1000! More seriously, he advocated a rival Unitarian dualism: 'Life in the body and life in the spirit.'

Ivon Jones detested the evangelical style, though he could not fail to have some sympathy with both the message and the social implications of the Revival. Some time before September, he filled his day-book with pages of reflection on it, clearly influenced by his encounters with Ethical Society people, his awareness of the social implications and his growing dialectical feeling for advance through contradiction.

Evan Roberts had been in the garden of his school in Newcastle Emlyn, downcast at the state of the world, when he saw the Devil leering at him over a hedge. He plunged into the Abyss, but then there appeared the Flaming Figure of Christ with a Drawn Sword . . . 'And from that moment, I assume, Evan Roberts became the possessor of a joyous, unconquerable faith in the omnipotence of Christ's healing virtue' (a faith which in the summer of 1905 David Jones might have envied!) 'Our first impulse when hearing of this vision for the first time', he adds, 'was doubtless to laugh outright.' He cautions against such a facile dismissal, citing Joan of Arc and the Luther who saw the Devil in his own soul 'with a large or a small d'.

'Now, I dare to assert', wrote Jones, 'despite our supercilious habit of sneering at those who believe in the personality of the devil, that there was a large amount of truth in that vision. In fact, the conception which the vision was supposed to symbolize is all true, one of the glaring truths of the creation. Whether we believe in the mere personality or personalities of the actors in the vision is a mere matter of taste.'

It is interesting that, by this time, Jones was describing the question of the personality of Deity as a 'mere' matter of taste. He went on to rank the various creeds along a spectrum. The Agnostic, he asserted, believed in two cosmic processes – the raw and cruel natural process of the survival of the fittest (which Jones, like many, identified in social terms with uncontrolled capitalism, the Law of Mammon) countered by an ethical process at continual war with it. The Unitarian believed in the ideal, but personified only the ideal, the divine ideal, in God the Father. The Methodist personified everything. He believed in personifying God because He personified Good; he therefore personified Evil in the Devil . . . and Jones pointed out that at least he was more logical than those religious liberals who got rid of one only to cling to the other. He asserted the primacy of the Unitarian who did not believe in a Devil because he believed in a God, but he noted, with clear approval, the

Ethical Society man or Agnostic who recognised the logic of the Methodist but shunned his conclusions, did not dogmatize on a God or a Devil, but founded his faith on the certainty of good, bad, virtue, vice, high ideal and low. Jones ended by asserting that there were 'opposing forces which tear the whole universe asunder betwixt their mighty clash of battle', in an endless struggle between opposites which shaped the human soul — and among the combatants were God and Mammon. His conclusion was an appeal to abandon all denominations and creeds which divided people by confusing real ideas with their metaphors. The latter were unimportant. He had uttered such a cry earlier after passing an 'enemy' Catholic church which God had girdled in natural flowers. This theme of world conflict between a multiplicity of beliefs and practices which were mere reflections and mystifications of the fundamental struggle he made the subject of his address to the meeting house on 24 September.

It was directed particularly to his own brothers in the cause. During the college vacation, they had been strengthened by the temporary return of some of their stars, notably J Park Davies, then a Hibbert Scholar in Oxford and D J Davies, then at Marburg university in Prussia. Discussions seem to have become more markedly 'theological' and there was growing tension with the agnostics and atheists in their midst. It is clear that David Jones had been exerting himself to preserve some unity of purpose. He was elected Secretary and Treasurer of the congregation in October and immediately faced a resignation from J D Stephens who could stand no more talk about 'the illusion of God'.

Ivon addressed an appeal to his friend, pointing out that there were many of Stephens's own mind, 'that Mr Drew has to take many things from our pulpit in the symbolic sense . . . We gather together, not from agreement on speculative beliefs, for of them we all have conflicting opinions — but on the reality of morality and goodness, that the spirit of man has in him something divine. That there is a fight of good and evil going on. On this rock we found our church, here is the centre of our gravity.' He rebuked the staunch J D for using the word 'supernatural': 'We could turn the same black bombshell against your — and our — pursuit of goodness.' For one man to believe in the reality of goodness and for another to clothe this goodness with a personality immanent in the universe, did not seem 'so vast a remove' to Jones '. . . both truths are one in their essence'. He called for Stephens's continued co-operation — 'even though God be an illusion — to bring men to conceive of a beautiful illusion . . . it is your duty to help us in our campaign against barbaric illusions which do have a debasing effect on the hearts of men.'

At about the same time, Ivon Jones addressed a declaration to himself in his day-book, breaking off from his sustained study of Martineau to do so, at the point where the latter was discussing God in Humanity: 'I have left the stage of experience when I pounced on every atom of evidence that would tend to prove the existence of God . . . I do not take a militant part in denouncing belief in a God, neither do I take an active interest in sustaining such a belief. I am now glad I have left that position when it was a continual, unreal straining to retain the faith in God, when it was "never glad, confident morning again" . . . the alternative to a belief in God then was to sink into a bottomless abyss.' He had been brought to glory in the Divineness of a Moral Ideal . . . 'and although I still think and feel this is a great argument for the Personality of God, I have ceased to make that Personality the hub of my happiness and aspirations'. He had 'relinquished absolute faith in a Personal God', saw moral ideals a concentric within a 'beautiful halo called God'. The inner gleam was his true solace and comforter; the outer halo, 'though not indispensable and perhaps illusory, is also a source of satisfaction and still keeps me a Unitarian . . . I can still worship the Personality but I worship it as a personification of all good'.

He had clearly reached something of a personal equilibrium but one may take leave to doubt its permanence; there is a strong whiff of the provisional. For David Jones, however, it clearly marked the end of a painful transition. What fills his day-book to the end of the year are the social implications of Unitarianism, which were beginning to concern them all as Wales built up to the radical surge of 1906.

On 29 October the meeting was to discuss True Citizenship and the challenge caught David Jones at a critical moment. He had broken off from Martineau to study Marcus Aurelius, the classical writers and even Buddhism and, while his thinking could hardly be termed 'political', he was certainly at that moment at grips with an ethical approach to citizenship. He was very struck by the renunciation preached by Buddhism. It was the absence of asceticism among the missionaries which explained the failure of Christianity in Asia. Jones saw it as the Sacrifice as opposed to the Survival of the Fittest (Law of Mammon). What appealed to him was the *activist* definition of 'renunciation' practised by the committed. He cited the Roman Emperor Sertorius who had renounced the offer of an island Utopia, 'to remain in the battle of truth with falsehood, of right with wrong'. This was a deep-rooted drive in him, possibly a product of his Calvinist upbringing, and it is surely not fanciful to see in it one source of his response to the Bolsheviks twelve years later?

On the 29th, Jones spoke after addresses by Drew and Pugsley and a prayer by Waylen. 'Citizenship', he said, 'I take to be the practical side — and to many the only side — of true religion, our duty to our fellow men. Personally, I cannot conceive of any worship of God apart from the service of man . . . The only way to raise the beauty of our particular street or town is to put our own house in order . . . to build the Golden City of the future, we must dig inwardly . . . What is the condition of true citizenship? To produce the soul . . . to follow the path of duty to the bitter end . . . through the mists of passion and of sense and through the tossing tide of chance and pain, to hold our course unfaltering in the great career of justice, and above all, to uproot the cancer of self-love. This is the greatest service of man and of God, this is the highest form of worship and this is the supreme prayer.' It is not enough, said Jones, to catch 'mutilated souls as they are hurled from the wheel of oppression and self-love. We must stop the wheel itself . . . the noblest citizen is he who lays the axe to the root of this spiritual convolvulus — self-love — and liberates human souls for their onward march towards the realization of the divine.' The corollary was inescapable . . . 'no smug renunciation of self-love in a cell or a convent or an upper room such as this can be anything but an evil in itself. Once having viewed the light, we must let it shine to the whole house, we must strive for righteousness in the hard jostlings of society.' His message was perhaps reinforced when Eyre Evans, returning from a visit to London, gave a follow-up talk on 'The poverty of Poplar and the wealth of Mayfair'.

Discounting all hindsight, it is impossible not to see prefigured in this young man of twenty-two, talking eloquently in the language of his time and place to a handful of friends in a shabby room in a small town among a people of no account on the western lip of Europe, that as-yet remote man who dedicated his life to the struggle for social justice in South Africa and found a martyr's grave in the Moscow of the Third International.

During 1905, too, he achieved a personal ambition; he launched his own little magazine. In May he floated the idea of a congregational magazine, four-page to begin with, written by the members and published quarterly. The first number was issued to the congregation on 18 June and six issues came out in all, edited by David Jones. He remembered it in Johannesburg in January 1912, when he promised to take copies of it to a liberal church there, run by Coverdale Sharpe . . . 'That was my very own . . . I remember sketching the proposed title page (exactly as published by the way) on the back of a tea wrapper whose front was a mass of foliated decoration and Drew laughing heartily at what he thought my joke when I presented him with that doubled tea wrapper showing "Garlands by members of a congregation" on the plain side, but what a "have" when opened — "garlands" of tea leaves!' What heights little we rose to then, Jones said seven years later . . . 'garlanded indeed by the bond of a common ideal and the spirit of the "catacomb"'

GARLANDS, ran the title page, Entwined by Members of the Unitarian Congregation, Market Hall, Aberystwyth . . . and it elaborated the metaphor into Keats's

Therefore, on every morrow are we wreathing
A flowery band to bind us to the earth.

Jones said he had come up with Garlands in looking for a symbol of unity which would not be harsh. No copy has survived, but it was intended to develop members' native talents and they kept it going until

November 1906. The year was not to end peaceably, however. On the morning of 5 November, David Jones delivered a laboured address which did not go well ... 'The general tone', reported Jones himself as Secretary, 'whomsoever the fault, the preacher may have been humdrum, the weather cold, no fire, possibly a shadow aforecast of what happened in the evening — was uninspiring to everyone. And the singing lagged ... '

This was as nothing to the disaster of the evening. Hector Waylen was scheduled to give a talk on George Fox, the Quaker. Still imbued with proselytizing passion, he conspired with his wife to transform the Unitarian service into a Revival meeting by *coup de main*. The resulting black farce was no doubt less fun to live through than to read about, but Ivon Jones, as 'recording angel', seems to have caught the spirit of the occasion.

'We had a highly interesting lecture on George Fox, the Founder of the Society of Friends, excepting for one or two outbursts in which he shouted too loud almost to be understood ... He brought the lecture to what seemed to be a close by repeating two or three times over the words "Thank God for George Fox". Then he committed the dreadful thing we all dreaded by proceeding to Test the meeting in an Evan Roberts fashion ... He put us in the uncomfortable dilemma of "standing up for God" as he put it, and inwardly acknowledging outward authority — a pope — or sit down and appear to foreswear our Unitarianism and our "Belief in God". When he gave out the edict that all who believed in God to rise to their feet, Mrs Waylen (was it pre-arranged?) stood up. All but she were level-headed (although embarrassed immensely) enough to keep their seats. In the uncomfortable pause following, Mr Waylen hysterically shouted at me "Won't you stand up for God, David?" Mr A J Pugsley, in the anger of his heart, had gone out, but not before whispering audibly in my ear also to come out. Failure to find my cap, coupled with a sense of duty, prevented this ... The meeting ended with the *Cambrian News* reporter stalking out, saying he'd come to hear a lecture not a Revival meeting and had not known it was a Unitarian affair anyway, with members denouncing Waylen for polluting the place with sacrament and ritual, with Mrs Waylen repeatedly shouting "Hector, put it to them, the existence of God" and Hector refusing to give out *Abide with Me* since none of them believed in a God to abide with.'

It was altogether, as David Jones put it in the Minute-Book, 'a landmark in the history and thought of the congregation'. It certainly marked the beginning of a sustained guerilla campaign of harassment which Hector Waylen and his wife waged against the Unitarians and particularly against their Secretary Ivon Jones, which pursued him almost to the foot of the gangplank of his emigrant ship. The annual Christmas ritual which he shared with Eyre Evans must have come as a relief. This time, after David took a morning service on Christmas Eve, they walked 53 miles over three days and spent New Year's Eve working together in the study. *Laus Deo!*'added George Evans.

With the close of what had been for him a memorable year, David Jones gave up his day-book and settled into a regular routine throughout 1906. He spoke more and more frequently at the meeting house and was a popular and effective secretary. He was constantly working with Eyre Evans, this time collecting and editing the letters of notable past Unitarians which he had bound by an old, skilled country craftsman who had never left his remote parish for more than a fortnight. The big event in an otherwise placid year was the congregation's move to new quarters, itself a measure of their growing strength and settlement. They took a lease on a pretty little building in New Street from the gentry estate of Nanteos whose Powell family were admirers of Eyre Evans and which had been serving as store to Galloway's, the town and university bookshop. Ivon Jones, loaded with lino and nails and hailing the skylight for admitting light direct from Heaven, took the lead in settling the place and, with many visitors in attendance, the Unitarians moved in on 15 April in as ceremonial a manner as they would permit themselves.

In July they were presented with a dramatic painting by one of their major patrons, Mrs Alice Evans, the artist widow of an Anglican clergyman who was then living in Paris. She ended her days in Geneva but spent some time in Nice — where she was to offer house-room to David Ivon Jones when he arrived desperately ill in France in January 1921 after a painfully slow, 58 day journey from South Africa. It was in her house, while he was recuperating that he wrote the *Report on Communism in South Africa* which he sent to the Executive Committee of the Third International (seemingly at the request of Karl Radek). Hardly with foresight but perhaps not inappropriately, her painting, which still adorns the walls of the meeting house, portrays Christ arraigned before Pilate by a gang of fat and evil plutocrats.

With the ending of his day-book, we once more lose direct contact with David Jones's mind, except for the occasional comments on sermons he entered in the congregation Minute Book. These could be lively... 'Mr Evans's sermons', he said of his own friend and mentor, 'are sometimes in danger of relapsing into the "dry-bone" state by his lack of the gift of knowing when and where to stop . . . This is, indeed, a free speech society!' On D J Davies the Marburg graduate: 'Mr. Davies has for many years held strong convictions on Women's Rights, Beef-Eating and Peace, so we always expect some burning question to be handled by him in a far from gingerly fashion. He extends women's rights even to the Deity; "Father and Mother God" are among Mr Davies's pet opinions. Mr Davies is an ardent champion of women, not yet having mixed much with females . . . ' (Ivon Jones, of course, is not known to have mixed much with any!)

Probably the most significant of his entries was in August 1906 on a new recruit: 'D Ernest Williams, a late convert from Calvinism, is a

Socialist, a co-worker and admirer of Keir Hardie and a member of the Independent Labour Party. A jolly fellow. A possessor of that virile positiveness which persons of liberal tendencies in theology are apt to lose. A dogmatist, not in theology certainly, but a dogmatist in the sphere of sociology, in burning zeal for the cause of reform and Communism, which for him are synonymous.'

Ernest Williams became something of a legend in Welsh socialism. Born in Breconshire, he lived for years in Mountain Ash in the Aberdare valley and worked as a miner, a hair-dresser and as a dentist, with one of the largest workingclass practices in Britain. A vegetarian, militant agnostic and patron of Welsh poets, he had worked closely with Keir Hardie and became a Communist, to suffer for it, not least in the crisis of 1940. He taught the craft of dentistry to one of Wales's best-known Communists, T E Nicholas, an Independent minister, a poet with 65 bardic chairs, Welsh-language spokesman for Keir Hardie, and founder-member of the Communist Party of Great Britain who ended his long life a Maoist.

Ernest Williams had considerable influence on David Ivon Jones, though it is undocumented. Certainly Jones took with him abroad, and cherished to the end, some of the earlier and revolutionary poems of T E Nicholas, *Bardd y Werin* (*The Poet of the People*), Williams's friend, who would have been only four years older than Ivon at the time. Nicholas's son Islwyn, also a Communist and a member of Aberystwyth Unitarian chapel, in his sketchy outline biography of Ivon, says that Williams led David Jones to William Morris, Tolstoy and other Socialist writers and did much to influence the young man's thinking. Certainly the Unitarians at one time distributed pamphlets by Tolstoy through the Aberystwyth streets.

It is difficult, however, to be precise about David Jones's specific political beliefs at this time. It is doubtful whether he had any as such. What is certain is that he was 'liberal' in the broadest sense, with a strong radical thrust, totally committed, to use his language, to the rigorous exercise of mind and spirit in the liberating service of humanity in a battle between 'good' and 'evil', impatient of ivory towers and ready to wrestle with society in his cause. In one sense, he was a dedicated man looking for a movement worth dedicating himself to.

Islwyn ap Nicholas's own assessment was: 'Ivon appeared to be a Christian Humanist, unless this is a contradiction in terms. Indeed, he was more of a Humanist than anything else and he always stressed the social and economic implications of the teachings of Jesus.' He was certainly sympathetic to an ethical socialism, not least because it might charge the Labour movement with ideals, which he thought it lacked. That is about all one can safely say about David Ivon Jones's politics at the moment when he left the country. The last thing he did before leaving was to go to a meeting to listen to the charismatic John Burns, Labour leader and democratic hero.

But leave he had to and the realisation struck him abruptly. On 16 September, 1906, the even tenor of George Eyre Evans's diary was broken by a terse entry: 'David with a hard cough, with me after evening service. Wish he could throw it off.' Over the next few weeks, he got worse, with severe bilious fits and vomiting. By the end of October, he had recovered enough to take a morning service and to help Eyre Evans move into his new house at Ty Tringad, on the landward slope of Pen Dinas. He was one of the drafters of a new constitution for the New Street chapel. On 11 November, he was re-elected Secretary under that constitution, in the teeth of disruptive clamour from the Waylens who were very bitter against him.

The next month, his condition suddenly worsened . . . 'It was a bleak December day', he was to recall, 'and I was in North Parade carrying a basket and nursing my fitful cough, when a great dull, heavy pain seized my left lung. I nearly gave up hope. The pain sent my temperature to 103° and drove me to the doctor.'

He was in fact succumbing to a family weakness, tuberculosis, the scourge of Wales, particularly west Wales, at the time. The doctor diagnosed weak lungs and told David he should choose between a sanatorium and a long sea voyage. The young man could not face the former. Anxious to restore his health, Eyre Evans abandoned the usual Christmas hike and urged Ivon Jones to go with him on a trip to Carmarthen. 'I would much rather have huddled in an armchair in Ty Tringad, with Miss Evans to talk to, Miss Thomas (the housekeeper) to make me cheerful with her jokes and Hannah Rhyd-y-Bont (the cook) with her rum and milk.' But he went to Carmarthen, walked Merlin Hill, snow-white under a brilliant sun, visited princely graves and old churches and took brass-rubbings. He felt restored and told the doctor on the 29th that he was cured. Within five days, however, the doctor summoned Eyre Evans urgently to tell him it was essential that David go on a long sea voyage and that he leave within a month. David, said Eyre Evans, took the news in his usual cheery and matter-of-fact way.

It seemed less catastrophic because it was assumed that his absence would be temporary. The intention was to pack him off to New Zealand, chosen because it was the longest feasible voyage and because Maria Williams, an aunt of David's, lived in Wellington, as did Dr Tudor Jones, a Unitarian minister and acquaintance of Eyre Evans. David was to make his way there, find a job which was healthy and earn enough to pay his passage home.

Eyre Evans went with Jones to settle the Bank loan; he and the Unitarian chairman Arthur Joinson each lent him £35 for the outward passage. He brought his books up to Ty Tringad and money was raised from friends. Those debts were to haunt Ivon Jones for the rest of his life.

At the service of 20 January, however, the Waylens again intervened. As Evans was preaching, Waylen shouted: 'Did you, George Eyre Evans, on the 7th October, deliver the message from me to David Ivon Jones, stating that if he made a clean breast, all his faults would be forgiven?' The congregation broke up in confusion and as Kitty, Eyre Evans's sister, was waiting for her trap, Waylen strode up whistling and shouting 'Here comes the chariot! Where are the dogs? Where's the bodyguard?' When he returned for the evening service, the congregation had had enough. They took him to Petty Sessions where both Waylens were fined ten shillings for brawling.

It was an unusual leave-taking, perhaps compensated by an emotional last service on 3 February. David Jones replied to tributes and gifts: 'The spiritual pilgrimage I undertook so many years ago has culminated at this point in my involvement and unqualified commitment to the cause of religious liberalism. Where I now stand can best be expressed in the words of Emerson: the new church will be founded on moral science. Poets, artists, musicians, philosophers will be its prophet-teachers. The noblest literature in the world will be its Bible — and instead of worshipping one saviour, we will gladly build an altar in the heart for anyone who has suffered for humanity.'

Eyre Evans lent Jones his aunt's binoculars and brown bag and arranged a code to signal his arrival. It is not clear what happened to the Bridge Street shop or to brother Tom who was to enter a university, but brother George thawed out sufficiently to see yet another brother off into the family diaspora. On 4 February, he and David set off for London, Eyre Evans going with them as far as Carmarthen, intending to board the ship when it docked at Plymouth. They spent a couple of days with another brother, John, in the Rhondda, who lived with his wife and child amid the grime of a colliery village. 'Nothing green in the Rhondda except the spirit of the Revival' — his brother took household prayers morning and evening. When the brothers reached London, they ran into William Evans and a bunch of other cousins at Tilbury Docks. After an evening of democratic rhetoric from John Burns, David embarked the next morning. Jones's cousin Emrys was going with him — a prospect he looked forward to with a wry scepticism since Emrys was thought a bit of scapegrace.

Evans's parents were upset at the leave-taking, but 'William and George gave me a jolly send-off with no Tommy Rot about it'. With a properly British stiff upper lip and to a chorus of fog-horns, David sailed down-Channel to Plymouth, where Eyre Evans came aboard and stayed for the last couple of hours.

When he got back to Aberystwyth, George Eyre Evans entered in his diary: 'We hope to meet at Naples on the homeward voyage.' In the event, he never saw David Ivon Jones again.

An informal photograph of David Ivon Jones

2

INTERLUDE IN NEW ZEALAND

5

THE JOURNEY

'There's a bit of style for you!', David Jones greeted Eyre Evans's sister on his first day at sea, 'You don't get a letter from the electric lighted third class saloon of the *SS Omrah* every day!'

His first reactions were of excited discovery. The cabin had an electric lamp, a wash-basin and water jug, with a little water tank for washing and a few pegs. There were plenty of spotless bedclothes and he had George's rug. Dinner was 'half a haddock shoved on you', while the spoons went 'toboganning down the table'.

He savoured the dubious joys of third-class travel... 'The third-class passengers are not allowed on the upper decks ... It is amusing to see how the toffs above walk about with a sense of their infinite superiority to the motley crowd beneath them. Sometimes they cast a condescending glance at their humbler brethren. Most of them dress stylishly, a lot of Hector Waylens, with fur-lined overcoats.'

'As for us of the lower deck, we are a motley crew' — many of them unlikely to benefit anything except the bar-room. Ivon Jones was uneasy in this respect about cousin Emrys and another young Aberystwyth man, Guy Hincksman. Both had taken the pledge, but they mysteriously vanished when the bar opened. Many of the others, however, were a novel and intriguing mix — plenty of Irish and Scots, two well-educated Hindu medics returning to Ceylon from an English university and already promised jobs in a hospital back home, two Swedes and some Germans. There was an Austrian coming back to his new home in New Zealand and a young, well-meaning Russian of 21, trying to learn English en route to Perth, who kept snatching David's binoculars with a breathless 'Please!' And as for the Italians — like the Welsh they could claim to be bilingual — 'Their hand lingo is really very good ... and I like their moustachios very much too.'

The Italians sang and played cards all day and in the course of the voyage, gambling became the major response to boredom. This appalled the priggish young Unitarian, but he took some comfort from the fact that his cabin-mate Mann had come a cropper at it . . . 'he is troubled with the Englishman's besetting malady — bounce'. David recorded Mann's wretched sea-sickness with considerable relish, while he vividly described his own exhilaration at the sight of the huge Atlantic rollers of the Bay of Biscay. That did not last. The fierce rocking of the ship had its effect — 'a touch of sickness, an occasional hiccup of the Mrs Waylen type! I am taking this like all other unpleasant things — lying down!'

It was to counteract the gambling that a sprightly old gent on board started to organise ship-board concerts. Emrys and David had to do their bit, singing *Hen Wlad fy Nhadau* (*Land of my Fathers*: the Welsh national anthem). The avuncular old man also started a ship's newspaper, pinned up every morning, full of gossip, comic verse and caricatures of the passengers (not unlike the 'topicals' which were a feature of student life at Aberystwyth and no doubt familiar to the young Welshman).

The sprightly old gent was a Mr Thornton, nicknamed Granddad, a 76-year-old veteran of the Crimean War, who knew a lot about Wales and went about flicking people with a wet tea-cloth. Uncle Jack was another old 'character' full of practical jokes. David Jones grew eloquent about Daddy Morse, an entertaining old gentleman going back to India, and even more so on General Sawdust, who looked like a general but was actually a cadger who sent people scuttling to their cabins. He always played draughts, always lost and always found an excuse.

'The times are too exciting for a quiet fellow like me', he told Eyre Evans and the first letters of his long odyssey bubble with good spirits. At Gibraltar, he first set foot on foreign soil. Unlike most travellers, he found it 'the most pretty town' he'd seen, with its painted houses, orange trees, goats, mules, lordly Spanish ponies and their even more lordly riders in broad Jim Crow hats. Salvador the guide took three of them around, but what most took Jones's fancy were the Moroccans . . . 'These Moors were the most interesting people I saw. They were tall and handsome with very clear and smooth complexions. They wore turbans of many colours, muslin cloaks or shawls and very fine knitted stockings with yellow shoes. They walk about without noticing anyone of the Europeans, as if self-sufficient in their own musings . . . I never enjoyed myself so much in my life. How strange it is to have nothing to worry about!'

On the way from Gibraltar to Marseilles, with the Sierra Nevada in view, David struck up acquaintance with a very learned and genial old gentleman who punctuated his conversation with repeated 'Oh Lor' yes!' He was an expert on Gothic architecture and knew all the Mediterranean ports. He told David he could get to Jerusalem in eight hours from Port Said. The young man brooded over the idea, but decided that 'my business now is to get straight to New Zealand', though he added: 'I have made up my mind to see a bit of the historic countries of the Mediterranean before I end my puff.'

His new friend was fascinated by what Ivon Jones had to say about Wales and its Nonconformist people. He was an Anglican himself, mainly because he loved the ritual. In what must have been a novel experience for the Welshman, the Gothic enthusiast dismissed mere preaching with contempt . . . 'Oh Lor' no! Damn it all, there is all the difference in the world between a man who's got something to say and one who's got to say something! Oh Lor' yes!'

David lost his friend at Marseilles, which he explored at the double from a four-wheeler. It was Naples and Pompeii he was looking forward to — 'seeing the place you've got to see before dying'. It was a disappointment. The ship ran into heavy weather, leaden seas and a raw wind. They came into the famous bay in the dark and left it the same way. He sent the usual shower of postcards praising the frescoes in the cathedral and calling Pompeii grand, but what stuck in his mind was the search for tea. 'We couldn't get a tea shop for nuts', he told Miss Thomas of Ty Tringad, 'When we found a café providing tea, we ordered two cups each, biggish like, until the bill came — for tea only — 5d a cup!! That was Naples. Now I suppose I can start dying!' He confessed that the Mediterranean had been a disappointment — 'not one really fine day yet'.

On the long haul to Port Said, the weather was still rough and he occupied himself with pen-portraits of his fellow-passengers. He made a friend, Jack Bartle, and was much taken with one of the Irishmen, 'an honest looking, brawny west country Irishman. It is like wine to the soul to meet one like this, un-enslaved by society's conventions and preserving untarnished the largeness of heart which is the peculiar property of all sons of dear Nature.'

Cousin Emrys brought him down to earth. To his surprise (and possibly disappointment?) Emrys 'was acting the fine fellow' and Hincksman too — though the latter had to be watched when the bar opened. A couple of weeks later, he reported that he was 'delightfully surprised' by his cousin who had been a man all the way so far. By that time, however, Guy Hincksman had gone to the dogs. He had taken up with dubious characters at the card-table, was squandering his money on whiskies-and-soda and rarely spoke to David. Emrys, on the other hand, had been appointed editor of the *Omrah News* in succession to Granddad! By the time the ship nosed out into the Indian Ocean, however, the world had returned to normal. Emrys gave up the newspaper after a fortnight and followed Hincksman to the bar and the card-table. The editorship fell to the waiting hands of David Ivon Jones.

Port Said brought excursions and alarms. The weather cleared and Jack Bartle and Ivon ventured ashore. They fought their way through hordes of Arab urchins — 'I shall never forget them!' — had 'big canal boats put on our feet' and visited a mosque. Then they went on a long hike to find a Turkish bath. 'It was horrible!!' — dank, dark, low, cramped and smelly. There were 'ten minutes of this, ten minutes of that' and they ended up being robbed. They went in search of another and found one in a restaurant. But only one person could use the bath at a time. Jack Bartle tried it, while David gibbered in incomprehensible French to the attendants but fearful of missing the ship, he fled. Bartle made it just in time, stuffing his shirt into his trousers as he came up the gang-plank.

After that, the Suez Canal was bliss . . . 'The Suez Canal was fine, the Red Sea sublime, the Indian Ocean heavenly', David wrote home early in March. In fact, as the journey dragged its weary length, the sun started to beat down mercilessly and Jones was taken ill. The overpowering heat drove him out of the Saloon where he used to write . . . 'The moist heat of the sea has not made it comfortable for my chest. I feel at times not so well as when I started. The five chaps who sit where I eat can't eat because of the heat. A young man with a bad chest loses his voice from the humidity.' The first hint of a doubt creeps into his letters . . . 'Perhaps the good effects of a sea voyage are not felt until after we land?' In fact, over the weeks ahead, he got worse.

The *Omrah News* was some consolation. He enjoyed editing it and sent copies home. The first two issues under his editorship were at once stolen from the notice-board . . . 'Without any lack of modesty, I may say that people are interested and amused by it. Nothing goes so well as a little mild banter at some of the passengers.' In fact Ivon Jones's squibs, yarns and verse were (to anybody accustomed to Jones's normal style) extraordinarily racy and vulgar, full of 'the lads' and 'their tarts'! The shipboard atmosphere was clearly getting to him. As they crossed the Indian Ocean, in a humid heat which drove many of them into a prostrate stupor on deck, that atmosphere became distinctly fey. There were mock trials; one Irishman went around painting the faces of sleeping passengers with burnt cork; another used to sew the sleepers' shirt-sleeves to their deck-chairs and shove ice down their backs. In this distinctly manic atmosphere, David Jones would sit on deck, watching the porpoises leap from a sea of glass, trying to forget his chest and to write home, with his sweat diluting his ink.

Colombo brought some relief. The cinnamon gardens were lovely, even in the sweltering heat of a tea-shop. 'Finer than all was the fine physique and meditative faces of the Cingalese (*sic*) men and women. I saw several Apollos today, wielding the pick and shovel in the street with only a turban and an ornamental shawl agirt the loins.' And into his writing, for the first time, crept a tone of voice which was ultimately to dominate it. He went for a rickshaw drive and looked at the drivers . . . 'Most of them had nice faces, some even noble, often of nobler stuff than the carcasses which they pull about after them for 2d an hour.' His admiration was clouded 'by the ghost of a struggle for existence. One feels that the apparent business prosperity of such places as Colombo for instance is made at the expense of native crowds made "wretched and forlorn" and our enjoyment everywhere is marred by sights which remind us of "man's inhumanity to man"'.

Back on board, he wrote to Eyre Evans . . . 'I think I am better. I'm sure I'll make progress once I land . . . I now feel that the best thing in the world has happened to me. This voyage has altered a lot of my narrow view. There is nothing like rubbing shoulders with people of other lands . . . ' He was right. He added that comment to a long account of a friendship which developed, after the ship had left Colombo, with two of his fellow passengers. That account fills pages; it seems to have been the most important emotional experience of his entire journey. It is, perhaps, a deceiving hindsight which charges those pages with a sense of premonition. For his new friends were Russian revolutionaries, who were refugees from the Russian Revolution of 1905.

'One of them is in the open berths, third class, the other in second class', he told George Eyre Evans on 12 March. 'The one in Third is Jacob, a simple fellow, that is, harmless. He seems very well read, although he cannot speak more than a few words of English yet. He seems to know the socialistic theories of Karl Marx minutely. The other revolutionary — Moses Blank — spends most of his time down on the third class deck. And every day, we have chats on deck. He can speak fair English and also good German. Moses is a most refined fellow, coming from a good family, rather tall, very finely proportioned, with a delicate face, the hands of an artist and the legs of a statuary. When Jacob can't make us understand, he says it to Moses, who gives it to us.' When something 'twisty' cropped up, Jacob gave it to Moses, who passed it to an Englishman who spoke German, who passed it via Moses to David Jones.

'Jacob tells me that he was a bit of a public speaker in Russia — as all the Russian revolutionaries have to do a little of it, to instruct the peasants. He was going one night to a secret congregation of twenty peasants in a cottage, to speak to them on socialistic theories and the rights of man. Presently there came a rat-tat at the door and in came the secret police. He was bound and taken to a prison, where there was only a small window of about six inches high. From there, he was sent to Siberia with forty-six other prisoners. He was put in a prison there, one in four in a small cell. From there, the four of them made their escape by digging a hole beneath the foundations and out into the open air. He escaped to Smolensk, Moscow and St Petersburg and from there to Finland. There, he lay hid for three weeks until a ship was found for him for London. Jacob put his thumb to his nose and his tongue out to describe his attitude to the secret police as the ship was leaving the quay!'

'Both Moses and Jacob', said Ivon Jones, 'took part in protecting the Jews in Odessa from the Black Hundreds, when the last great pogrom took place there. He says that all the young men are revolutionaries. That 500 Jewish young men and 1,000 Christians joined in a secret committee in Odessa to protect the Jews from being massacred. The Jews are massacred because they are the prime movers in the revolution. He tells how the Governor of the place instituted a pogrom. His son — a student — was of the revolutionary committee to protect the Jews. So when the Governor sent his mercenary Black Hundreds out to massacre the Jews, sixty student protectors were killed with the Jewish men and women, old and helpless people. Of that sixty, one was the Governor's own son. A more tragic retribution was never told in a novel!'

Jones was still under the spell of the Russians when the ship at last touched Australian soil at Fremantle on 14 March. He took the short trip to Perth, to be surprised by the density of the woods along the road — and by delicious black grapes at 4d a pound (they were 2/6 at home!). It had been bad weather all the way. 'I felt shaky yesterday and am not right today.' The atmosphere in his cramped quarters was hot, close and uncomfortable. Another interminable haul then to Melbourne, across a 'glowering dark sea' troubled by dreams . . . 'If dreams have a marketable value in New Zealand, they will find a most industrious producer of them in David Ivon Jones!'

Most of the 'cheery souls' left the ship at Adelaide, to be succeeded by a big bunch of 'Colonials, all on the make, all with big talk'. They reached Sydney on 22 March and 'at long, oh so long last!' left the *SS Omrah*. Moses Blank quit with most of the others. David Jones and cousin Emrys, with whom he now barely exchanged the minimal courtesies, boarded another vessel, which sailed the next day.

It was frightful, rain and wind all the way to Wellington in the North Island of New Zealand. The food was better than on the *SS Omrah*, but still pretty dreadful: 'They spoil the rice, it's underboiled.' And it was nothing compared to the grub dished up to the inescapable First Class: 'There is one cook for the Third Class, five or six for the First!' The journey had left David Jones 'weary almost unto death' and as it finally approached its destination, he at last let rip at George Eyre Evans: 'We are the SUBMERGED TENTH! The alleged benefits of a sea voyage are ENTIRELY VITIATED by THIRD-CLASS TRAVEL!'

It was a wet, wind-blown, sick and fed-up David Jones who, on 28 March, was finally carried into Wellington harbour. The first ship he saw there was the *SS Ivanhoe*, which had been built in Aberystwyth.

6

NEW ZEALAND

'Ah!, not blind yet then?', said the doctor at the shipboard medical examination as he eyed David's glasses. He pulled a face when he heard the young man was a grocer, thumped his chest, shook his shoulders and let him pass. Through pouring rain and feeling like death, Jones took what looked like the Constitution Hill tramway in Aberystwyth up to the heights of Wellington, to find sanctuary in the Bryn-y-Môr study of Dr Tudor Jones, who gave him dinner. He was lodged nearby in a Unitarian boarding house, with four carpenters, an ironmonger, a pattern-maker and a clerk. The clerk played the piano and the son of the house a violin, so the evenings were musical. His room had a splendid view of the harbour, with its seven-mile sweep of placid water and three Japanese warships at anchor. Wellington's business district formed around the harbour, its residential quarters were on the hills, wooden houses with bright red zinc roofs and gardens glowing with the blue-gum eucalyptus. His spirits rose.

He was astonished to hear Dr Tudor Jones preach at the Masonic Hall on his first Sunday. 'Ruggedly Cymric in tone', with a strong Welsh accent and in Geneva gown he left the rostrum and, in full flood, strode about the hall. It was if a voice from the Cardiganshire hills rang out among 'the American-like nasalities and banalities of the Antipodes'. The congregation — even 'these prosperity-seeking Colonials' — loved it. Dr Taff was out in the streets afterwards, stalking through his forty followers, all drawn from the 'most cultured class', shaking hands, laughing, calling out cheerily in Welsh to David. He introduced him to two influential figures, Professor Mackenzie of the University and Mr Geddes who owned and edited the *Freelance* newspaper. They promised help in finding a job.

The next day, he went to a picnic on the coast — 'Colonials are very fond of picnics.' Fourteen of them humped hampers and set up 'a cooker called a Billy', shielded from the wind by bullrushes. They spent the whole day playing cricket — the universal passion — and David acquitted himself as well as he used to with Tommy Llandeilo and Tommy Marina back home.

But he had to be about his business. He traipsed around the grocers whose names Geddes had given him, but had no luck. Professor Mackenzie took him to one farmers' co-operative and Dr Tudor to another. They had nothing but thought there might be assistantships going up-country. It was the same story at the biggest ironmongers in town. Dr

Tudor took him to a soap factory run by a Unitarian. Jones did not fancy this. The atmosphere would be bad for his health and anyway it paid 'only a boy's wage of 20 shillings a week' (he was soon to change his tune on this subject!).

At that point, his formidable aunt Maria Williams was at the door, calling him a 'naughty boy' for not calling on her and telling him he looked like his mother. Her household was equally formidable; both her daughters were Methodists and school teachers, Enid a university graduate. It was to their house that his delinquent cousin Emrys had rushed on landing, abandoning David at the quayside. They found Emrys lodging with a Congregationalist minister, but found his person disconcerting . . . 'somebody has taken his measure at last', commented David in proper cousinly style. Emrys, in addressing these 'highly cultivated ladies', had been 'as talkative and cheeky to them as to the rude girls on board ship. Thank you, sweetie, he'd said to Miss Ethel as she passed him the sugar. She gave him a withering look.'

Evidently the joys of respectable Welsh family life were catching up with him! Two letters came through from his sister Florrie in South Africa but because the mail was so slow, they were hopelessly out-of-date. And by the time he sent his first letter to George Eyre Evans from New Zealand on 3 April, he was still stuck for a job.

Then he spotted an advertisement in the *Otago Daily News*. The Medina Apiary of W C Brown at Mosgiel near Dunedin, was offering a job to a young man who wanted to learn orchard work. This took David's fancy. His aunt was dubious. Dunedin was way off in South Island, hundreds of miles away. And what was the climate like? Somewhat to David's surprise, the Medina Apiary responded promptly. They were prepared to take him, but hesitated to drag him all that way for an interview. He went to a doctor, who told him he had evidently been very much worse, advised him to take cod liver oil and reassured him about the Dunedin climate. David booked his passage that night. He landed at Littleton at nine in the morning, took the local train to Christchurch and the express to Dunedin. He arrived that night at nine-thirty. He'd been advised to stay at the Leviathan Temperance Hotel, but a surly van-carrier demanded an extortionate rate which David refused. They stood glaring silently at each other in a deserted square till ten, when they settled for a bob. The van promptly whisked him to the hotel just across the square, two minutes' walk away. After a night spent brooding over the morality of Colonials, David set off for Mosgiel in the morning.

Mosgiel, ten miles south-west of Dunedin in a fertile but rain-washed plain, was a one-horse township of 1500 people, little more than a couple of long streets and a woollen factory: 'Having heard the factory steam whistle', David told Eyre Evans on 18 April, 'you may safely say you have seen Mosgiel.' The place had a gaggle of 'patent sects', distressingly similar to those at home, and a Catholic convent, whose dinner bell tolled in counterpoint to the whistle.

The Browns, Londoners by origin but thirty years in New Zealand, had the biggest place, a fine though isolated house, with two and a half acres of orchard, a vinery, a big tomato house and fifty colonies of bees. At first, David found them congenial. Brown had worked himself up from a packman to buy his orchard and to become manager of a soap factory in Dunedin. Though he had the last word he was away all day, and management fell to his wife who was tough, hard-driving and avaricious. But for the moment, all seemed pleasant. David lived at the house. He was compelled to become a vegetarian and denied tea with his meals. It was a six-month struggle for him, relieved by the occasional fish and a rabbit he surreptitiously shot himself. The evenings, however, were musical, with singing to a piano and an organ. He thought of taking up the violin. And the house was full of books on horticulture.

He revelled in the work . . . 'The Managing Director of Messrs D and T Jones has just come in from topping hedges and pruning 1000 black-currant bushes', he greeted George Eyre Evans in June . . . 'I have done something I never thought I'd be able to do — clip a hedge and clip it straight.' He threw himself into his job, nursing fruit trees, trenching, raising fences, weeding, weeding, weeding and enthusiastically reading up on every new project. His letters begin to read like horticultural tracts. He conceived a genuine love for gardening which he never lost.

'It is most wonderful, face to face with the awful mystery of perpetual creation . . . why even the blights are interesting', he told his Aberystwyth friend, while giving him precise instruction on how to plant cabbages. He renounced the indoor life: 'Never again shall I endeavour to ape the merchant.' He was syringing the apple trees, digging, hoeing, splitting wood; next would come the bee season, the soil to barrow out of the tomato house — and he had to read up on vine-growing . . . 'I simply glory in the race with the orchard and its seasons . . . gardening is the purest of human enjoyments'.

In fact, the work was back-breaking and without remission. He was up at seven, woken by the factory whistle. An hour's work before a half-hour breakfast opened a day of hard labour which ended only at nightfall, later if there was a moon. A wash and tea took him to near eight o'clock and bed-time was ten — in a room denied a light 'because of the sins of my predecessors'. There was no half-day holiday. And as some kind of apprentice, his pay was a pittance — ten shillings a week. 'I came here for my health, only secondly to make money', he wrote defensively to his Welsh friends — who were also his creditors. He claimed his health had greatly improved. He admitted in July that he'd thought he couldn't stand it. His cough got worse and he spat blood for days on end; 'hard frosts in the mornings froze the pluck out of me'. But he'd stuck it out, his permanent back-ache had gone and 'now every-thing is a pleasure', above all 'the thrill of actually producing something'. A couple of months later, however, he was driven to admit . . . 'I like the work more than ever, if only there were not so much of it . . .'.

The Browns were exploiting him as sweated labour. He learned that he'd had six predecessors, none of whom stayed for more than four months. And it was unspeakably lonely, days spent among trees listening to the distant cries of children and far-off laughter, with blackbirds his only 'companions in exile'. He discovered that the Browns, regarded locally as 'grab-alls', looked on their neighbours with suspicion. No-one came near the house, not even their three children. An adopted thirteen-year-old had been worked near to death and had finally escaped at the sixth try.

It was weeks before he made two friends, Aitken, the Presbyterian minister, and Charles Stewart, the station-master's son. That was the trouble with being a Unitarian, there was never any big chapel community to join. He made one trip into Dunedin to meet William M Roberts, a town grocer of Welsh descent whose grandfather had actually worked in John Ivon Jones's old shop in Bridge Street, Aberystwyth. They caught the second of two lectures which a visiting Dr Tudor Jones was giving — a lecture which generated tumultuous and welcome argument. But mostly David was 'barred out in gloomy tomb'.

All the time, he was being bombarded by George Eyre Evans's weekly cards, his giant envelopes full of clippings and his rebukes at the absence of any word from David, rebukes echoed by Evans's sister and even by Mrs Emily Evans, the Unitarian patron who had moved to Geneva. When his letters finally got through, the response was invariable. Why were they so listless and empty? Where was the old David Jones? His shipboard friends, Jack Bartle and Moses the Russian wrote. He had to try to keep in touch with his brothers.

He made an effort, learnedly debating with Evans whether British and Foreign Bible Society support might corrupt Unitarian missionaries and whether the New (and socially progressive) Theology of R J Campbell was a form of Unitarianism — the people of the Aberystwyth Meeting House were still 'we' to David Jones. The intensifying political struggle at home was beginning to engage him. He delighted in the anti-Tory cartoons of F C Gould, religiously sent on by Evans, and asked him to forward the Saturday edition of the Liberal *Daily News* so long as (the then very radical) G K Chesterton wrote for it.

There seems to have been some shift in his attitude. He expressed admiration for the dramatic way Campbell had announced 'I am a Socialist', and while New Zealanders' aping of British ways 'nauseated' him, he noted that their government sent aid to areas suffering from drought, and that the railways, under public ownership, let students travel free — 'manifesting the benefits of a socialist-minded government'. In one intriguing comment, he suggested that the socialist Campbell did not declare himself a Unitarian because he was reluctant to identify with 'a sect which is select and undemocratic'!

There were some flashes of his old spirit. He planted some Welsh leeks 'with full military honours' and gleefully reported his pride 'when these Colonials prick up their ears at my rugged accent and ask my nationality and I say that I come from the country that played the devil with the All Blacks!' But he sensed some decline in himself. He bought an Emerson and a Keats in Dunedin. Keats and Omar Khayam he cherished as 'good old friends', but he dismissed George Evans's renewed interest in some poems he'd sent to the Aberystwyth *Garlands*: 'I have now renounced all mawkish notions concerning poetry . . . when I live through days like these when all seems futile, I turn to humble and ignorant versifying as an antidote.' The serf-like labour was grinding him down. He had little to say and no energy to say even that. His letters dribble away into hurried postcards: 'Fine invention the weather, said a Scotty the other day. It gives even the black'ardest fool something to talk about.'

At the end of September came the inevitable explosion. 'There are two classes of employer — those for whom you can never do too much and those for whom you can never do enough. Mrs Brown is the latter.' She had grown suspicious of his persistent cough and began to question him closely about his family and background — 'not in sympathy but as if asking the price of sugar . . . I am a long suffering ass, but even he will make a sudden fling sometimes. So I broke out into open rebellion with the righteous anger of one who knows he's doing his money's worth. Go to . . . well, call it blazes! I told Mrs B to look out for someone else.'

When 'little Brown' got back, he would not hear of David Jones leaving, but during what was evidently an unholy row, the truth about David's tuberculosis came out. The Welshman had deliberately concealed it, he claimed, to prevent people making allowances for him which would have hurt his pride. A couple of weeks with the Browns and he'd learned to keep it dark for quite other reasons! They were horrified at the prospect of 'infection from the horrible disease'. They reached a compromise. David did not want to leave just as spring was bringing the fruits of his winter's hard labour. They gave him a two-shilling bonus but banished him to an old wooden cottage at the end of the orchard. Only meals would bring his polluted person into the 'holy house'.

Now he was lonelier than ever, with only a cat and a dog for company. After getting a letter from Mrs Evans in Geneva, he began to talk wistfully of trying his luck as a gardener in Europe — gardeners would always be in demand, unlike grocers with only a weird Welsh lingo to commend them. In October, he caught pleurisy, working in his shirtsleeves in the rain. Mr Brown told him a doctor would cost money, so he stayed at work in bad weather. On 26 October, he had to break off and lie down. At dinner that night Mrs Brown called him a scrounger and sent him to cut wood among the draughts. David had had enough. He quit. As usual, he experienced this as a personal failure on his part. He had thought he was self-sufficient. He went 'back into human society' — to William Roberts in Dunedin. When he got there, Roberts could hardly get him up a hill.

He had barely two weeks in Dunedin to recover. William Roberts turned out to be a lively and open-minded young man; so was his friend Harold Guy nicknamed The Saxon. A small group of young men with intellectual aspirations began to form around this 'brilliant comet' of a David Jones who had flashed into their world.

Brilliant or not, Jones still had to eat. Roberts put an advertisement in a local paper and a farmer of Welsh descent responded, offering 15 shillings a week. At this moment, however, David met another friend of Roberts, Robert Fyfe, 'a fine manly Scotsman with a genial face' and a fatherly way with young men. David had a gift for making long-lasting friends at first encounter. Fyfe was one. A wool-classer, he offered the young Welshman the chance of going up with him into the Southern Alps to work among the legendary sheep-shearers at 25 shillings a week. David immediately bought a second-hand bicycle and headed for the train.

That train, traversing bends even more hair-raising than those of the Devil's Bridge railway at Aberystwyth, took him up, out of the foetid plains into the clear, crisp, invigorating air of Otago Central, barren but beautiful mountains broken by brilliant green plateaux, thick with imported British willow, poplar and hawthorn. The railway ended at Lawrence, some seventy miles from Dunedin. There was a horse-drawn coach to Miller's Flat, but this cost ten shillings, which David could not afford. So he got on his bike and cycled thirty-two miles through Miller's Flat and on to the sheep-run, against the wind, through dust three inches thick, past mountains higher than Cader Idris and along roads which would not have been approved by Cardiganshire County Council.

He came up into a run of 30,000 sheep. In New Zealand, they did not have flocks of sheep, they had 'mobs'. The stone-built shearing shed was the largest in the country (he supplied Eyre Evans with a neatly-drawn plan), 200 feet long with a fine half-circle roof, whose shepherds ranged fifteen miles out. Those shepherds and shearers — a 'rough, roving class' — Jones found congenial. 'They never read, but some of them give you the impression that they have inarticulately thought all that we read of in books.' He'd brought books with him, but he abandoned them in favour of the 'confabs'. Scottish humour was pure, he noted, whereas the English and Colonials were 'unclean'. A particular pleasure was 'Old Mac', a Scottie with his 'wee dawgie', who seems to have been a fount of folk-wisdom and whose 'wicked language reminds me of the music of saints'. Mac took him up to the hut of a rabbiter in the mountains. A Lowland Scot, the rabbiter lived in a fabled canvas 'house' with a clod chimney, his horse Nell tethered in a dell and his dogs at the door. The novels of the Cardiganshire writer Allen Raine filled a shelf over his bed!

Jones was captivated, both by this kind of life and its prospects. Rabbits were a plague in New Zealand, rabbiters an honoured profession;

there was good money to be made. An idea lodged in his mind and was soon to dominate it. In the meantime, he had to master his new craft. He began as a fleece-roller, humping the fleeces from the often frenzied shearers, picking them clean, rolling them tidily for the wool classer. In a couple of weeks, he was promoted to 'piece-picker', a job needing more skill and dexterity. He had to sort the wool out — Merino, Leicesters, Belly-Wool — there was talk of training him as a wool-classer. He had a jolly, fat lad, 'John Bull Junior', as a mate. They disagreed only over the door of their hut; David liked it open at night, with sheep framed in moonlight around the doorway and hundreds more nearby, 'bleating away like a pack of Welsh deacons saying "Amen"!'

He thought his health had picked up. He played cricket every day (not to play cricket in New Zealand was a species of Original Sin) and could 'field as fast as any'. The cough was still there, but 'I am master in my own house, so to speak'. So enthralled was he that a letter of Eyre Evans carrying news of Aberystwyth brought him out in nightmares. He dreamed he was back in the Bridge Street shop . . . 'with bills all over the place. I was just getting bankrupt when I awoke to find myself rich on ten bob and good friends to remember me . . .' Other home news was more welcome. 'I say', he replied to Evans, 'what a fine peroration that was of Lloyd George at Cardiff! I should not wonder if those words of his became famous. They sent a thrill through me. *Duw sydd yn gwybod mor annwyl yw Cymru lan i mi*! (God knows how dear little old Wales is to me!)'

By now 'Skipper' Jones was serving sixteen shearers, against the average picker's eight. But he kept his options open. When the work was finished, Fyfe took him on to Roxburgh, which David at once observed was the centre of a great fruit-growing district. On then, to remote Galloway station, thirty miles further into the mountains, for more shearing. The air was bracing, hot but not oppressive and though the place was very isolated, David felt fit and 'was gradually winning back the art of laughing'. It was January 1908 before the work was done. He went on to the nearest township of Alexandra and there, within a week, 'landed on a job' with a pioneer family, the Iversens, who ran one of the most famous orchards in New Zealand. He was to put in two long stints with them, six months in 1908 and nearly a year over 1909-10.

David never forgot 'old man Iversen . . . The Boss'. In South Africa three years later, when he heard that Iversen had died, he was so moved he wrote an elegiac poem *The Boss is Dead*, signed from 'One of the Boys', which was published in the *Otago Witness* in February 1912.

Andreas (usually called Andrew) Christian Iversen had been born in Denmark in 1836. He joined the gold-rush to Australia in 1854, farmed and learned irrigation in Victoria and moved to New Zealand in 1863, where he married an English woman, tried gold mining and became a pioneer of irrigated fruit growing in Otago. By the time David Jones met him, Iversen was in his seventies; he owned some 900 acres on the Earnscleugh plateau, 50-60 acres of it the celebrated Varde orchard, the rest Sycamore farm with grazing for 900 sheep, 80 acres of oats, some cattle and a dozen horses. His homestead nestled at the foot of steep hills, with irrigation races dug from a terrace above. His fruit had become a by-word for quality. His early apricots fetched the record price of 10d a pound; five of his apricot trees yielded three tons of marketable fruit in one season. Three years before Jones met him, he had rejected an offer of £25 an acre for his estate and another of £100 an acre for sixteen acres of it. And in a New Zealand which periodically panicked over the Yellow Peril, Iversen cheerfully leased and then sold a substantial chunk to a Chinaman (a universal term at the time) who had worked well for him.

He and David got on famously, though they argued endlessly . . . the Welshman's poem spoke of 'well-spent hours which, bruised in anger, yet may bloom'. For Iversen was 'a materialist who through ignorance, carries atheistic sentiments to extremes' and brought up his children to have no religion of any kind 'like a mere brood of porklings'. They used to make themselves hoarse, shouting at each other on long walks. But Iversen took immediately to the young Welshman, was fascinated by Wales and hypnotised by Lloyd George, at that moment beginning to blaze his way through British politics. The Boss was avid for all the political news Eyre Evans sent David and the whole family revelled in Gould's radical cartoons; Iversen's daughter Thereza made an album out of them (though cartoons had to be explained to Colonials, Jones loftily commented). Iversen was a 'great politician' himself, a devoted Danish patriot who thought Denmark's social legislation immeasurably more advanced than New Zealand's and tried to introduce it into his adopted country. 'Rise up! Rise up! Great Holger Danske!' he used to sing, celebrating Denmark's legendary hero, 'their version of the Welsh King Arthur'. When David ribbed him that Holger Danske had not risen up much during the war against Prussia over Schleswig-Holstein, he touched a raw nerve. Iversen hated Queen Victoria for her pro-Prussian stance during that war . . . 'Ah! if only Lloyd George had been there at the time!', he cried, 'He'd have told the Queen to go to hell and carried the declaration of war himself, to succour a small nation fighting for existence!'

David had not been very interested in New Zealand's politics (and never made any contact with its labour movement) but this changed under the tuition of Iversen who carted him off to local election meetings and preached him sermons on the inadequacy of the Liberal government of Sir Joseph Ward. What struck David was the intensely democratic nature of New Zealand: 'Every party here is liberal . . . all are for popular reform.' Women had the vote and the suffragette struggles back home were viewed with stupefaction. Sir Joseph Ward, the premier, had been a telegraph boy, Massey, leader of the Opposition, a ploughman. And, added David, quite evidently with himself and Iversen in mind ... 'A farm labourer would not be expected at dances, tea parties or mixing with his betters at home. Here, they are sought after according to their merits.'

The local government candidate was a Dr Chapple, a former member of Dr Tudor's congregation in Wellington like the former premier Sir Robin Stout. Driven to the meeting by Iversen, David put two questions and was answered with a ten-minute lecture. It was probably about this time that he conceived his admiration for T E 'Tommy' Taylor, the great 'independent freelance' of New Zealand politics, a maverick whose twin causes were Prohibition and Labour. When Jones heard of his death in South Africa, he again burst into verse, this time a sonnet, hailing Taylor as the Lloyd George of the Antipodes. For it was Lloyd George who dominated the politics of both the Welshman and his new-found friends. When the pro-Boer, Nonconformist radical and Welsh patriot became Chancellor of the Exchequer, David Jones could scarcely contain himself. To think that the great outsider — and one of the unjustly despised Welsh to boot — had got to the centre of power! He begged his brother George to send him a biography of the hero. The book bowled him over — a thrilling romance ... such dare-devilry in the cause of righteousness!' He passed the book to Iversen and they used to swap titbits of wit from LG all day. As the spokesman for the People's Budget went to battle against The Lords in his raging, tearing populist campaigns, both David Jones and Andrew Iversen became fanatical Lloyd George men. David wrote his first political letter in a blistering attack on a New Zealand liberal paper which had dared to question the Asquith government's sincerity in its campaign against the House of Lords.

Islwyn ap Nicholas, a knowledgeable Aberystwyth communist and a member of New Street Unitarian congregation, in an unpublished memoir on David Jones, states that Iversen and his family were socialists. There is no direct evidence of this in David Jones's letters, but there are hints that Iversen had broad and radical social sympathies. Jones's poem spoke of this 'Great Dane' in whom 'the yeoman and the viking fought to mould his blood' as a man who inscribed his unbeliever's faith on Nature ...

Planning for the common weal
Even the politician's zeal
In mad career of viking blood
Reveals the truest will of God.

A New Zealand encyclopedia of 1905 recorded that it was Iversen who had persuaded the government to introduce the little owl which wiped out the bud-eating birds which had threatened ruin to all the fruit growers of Otago Central. It also stressed that it was he who had got the Earnscleugh block opened up for settlement and 'was successful in preventing the property from being surveyed in a way which would have made it useless to small settlers'. An old sailor who never wore a watch, Iversen was certainly a good boss, working with his men, sharing his table with them, having them join the family evenings. Though the Book of Books was an 'absentee monarch' on his shelves, he would have no-one work on a Sunday and his regime was generally relaxed. David Jones enjoyed fruit-picking so much because the pickers ate great loads of it! In one comment on an *Otago Witness* photograph he sent Eyre Evans, he said: 'Harvesting fruit has all the romance of hay harvesting, with the additional excitement of having it ooze out of one's "chops" in luscious juice! The free air, the bountifulness of the fruit and the *Principles of the Boss* [my italics] were all against "muzzling the ox on the threshing floor"!'

Whether this constitutes proof of Iversen's socialism is another matter. And whether it directly influenced David Jones is more problematical still. One remembers the endless arguments! David at this time would probably have echoed Tommy Taylor's deathbed message to his Labour friends . . . 'they have Divine chances here if they will only recognise the religious element and lift the movement to a higher plane'. At least he would have echoed it during his first stint at Iversen's; by the second, he would probably have jettisoned 'religious' for 'ideal'.

Taylor's battle against the Liquor Interest and Lloyd George's against the Beer Barons certainly enlisted Jones's support in what was in fact a major problem for working class movements — though he had become far less fanatical on the subject of drink. When he heard that his brother George was moving to Canada, he feared that the 'thirsty climate' would worsen his brother's addiction to the bottle but he added he was not too good on that score himself and now felt that moderation was more effective than prohibition!

What is certain is that, with the Iversens about him and Lloyd George thundering on the far horizon, David Jones began to commit himself more whole-heartedly to social action and lurched decisively into radicalism. 'I do not read as much philosophy as I used to', he told Eyre Evans in June.

Nor was old Iversen his only friend. Ned, the son of the family who lived with his wife in their own house on the estate, became a mate. So did Thereza, the crippled thirty-one-year-old daughter who devoted herself to painting and the Opposition cause and, despite repeated arguments over religion and politics, was an admirer. 'He ought to be something higher', she told Evans in October 1910, 'Dave brought more out of me by his influence, that I never knew I could do . . . He is too straight — it don't do to tell people what you think, not always . . . Him and I had our own misunderstandings, but I will take no notice and I will try always try to be his friend.'

Dave shared a cramped but comfortable tent near the house with a 'cowboy' and worked with two Chinamen. The Boss had no 'side' at all.

They all ate together at the house and were expected to join in the games and conversation of a 'jolly household', even sometimes the Chinamen. . . 'and why not?' Jones was fascinated by the Chinese, the first he'd seen, particularly the older one, a 'yellow brother' called A-chu (make a sneeze and you'll get the pronunciation right, he told Evans). A-chu was brimming with pidgin English, 'yellow oaths' and wizened humour . . . 'You go churchee?' he asked David Jones . . .' No more bad talk, no more lollikin, no more stinkum whishkee — bye and bye, no more eatum tucka.' (Tucker, David explained to the stay-at-homes, was Colonial for food). The Chinese could not keep up with a machine and worked with less bustle than Europeans. But they slogged away relentlessly, easily outpaced their colleagues and earned much more. Jones had to compete once with A-chu in bagging chaff. It left him in a desperate sweat: 'You can't be beat by a Chow!'

In this encounter with an alien people, as in those on his long journey, the Welshman, almost inevitably in his time and circumstance, was steeped in a mild but persistent racialism. Never aggressive or contemptuous, it could be patronising and he may never wholly have lost it. But, from the first, it was qualified by warm human sympathy, a strong sense of justice and an intense respect for individuality.

Jones enjoyed his six months with the Iversens. He earned a pound a week. The work was hard but varied and the lightest he'd yet done. Sundays were idle and delightful. His health was better. He felt as strong and as gritty as he'd ever done, nobody suspected he had TB, and they put him to the toughest jobs. 'I am, you might say, cured.' His letters to Aberystwyth, however, grew more infrequent, Eyre Evans's jibes on the envelopes more pointed, David's apologies more abject.

What haunted him were his debts. He was simply not earning enough money to pay off his creditors. George Eyre Evans had started urging him to come home, offering prospects of a job with Galloways the bookseller. David put him off with chit-chat about the old days and warm, personal commiseration over a fall-off in numbers at the Meeting House, but finally told him baldly: 'What prospects are there for me at home? To think of earning my daily bread in the same old ruts is to me nauseating. Nothing spells home yet. I cannot come home until I have paid my debts and made a place for myself in the world.'

He was still reading Emerson and had introduced Thereza to that great thinker, but music was now engaging him. He asked for Welsh song collections, bought a fiddle for a quid and started taking violin lessons in Alexandra. But as the New Zealand winter approached and his term at Iversen's drew to a close, it was money which occupied his mind. He was put to trapping rabbits. The whole trade operated under strict government regulation, he explained to his friend. The freezing factories shipped out thousands but only over three months of the year in the 'great rabbit rush'. For the rest of the year, they trapped for skins only, but at 12/6 a hundred. He knew of a man trapping on a block above

Earnscleugh who'd bagged 20,000 rabbits last summer — and got 20 shillings a hundred! As soon as his stint with old Iversen ended late in June 1908, David Jones was off up into the mountains, after his rabbits.

He and his mate Williams (presumably the 'cowboy') took a coach for fifty miles and then hiked up into the mountains to camp on the slopes of the seven-thousand foot Mount Pisa. After a quarrel with his first boss who was doubtful about his eyesight without glasses, he found a job with a Dutchman who lived nearby with his mother. Trapping was useless in this season, because of the ice. They poisoned the ground instead. Their block, six miles wide, ran to the top of a mountain which would dwarf Snowdon. They split the block into two beats of three miles and worked in a regular rhythm at fixed intervals, spreading pellets of pollard and phosphorus, doubling back and then going out again to pick up the rabbit corpses. They skinned the rabbits as they walked, keeping an eye out for others. Jones had been very clumsy at this, but soon picked up the knack. He described the whole process with so much gusto that Miss Evans in Aberystwyth, a renowned animal-lover and crusader against hunting, was appalled and in due course (letters took six weeks each way) David had shamefacedly to apologise. He did so in a light-hearted but accomplished set of three *englyn* — Welsh verse in the ancient, strict metres!

He'd had to walk eight miles to get his letters and cards posted and he was working through heavy snowstorms. His writing tailed away. Even in his remote camp, however, the massive envelopes of George Evans, forwarded by Roberts in Dunedin, kept coming. The latter's book on Lampeter got through, to send Ivon Jones into paroxysms of nostalgia for the place, coupled with renewed expression of distaste for Aberystwyth. He was painfully embarrassed when Evans's edition of the *Lloyd Letters* reached Roberts with a preface which described David as a 'writer of verse'. Roberts and Harold Guy in Dunedin immediately broke into verse themselves and started bombarding Jones with jocular postcards about a Royal Otago Cambrian Society! 'Here I am going to be feted as a mawkish, curly-haired "writer of verse"', he complained to Eyre Evans, 'really, you must be more measured in your compliments!'

In fact, he was flattered, as the little circle back in Dunedin conceived a passion for Allen Raine and all things Welsh, and William Roberts sent glowing praise of David in his own letters to Aberystwyth. By September, Jones was writing sonnets, in between rabbits and snowstorms, on mountain slopes with breath-taking views over the great lakes of the Southern Alps. In one he talked of the 'days of despair'.

When 'competition's' sordid strife besmeared
My bread with cankering care.
In freeman's land, my body found new life
Although my soul has lost its lyre.

He repeatedly spoke of his rude health. The cold, the clear air had worked wonders. He'd played rugby down in Earnscleugh — 'rough and tumble scratch' — and coughed no more than the others. Roberts confirmed, in a letter to Evans, that David could now run up and down precipitous hills with ease. In September, David went higher up still into the mountains, to do his rabbiting at Glendhu sheep run overlooking the beauty of Lake Wanaka, 50 miles long.

But in fact, the game was not paying. Rabbits were scarcer than usual. In his first block, he'd made £12. Food and necessary clothing had left him only £3. This satisfied David Jones, but how would he pay back his creditors? It was at this moment, in a letter of 15 September, which took two weeks even to reach the post and was obsessed with money, that he wrote . . . 'Besides, dear Florrie needs help. Now that Eben has married, she has one less to depend on.' This is the first direct and personal reference to South Africa to appear in his correspondence.

His sister seems to have been widowed. One can only guess at what information had reached him from his brothers in South Africa, but it certainly unsettled him. And, for the first time, a basic disenchantment with New Zealand begins to creep into his mail. In that same letter, he wrote to Evans: 'In these backblocks, people are indifferent to the great problems and strife in which I used to take a humble but active part. I am getting satiated with this life without responsibility, life without Duty, this life where Darkness and Light are not clearly and distinctly divided'. He talked of 'existing amid the "alien corn" and dead machinery of Colonial life'.

No doubt, disappointment at the failure of the rabbiting 'gold mine' was a factor and his spirits were to pick up. But this was the first sign of a sense of disillusionment and defeat which were to grow on him. By November, Roberts, suspecting something, came up from Dunedin to see him. In another idyll in the companionship of a young man which Jones cherished, they spent some weeks camping on the shores of Lake Wanaka. The idyll ended abruptly. In November, at the camp, David learned that his sister Florrie had died. The news shattered him.

'A great void has opened in my life', he told George Evans in December. He spoke of 'the departure of dear Florrie (where? I would fain know)'. It had taken Cruel Death to reveal how indispensable she had been in holding the brothers together. 'She knew all the burdens of life and tasted none of its joys . . . that she should die ALONE among strangers . . . the thought is harrowing.' The sense of loss, which surprised even himself, since he had not seen her for six years, generated a crisis of faith. 'May the hereafter be a compensation for dear Florrie. I hope that He, the Eternal Immanence IS as just as our hopes say . . . But all as yet is dark. No vision yet appears except that of dear Florrie dying alone. One tear drowns all philosophies. Oh! for a philosophy based on REALITY which will give us a serene view of "God's dark ways".'

He was utterly miserable and had no idea what to do, so Roberts took him back to Dunedin and gave him a job in his shop over Christmas. A photograph of him in front of the shop survives, prim and respectable in his white coat and apron, standing a little apart from the others. 'It seems little short of cruelty that one of his gifts should have to waste his talents among (very often) rough and uncultured people', Roberts wrote to Eyre Evans . . . 'The greatest difficulty is himself. He knows more about literature than any around here. He has more brain power than the young men here. But he persists in hiding and denying these truths!'

Roberts tried to get him a job as a school teacher and the local Education Board did in fact give Jones to understand that the post of assistant teacher in a county school would be found for him. Meanwhile, he worked through Christmas in the shop. He sent Evans some material on a local election fought mainly on the Prohibition issue . . . 'Every man and woman over 21 has the vote here, even though he does not own so much as a pigsty . . . The woman's vote has done a lot of good here. . .' The Gould cartoons went down well in Dunedin, where they were promptly adapted to local purposes.

But the spirit had gone out of him. He was obsessed with the sheer loneliness of Florrie's death. George Evans complained that his letters were getting shorter and the gaps between them longer. In January 1909 there was still no news of the teaching job and Roberts could not afford to keep him any longer. There was nothing for it but the mountains of Otago Central again. By early February, he was working on a farm at Beck's in the Leander district run (inevitably, one feels!) by a Colonial of Welsh descent.

Up in that rainy corner of the hills, Jones came across Welshman's or Cambrian Gully, a sparsely populated valley still served by the Welsh Harp inn. Its people were survivors of a colony of Welsh first established after the mid-century gold rush. He was astonished to find these Griffiths, Morgans, Hughes using hardly any English, still speaking Welsh and cherishing the old ways. A clutch of Hugheses ran what was left of a small gold mine and farmed fertile holdings. The patriarch Thomas Hughes was a grand and dignified old man. The works of Thomas Charles of Bala, an eighteenth-century Methodist father, graced his shelves, but his favourite poet was Talhaiarn, whose themes were war, women and wine, none of which figured much in Hughes's own life! Rhys Hughes, his brother, on the other hand, responded more directly. Ten years younger than Thomas and a mere 27 years in New Zealand as opposed to his brother's 40, he was the great wag of the district, an 'overgrown puppy', whose witticisms convulsed his neighbours (Welsh Colonials, Jones observed, were wittier than the stay-at-homes). When the drink was on him, Rhys Hughes would explode into Welsh patriotism, roaring martial songs through the hills. With them, in their three stone cottages in a pretty dell, was a sister-in-law, Mrs Thomas, who spoke of Wales as if she'd left it only yesterday.

David's arrival plunged them all yet more deeply into Welshness. He was virtually compelled to give public readings of the poet Ceiriog and sing the newer Welsh songs. When they raised an oat-stack, old Thomas 'crowed' on the top in traditional peasant style, something he'd last done in Wales, fifty-two years earlier. In this remote district of New Zealand Jones was thrown back into rural Wales, even as his boss's daughter repeatedly played 'Home Sweet Home' on the piano and the weekly mail brought reiterated pleas to return from George Eyre Evans. It did little for his peace of mind.

He worked for Hugh Hughes, Thomas's son, who ran a farm a few miles from Welshman's Gully, a jovial enough man but, 'like most good-hearted fellows', too fond of the bottle. Once, driven by the startling premonition of his wife (which decidedly unsettled David) he and a mate went out in a snowstorm to look for missing Hugh, to find him pitched drunkenly from his horse with his head in an icy puddle. The farm was going downhill in consequence and when Jones left, he was owed £12. 'I will get it, so don't mention it again', he curtly told George Evans.

His tone, indeed, got more acerbic with every letter. Eyre Evans's endless pleas and rebukes, written for all to see on his cards and envelopes, were irritating . . . people would be convinced 'that such shrill calls can only come from a young lady'. Jones's own letters, heavy with guilt, grew more infrequent: he wrote once a month on average. And they chronicle a descent into depression. 'I have been here nearly two years now', he wrote on 7 February. 'They have not been very happy, although I have regained a measure of health. It has meant hard work all the time. There is a tincture of bitterness in my view of things at present which I cannot account for. The past seems irrecoverable. We would that we could bring it back unchanged. But death, disease, the breaking of old associations, partings, bitterest of all perhaps, changes within ourselves, all allied, muster themselves to drum into us the hideous fact that we are ALONE . . .'

To take his earlier letters at face value, he would seem to have been exaggerating his unhappiness, at least during his first year in New Zealand. Clearly, it was the death of Florrie and, perhaps more significantly, the gloomy reflections it precipitated which had unhinged him — coupled, of course, with his growing frustration. The standard farm work at the Hugheses was tedious and ill-paid. 'I have nothing to say' became his standard refrain.

At the end of February, he was stunned to learn that the Meeting House people in Aberystwyth were disappointed because no message had come through from their former secretary. Saddled with yet more guilt, he said he had not realised one was expected. He blamed the apathy which had engulfed him since Florrie's death: 'It is not easy to keep the enthusiasm unflagging when one is conscious of a glory that hath departed.' The backblocks were good for his health, but he had become an 'exile from things intellectual'. He had spent two years in menial labour: 'Two years spent among an honest and industrious class of people certainly, but among a class where it is idle to attempt a conversation on anything higher than the next trotting match, the last successful ball held in the township, the ordinary newspaper topic and the tittle-tattle of neighbours.' Over two years he had been unable to discuss a favourite author without being stared at (the Dunedin circle had presumably slipped his mind!) . . . 'One's views become more practical, perhaps broader, but certainly the reverse of profounder. How hard it is to adhere to old enthusiasms! Swans become geese. The past gets pale.'

There were some consolations. He continued to be transfixed by the political struggle at home and enjoyed a brief trip down to Dunedin to hear the Royal Welsh Choir. He discovered Macaulay's *History of England* which entranced him . . . 'I am losing interest in the metaphysical philosophizing of the nineteenth century in which I used to take a feverish, but in its results, superficial interest', he added. Now he was dipping into Ruskin and looking for books on economic problems.

By May, money was obsessing him again. His pay had dropped from thirty shillings to a pound a week, now that the work was threshing, ploughing, carting oats and digging potatoes. This might be a good wage at home, but didn't go far in New Zealand which, while a good country for working men, was no Eldorado. His mates were getting on his nerves as they made spud-digging into a race . . . 'The Colonials invented the word blatherskyte for a braggart. No wonder!The Colonies teem with them!' The weather in Leander was not good for him, wet, windy, with snow coming on. On the other hand, rabbiting was starting. Then, abruptly and apparently without warning, Jones added: 'Sometimes I have a fancy for going over to South Africa to see a little of that part of the world, or over to Canada.'

This is the first hint that he might quit New Zealand. Later evidence suggests that his brothers had been working on him. If they had, he kept the information secret from the George Eyre Evans who weekly begged him to return to Wales. Jones had begun to ration the words he sent Evans! Money was the crux. Two postcards in May mentioned that he was doing some rabbiting for Hughes, but at the end of the month, he left, £12 arrears notwithstanding. He signed up with a mobile threshing machine crew going around the farms, sleeping on straw in weather so cold that frost formed inside the canvas and fell on their faces.

Then, after a silence of two months, he wrote to Evans on 27 July. He was back among his friends the Iversens at Earnscleugh and the comforts of a feather bed and a table. He and Ned Iversen were going up into the hills to hunt these miracle-working rabbits. He felt unable to write more than a couple of pages to his old friend and mentor: 'Something is out of joint'. Something must have been. Jones ended his letter: 'What evil in this world lays low the good and makes the evil flourish?'

Ned Iversen and David went into the hills in August. They planned to trap rabbits for months, take a break of a couple of months at the farm and then go up again for a final stint. Ned lent David an old horse, Jim, and a sheep dog. They lived in tents and worked 300 traps in a fixed alternating rhythm, David making the 'scrapes' in the ground, Ned inserting the traps, David covering them up. Then out again, along alternate lines, picking up the rabbits . . . 'I will not shock you with what happens next.' They were at it right through to November. Towards the end, David was left alone, among the grotesque rock formations of Otago Central, guided often only by old Jim. Every so often, they'd descend to Earnscleugh to stock up. It was there that David wrote his cards and letters, roughly once a month.

He found the work brutal and uncongenial and had to face a barrage of shocked complaints from Eyre Evans's sister. He could plead only the justification used for Chinese labour on the Rand — 'Regrettable necessity!' You must understand, he said, that rabbits here are vermin, a pest. He knew it was difficult to conceive of such delightful creatures as 'pests'; he understood that they were such only in a world subject to Man. But he had to get money if he were ever to make his way. And he was not entirely passive: 'Maybe a beautiful little doe of my skinning will be the kid gloves of Miss Evans or Miss Thomas?'! And George Evans could hardly complain when he 'goes round the country on the far from humanitarian work of killing Town Councillors!' His mind, however, was seizing up and perhaps being brutalized. Letter after letter echoed the same complaint: 'I suffer from a paucity of ideas . . . my mind is impoverished . . . I live in the Land of Hogs, a man very soon gets Hoggish . . . I never see a daily paper . . . my mind is as empty as a saucepan.' There were some glimmers. The Dunedin group were now obsessed with Allen Raine and busily corresponding with Eyre Evans about her and David Jones started to read Balzac.

But what possessed the Welshman was the imperative need to make money to pay off his creditors and take his place in the world. Increasingly this meant to get away from New Zealand. On 8 August, he at last admitted to George — 'My brothers in South Africa want me to join them there'. Evans wanted David back in Wales — and Evans together with Joinson were his creditors. What was he to do? William Roberts confirmed to Evans on 8 September, that a move to South Africa was much in David's mind. The greater the shock then when Evans received a letter from David dated 10 September which baldly announced: 'I am going to Canada next autumn, that is April or May 1910!'

The key was another brother, George, who had moved to Canada. He'd taken an upland farm of 160 acres and needed David's help to run it. He argued that David could 'pop home' much easier from Canada. The winters were severe but the air was bracing and, at 3,000 feet, the farm would be good for him. David had come to agree, a decision he re-asserted on 24 September: 'South Africa drew my attention for a long while here. I wanted to shift somewhere from here. But the only attraction there was my brothers. The country itself did not commend itself to me. A man's work there is confined to the counter and the office.' (An interesting perception of the place from the point of view of a former Welsh grocer!)

'I have become enamoured of the soil and the fruits thereof.' He was finished with mere 'distribution', it was 'production' which had captured his enthusiasm. Besides, land was getting more and more expensive in New Zealand, in Canada, there was room to breathe — a notion he repeated in October: 'New Zealand is a trifle parochial. Like Joe Chamberlain, I want my spirit enlarged, if not by the illimitable veldt than by the illimitable elbow-room of Canada!'

Whatever the choice, he was now fed up with New Zealand. By January 1910, in writing to Evans about a walk he'd taken up to the Galloway sheep run to see his old wool-classer friend Robert Fyfe, he could say: 'Every rock and turn of the track along the breezy, rugged upland brings back sharp memories of two weary years gone. I suddenly saw how UTTERLY PROFITLESS my sojourn here has been. Mentally, spiritually and even monetarily, I have made no advance. The conviction rudely struck me that it was time to get out of it.' At the end of October, Jones, now alone, packed his stuff on old Jim and went down to Ned Iversen's farm. He was to live there and work in old Iversen's orchard for a few months before what he hoped would be a final stint at rabbiting to raise his fare to Canada. He found the old man and Thereza and A-chu as genial as ever, but the work in orchard and farm had lost a lot of its charm — only tree planting really excited him now. 'Hard labour is not good food for ideas', he wrote in December, 'Let these pseudo-Ruskinians try the soil! With a sore back, appetite, pick and shovel as companions, the only musings in the silent grove are on how soon the dinner bell will ring! As the sun beats down, you think of nothing but dinner and knock-off time.' Certainly his health was adding to his gloom. In the following month, he made the ominous confession: 'I am sorry to say that for the last two or three months I have not felt so well. They tell me I am thinner than I was . . . He added: 'That makes me afraid of Canada'. But labour and health were in no sense his only worries. Early in December, his letter-writing was interrupted by the arrival of two packages from his brother Will who ran a store in South Africa. The first told him his eldest brother Arthur, who was Will's partner, was very ill and almost begged him to go over to help. From the second, he learned that Arthur had gone into hospital. In mid-December he heard that Arthur was dead.

This was Florrie all over again. He wrote of his lost brother in much the same terms. It was fourteen years since he'd last seen him when he'd come home from his work in north Wales to say goodbye before sailing for South Africa. He had fought with an iron will against his disease, but venture after venture had failed . . . 'like poor Florrie, he experienced all the burdens but none of the pleasures of life'. And before breaking off his letter in despair, David Jones cried in desperate rage: 'How bitter and unrelenting Nature, God — call it what you like — is!'

He was now distraught. He had written to George to say he'd go to Canada. After a long delay, George had acknowledged it, but had said nothing more. But now so much had changed! David was seized of a need for the remaining brothers to get together. Will wanted him, but in Canada, George was alone. And there was Eyre Evans, still hoping David would return but reconciled to Canada to the extent of planning a meeting there on Evans's projected tour of British Columbia . . . 'I am like a mariner's compass whose pole is at three quite opposite directions.'

A little rest would see him right, but 'if I go to Canada, it will mean hard work to establish a home. Yet I delight in hard work. Still, from a health point of view, South Africa would be better for me. The work would not be so arduous all the time. I feel it cruel to desert George and I am sorry to disappoint Will. Silly fool that I am!'

By February 1910, news from George began to tip the balance. George had found it very hard work clearing the brush from his land and had taken a job with a baker's van in town. He was now worried about the effect of farmwork on David's health, but was himself eager and happy. 'I am not in that state of mind at present', reported David. He was in fact in deep melancholy. His health had not improved much and the hard labour was getting him down. New Zealand was a nice place with nice people, but it had been a constant grind. He needed a rest and wouldn't get one in Canada. And he was now bored stiff — once the decision to leave had been made, 'everything BORES!'.

His intellectual crisis was getting worse. A batch of mail from his aunt in Wellington in March brought news that Dr Tudor Jones was leaving. This unleashed in David Jones a passionate reaction against his earlier enthusiasm for the preacher. It became a shout of despair: 'I was enthusiastic in the cause then, but I have not been able to preserve the dogmatic stage of Unitarianism.' Tudor Jones was terribly dogmatic, had no sympathy for lukewarm Unitarians: 'Some of us are content to let principles make their own way like a tide. We are reluctant to probe too deeply into metaphysical knowledge (so small!) and problems of destiny — the CHAOS, blind, weltering chaos of agnosticism into which these probings have landed us.' It seemed hardly worth the effort to prise men free from their comforting old religion to force them to contemplate the abysses, so deep, so utterly hopeless.

This was precisely what Dr Tudor's sermons did. His preaching was brilliant, at one moment seeming to accept the most extreme atheistic teachings of science, at the next seeming to negate them. 'The effect on me (though I would not admit it at the time) was of lurking hopelessness and despair.' David could still remember the sense of insufficiency they produced: 'I have heard dread atheistic propaganda without experiencing this hopeless, despairing feeling.' The preacher, like himself, seemed 'to be performing the Highland Fling above crumbling precipices'. Since then, David had stared into many abysses and now he did not know what his place was in the Chaos. By this time, David Jones was exercising self-censorship in his letters to George Eyre Evans. One would like to know what he said to his other regular Aberystwyth correspondent, that doughty rationalist J D Stephens. To Evans in March 1910 he was not specific, but it is clear that he was fast losing, if he had not already lost, his religious faith.

'I have always tried to get Dave to go to his brothers ever since he spoke of it, although I knew I would miss him', Thereza Iversen was to write to George Eyre Evans. 'He has told me many passages of his life — they seem so sad. I often wish he would look at things in a more brighter way. Dave thinks everything seems to go wrong for him. But we make our own world.'

To make his, Dave needed the fare. He'd made some money from the earlier rabbiting and had hoped to send some to Eyre Evans and Join- son, but mere living had swallowed it up. 'I am in a ferment of unrest', he wrote on 25 April, 'I might pop off to South Africa any moment. But I lack funds. The fares from Dunedin are higher than I'd expected.' He was then just down from the hills, where he'd been rabbiting for weeks. He went back up. He was to be in those hills until June.

He left one record of the experience, an extraordinary twenty-two page letter which took him most of May to write. By then, he'd been rabbiting for three months. He wrote his letter at the door of his tent, a lean-to by a stone chimney, with a rabbit hopping about outside. He wrote by the light of an acetylene lamp, with two sacks of rabbit skins as a coverlet and another as pillow. Old Jim the horse was tethered nearby but sometimes he broke loose and had to be chased. The dog was snuf- fling about. Great batches of rabbit skins which had to be cleaned and stretched on wire frames lay all around him. The winds of heaven were his bed-mates. Of a morning, he had to feed the horse and collect sticks for his fire and billycan. Porridge, bread, cheese, rice, mutton, peas were his food.

When he'd first come up he found that a couple of toughs had jumped his claim, but he saw them off. He'd sunk everything he had into this venture, but thought the skins plus the sale of his kit would see him right. He was hard at it day and night, on a rough ridge two miles away. The country was all rocky gullies and abysses; he let the horse guide him. One night he got back by holding on to Jim's tail. In three weeks, he'd got 3,000 rabbits, but this was only a medium tally, worth perhaps £25; he needed more and would have to do some farmwork to make up the money. That morning he'd bagged 57 . . . 'How would you like to skin 57 rabbits, Miss Thomas?' He'd done it in half an hour.

David told the Evanses that his cousin Jack had suddenly appeared at his tent and dubbed him Dai Rabbitskins! Jack was going home; he'd found no friends in New Zealand. David had. Even now, once a week down on the Flat a woman with 8 or 9 kids cooked his meat and gave him milk and counted herself well paid on pittance, though he did take lollipops for the children. But he had to get away. Will in South Africa had written to say that wages were much higher there. His brother Jim got £17 10s a month and all found and was expecting £20 for counter-jumping — 'far more than I get for toiling incessantly night and day'.

The mail which regularly got to David up in his eyrie evoked little response beyond a sad nostalgia for old hopes gone beyond recall, but the sighting of Halley's Comet excited him enough to conjure verse out of him — Ye Comet y-clept Halley (perhaps he'd been reading Chaucer!) — which was ultimately published in the *Otago Witness* and certainly expressed his current mood:

Gone is the romance, the hush of ancient night,
The know-all day is here, sans God.
Man's at the perihelion now, like you.
Ye stars around! What course will HE pursue?

At the end of May, he came down. He needed more money and had the choice of three jobs. The one he chose was at the farm of Pat Weaver, where he was to plant 2,000 fruit trees. On 24 June, he wrote to say that this would be his last job in New Zealand. And at that point, David Jones virtually disappeared.

Eyre Evans heard not a word from him for three months. It looks as though David did not write to anybody. During those months, at Aberystwyth, Miss Thomas the old housekeeper died. Evans at once sent a cable and a letter to Ivon Jones. Silence was the only response. The people at Aberystwyth were beginning to get desperate when suddenly a cable arrived from David at Dunedin dated 29 September. It carried the brief message: *Booking South Africa.*

On 1 October in Dunedin, David sat down to write. He'd had the news of Miss Thomas's death, written a long letter about it and had then let the letter stare him in the face for two months. He apologised, but with none of his customary effusiveness. The letter had waited on 'a certain decision'. For at the last moment, the attraction of South Africa had been balanced by an almost equal temptation to stay in New Zealand. 'I found an ideal home in the Weaver family, who came to look upon me almost as a son.' He then told of an experience which is best described in his own words:

'Moreover, I got entangled in the charms of a quiet, retiring girl, their adopted daughter, a niece who was engaged to another man whom she would willingly have thrown over for myself. In the letter I have mentioned, I had decided to stay in New Zealand and settle down. My brain was in a continuous turmoil — regrets, attacks of conscience about Will and yourself, the uncongenial nature of the society outside the Weavers. The tension became so great that I was unable to work.'

In fact, David Jones broke down. For two weeks, he was nursed with tender care. 'I came back again to the only possible decision — to do my duty and go to South Africa. I might laugh at this in years to come as mawkish and sickly. If I do, it will be with the laugh of the hardened cynic. But, at present, it is a case of wrenching myself away from a simple, uneducated yet refined and loveable girl who, to put it plainly, loves me as I was never loved before and, I fear, as I will never be loved again. The quiet tears of Ethel Weaver as I left haunt my mind.'

Three weeks later, on a ship out of Sydney, David Jones wrote to Eyre Evans . . . 'I spoke to you in my last letter of some things which I need not go into once again. Nor need you make any further reference to the matter to anyone, least of all to myself.' Neither man ever did.

When he got to Dunedin, in a state of mind we can only guess at, David found that William Roberts was on holiday in Australia. They arranged to meet in Sydney. On 4 October David posted off dozens of New Zealand postcards to Aberystwyth and on the ninth, seen off like a son by Robert Fyfe and his wife, he sailed for Wellington. He stayed four days there with his aunt and learned that his cousin Emrys had been drowned in a drunken boating accident off Auckland.

He reached Sydney on the 19th, 'ran around' with William Roberts and left the next day. Roberts was distraught. In an anguished letter to Eyre Evans, he blamed himself. If he'd been in Dunedin when David got there, he'd have talked him out of it. In Sydney, he said, David was already half repenting his decision. On board ship on 20 October, Jones told Evans he was going 'breast forward certainly, but many a regretful look I cast back . . . Some strange power seems to have impelled me, not purely from inclination . . .' He talked of Otago Central as a 'barren land of uncongenial spirits' but, in fact, his first months in South Africa were full of nostalgia; he even infected his brothers with New Zealand fever. A year later, William Roberts was convinced that Jones was on the point of returning. He never did.

After a stop at Melbourne, the ship put into Adelaide — 'the most beautiful of Australian cities, the Dunedin of Australia'. He left there on the 27th on the last leg of the journey. His decision was now irrevocable. In the last resort, it was a family crisis and a sense of duty which drove a half-reluctant David Jones to South Africa and he paid a price for it. What did he expect of his new country . . . 'I incline to the melancholy view . . . What I need is something to occupy me intensely, something to give me a zest in life'.

After a fine voyage without a glimpse of sail or island, he landed in Durban and sent the obligatory postcard to George Eyre Evans on 17 November. The next day, he was off inland to brother Will and his store. David Ivon Jones had at last set foot in the land where, in a manner he could not have foreseen, he was in truth to make a place for himself in the world and in history.

3

A SOCIALIST IN SOUTH AFRICA

7

A FRESH START

Government of the People, For the Whites, By the Whites.

When Ivon Jones arrived in South Africa on 17 November 1910, the Union of South Africa was not yet six months old and the first session of the Legislative Assembly had only recently been opened.[1] According to the census of 1911, there were 1.3 million whites, four million Africans, and 680,000 Coloureds and Indians.[2] Government was the preserve of the white man headed by the one-time Boer Generals, Botha, Smuts and Hertzog. Their comrades of the Anglo-Boer war, Generals Beyers, de la Rey and de Wet, were in command of the army.

Sixty-seven Members of the Legislative Assembly (MLAs) were members of the South African National Party (SANP). They faced a divided opposition of thirty-nine Unionists, eleven Independents and three Labour members but the contending parties agreed that South Africa was, and should remain, a white man's land.[3] The first differences on political policy came from within the SANP (in 1912-13), when a section of the party defected and formed the National Party under General Hertzog. It was ostensibly a matter of language and of flag but behind these symbols lay the question of the country's economy and the discontent of those who felt they had been dispossessed by the British in the war of 1899-1902.

The wealth of the country depended mainly on the extraction of gold from the mines on the Witwatersrand. The discovery of these mines that had led to the importation of thousands of white miners from Europe and across the world and hundreds of thousands of black labourers from southern Africa. The perceived need to control the supply of gold (the 'money commodity') lay behind the struggle for control of the independent South African Republic under President Kruger. This culminated in the Anglo-Boer war of 1899-1902 and, after the defeat of the Boers, the control of the country by the British. The bitter memories evoked by that war were to affect the political and social development of the country over the coming decades but, ultimately, it was the existence of these mines that initiated South Africa's industrial revolution, opened up the country and led to the unification of the sub-continent.

The speed of development and the concentration of capital in the mining ventures was not an unmixed blessing. General Smuts, then Minister of Finance, addressing the Congress of the South African Manufacturers' Association at their dinner said:

    . . . without the mines the country would have stagnated and he wished them well, but the extraction of minerals had changed the

face of the country, and introduced new problems. It had transformed one of the cheapest countries in the world to one of the
dearest. This retarded the development of industry, because the
high cost of living made any far-reaching alteration in the
economy impossible. The only solution was to cut the cost of
production by reducing wages and the cost of living.[4]

For Smuts, as for the mining houses, the problem lay in cutting working
costs and the cost of living. It was to keep down costs that the mines
opposed the development of local industry (at least until the First World
War), finding imported goods cheaper than local products — and, to
keep down production costs the mines aimed at cutting wages . . .
primarily those of the white workers.

These were unsettled years. The newspapers carried news of fighting
in the Balkans, rumours about imminent war in Europe, and fears of
impending black rebellion in South Africa. There was also news of industrial unrest and of militant action by white workers on the Witwatersrand. Yet the issues that aroused most passion in the legislative
assembly were the language question (or the primacy of English over
Dutch) and South Africa's standing in the British Empire.

The first tasks of government were to present a budget and build a
local army and citizens' defence force. The legislature had to unify,
centralise and develop the railways and harbours, administrations and
local infrastructures of four previously separate territories;[5] define an
educational policy (for whites), regulate the labour supply for the mines,
and delimit the extent of African land holdings. These issues were not
questioned by the white electorate irrespective of the party in control.
The economic debates in the years to come were concerned with
methods of increasing the local holding of capital and the problem of
restructuring the country's economy to lessen the dependence on gold
— which was known to be a wasting asset. There was also the problem
of rising unemployment in the white community. Yet every step taken to
increase production through rationalisation led to the displacement of
more skilled and semi-skilled workers. On the farmlands the development of agriculture, both for export and to feed the growing urban
population, led to the concentration of production in fewer hands and
the displacement of the poorer white squatters. The expansion of
manufacture to diversify the economy and provide new centres of
employment was a slow process that advanced fitfully, subject to booms
and depressions and the shortage of local capital for investment.

These were problems with which Jones was to grapple in the years to
come, but his first concern had little to do with the state of the new
nation. He needed to reach his brothers in the countryside, through
whom he was to secure both work and lodging. Not always congenial
work and never giving the opportunity of earning enough money to
repay his debts, but giving him time to find his own place in the country.

He set out at once for Oosthuizen (near Kroonstad) in the Orange Free State where his brother Bill lived, and in his letters to George Eyre and Kitty Evans recorded his impressions of the scenery, lyrically about Natal, but less enthusiastically about the Free State. He contrasted the 'snow-white peaks, blue with translucency, noble and distant', of his youth, with the local heat: the air 'charged with electric oppression, thunder ever present, rumbling angrily'.

From the outset it was obvious that Jones came to South Africa with decided views on the Boers and their fight against the British. Writing of his train journey out of Natal he said:

As morning broke we were nearing the scenes of those harrowing fights where so many men and so many reputations were buried in graves of glory and disgrace respectively . . . Here and there, unbounded by nought but a neat border of white stones . . . lay the graves of the men of England, and their fellows against whom they waged unrighteous war! Those white memorials gave a strange meaning to the landscape, a portentous one, for were they not everlasting reminders of oppression to the oppressed?

For over two years Jones held that the Boer cause was just and their leaders worthy of support, although he criticised many Afrikaners for their narrowness and lack of culture. His concern for Welsh rights and the Welsh language predisposed him to sympathise with the Boers, but whatever the source of his sentiments, he knew little about the history of the country. Many of his attitudes, at least in the first years, reflected the views of the local press. Many of the issues that preoccupied him later, and for which he offered pioneering solutions, were still opaque. His early attitudes persisted until he witnessed the Boer leaders' rejection of legitimate workers' demands in 1913 followed by their support for the Allies in the First World War.

He went to the general-purpose shops in the Free State owned by his two brothers. His first stop was with Bill Jones at Oosthuizen and then with Eben Jones at Riviera, near Heilbron.[6] He had grown accustomed to village life in New Zealand, but here he felt both isolated and cramped and had little love for shop work. Yet, in retrospect, there were compensations. He had a vantage point in the countryside from which to acquaint himself with some of the social problems that beset South Africa — of black labourers, of small (white) farmsteads and of 'bywoners', or white rural tenants.[7]

He had to cope with two new languages and he complained that there were no primers available. The Afrikaners used a Dutch patois and the spoken language differed from the 'High-Dutch' of the printed word. Nonetheless, he soon learnt enough to conduct a broken conversation, half Dutch, half English — well enough, he wrote, to be sent by Bill Jones as a *smous* (or travelling hawker) to surrounding homesteads. The Sotho [or people of Basutoland/Lesotho] spoke a language that differed from any he had heard before. It was, he noted in a letter on 1 January 1911, a 'strange collection of sounds', but there was a double-ll sound which was similar to the Welsh and also a click 'which was the same mode as the Ll but in a condensed form'.

'The county is pretty scattered', he wrote. 'We can only see one farmhouse from the *winkel* [shop] door . . . Yet every day business is brisk; and one wonders where the people come from.' The Dutch came into the shop first, the Sotho sat outside, 'conversing, now soft, now vehement', until the whites had finished. Only then would they barter their fowls, wool, hides and eggs for goods they wanted. Mainly they brought eggs, carried in woven straw baskets, or pottery, balanced on their heads. He helped with the serving and was not required to do any manual labour because he was white, and he commented on the servility that was required of black customers, an issue that he returned to again and again.

The first reference to events in South Africa was incidental and without political significance. Jones urged Evans to keep the stamps he sent, because they were a special issue commemorating the Union of South Africa. However, he had still to learn more about the country and this would take time, particularly as he became even more isolated and cut off from news when he moved to his brother Eban at Riviera, where mail was dispatched and delivered only once a week. His letters were dotted with comments on what he found in the columns of the Welsh newspapers. The only other reading, he wrote, was of Wordsworth and a 'peep into a Dutch grammar'.

He gave no explicit reason for his move but did say he was happier at Riviera than he had been at Oosthuizen because Eben was married and had a child. He had not relished bachelordom, he wrote on 5 April, and the transition to family life was welcome, offering more regular meals and the presence of women in his life — although he seems throughout his adult life to have coped better with women at a distance! He gave no details about the family nor about the household, but said that conditions were easier: working hours were shorter and he was learning 'a good system of book-keeping'.

Letter Writing

Jones found little companionship in the Free State villages and he only stayed for six months before moving to the Witwatersrand. He said little of his brothers or of Eban's wife and there seems to have been little communion between the brothers. It was not until he moved north to Johannesburg, where he found small Welsh communities, as well as a Unitarian centre, that he found some kindred souls. But he went through periods of doubt and depression and was sustained only by letters from friends, most particularly from the Evanses, who also sent him copies of the *Welsh Gazette*, the *Inquirer* and occasional British journals and papers. They wrote about events in Aberystwyth, of George Eyre's travels and his archeological work and the Unitarian community. Jones wrote about personal and political decisions (even when he was certain they disapproved) and sent press cuttings of some of his writings. In later years he wrote less. Instead he sent some pamphlets and, after 1915, copies of the *International*, the anti-war paper he edited. He was also less inclined to write as he distanced himself from his youthful ideals. He knew that George Eyre could not respond to his feelings of revulsion against 'mammon' or his involvement in the Labour Party and his increasingly rebellious stand.

Jones's lyricism, remarked upon by his political associates long after his death, was apparent in the letters he sent. If his writing was sometime over-flowery he said, it was because Kitty Evans encouraged him to 'dip oftener in the cup of sentiment'. That was not the whole story. Ivon Jones was steeped in the language of the bible and his writing reflected that absorption. His letters also had more than one purpose. On 13 October 1912, writing from Germiston on the Witwatersrand, he felt it necessary to explain:

Letter writing has been of great good to me, not only directly by keeping me in touch with friends, but incidentally it must also train one to readily express himself. Given the ideas . . . to commit them to writing presents no serious difficulty now, as was the case with me before I left home. I attribute this to letter writing.

Many passages first found in letters reappeared in articles he sent to the press. In his letters he wrote about the people, their occupations and their conflicts and he showed a growing (if sometimes slanted) understanding of the social and political problems of South Africa. He wrote about his first meeting with the Afrikaner and the division of labour between black and white in the countryside. These merged with articles in which he wrote of the problems of the gold fields and the ruthless drive for profits by the mine magnates. He spoke about his involvement in two major strikes and about his anti-war agitation. Ultimately, he discarded many of his old tenets and, welcoming the Russian Revolution, he wrote about and called for a Bolshevik party in South Africa.

Yet his changes in attitude came slowly. In 1912 he still wrote approvingly of Lloyd George's activities in Wales and in the House of Commons. It was not only the content of Lloyd George's speeches that he applauded. He was enthusiastic over the oratory that was 'glowing and daring . . . teeming with apt scriptural allusions which make it a sermon and him a preacher rather than a political speaker'. As his own interests changed, the sentiments in the correspondence altered. On 23 June 1912 he wrote unusually sharply to say that he was no longer interested in archaeology. He added, in conciliatory tone, that he was still a Unitarian,

. . . but something more, For I should not consider foreswearing of national ideals and aloofness from Welsh life and thought warranted by the embracing of views on religion which do not agree with those of the chapels and of the *seiat* [Methodist meeting].

Yet he was to break with the Unitarians. On this there is no information. When he arrived on the Rand he had written about attending services. He also announced in the *Inquirer*, of 26 August 1911, that in the census of May 'he was proud to have signed himself a Unitarian', and on 3 July he wrote from Boksburg, that

no writer now is bare-faced enough to say, as so many were fond of saying only five or six years ago, that the resolving of matter into atoms and electrons explained all that there is to be explained in God's universe.

However he found less time for going to chapel. When he wrote on 3 August 1914 to say that he had come to South Africa 'without a God in the world', he added:

You know what I mean. With frequent spells of depression and pessimism, unaccountable. Life a futility. I found S. Africa permeated with a feeling of snobbery. The cure for my pessimism and S. Africa's snobbery has since been found in the entirely spiritual enthusiasm for a new Heaven and a new Earth, in which the publicans and miners do share, with which Labour's awakening fires us.

Did he lose his faith and regain it for a time? Did he perhaps feel that he had to meet the rebuke from his former friends of the chapel for not having sent a message from New Zealand, or was this the start of a change in life philosophy that led to a break? Ultimately he wrote, in October 1914, that:

The question of Unitarianism versus Trinitarianism has become obsolete and futile to me. Unless your religious revolution is going to reflect itself in a complete change in the life of Society, in its structure, what good is it? Therefore all liberal thought has become stale, bourgeois, palliative, merely ameliorative. Periodicals which accept the revolution, whether in art, society, religion, or life as a whole, are alone interesting now.

Nonetheless his ingrained religiosity shaped his language in his letters and his political tracts, and he applied its puritanism to all his activities. Soon after arriving on the Rand, he wrote to the *East Rand Express* castigating their critic for praising frivolous films. He condemned the 'bioscope' for its crudities and commended the moving picture only in the application to scientific pursuits. He was also uncompromising in his political pronouncements, condemning all opponents, and this must have brought a sigh to George Eyre as he read his letters. Nonetheless, throughout his life, David Ivon wrote with great warmth to

his friends and even after he confessed his 'apostasy', he looked to them
for the friendship that meant so much to him.

Prayers of their Fathers

Despite Jones's initial pro-Boer position, he felt cramped by the
Afrikaners. Shortly after arriving in Oosthuizen he complained that he
found nothing

> to indicate aspirations after a higher life. The best Dutchmen as a
> rule is the least strict in religious matters . . . As far as I can see,
> [he] attends 'kirk' [church] and keeps the sabbath purely for the
> same reason as he ploughs with oxen and reaps with a sickle,
> simply because his father did so . . .

At Riviera he reacted sharply to the Afrikaners he met. On the one
hand, he wrote on 23 April, they were less enlightened than those at
Oosthuizen. Yet, on the other hand, they had 'virtues' being part of that
'famous commando' called the 'bitter-enders' [fighters in the Boer war
who opposed surrender] who had shown 'superb bravery'. Nonetheless,
their only other interest was the perfunctory one of going to 'kerk' every
'Nachtmaal' (the Lord's supper, or the sacrament of Holy Communion
held quarterly). He continued:

> Unlike the Welsh peasant . . . he has no ideals. A love of liberty,
> certainly, but that liberty must be his own. I could never imagine
> him giving up farm and home for such a comparatively abstract
> principle as the ballot or Home Rule for another country, as Car-
> diganshire farmers did in 1868. He is not a reader. A devout
> Dutchman has prayer certainly and grace before meat and after.
> But no literature. His gallery of heroes are military and political.
> No equivalent of Charles of Bala, John Elias, Christmas Evans
> [radical Welsh dissenters] adorn the walls of his ancestral home.
> He is a peasant of exotic growth, torn from ancient welkins centur-
> ies ago, remaining a peasant but lorn of those thousand and one
> generous illusions, folklores and moral heroes which make a
> peasant lovable. I suspect it is the inevitable result of all colonizing
> to make the colonial worldly.

Writing from Oosthuizen on 31 January 1911 he said he had much to
learn about his 'dark neighbours' . . . particularly as the mode of treatment by 'most Colonials [foreswore] all the attributes of good
behaviour'.

> The Kaffirs constitute a problem which it is difficult to solve. Ac-
> cording to my tutors, I must forget all feelings of compassion and
> humanitarian ideas in dealing with [them] . . . It remains for me to
> find out how far this is true. If honesty, trust and fidelity count for
> anything, the Basuto is in the main a credit to his Maker. If . . . an

honest man is God's greatest handiwork, then many of our dark customers are greatly superior beings to some of our white.

Despite his move North, his spirits remained low. Writing from Boksburg, near Johannesburg, on 18 June 1911 he spoke of returning to New Zealand, not only because conditions there were much more congenial but also because the Dutchman, contrary to his 'previous idealised opinion' was:

> not an attractive personality . . . He is a peasant transported. But having lost the virtues of peasantry in migration. He has no taste for books. He is a bore. His virtues are negative and consequently his vices are negative as well. Long association with the Kaffir has woven on his fibre some of the traits of the black man. They have severed for centuries, except in language, with the life of their mother country, knowing nothing of her literature and having none of their own. Bred of one bone for centuries, a comparatively small clan, they seem to suffer from the inexorable result of in-breeding, receiving no fresh reinforcements of new ideas, new hopes and new strengths as has been the lot of the English colonists.

He had found little cause to change his mind when writing next from Germiston eighteen months later. He mused on the 'suspicion and distrust which are the aftermath of [the Boer] war'. The Boer was uneducated, narrow, devoid of humour and 'wholly incapable of discussing points of Calvinist doctrine . . . He can talk commonplaces about his farm and exchange tobacco with you and say that the weather is dry, and then silence reigns supreme.' Jones could find little to praise. He said that the Dutch were 'not lovers of Nature as a whole' because farm names were taken from 'abstract experience', like *Langverwacht* (Long Expected), *Goedehoop* (Good Hope), *Nooitgedacht* (Never Thought of), *Twisnietmeer* (No More Trouble).

In his impatience Jones condemned the Afrikaners as a people but had the good grace to speak of 'personal knowledge of many fine exceptions'. He added that in so far as this was a 'wrong estimate of character [it reflected] . . . the general prejudice of the Uitlander'. The other more pervasive prejudice shown against the African — was shared by all whites. Jones was ambivalent but he generally accepted the stereotypes of the society in which he lived. He only partly made amends when, contrasting conditions in South Africa with that of New Zealand:he stated that:

> South Africa has no public opinion. One race has its own interests and each one pulls like a scratched up wagon team, one this way and the other that, after each other. When the gold rush calms down and the mines are closed and the various nations get fused together, then it will be a country.

Jones was to return to the Orange Free State in October 1913, but under very different conditions. He was forced to resign his job after speaking in defence of the striking miners in June-July and, unemployed, he was on hand to help Eben set up a new store in Frankfort. Once again he was scathing about the Boer. He could find few kind words for these people whose heritage was lost, he said, because of their 'ignorance of and indifference to the outside world of ideas' . . . and whose

> political leaders seem to conspire to keep him so for they never fire him to achieve and make his language the vehicle of a new message to South Africa and the world, while his religious leaders, the 'Predikants' . . . exercise the authority of priests over his mind, dish up the old old dogmas of Calvin . . .

Besides weddings and funerals and perhaps political meetings, he said, they gathered at Rifle Associations and shooting competitions — and at their annual commemoration of the victory over the Zulu Chief Dingane on 16 December. Inevitably, Jones's discussion of the Afrikaner became a discussion of the position of the African and, although he was still far from breaking with the views of South African white society, his ideas differed from that of most of his contemporaries.

The Blacks — 'Slaves in All But Name'

The race hatred that flowed through South Africa was fed by many streams and, although Jones's perceptions were not typical, his grappling with the issue is illuminating. His first observations of the Africans, outside the store in Oosthuizen, while sympathetic, were distant. It was not only language that stopped him making close contact with the women who waited patiently for the whites to finish their shopping. There were cultural barriers separating them and, ultimately, Jones was trapped in an impasse that it would take him some years to unravel — how to separate out prejudices that had no rational base, from his instinctive sympathy for the oppressed.

He grappled with the issue and in the first instance sought the answer in moral terms. There were few studies that might have provided real evidence of the thoughts of the African people and Jones mixed his own observations with popular prejudice. The 'Kaffirs',[8] he said, were 'slaves in everything but name, almost. Yet happy enough I admit, although he cannot own land nor rent it.' He found a parallel problem in the local church. Religious thinking, he claimed, was 'a thing far, far away from the tenor of South African thought', and this gave the 'brotherhood of man' a hollow ring. This, he said, was a natural consequence of the situation in South Africa. 'Strenuous thought . . . is a necessary corollary of strenuous work, or should I put it vice versa. Kaffirs do all the work here . . .' That 'glow of high thinking or high feeling [followed] the proud consciousness of an arduous job well done . . . ' The solution was for people to become religious liberals, but they 'must first be *religious*'.

Jones worked his way through every possible answer to the colour question. He started with few biases and sympathised with the lot of the blacks before joining the South African Labour Party (SALP) — which prided itself on being the first party to advocate total separation of the races. He adopted the party policy opting for complete segregation and, in this respect, his move to active politics was a retrograde step. His change in attitude was signalled to the Evans family in a cutting from his letter in the *East Rand Express* signed *Cincinnatus*.[8] Jones had undergone a change of attitude over the brotherhood of man. Taking as his example the arch segregationist in Natal he urged that there could be no success for the white labour movement and no relief from racial extinction

> except by drastic and stupendous reform lately advocated by such an authority as Mr Shepstone be adopted. Nothing less than the complete segregation of the Kaffir![10]

Jones wrote in praise of manual labour and claimed that

> no respectable white is going to labour on equal terms with the Kaffir, or when there is a possibility of black loungers in large numbers looking on. Under present conditions both races are prevented from working out, each their own salvation. Segregation, then, seems to me to be the only remedy.

Yet, his views on the colour question were ambivalent. A few weeks after this letter appeared, on 26 July 1911, the *Star* printed an interview with the African lawyer, Pixley ka I Seme, announcing the coming formation of a Union-wide African Association (known first as the South African Native National Congress and later renamed the African National Congress). Seme said the new body was to express the black communities' ideas but, in accord with white prejudices, much of the newspaper's report was devoted to the question of polygamy![11] Writing to the editor, Jones cut through the cant, saying the interview was a 'revelation' and Seme's description of the new movement's function as 'Thinking Loudly' was an 'appropriate term for the process of striving towards national self-consciousness'. He continued:

> 'Exeter-Hallism' [the London based meeting place of the anti-slavers], as the stock sneer for any recognition of the image of God, though black, in man, is becoming vulgar and ill-timed. It is a mistake to think that the real and best interests of white and black are antagonistical. South Africa's economic salvation lies in the salvation of the native. And now that he is beginning to undertake his own salvation, all things are possible.

Those who, unheeding the taunt of quixotism, dream of South Africa standing abreast of the other white dominions with a great race of virile, pure-bred yeomen, may also imagine as the counter-part of such a dream that of a sub-tropical Kaffir Empire — on the pattern of India — where the black man may ultimately work himself into an honourable place in the South African federation.

This was not a break with segregation, but it broached the possibility of co-operation across the colour line and, for its time was remarkable in being a message of support for the formation of a black nationalist movement. The editor of the *Star* disclaimed any support for Seme.[13] Jones sent a cutting to GE Evans and wrote condemning the curt and abusive language used by whites in addressing blacks.

And yet, the white man only considers his marketable value. When he begins to find that he has responsibilities towards the black man other than sending him missionaries, there will be a changed South Africa.

'Gold, Rusting Not Itself . . .'

Jones had been in the country for barely six months when he wrote from Riviera, on 17 May 1911, to say that there was little to excite his interest in this impoverished environment, where he 'blurted out incoherent scraps of Dutch to unappreciative Dutchmen's ears'. Furthermore, he was penniless and the only toil he might have wanted was the preserve of blacks because 'in this land of snobs' any whites who worked with the shovel were 'denominated . . . as poor whites'.

Jones's financial situation was always precarious. He does not mention any salary from his brothers Bill or Eban, but later, in June 1911, when he was in Boksburg he wrote to say that his wage was £12 10s per month, £8 of which was for board and lodging, and he had to save for clothes.[14] He saw little possibility of earning more and commented wryly on his materialism, 'bound up in the acquisition of a pocketful of coins'. He would not countenance any further loans (being unable to repay long standing debts to friends) and, although tempted by Evans' invitation to act as his secretary for a year, he felt it would only postpone the need to make his own way in the world. Even his contemplated return to New Zealand was impossible in his current impecunious state.

The next letters came from Vogelfontein, on the outskirts of Boks-burg, 'half an hour by train from Johannesburg'. Here Ivon had found his brother Jim managing a coal agency and worked for him as a book-keeper. Boksburg was a larger town of some 43,500 (11,600 white and the rest black),[15] situated near the gold mines. He was to confront problems which would change the direction of his life.

Jones now discovered and read the *East Rand Express* which was published in Boksburg and carried local news and gossip about the escapades of the town's elite. It also included endless debates on

whether trams or trackless trams should be installed in the town, discussions on additions to the Germiston railway station and reports on
Council meetings of the four East Rand towns (Germiston, Boksburg,
Benoni and Springs). He described the paper as a 'weekly-rag', but he
was less than kind. There were letters on phthisis, the scourge of the
miners, and information on the cinema, theatre and other enter-
tainments. There were reports of election campaigns, including that of
WH Andrews for the Georgetown seat in parliament. The 'Fighting
Platform' of the South African Labour Party (SALP) containing demands
that Africans be discouraged from immigrating to white centres, was
printed on 6 January 1912, and letters from 'DIJ' supporting the Labour
Party on 3 and 10 February 1912. The *Express* reported meetings of trade
unions and the local Labour Party and on 27 April 1912 the journal
reported the first meeting of the Germiston Literary and Debating
Society where Col Stallard (a Natal advocate, on the right of the South
African Party) spoke on the need to keep Africans out of the towns. This
was to be his constant demand over the years and coincided with the
policy of the SALP, whose ranks Jones had recently joined. Jones wrote
to Evans about the Society on 14 July and said he had spoken there on
Irish Home Rule.

The *Express* also conducted a virulent campaign, together with local
citizens, against Indian traders in the Transvaal. An article on the Vogelfontein location that seemed to be in the best tradition of journalistic
muck-raking and exposed the area as a 'moral plague spot' and a centre
for crime, pimping and illicit liquor. Houses that stood on 50 square feet
contained as many as ten rooms clustered around a tiny yard with a well
into which the filth of the houses drained after the rains. However, this
picture of squalor was not intended to secure redress for the African
residents. Rather, Indians who owned the properties were accused of
rack-renting. This was part of a campaign against a Mr Bhyat who had
used a legal loophole to open a store in Boksburg and whom the 'good'
citizens wanted removed.[16] These articles appeared before Jones arrived in the Transvaal but the views expressed in the journal coincided
with the anti-Indian views of leaders of the Labour Party.[17] It does seem
that Ivon might have acquiesced in 1911.

Jones first wrote from Vogelfontein to Aberystwyth in June 1912, and
ventured into new fields. He described for the first time the vast saucer-
shaped Rand. He wrote of the mighty shaft gears towering over the
mines and he spoke of the mine dumps that dominated the skyline as
debris heaped in man-made hillocks.

> And around the edges of this mighty saucer of gold and quartz
> nibble these thousands of two-legged rats, where it crops to the
> surface, following it down to the depths as far as they dare —
> about 4000 feet.
> . . . Rims of saucer dip sudden to ends of Reef and geologists
> think it must resurface in the Orange Free State. Marvellous to

watch surface workings. Shafts go down at an angle. Men have to
half recline and a railing is slammed on them . . .

The black man has to do all the work of course. And I saw cages
coming up with a load of Kaffirs jammed in on one another like
sardines; like sardines would be a tame expression.

The description of miners as 'two-legged rats' was bizarre, even if
Jones was only using it metaphorically. But the mines were central to the
Witwatersrand and he saw mammon behind the industry. Or so it seems
from his next letter of 18 June: 'Today is Sunday. Even on the Rand, that
is given us. Although such is the greed of magnates, the mines never
stop.' Jones was depressed, dejected and possibly ill. Work in the store
was onerous, he said, the rewards small and he was too tired even to
read after the supper meal.

He despaired at the sterility of the gold fields. There was no idealism
and he foresaw the eventual desolation on the day the mines closed,
'leaving hollow caverns in the deep and huge mounds of battered debris
and wrecked shaft-gearings above'. Even in Johannesburg, the centre of
all activities on the Rand, there was little of interest: only 'two or three
churches and a theatre'. This was a land of snobs 'with a dearth of good,
simple folk'. Character was judged by clothing which 'must not bear the
least testimony to the toil'. He wrote of walking 'in vain the streets of
Johannesburg looking for a bookshop' and of loneliness which left individuals to their own devices. Citing the case of a miner who had died
in his room, but had not been discovered for a week and was then buried
and forgotten, he lamented:

Gold, rusting not itself, is here rusting into the soul of a people. . .
I do not think I shall make any friends here. The atmosphere is
against it.

Worse still, he continued, his job provided no satisfaction, but he was
glad he had stuck to it,

because times on the Rand [are] not good now . . . Men seem to be
quite as much afraid of losing a job as in the old country. Certainly
it seems just as hard, if not harder, to obtain one.

Labour with a White Skin . . .

Although Jones was pessimistic about finding friends on the Rand, he
was about to find a group of persons with whom he established and
maintained a life-long intimacy. Some time in 1911 he joined the South
African Labour Party (SALP), and it was there that he was to meet the
men who gave him a new sense of purpose.

At the time there were two main (exclusively white) groups that
claimed to speak for labour. The SALP, established in 1908, was
modelled on the British Labour Party and included socialists of a variety

of hues. Like its counterpart in Britain, it believed that socialism would
be achieved by parliamentary means. The British model was reinforced
by the affiliation of trade unions, some (like the Amalgamated Society
of Engineers), being branches of British unions. Yet, by claiming to have
been the first party to demand total segregation in the country, the SALP
showed its specific South African character. The party also called for
the repatriation of Indians, and ignored their campaigns against discriminatory laws. The only exception to this narrow racialism seems to
have been the acceptance of Coloureds as members (although this was
not put into effect), because their vote could decide success in some
Cape constituencies.

On 13 December 1911 the *Rand Daily Mail* reported the resignation
of George Ferrar, President of the Chamber of Mines, from the Legislative Assembly. This followed a scandal over the bungled amalgama-
tion of the East Rand Proprietary Mines (ERPM). Fortuitously for Ivon,
he was asked to assist W H Andrews in the by-election that followed in
Georgetown (Germiston district). Andrews won and their joint work
was to ripen into friendship. Together they participated in the leftward
move against the war in 1914 – but much was to happen in the few years
before Europe burst into flames

Jones wrote of the magnates using 'their power to perpetuate racial
animosities . . . to hinder that permanent entente between the two white
races which the good [General] Botha strives so much to accomplish
against the extremists of his own side and the machinations of
Randlordism'. It was strange, he wrote from Germiston on 19 December, to find that the Randlords – the mining magnates – 'who had no
political ability, save the almighty dollar' got the miner's vote 'but disillusion is coming to him and the Labour Party, comprising both [white]
races, will very shortly sweep the polls on the Rand'. This was to be one
of the few occasions in which Jones wrote of the expected role of
Afrikaner workers yet Labourites had high hopes of winning these
newly urbanised workers to their ranks.

Alongside the SALP, the other movement on the political left was
associated with the *Voice of Labour*, which appeared weekly from October 1908 until December 1912. It printed extracts from those who
called themselves Marxists, syndicalists and British Labourites,. It included occasional articles by blacks and by suffragettes and carried
stories of Tsarist terror and news of working class activities across the
world. There was little stress on formal organization and the journal
supported several bodies which appeared under a succession of names
including the South African Socialist Federation, the Socialist League,
the Socialist Party, and the Industrial Workers of the World (IWW). Most
were averse to parliamentarianism – having suffered heavy defeats in
the elections of 1910 – and many tended towards syndicalism: their
stress was on trade union organization and the use of the general strike

to abolish capitalism. They did not accept the division between craft and other workers and called for one big industrial union to represent the interests of the whole working class. However, there is no evidence that they had any support from workers and there was no effective syndicalist movement in the country.

The *Voice of Labour* recognised only two classes in society and rejected any policy based on colour differences. However, this was not translated into practice, even when the journal publicised the campaigns led by Gandhi against discrimination or black industrial unrest in 1911. On 12 January 1912 it also welcomed a resolution by an African named Zini, at a conference in Johannesburg, calling for the formation of a black miners union. Its most frequent contributors included Archie Crawford, Mary Fitzgerald (who owned the press), LHH Greene, Andrew Dunbar, Jim Davidson and Arthur Noon. However, it was Mary Fitzgerald who received most publicity. She was dubbed 'Pickhandle Mary' after retrieving a pickhandle that a mounted policeman had dropped and leading irate citizens with these weapons against the police. Thereafter her followers used these pickhandles against police, scabs and political antagonists. The *Voice of Labour* proudly referred to her cofighters under the headline 'Pick Handle Politics'. Fitzgerald was also acclaimed for stopping the trams in Johannesburg by placing detonators on the tracks during the tramwaymen's strike in 1911.[18]

There was no love lost between members of the SALP and the Socialist Party. They opposed each other in the 1910 elections and after Georgetown, Crawford used the journal to attack Andrews and the SALP for nominating candidates in 1910 and 1912, in constituencies already chosen by the Socialist Party.[19] Nor did the leaders of the SALP approve of 'Pick Handle Politics' or some of the escapades for which Fitzgerald was blamed Furthermore her espousal of suffragettism on 9 July 1909, and in subsequent issues of the *Voice of Labour*, probably earned their disapprobation.

Jones was not attracted to these people. He did not mention them in any of his letters and this omission was probably deliberate. Their activities in 1911-12, and particularly the pickhandle tactics, were very different to his. Contact with them was precluded by his friendship with Andrews. The attacks on syndicalism by Lloyd George (on whom Jones still doted) would have made their mark, although it is not certain what he thought of Lloyd George's statement in the House of Commons, on 19 March 1912, that parliamentary socialists were 'the best policemen for the syndicalists'. During the strikes of 1913-14 the paths of Jones and Crawford converged, but there was still no intimation of a rapprochement. Crawford was amongst the men deported by Smuts in January 1914, during the second general strike in six months, and Mary Fitzgerald (now his wife) joined him in Britain. During that fateful year, as Europe moved to war, Jones moved leftwards, altered his attitude towards segregation and even adopted de Leon's syndicalist views, but the Crawfords moved to the right — and their political paths did not intersect. Perhaps Jones and the Crawfords could never have worked together amicably, even if they had belonged to the same party. — there was no compatibility in lifestyle, in values, or in philosophy. Yet, in the regrouping of socialists after August 1914, Jones worked not only with SP Bunting and WH Andrews, who had been in the SALP, but also LHH (Laurie) Greene and Andrew Dunbar who had been regular contributors to the *Voice of Labour.*

Phthisis — the 'White Death'

The first distinctive mark of gold production seen by every newcomer to the Rand was the white mine dumps on the outskirts of every mining town — the 'debris' once mentioned by Jones. During the windy season, before the rains came, showers of sand from the dumps filled the air and lay like a thin white blanket on floors and furniture in nearby suburbs. It was therefore not exceptional that Jones should write from Boksburg in October 1911 about the relief that the rains had brought, after several weeks of winds which left people 'choking with dust'. 'The white ore dust overlays everything', he wrote, and a close examination revealed that the 'particles were like glass':

> You can imagine how it must be underground for the miners who inhale the stuff daily. No wonder that Rand profits are made out of the lives of thousands of men who are hurried off into a premature grave by the scourge of miners' phthisis. The average working life of a Rand miner is only about ten years. Many drop off in twelve months or two years. I was talking to a strong looking miner yesterday who prided himself on being a rare exception, having worked at the drills for 15 years. It is said that 20 per cent of the white miners on the Rand suffer from the disease, knowing that nothing in the wide world can help them. The mortality among the Kaffirs must be appalling, but no statistics are available, for they go home to their kraals to die.

The life expectancy was even shorter than noted in this letter, but the central point was clear. Phthisis was a deadly malady and Jones, who had left his native Wales in search of a cure for consumption, observed in a letter from Riviera that Johannesburg would not suit him because of the 'peculiarly malignant' dust and because the high altitude had an 'asthmatic tendency' on him. For people who did not work on the mines the all-pervading dust was an inconvenience — for the miners, their dependents and their associates, the White Death was a scourge to be fought.

A post-graduate trainee, Lewis Marino Nesbitt, worked from 1912-16 on several mines on the Witwatersrand as surveyor, shift boss, and finally as mine-captain at the New Kleinfontein mines, the epicentre of the general strike of 1913. In an account of the hazards of mining and the threat of phthisis,[20] Nesbitt said that the disability was bound to strike the men down. He put the average working life of engineers and miners at no more than eight years:

The deadly quartz dust hung like a fog always in the air; we breathed it continually, and the lungs of many were destroyed. Only a strong constitution could resist the changes of temperature, for it was very hot underground, especially in the lower levels. The atmosphere was continually fouled by poisonous gases, and fresh air had to be forced by mechanical means into the workings and galleries. Moisture, too, was artificially diffused there, in an attempt to allay the quartz dust, and in some parts of the mine this moisture became excessive, so that the levels and workings were filled with a curious sickening mixture of dust and water-vapour. In other parts the air was so dry that the men were half suffocated at times, and their eyes and throats were parched by the thick dust.

The commonest illness was pneumonia followed sooner or later by phthisis — a disease 'which often caused the death of its victims in a very few weeks'. In a passage that echoes Jones's description, he said:

The fine grit, so light that the movement going on in the air was quite sufficient to hold much of it floating in suspension for an indefinite time, consisting of minute particles with points far finer than that of any needle and edges infinitely sharper than that of any knife. With each breath the miner drew, thousands of these glassy splinters rushed into his lungs, piercing the tissue and causing lesions that could never heal.

Furthermore, in some mines charges were ignited in rotation and rock faces were inspected to determine stratification while the gallery was filled to suffocation point by dust and dynamite smoke. Each inspection shortened the miner's life by a month! The mine owners supplied special masks; sprayed molasses while the drills were boring and had special vapours diffused to cause the precipitation of the particles but to no avail. The men worked their terms and, if not killed by rock falls, premature blasting charges or other accidents, died from phthisis. Consequently, 'no insurance company would do business with a Rand miner'.

The number of miners, white and black, killed by phthisis is unknown. It was the white fatalities that were usually reported. However, in a rare exposure, John X Merriman, who had been favoured by many for the premiership of South Africa after union in 1910, spoke in parliament on African fatalities. He quoted the Minister of Native Affairs' statistics for the years 1903-1912 to show that including accidents 'no less than 100,000 Kaffirs have been virtually murdered since the [Boer] war'. On

3 August 1913 the same paper said that many Africans never reached their kraals, but were found dead on the roads. The 'White Death' knew no colour bar yet the *Rand Daily Mail* of 28 May 1913, quoting official figures, said that only seventy-two Africans were receiving compensation for disablement under the Miners Phthisis Act, and twenty for partial disablement. Only one dependent was receiving compensation.

Officially, 4,500 men were said to have contracted the 'White Death' every year — a gross understatement. Jones wrote of this human toll in a letter to *Reynold's Newspaper*, [21] quoted in an editorial on 14 September 1913, after the strike of white miners (discussed below), in which the main demand was for the incidence of phthisis to be cut. He said that of the members of the strike committee of 1907, ten had died of phthisis, three were living but had the dread disease, one had died in a mine accident in Canada and one was alive: the fate of two or three others was not known. He added that at a recent meeting a union organiser 'dropped the remark, "I've got it. We've all got it"', 'it' being the spectre that lays low all miners'.

Of Bawdy Houses, Alcohol, and Whippets

Johannesburg was unique in many respects. Founded in 1886, it had a population of 237,000 in 1912/13. Half were white, the rest black. For the first decade there was a preponderance of males among the whites but, by 1910, the sex imbalance had narrowed. The mainly white-serviced brothels still operated but trade dropped as men found wives.

The black sex ratio was between 10 and16 to1. Almost half the blacks worked on the mines, housed in unisex compounds. Africans were not yet forced into segregated areas although Pimville, one of the first 'location', had been established in the region that was incorporated at a later date into Soweto.Another 37,000 were employed as 'house-boys' and 6,000 in factories, workshops, or warehouses. Owing to the controls set up to restrict African women entering towns, most of these men found sexual gratification through prostitutes or homosexuality.

Whites remained inside the all-white suburbs and rarely entered the locations. Nesbitt, in his recollections, [22] said that most white miners on the Rand were accommodated on mine property in terraced bungalows, each one 'squalid and depressing'. They were rooms rather than apartments, furnished with a small iron bed, an enamel basin resting on a packing case and a chair or two. Clothes hung from the walls, or were stored in boxes. Despite this, there was a measure of comfort. There were separate bathrooms with a plentiful supply of hot water. Cleaning, cooking and laundry, were done by African men.

But the white miners were unable to relax. At night their sleep was fitful and broken by nightmares or the cries of other men, or the racking cough of those whose lungs were already affected. They found relief in induced stupor:

> In these dreary cubicles each miner sat amongst his bottles, for in almost all of them there were bottles of liquor everywhere — on the floor, in the corners, lined up against the walls, some upright, others overturned, full bottles and empty bottles. The depression of mind caused by his hard toil, and its foreseen or suspected result, an early death, made the miner long for oblivion, for a little respite from full consciousness of the grim world in which he lived.

Nesbitt believed that 'scarcely a dozen of the white miners could be said to be moderate drinkers' and many would finish a quart of brandy or whisky in one long draught — frequently before breakfast. Many were seized by delirium tremens and when they reached this stage they ate very little. The (all white) pubs were for men only, were tastelessly decorated and 'filled with customers at all hours of the day and night'.. Money was of little account. Discarding life-long habits, miners pulled out handfuls of tobacco from their pockets to fill a pipe, and threw whatever remained on the ground. Never once had he seen a man return any surplus to his pocket.

Conversations were mostly of betting on horses or dogs and the miner's passion was his dog. These were kept 'with jealous care in the room of his owner' and, at the end of the day's work, there was a hurry to get home to feed, groom and exercise it. Men would meet on open spaces behind their rooms and try out their dogs and when they went into town they took their dogs with them. They met in parks to discuss the respective merits of their animals and sometimes ran a trial, always with stopwatch in hand. They trained the dogs for the races, betted on the results and nobbled the animals without compunction. Despite the obvious doping and 'fixing' of the whippets, there was widespread interest in the races:

> On the public holidays important races were held, and whole families would travel from one end of the Rand to another, each with its dog in its arms, as it were; first the father holding it, then the mother, then one of the children; and throughout the long railway journey the conversation was of nothing but dogs, of their performances, their victories, and the prizes they had won or would win.

The men and their wives found their pleasures where they could and the conviviality of the whippet racecourse — and the excitement of the race — added spice to their lives. These men (or their wives) were not usually to be seen at political meetings and Jones did not meet with them. However, there was a time, in 1915, when a particular type of 'sportsman' would play a significant role in Labour Party politics. Jones was later to recall that, owing to the introduction of Betting Legislation in the Transvaal Provincial Council and 'favours received or yet to come', a number of 'racing scribes', 'bucket-shop delegates [and] white waist-coated straight-from-the-horses-mouth men' supported the right-wing of the party to vote the left out of office, and eventually out of the party.[23]

Yet the whippet owners, together with their wives, would shake the Witwatersrand when they were driven to a fury by the actions of the mineowners. Then the dogs took second place, the bottle was put aside (at least partly), and the power of the state seemed to be threatened by men with a new will and determination. It was then, as we will see, that Jones felt an accord with these men and it was to become one of his enduring beliefs that the future belonged to them. This misplaced belief in the social potential of the white miners, held by most leftists in the early years of the century, provided the energy with which to launch the communist movement.

A Time of Changing Values

Events that were to move Jones to the left started quite fortuitously. Seeking a better post he learnt book-keeping, shorthand and typing, at a local evening college and he got a job in December 1911 with the Victoria Falls and Transvaal Power Company (VFP). This company had been established to transmit power overland from the Victoria Falls, in what was Rhodesia, to the gold mines, but it proved more economical to use the abundant coal seams near the mines. Consequently the company built generating plants at collieries in the southern Transvaal. Jones worked in the company's offices at Germiston and he wrote in December 1911 that this town was

> larger than Boksburg, dreary and featureless, whose only institu-
> tions, in a population of many thousand people, are two theatres.
> Life truly runs into a vein of pumice and scoria here . . .

Jones was referring only to the 15,315 whites. The population of Germiston was actually 53,559 — 32,865 Africans worked on the mines, and others worked on the railways or in domestic service. There were no theatres for Africans, nor for Coloureds or Indians. The shift to a new town involved new surroundings and new people. Jones, now a member of the SALP, reappraised old values, although initially, involvement in politics seems to have strengthened his religious affiliation.

His church work continued in tandem with his awakened interest in South African politics and in both he did find 'good men'. On 7 January 1912 he referred in a letter to an article he wrote for the local press in November in defence of liberal theology, in which he mentioned the Liberal Church and the preacher Coverdale Sharpe. He had attended his services in Johannesburg and was 'surprised to find 50-60 people of the intellectual type' present. Sharpe spoke on 'Why I Believe in God', using 'only intellectual arguments' and Jones was impressed.

Writing on 21 January he said it was the most conclusive he had ever heard as proving the existence, after all scientific deductions, of infinite lacunae which can only be filled by the Divine which rolls through all things. Taking up the cudgels for labour and propounding the claims of 'liberal theology' were both seen as advancing man to a better world — literally and metaphorically.

But Ivon did not exist in a vacuum. Many of his ideas in 1911 were taken from the newspapers he read. A survey of the November and December issues of the *Rand Daily Mail* — the paper he dubbed the *Manchester Guardian* of South Africa — provides some clues. A biography of Ruskin which he praised as 'the first bit of good reading for a long time', was reviewed and acclaimed in its columns and the scandal at the ERPM (which led to the Georgetown by-election) was analysed and lambasted in articles and editorials. There is a strong similarity between Jones's comments and an editorial of 13 December 1911:

At the moment everything is playing into the hands of the Labour Party, or any other party that is evidently absolved from the influence of men whose only claim to political distinction is the wealth that fortune has placed in their hands.

Writing on 17 December to Miss Evans — he seldom referred to her by her first name —he said he dated the letter as the 16th, to explain 'a holiday we get in South Africa which you do not enjoy at home'. Summarising an article in the press, he wrote of the great Boer pioneer General Pretorius who defeated the Zulu hordes of Dingaan [Dingane] in 1838 after the treacherous massacre of Piet Retief. The barbarians were halted by the gallant trekkers, with the help of the Almighty and civilisation had been saved for South Africa. Ivon was only following the story that most whites believed and there were few texts that gave a different account. He told a very different story when he wrote about the subject again in 1921. By then he had been transformed by his local experiences and had time to rethink his approach. However, in this his last letter of 1911, he tried to give his impressions of the country after a year of residence. Despite his note on Dingane and the Zulus, he was not reconciled to what he saw of white society around him. He finished on a note of bitterness, saying that the omnipresent corrugated sheet roofing on the houses of [white] residents in the Witwatersrand represented . . . 'the hard tone of Rand life'. It was a community in need of good men, he said, but not one he could recommend to any of his friends.

8

WHITE LABOUR UNDER SIEGE

A Paul with a Gospel of Robust Hate

Jones's philosophy did not alter appreciably when he joined the Labour Party. His ideas and inspiration came from Emerson — one of the fountainheads of Unitarianism — and from Ruskin, whose humanism he found congenial. To this he added Welsh nationalism and an interest in social welfare, inspired by Lloyd George's piloting of the National Insurance Act of 1911, against the opposition of British employers and Labour leaders alike[1] This led to Jones's enthusiastic report of an address by Patrick Duncan, South African Party member of the Legislative Assembly and future Governor-General, on the question of 'Workmen's Compensation' at the Germiston Literary and Debating Society.[2]

He wrote admiringly of Lloyd George to the Evanses, and, on 21 November 1912, wrote to the SALP paper, the *Worker*, urging that the party and its paper be Liberal as well as Labour, deprecating the 'sneers for Lloyd George's endeavours at social regeneration, though we strive might and main to achieve here the half of what he has done'. Jones was obviously not yet a socialist. Furthermore he criticised the party for being too narrowly interested in class issues, saying:

> If the Labour Party looks forward to a time when it shall guide the whole State and its destinies, it should begin now to include the whole State, every phase of its feelings and activities; all its frailties and foibles, and all its best and noblest, within its concern. Rebuking what is unworthy, not with vitriol, but with firmness, and acclaiming all that is fine from whatever source it comes. But then, that is Liberalism.

Jones was not yet anti-capitalist, but his deep-seated hatred of the Randlords reinforced his pro-Boer position. He commemorated the second anniversary of Union by sending a post card to Evans with a picture of Botha, on the back of which he wrote:

> Botha the Peacemaker. General Botha needless to say. Foremost in war, foremost in peace. Who stills the rankling sense of wrong still burning in the hearts of his countrymen and that not to great applause, but in spite of the racial yelping of the mediocre breed of Rand politicians. England was great when she entrusted this, her erstwhile enemy, with the reins of government. How grandly he has responded to the trust!!

This followed a letter he wrote from Germiston on 2 June 1912 saying that reconciliation between Boer and Briton was still to come, 'But good men are at the helm . . . of which the kind General Botha is the prophet whose "forget and forgive" resounds through every utterance of his.'

On 14 July, he wrote again to Evans saying that he wanted to win Welsh support for the Boer leaders 'in their single-handed endeavour, against the vitriolic attacks of Randlord subsidised papers and politicians, to bring about a real reconciliation of both races.' The disillusion that was to come transformed his ideas — on the state and social welfare, on his church, and on Lloyd George. What remained, was his compassion for humanity, with 'all its frailties and foibles' .

Precisely when he moved away from from his church is uncertain. Six months earlier, he had written to bewail the lack of spiritual sustenance on the Rand. He had suffered a personal setback with the death of his brother Bill — the second member of the family to be buried in the Orange Free State and he invoked the lament of the psalmist: 'It is for us the valley of the shadow.' His liberal church did not provide the solace he sought. It was, he wrote to George Eyre on 30 April 1912, 'rather too feverish about getting quickly prosperous. This band of really thinking men are small and their job is finished when they have listened to the sermon. This is not the ideal of a true communion.' He fought off cynicism with difficulty, he said, because:

> our Liberal Church is a community of opinion only . . . to preach tolerance and liberalism in the camps of indifference . . . What is wanted here is an uncompromising moral trumpet call to the old fashioned creed of home and duty and honour and self-sacrifice and public spirit. A Charles Beard. But not a Martineau. A Paul with a Gospel of robust hate, not a John the Divine. Someone to make Rand magnates and snobs cower into shame at their glittering badges of the nether world. I am afraid that Unitarianism is too much engaged in defining, explaining and defending. Forgetting that when that is done, there is still a mission left to preach. It is not enough, in attacking the forts of iniquity, to spend the time in arguing over the superiority of our artillery to that of the Orthodox allies. Some time or other, surely, the fight must begin, for the guns to pound away.

Not insignificantly, he opened this letter with reference to the blight on the Rand, wrought by nature — and by the mine-owners:

> Not a drop of rain. Blades of grass parched bare by night frosts and midday heat. Storms of choking cyanide dust from the mine dumps and not a drop of rain. Not a drop.

Politics was now 'alive and burning', he wrote just three weeks later (19 May 1912), but it was October before he spoke of his work in the Labour Party. Then in two letters he wrote of his involvement, sent press cuttings, and gave his reason for joining the party. On 13 October he said that he was the 'official reporter' for the Germiston local branch:

There is no other party in South Africa worthy of the enthusiastic support of anyone who feels strongly the need for a revolution in our social system here. The Unionist Party is a party of vested interests, mine magnates, etc. The South African Party, what was the National Party, now in power under General Botha, deserving of sympathy in many things because they represent the legitimate claims of the national ideals of the Dutch people, is also impossible to the sympathy of us impatient reformers, for it is mainly composed of big landowners and farmers whose interest it is to maintain the status quo.

Foreshadowing his letter to the *Worker*, he continued: 'The Labour Party, though extreme and narrow in many respects, advocates Liberal principles, though it will not call them so.' This was reiterated on 27 October, when he announced that he was secretary of the Germiston District Committee of the SALP, and said: 'There is no Liberal Party. Labour is the liberal here. The whole country wants a Lloyd George to shake it inside out like a dusty sack.' More specifically, Jones explained his own adherence to the SALP:

I look upon it as a kind of religion. For nowhere is reform more urgent. Nowhere is political serfdom more rampant. Nowhere is social injustice and inequality more unashamed than in South Africa. Men on the Rand dare not openly express their political principles if they are at variance with those of their employers.

He wrote further of 'rampant political serfdom' on the Rand, worse than in any other town in the British Empire. If his employers, the Victoria Falls and Transvaal Power Company, knew of his activities in the SALP he would be sacked immediately. Social conditions on the Rand were deplorable, he had written earlier, and though wages were high everyone wanted more in order to build up a nest egg, and then clear out. But few achieved this, despite attractive salaries, because the cost of living was high and many resorted to underhand means to buy those things 'considered indispensable to life here'.

Jones also stated the viewpoint of the SALP on the Africans, speaking uncritically of the party's colour-bar.

Black labour is encouraged everywhere. Government enactments encourage it, while many whites have to sink in the midst of plenty. There are white men working on the railway, they are called 'poor whites', those who handle picks and shovels, for the pittance of five shillings a day. In New Zealand where the cost of money is one-third, the minimum for such work, indeed for any work, is eight shillings a day and at a maximum day of eight hours at that. It is an iniquitous system! A land of plenty, millions of acres lying idle, while men trudge the weary streets of the cities, seeking in that narrow sphere left between black labour and the white professions, for some thing to earn their daily bread. South Africa is waking up to the fact that there is something amiss in the social structure and the next election will see a clean sweep for the Labour Party, with its policy of segregation of the natives to their own territories, a white society, minimum wage and an honourable life for all, and the land thrown open for production by the people.

Jones at this stage wrote as a good member of the Labour Party and combined its racial obscurantism with a militant programme for the white worker. He was in close contact with Andrews, the most militant Labour MLA, who campaigned for the right of white railwaymen to belong to a recognised trade union, and the need to restrict miners to an eight hour 'bank to bank' day if they were to be saved from the worst ravages of phthisis.

It was no coincidence that Andrews used the same extract from Ruskin in the House of Assembly,[3] as had Jones in his letter to the *East Rand Express* of 10 February 1912, namely

There is no wealth but life. In fact it may be discovered that the true veins of wealth are purple — and not in rock, but in flesh — perhaps even that the final outcome and consummation of all wealth is in the producing as many as possible full-breathed, bright-eyed and happy hearted human creatures.

Jones capped this with a quotation from Emerson, 'the only interest for the consideration of the State is persons, and the highest end of Government is the culture of men'. From these words to Jones's conclusion was only a short step away:

Instead of gloating over 'monthly returns' of gold output, South Africa is awakening to the fact that her greatest pride will be to 'lead forth her sons' and say 'these are my jewels'.

On 8 March 1913, the *Nation* printed a letter 'The South African Political Situation', signed 'Anti-Jingo, from an up-country dorp', which commented on and condemned all sides in the split in the Botha-Smuts-Hertzog camp, and took the government to task for governing in the 'interests of the Rand mines and De Beers'. Jones informed Evans on the 8 March that he was the writer. He said he had become so involved in Labour that he had neglected everything else. Yet, he had few regrets:

I have theorized so long and to so little purpose that a little reality is a bit satisfying. Moreover you should understand that the Labour cause here is an issue between grovelling to the Clawing Beast of vested interests which ramifies the whole of South African life, on the one hand, and defying it and its soul destroying influence on the other. Whoever sees this beast in its most unashamed form can never rest but, though at the risk of material prospects, must forever be doomed to battle with the most bitter and uncompromising hatred.

He assured his friends that although they might read his letter as the work of an extremist, he was the 'old, docile peace-loving fellow' willing to see change through constitutional means, but he wanted:

a true republic . . . where the strong of arm will find no energies expended in vain, and no one shall go without bread, nor be tormented in waking thoughts by the spectre of hunger, where the common labourer shall be king and the slothful shall not be rewarded by another's toil. These things are not chimeras but the Ordinances of Nature, temporarily abrogated by deceitful men.

. . . I work for a Political Company [the VFP], which, in conjunction with the mining houses, seeks to obtain control of the souls as well as the bodies of their wage earning dependents by holding the sword of dismissal and unemployment above the head of anyone temerarious enough to think that he may have ideas of his own or on how his own land should be governed . . . A man on the Rand dare not show Labour colours going to work. The Chairman of the Labour Party, immediately he was elected to that post . . . was dismissed his work and 'blacklisted' . . . through all the mines; with the result that he has tramped and tramped the 60 odd miles of the Rand reef in vain search for the right which Nature extended to every man . . . the right of sweating for his daily bread.

To call the VFP a 'political company' in 1913 can only be understood against the background of antagonisms building up on the Witwatersrand. The miners were in constant conflict with the mineowners or their managers. The VFP was perceived by its employees and by the Labour Party to be closely allied with the Chamber of Mines and consequently part of the 'enemy'. By a twist of fortune Jones's position in the VFP was to affect his political stance and his life in the coming months.

Time to Change

On 22 March 1913 a postcard to Aberystwyth said tersely: 'Getting shifted to Vereeniging. Kick upstairs.' But in his next letter, on13 April, he said the company had treated him well — in fact promoted him and given him a substantially higher salary. Yet his friends in the SALP were quite certain he had been moved for political reasons:

It was considered cheeky, to say the least, of me to engage in so much political discontent, while working for a concern like this supposed to be hand in glove with the huge trusts which seek to intrude their iron hand into the liberties of South Africa, to manipulate its legislation for financial ends, and to blight the prospects of any helpless unit daring to make public protest against its machinations. This is the policy of that Combine of Capitalism — a blind aggregation of personally worthy and well meaning men.

Yet he was not certain, although the VFP was obviouly working 'hand in glove with the huge trusts'. Perhaps 'the Company's identity with the "beast" had been exaggerated', and he repeated that he had been well treated. He added that, quite unaccountably, members of the staff thought he had been sent down to convert them to the Unionists — that is, the party of capital!

Initially his letters were filled with descriptions of his new location. Jones found little enchantment in the town, in its activities, or its inhabitants. Vereeniging, he wrote, was a backwater, a 'dorp ... something between a village and a town' and Jones believed that if he stayed there a year 'with few temptations for extravagance' his financial position would be much improved. He would have leisure to read and to learn French, which he had started studying ... 'in a desultory sort of way'.

Vereeniging was in fact a 'company town', controlled by the mining and finance house Lewis and Marks. President Paul Kruger had given them control of the mineral, agricultural and other rights, and an area of 1,000 morgen or over 2,000 acres within the town in 1899. Jones knew enough of this when he arrived, to write:

Coal mines, land, trees ... all wait patiently as the year roll by waiting for land values to increase ... and all the time it gathers money for Mr Sammy Marks who simply has to sit and wait, and barb wire the Gift of God.

[The town was bleak] ... a few straggling shops, mainly Jews and not a few Indians. There seems little to redeem it. There is no civic pride; no high aims ... an utter absence of that calm leisure for higher pursuits, for the delights of literature and poetry ... no class of men embodying high ideals of what a state should be, bent on producing an atmosphere of true culture amid our too Commercial banalities.

Nonetheless Jones looked forward to finding 'a few of the faithful', and even of starting a literary and debating society 'now that winter is coming'. It was a sudden quietness after the bustle of Germiston and this, said Ivon, led him to think of friends and family, many of whom 'have disappeared long since into their past'.

Reading the letters with hindsight, it is remarkable how far they were from the storm that was about to break on the Witwatersrand. On 11 May, and again on 1 June, Jones wrote long letters describing the Vaal river and the town ('Vereeniging is all shops, Post Office, Police Station and a tin shed they call the Town Hall. It used to be the Custom House between the Free State and Transvaal.') He wrote of his brothers, enquired about the Meeting House at Aberystwyth, and spoke of the 'inspiration to look back on that time, the time when we were "saved" in a sense that Methody parsons cannot understand'. These were letters that covered events in South Africa as well as Aberystwyth, included solicitous inquiries about Kitty Evans's health, and also included information of a crowded Eisteddfod that had recently taken place in Johannesburg.

Yet Jones was silent on the strike that had started on 27 May at the New Kleinfontein mine in Benoni and was spreading across the mine fields. Perhaps he did not wish to alarm his friends, or believed the issue would be settled soon. But although it was a strike that was bound to affect the VFP he only said that it was quiet despite there being about eighty whites and three hundred blacks employed by the company. On 1 June he was still writing reassuringly. He said only that if he stayed he had been promised, confidentially, a higher post. There was still no intimation of any difficulty then facing the trade unions in their struggle against both the mining houses and the VFP.

However, the strike spread and the white workers at the VFP in Vereeniging walked out. The clerical staff stayed aloof, but Jones could not stay silent. He showed his sympathy for the strikers and was sacked. On 3 August, in a short note, Jones wrote:[4]

> Suffice this to assure you that I was not shot. Only pressure here in Germiston is sufficient proof that we are fighting a big monster that seeks to retain its monopoly of men's bodily labour by cramping their souls. I did not come on strike, but was forced to resign, having exercised a man's inalienable right to convince and enlighten those of his fellows who were not alive to the dangers of Randlordism.

He sent leaflets advertising meetings on 'Political Action in the Industrial Crisis' (in which he was listed as being in the chair) and promised a longer letter at a 'calmer time'. But there was no such time on the Rand, or even at his brother's in Frankfort, where he went next and that longer account was not written.

The Turbulent Years — 1913-1914[5]

The events of May and June 1913 on the Witwatersrand had far reaching effects that altered the lives of Jones and many of his friends. Yet until the end of May it would seem that most of the men who dominate this story were not fully aware of what was happening. They remained remote from much of the action and they had not sensed the mood of the miners and their supporters.

There were 38,500 white workers employed on the Witwatersrand in 1913: 22,000 on the mines and 4,500 on the railways, the rest distributed in the building trade, tramways, print shops, electric power works and small workshops.[6] There were about 200,000 Africans on the mines, mostly underground labourers. Other Africans on the Rand were employed in domestic service, as washermen, or in workshops. Nearly all were unskilled and most were manual workers. The trade unions

were minuscule, restricted to whites,[6] mostly craft dominated and concerned with wages and work conditions. If they had political aims, it was
for the reservation of certain jobs for whites or, more ominously, the
removal of all Africans from the towns. Only the Transvaal Miners Association (TMA) argued differently. Fearing competition if unskilled
whites were employed, they wanted black labour, but restricted to unskilled jobs. The TMA's main aim was not higher wages, but recognition
of the union and an eight hour day bank-to-bank. That is, a shorter time
at the working face to counter the dreaded 'white death'.

The fight against phthisis was a central issue for the TMA and for
individuals who had been brought into the socialist movement through
contact with the miners and their fight against the dread illness. Mary
Fitzgerald, addressing a meeting in 1912, said that when she had been
employed at the TMA, three sets of photographs were taken of members
of the union's executives. 'Of the thirty-six men, all in the prime of their
lives, only four were still alive. The others had all died of the 'white
plague.'

The effects of phthisis were well known on the Rand. The *Evening
Chronicle*, of 5 June 1913, said the average working life of a miner was
reduced by phthisis to four years, and many died after a further three
years on disability allowance. Nor could the governments of South
Africa and Britain claim ignorance. In a dispatch to the Colonial Office
on 20 July 1913, immediately after the strike (see CO 27645) Gladstone
wrote:

> The principle factor [for the unrest] has undoubtedly been the
> growing realization . . . of the frightful risks from the ravages of
> miner's phthisis to which their work exposes them . . . They gamble
> with their lives for high wages, but there remains the haunting
> dread of the future, and to earn £100 a month is for them no
> soporific[7]. . . phthisis has made their life abnormal, and the
> capitalists who are the only visible beneficiaries under the system
> . . . have become . . . the focus of a bitter class hatred on the part
> of many of the men.

The issue was summed up by the Johannesburg *Evening Chronicle*, a
pro-labour paper, on 4 June 1913: 'Phthisis must be destroyed or it will
destroy the mines, and with them the Rand. This is where the length of
the day comes into the discussion', and the *Daily Chronicle* correspondent in Johannesburg said that the principle causes of the strike was the
'terrible mortality in the mines'.

Although phthisis was undoubtedly the central issue, the fight against
the mineowners included other demands. There were reports of deep
resentment among Labour supporters against the government, the mine
magnates and the press (which was rightly regarded as being in their
hands).[8] Since 1911 the TMA had fought the Randlords over the reduction of overtime pay and retrenchment, victimisation of union officials,

and the refusal of management to recognise the union or communicate with union officials on conciliation boards.[9] Buss Melman, in a letter to the *Evening Chronicle* of 1 September 1913, said he supported the demands of the 'world working class' and the SALP. But, he said, the struggle was for security of tenure . . . if South Africa was to be kept a 'white man's country'.

Black Friday . . . And Bloody Saturday[10]

The clash on the mines was bound to come. When it did, it was at the New Kleinfontein mine in Benoni, where the militants were centred. The management, determined to confront the miners and root out the trade unionists, who were held responsible for the drop in profitability, appointed EH Bulman as manager.[11] His methods had all the hall-marks of provocation. He dismissed or secured the resignation of 'redundant' miners, and cancelled the traditional mechanics' Saturday half-day holiday. When the men protested, he replaced them with non-union labour.

This was 'a hotbed of idealists', said Jones approvingly, writing on a strike ballot paper issued by the federal body, the Transvaal Federation of Trades (FoT), and sent to Evans. The unions demanded the restoration of the half-day, the reinstatement of those sacked and recognition by the Chamber of Mines of the TMA. This was rejected and a strike committee, elected on the initiative of the FoT, called the workers of New Kleinfontein out. On 27 May the miners downed tools and two weeks later, when engine drivers and others joined them, the strike was complete. Scabs were brought in, and the owners demanded 'the fullest protection and assistance from the Government'.[12]

All eyes turned to the Witwatersrand and even the Balkan crisis took second place in the newspapers. In Britain, most newspapers expressed alarm: only the *Financier and Bullionist* of 4 July 1913 remained sanguine at first: 'Without adequate financial preparations being made,' it said, the strike could not last but the editorial in the next issue said that even if the strike was settled soon there would still be political uncertainty, and a 'somewhat dubious outlook for money'. The *Daily Chronicle* of 4 and 7 July, noting that 42 per cent of the world's gold (£38m ex £92m per annum) was produced on the Rand, predicted 'dire financial disaster' if its flow were interrupted. There would be 'grave difficulties on the [world] money markets . . . and a crushing blow to South Africa whose . . . gold industry is [its] keystone'. The *Daily News and Leader* of 3 July, fearing war in Europe, urged the Botha government to stop the strike spreading, lest the gold supply be temporarily curtailed and the *Financial Times* of 4 July spoke of 'financial crisis' if shipments were suspended for long. On 7 July the paper spoke of an 'immense sigh of relief' because the strike was over.

The strike spread first to neighbouring mines. Thereafter miners responded to columns of workers and their womenfolk (or widows) marching to the mineheads. In the lead came the miners' leaders, J T Bain, George Mason and Archie Crawford and, with them, Mary Fitzgerald. When he addressed the assembled miners, Crawford's stratagem always worked. Declaring: 'Strikers stand on this side — scabs over there', few men would join the shift. By the end of June nine mines were idle. The government brought in 540 Royal Scots in a show of force but by 2 July the strike had spread to VFP stations, including Vereeniging. A new enlarged committee took control of the strike and called a meeting at the Johannesburg market square for Friday 4 July, where a general strike was to be announced.

The meeting was banned under the old Transvaal Republic Law 6 of 1894 forbidding meetings, and allowing troops to disperse more than six persons on a public square.[13] A similar ban had been defied in Benoni on 29 June and no one believed it would be any different in Johannesburg. No sooner was the meeting underway, however, than troops and mounted police, wielding batons and pickhandles, charged and knocked people down indiscriminately. When the crowd retaliated with stones and bottles, Dragoons and mounted police drove them back with pickhandles and the flats of swords. After several such forays,[14] the crowd scattered and stopped trams and trains running, burnt down the central railway station and the *Star* newspaper building, looted gunsmiths and broke down shop fronts. In Benoni, where the strike began, crowds rampaged through the streets, burnt down buildings and beat up scabs. In other mining towns there were running battles between police and those who had seized guns.

On the 5th, the general strike on the Rand was complete and, in the early afternoon, as crowds collected near the Rand Club (the Randlord's centre), the Dragoons formed a square and fired. Press reports and Gladstone's dispatches exonerated the troops but eye-witnesses told a different story. The *Evening Chronicle* of 9 July 1913 printed a letter from 'For Valour' saying:

Opposite the [Rand] Club the cavalry came to the halt and dismounted, the crowd flying for safety to the pavements. The crowd finding the military did not pursue, halted and watched the scene, and whilst some were thus standing and others trying to get away, a volley was fired (blank so I am informed). Seeing that no harm was done the crowd still watched. Practically without an interval another volley was fired — ball this time — and they dropped. Altogether eight or nine volleys were fired and I believe everyone in the vicinity will agree that there was no appreciable pause between any of the volleys. It was load and fire. The crowds were running, and as they ran the shots were pouring into them. I saw the firing, saw the people drop. I went through the war with the first Cavalry Brigade, but I have never seen such a sight as the indiscriminate shooting of men, women, and children.[15]

Over 20 lay dead, and some 200-400 were wounded. Among them was a young miner, Labuschagne, who became Labour's first martyr. A leaflet issued after the strike said of him that he stepped off the pavement opposite the Rand Club and shouted 'Don't shoot more women and children — shoot a man!' The soldiers fired and he was silenced. The *Evening Chronicle* of 7 July said the real total would never be known, as many had sought their own medical attention. Ultimately on 26 September the paper reported that about 170 were treated at the Johannesburg Hospital for wounds on 4 and 5 July, 89 were detained for treatment, 12 had died and 12 were still in hospital.[16] Meanwhile the *Evening Chronicle,* on 9 July 1913, spoke of lumpen elements looting the stores of Indians in Vrededorp, Fordsburg and Newlands. In Benoni, the centre of greatest violence, the goods station was burnt to the ground, scabs assaulted and their houses or possessions destroyed, wagons held up or destroyed. One report said that 'The Red Flag has been supreme . . . it waves from hundreds of houses and stores. The police and military have been impotent . . .' The government summoned 800-1000 cavalrymen to the Rand the following morning and the red flags disappeared.[17]

On the Saturday afternoon, 5 July, Botha and Smuts travelled from Pretoria and agreed a truce with the Federation — but apparently (it was said by the men deported to Britain in 1914) not before Bain held a pistol to Smuts' head.[18] The strike was called off. All disturbances were to end, there was to be no victimisation and workers' grievances would be investigated. The *Daily Chronicle* reported on 7 July 1913 that part of the waiting crowd rejected the truce with cries of: 'What about the shooting?', 'What about the dead?' and 'You've been bought!' However, an attempt to continue the strike failed, and men returned to work.

After the capitulation Smuts resolved never to be caught unawares by the unions again. Within a month things were in place to counter renewed strike threats. The South African Defence Force had been reorganized, and contingency plans were drafted requesting that all available imperial troops be placed at the disposal of the government. Mayors were advised on procedures to be followed and control officers and headquarters were allocated in twelve central areas. Gladstone's dispatch, dated 25 July (CO 29414), enclosed letters from the Prime Minister's office, drafts on the enrolment of special constables and of proclamations specifying measures to suppress disturbances and maintain order and public safety. These were to be signed by the Governor-General and Smuts when required.

There was talk in the unions during July of resuming the strike, then of a 'suspended strike' (allowing for a walk out at any time). Finally it was reported in the *Transvaal Leader* on 1 August 1913 that the Federation of Trades had decided to abandon further strike action and 'rely upon our industrial and political organisations to remedy our grievances'.

The trade union leaders had little option. Despite the apparent victory in July the mines exercised a firm control on its work force. This was summed up by Jones in the *Worker* on 21 August where he linked the three factors that kept miners under control:

It is a blunt commentary on the ravages of disease, and on the fell work of the black list and the sack as a political weapon that so few miners are able to appear on political bodies.

The General Strike of 1914

On 1 January 1914 Jones wrote that he was now at the Johannesburg Trades Hall, having been invited by the Transvaal Mining Association to help reorganise their office. He was at the centre of 'stirring possibilities', the situation being ripe for 'a huge general strike which may eclipse the other one in intensity and violence'. South Africa was 'an unhappy country' governed by men who knew 'of no remedy for social ills but the force of arms'.

During this period the government was condemned by both the Federation and the Amalgamated Society of Railway and Harbour Servants (ASRHS) for refusing to recognise the railwaymen's union and not investigating workers' complaints. The hours worked by train crews were excessively long and the pay of unskilled white workers — 3s 4d, 4s, or at most 5s per day — was below the subsistence level, said to be 8s per day.[19]

There were reports during July of dynamite being found on railway platforms, in culverts and elsewhere but trade unionists claimed that this was largely the work of provocateurs aimed at adding to the state of uncertainty. The government also proceeded tardily in investigating workers' conditions (in fulfilment of the July agreement), and in September, before any report was available, the minister for railways called for retrenchments. Provocatively, despite a holiday rush and men working overtime, the first dismissal notices were handed out on Christmas Eve. J H Poutsma, the union secretary, who had warned against such a step, called a strike for Friday 8 January.

On 2 January white miners in the Natal collieries came out, demanding 20s per day, a 57-hour week, overtime at time-and-a-half and the reinstatement of four men, laid off because there was a shortage of black labour. Over a thousand black workers also took action, demanding £5 per month, but, warned that strikes by Africans were illegal, they returned to work. The whites also went back and called for a general strike. Although vetoed by their executive the *Transvaal Leader* of 2

January 1914 said that the threat of a strike and a coal shortage remained.

The railwaymen came out on the 8th, but, although most workshops closed the strike was ineffective because too few of the train crews joined them.[20] There were unsuccessful attempts to pull train crews or signalmen out and attempts at sabotage.[21] The government had also taken steps to stifle the strike. On the 7th, troops had occupied railway stations and workshops in Johannesburg, Germiston and Pretoria. Poutsma, Justin Nield (his deputy) and Colin Wade of the SALP were arrested on the 10th, and held incommunicado.

There were doubts about Poutsma's role. He had not consulted the branches of other unions with members on the railways, and there were few signs of preparation, locally or nationally. Members of the Federation had advised against a strike and were furious when it was announced[22] and Poutsma was generally suspected as being the witting or unwitting tool of the government.

There were sympathy walk-outs by building, municipal and colliery workers and by typographers, indicative of the depression and discontent of the time. The miner's strike of May-June had not been finally settled and just over 9,000 gold miners now came out. The total number of workers who responded to the strike call remains unknown, but in the confusion numbers had little meaning. The Federation now closed ranks and after a ballot called a general strike for the 14th. This was countered by a declaration of martial law on the 13th. Smuts had planned for this moment and published the proclamations and issued special passes for movement in proclaimed areas. These had all been printed in anticipation in December.[23]

Creswell, effectively silenced, answered in a leaflet. Stating that he was not allowed to address any meeting, he called on the workers not to be terrorised into working, nor provoked into violence. He appealed to the 'Dutch workers' to remember how their forefathers had defended their liberties 300 years before, by opening the dykes in Holland and he appealed similarly to the British workers to follow the examples of their forebears 'in the cause of liberty'.

Six leading members of the SALP, WH Andrews MLA (President), HW Sampson MLA, W Wybergh, SP Bunting, FAW Lucus and D Dingwell, sent a letter surreptitiously to the Colonial Office on 21 January, after all previous communication had been blocked by the Smuts government.[24] In it they stated 'that the crisis had been deliberately sought and prepared by the government to destroy the trade unions and the Labour Party'. They continued, hoping no doubt to get the measures reversed:

> The situation prevailing here is intolerable, and quite unprecedented under the British flag and constitution.

The story [in] . . . the South African press, and no doubt cabled home, of a Syndicalist Revolution, is entire rubbish . . . being designed partly for British consumption, and partly to enlist middle class sympathy out here . . .

It is a deliberate effort to suppress their political opponents by removing the leaders and terrorising the rank and file, and at the same time to swamp Hertzogism by exciting Dutch racialism against the 'common enemy'.

The whole affair has been on our side a peaceful industrial dispute: the Mass Meeting on Sunday, January 11th on Market Square was not only perfectly orderly, . . . but it afforded a dramatic proof that the disturbances of the previous July were directly due to the action of the Police and soldiery in charging the crowd.

On this occasion not a Policeman or soldier was to be seen, and although the Authorities had suspended the local tram service, the crowd was greatly larger than the one that had collected on July 4th.

The authors then listed the measures imposed under martial law. The offices of trade unions and the SALP had been raided, as had printing shops that produced leaflets for the labour movement — and their machines destroyed. There were mass arrests, with no legal help allowed, including MLAs (FHP Creswell and T Boydell), provincial and town councillors, candidates in forthcoming elections and the entire executives of the ASE and the ASRHS, although all opposed violence.

The severest sentences are anticipated and the deportation of the leaders is believed to be imminent. Railway and mine workers are being evicted everywhere. It is an offence . . . to advise any person to strike or to continue to strike or to assist a striker or his family in any way. The police also looted the Strike Distress Committee's food supply in Pretoria.

There were bans on wearing SALP colours or the red flag or using the words 'scab' and 'blackleg', said the writers. 'A man got two or fourteen days for looking "sneeringly" at a Policeman . . . ' Meetings of more than six persons were banned; news was censored; prominent persons restricted to their houses or shadowed by police spies. Permits were needed to cross magisterial boundaries or to use wheeled vehicles (and these were usually refused).

The letter continued::

All centres are swarming with Burghers [commandos or armed volunteers], who are to be allowed to retain their arms and accoutrements permanently.

Racialism [that is English-Dutch antagonism] has been directly revived by the Government through this means and has received great impetus . . .

The public is menaced everywhere by Police, Burghers and Civilian [Defence} Force with fixed bayonets. Unoffending people walking the streets are ruthlessly handled, herded into arcades, and driven like cattle to the Charge Office under Police guard.

Apart from all questions of detail, the serious features are that, as in the case of the Indians, the armed forces of the country are being used, not to suppress violence, but to terrorise men into working. . . .That the public services of the country, such as post, telegraph, telephone and the public press are being controlled under the pretext of Martial Law not merely so as to prevent incitement to violence but to prevent any criticism of the Government and to avoid any information being made public either here or in England. . . . That these things are being done for Party Political purposes, relating partly to the domestic issues between Botha and Hertzog, but still more to the tacit combination of Botha and the capitalists to stem the rising forces of the Labour Party, in particular of Botha's public and repeated assertions that 'socialism cannot be allowed in South Africa'.

After commenting on General de la Rey's statement that his men had responded 'to the call of *their party*, which was represented by the Government in power', they concluded that the government's actions would 'undoubtedly be endorsed by the Union Parliament' and they hoped the Indemnity Bill would be vetoed by the King.

Gladstone said in his dispatch of 22 January that about 70-100,000 men from the army, defence force, police, and burgher 'commandos', were called up by the government – including many strikers (CO 4990, p 16) – and special constables were enrolled to supplement the police force. All railways, communication networks, power stations and mines were placed under guard.[25] On 15 January the mass round-up of trade unionists began. First the Pretoria and Johannesburg strike committees and hundreds of 'strikers' in Benoni, then activists in the main centres were arrested. The armed forces were instructed to root out the forces of 'anarchy', and 4,000 troops surrounded the Trades Hall, trained a field gun on the building and demanded the surrender of the occupants – eleven members of the Federation executive, and thirty-two pickets.

Jones was distributing the syndicalist leaflet 'Don't Shoot! Address to Soldiers',[26] to the mounted and foot police with an appeal for class solidarity, and, at about 4 o'clock, he left the Trades Hall and went for further supplies. The printer was afraid of being raided and arrested and it took Jones an hour to persuade him to retrieve the form from its hiding place. When he returned there was a tight cordon around the Trades Hall and troops barred the way with drawn bayonets. He was 'rather fiercely ordered back' and 'discreetly' he made for the Labour Party offices. Jones made little of his participation in the January strike – whether through modesty, or because he still worked behind the scenes is not certain, but, as a party official, in close contact with the leadership, he would have been in the centre of activity. That he went to the printer to obtain more leaflets demonstrated his involvement; his temporary absence saved him from deportation.

The use of the army was not without its own problems. With 30,000 burghers under arms there was open talk of the commanders arresting Botha and Smuts and proclaiming a Republic. Denys Reitz, a Botha man, recalled that the troops he led from Heilbron, in the Free State, had to be harangued for two days before they would cross into the Transvaal.[27] Reitz also reported that some army officers were bent on discrediting the government. General Beyers, on the other hand, the newly-appointed commander-in-chief, gave orders in Germiston to arrest 'every man if he looked like a striker. . . ' He marching at the head of his troops who wielded sjamboks and rifle butts indiscriminately, herding innocent men and women into cattle pens, or marching them several miles to gaols and so on. Whether other brutalities were similarly motivated is not recorded. By way of contrast, members of commandos fraternised with strikers in some districts after hearing their complaints.

The strike was over by 21 January and the men went back defeated. Nearly 700 railwaymen were retrenched and many had to accept lower rates of pay. The position of the ASRHS was precarious, with the men 'crushed and dispirited', and working under conditions that left them in despair. . . J Nield of the railwaymen's union wrote to say they could 'not cease work, nor absent themselves from duty, nor write to the press, nor in any way communicate their grievances to the public — under the threatened penalty of six months hard labour, or a fine of £50, or both'.[28] There was also widespread victimisation: hundreds of strikers were blacklisted, former executive members of the ASRHS were dismissed and, in some regions, membership of the union was proscribed.

On the night of 27/28 January, Smuts secretly moved nine imprisoned men (JT Bain, Archie Crawford, William Livingstone, David McKerrell, George Mason, William Morgan, JH Poutsma, Robert Waterston and Andrew Watson), all executive members of the FoT, from Johannesburg. They were taken at night to Durban and placed on the ship *Umgeni* on its way to Britain. Despite attempts by members of the SALP to stop this illegal deportation, the boat could not be turned back.[29] Smuts made great play of a 'syndicalist plot' and was indemnified by parliament.

J Davidson, a socialist of long standing in Parliament, commented in a letter to *Forward* of 21 February 1914:

> The home [British] press, I note, are making much play of our Syndicalist tendencies. There is no country where less theory has been taught to the workers. What line has been taken has been forced upon them by the most brutal and callous set of employers that has ever cursed any country . . .

Smuts had antagonised many people, and, in the 1914 Transvaal Provincial Council elections, the SALP won 23 seats, one more than the combined opposition, but without gaining control of the Provincial Executive. Labour was on its way to winning the north, and only the coming of war shifted the political balance back to Botha and Smuts.

An Injury to the Most Humble of Their Race

Jones had sent a copy of the 'Don't Shoot' leaflet to Evans. On the back of it he wrote that at the Labour Party offices he had 'pleasant memories of working with Creswell, one of the loftiest characters it has been my lot to meet.' When Creswell anticipated arrest he scribbled a note saying 'Can't get down, too busy — But stick to it. Very Solid, FHP Creswell', and asked Jones to deliver it to the men at the Braamfontein [strike] Centre. Jones kept the copy and writing on the back sent it to the Evanses, describing events leading to the arrest, and concluding: 'Half the government's operations were directed at destroying his political influence. He is the Randlord's arch-enemy.'

Nor was Jones alone in his praise. Bunting and Andrews (among others who later turned leftwards) were Creswell's intimate friends and praised his policies and his leadership. This uncritical endorsement of the leader of the party indicated that, despite the new radicalisation, there were still many political lessons to be learnt before a left-wing could emerge in the SALP. In just over a year Jones would oppose most of what Creswell represented: total segregation, the pro-war policy, the reformism that accompanied this social patriotism, and so on.

Jones still had to rethink Labour's colour policy and he had not yet reached that position. At the end of July 1913, Waterston, Wade, Andrews, Dingwell and Jones all spoke at an open-air meeting in Germiston on the strike and phthisis and the grievances of the railwaymen and other workers. In a report written by Jones it was said that the government was attacked for using the military against striking workers, and, in defiant mood, the meeting rang with cheers when Botha was called upon to resign, being 'branded with the brand of Cain'. Jones's specific message was 'that they were not engaging in a revolt merely to raise the standard of wages, but to raise the standard of manhood'.[30]

The report seemed to be in the best tradition of Labour agitation but, included in the speeches, without any dissenting comment, was that of J D Jooste (in Dutch). He condemned the government in no uncertain terms and then added:

General Botha at Potchefstroom told the farmers that people in Johannesburg wanted to make another war. That was untrue; they only wanted their rights. They had been treated worse than Kafirs, and not allowed to be in the streets. (Hear, Hear!) If Lord

Gladstone had the right to say, 'shoot to kill', they had the same right. They insisted upon being handled as white men. If they called a meeting and the government said they must not hold it, were they to sit still in their houses (Cries of 'No') . . . Five shillings a week would not break them, and by joining the Union they would make victory certain (Applause).

Jones perceived the fight in 1913 as being against the perpetrators of the worst outrages: the government, the mine owners and the British army. Yet the actions of white workers, which made them agents of repression, were overlooked. He made no mention of the looting of Indian shops during the riots of July 1913, the shooting down of black workers at Jagersfontein and Premier mines; the acting as temporary warders to arrested Indians in the Natal colliery strike and the forming of vigilante groups to stop Indians crossing into the Transvaal.[31]

Some white socialists did criticise the colour line but this was exceptional. JT Bain, secretary of the Federation of Trades, was among the first to support openly the Indian workers. As reported in the *Evening Chronical* of 13 November, he hoped that

at a later date the party of which he was secretary would endorse [his statement] that an injury done to the most humble of their race was an injury done to humanity. They must fight for human rights, whether for the coloured or white people. Race must not tell.

He characterised the indentured system as 'slavery glossed over and disguised by law'. Several white socialists appeared on platforms to express solidarity with the Indian people in their resistance movement, but they represented only themselves. TW Ward (one of those arrested in July 1913, but then released), speaking for Bain at a meeting attended by several prominent white trade unionists in Johannesburg, was reported in the *Transvaal Leader* on 13 December as saying that the Indians' resistance was

an expression of their revolt against oppression. But the real cause was economic . . . He was not going to advise them against passive resistance, but he warned them to be careful, and to be ready to be shot down. He was not there to stir up race prejudice, but came as representing a small minority of white workers on the Reef, who realised that the Indian's fight was the white workers' fight . . . Your brothers [fight] in Natal . . . will be your fight tomorrow. Do not forget there were a few white men willing to forego all questions of colour to help you.

Bain was vilified in letters to the *Evening Chronicle* and the Natal Federation of Trade and Labour Unions, at a meeting of delegates, reaffirmed Labour's standpoint and called on the government to speed repatriation. Herein lay the tragedy: white workers, embattled in 1913-14, strengthened their unions but at the expense of the blacks.

Gladstone's dispatch (see above) said the government was aware of this conflict, and was not displeased.

The Ethnic Divide

On 21 July 1913 the *Cape Times* reported that Rev R Balmsworth, speaking at a protest meeting in Cape Town, condemned the shootings in Johannesburg in scathing terms.

> If you ask me who were the worst enemies of the town . . . I would say, the military, and those upper class hooligans who directed this cruel work. It is a strange thing to say, but nobody seemed afraid of the strikers, everybody was afraid of the soldiers.

Olive Schreiner, novelist and socialist, sent a message to the meeting saying that the massacre

> should have served to show the mass of our people in this country the true conditions under which we are living. The death of those innocent persons will not have been in vain, if we make the light it has shed on our position as citizens of South Africa one which will dominate our future actions, political and social.

In a prescient letter to Edward Carpenter she wrote:

> If they shoot us down in this way the moment WHITE labourers strike, what will it be whenever the native moves? And they are bringing in more and more oppressive laws against the latter. We have just passed a terrible native Land Bill — the worst bit of work we have done for years.[32]

It was too much to hope that whites in South Africa would have learnt 'the true conditions under which [they] were living'. They were indifferent, or openly antagonistic, to the struggles of other ethnic groups. Africans were almost alone in protesting over the Land Act, and whites did not join Africans and Coloureds who condemned the arrest of black women protesting against the pass laws in the Orange Free State in 1913. In the campaign against a three-yearly tax which led to mass walk outs of Indian workers, only a handfull of devoted white intellectuals supported Gandhi but they were isolated. Later, when colliery and sugar field workers were on strike, Bain and a few other white trade unionists sent messages of solidarity — but most white workers and socialists were antagonistic.

Schreiner's fears of what would happen when the black workers moved was tragically borne out in strikes at diamond mines in 1913-14, at Koffiefontein, Klipdam, Randfontein, Kimberley, Premier Mines and Jagersfontein. Conditions on the mines were miserable. Blacks in diamond mines received 78-89s for a 26-day month; higher than gold mines', 52s, or coal mines', 41-43s, but pitiably low. Working conditions were onerous: underground tunnels, only 1.1 yards wide, were hot and sweaty, with mud underfoot. Lighting was only from lamps on helmets. Wagons were hand pushed. Roof-falls were one of the hazards and there were always fatalities. Humiliating body searches were frequent. Only the shootings at Premier mines — four dead and twenty four wounded — and Jagersfontein (where a hundred white workers shot and killed at least sixteen and wounded thirty-six) received significant publicity. Yet strikes were ascribed to 'tribal' friction, illegal beer drinking and so on, trivialising the events, and exonerating the authorities.

Ethnic antagonisms took precedence over cooperation and these were usually two-sided. The statements made by black leaders were as narrow as those of whites. How far they reflected the attitudes of their followers is a matter of conjecture, but from their context it seems that there was a vocal opposition. This might have indicated class differences inside the organizations but, once again, this is only a guess. What is on record is that in July 1913 Sol Plaatje, Secretary-General of the SANNC, blocked a Congress move of solidarity with white strikers.[33] Dr Abdurahman, president of the (Coloured based) African Political Organisation, despite his gibes against white repression, did this for narrow ethnic reasons and ignored the massacre of whites. Gandhi called off his campaign in 1914 when white workers were on strike, in order not to embarrass the government.[34] The white workers were worse. They ignored the struggles of blacks or turned their guns on them. The party that claimed to represent their interests, the SALP, wanted all Indians repatriated and, calling for the removal of Africans from the towns, supported the Land Act because 'the government was carrying out one of the planks of the . . . Party platform'.[35]

Struggles by different ethnic groups did not reinforce each other but set communities even further apart. The whites who were out on strike demanded that blacks be kept out of some occupations; black women opposed passes that whites insisted they carry; black miners wanted bullying overseers removed, and, in all the conflicts with management, white workers and their supporters showed only contempt for the Africans. The separation was near complete. Yet of the many cynical statements of the time, that of the *Evening Chronicle*, sturdy champion of white miners, surpassed all others. An editorial on 3 June 1913, calculating the cost of shortening the working day to provide an 8 hour bank-to-bank day (deemed essential to cut the incidence of phthisis), estimated that if applied to all workers the annual cost would be £600,000, but if only white workers were considered, the cost would be only £300,000. The editor, addressing his white readers, concluded: 'Our own view is that there is very little objection to such differential treatment if the true losses can be adjusted.'

Some Africans stopped work in June, at times encouraged by trade unionists who grasped the need to bring the African workers out. RB Waterston, a strike leader, called on black workers (in a poor rendition of the artificial mine language, Fanagalo) to: *'Tchella lo Baas wena funa maningi mali and picanniny sebenza'* ('Tell the bosses you want more money and less work'), and the *Cape Times* (9 July 1913) reported that Dan Simons, a member of the strike committee, caused a stir when he addressed a Benoni open-air meeting on 13 June, with the words, 'Ladies, Gentlemen, and Kaffir Brethren.'

After the 5th more black workers came out, demanding 5s per day, (compared to the going rate of 2s), or payment for those days on which the mines had been idle. Once again, British troops confronted the workers, with bayonets drawn or firing overhead, or 'into the ground near their feet' or charging with pickhandles. One eye-witness reported in the *Evening Chronicle* on 11 July, that men of the Staffordshire Regiment killed two workers at the Meyer and Charlton mine. Some workers demanded the release of imprisoned colleagues and, according to the *Transvaal Leader* of the same date there were shouts of 'Kill the Police!', but the strike was over. 'Ring leaders' and those who would not resume work, were arrested.

Report on Communism in South Africa (front cover)

9

THE WAR-ON-WARITES

General Secretary of the Labour Party

Having avoided arrest in January 1914, Jones immersed himself in the work of the South African Labour Party. Under constant police surveillance, the SALP was searched for incriminating documents and strike bulletins which were brief and issued as 'Manifestos'. A copy was sent to George Eyre and Kitty Evans with a note saying that the objective was to 'counteract the manufactured reports of the censored press'. It read:

Sunday 2 p.m. Pretoria
Messages through this morning state that no men are going back.
All are cheerful and solid.

Jones also wrote to say that printing and distribution over an extensive area was difficult but was overcome through the support of several Jews, who provided money and their Russian experience: 'and against their organization no martial law restrictions could avail'. He continued:

The printer was known to myself and two others (George Kendall who escaped to Australia being one). The printer took them hot to an isolated room as they came out of the press. From there they were taken to a dust heap in another part of Johannesburg . . . picked up by fellows with motors and bikes carrying official permits, some even conveyed in unwitting police cars!! To all parts of the disaffected area.

On 27 March 1914, in a letter from Johannesburg, he gave more details:

The secret publication of manifestos to the men. The shadowing, the spying, the tracking which we had to undergo by hundreds of Government [agents] . . . Russia was not in it. Printer after printer was kidnapped and his press seized until we were left without our last and faithful one, and we had to resort to typewriters and duplicators, until the retreat came, none too soon for us. The thing simmered and boiled until the end of the month, the authorities refusing us re-entry into the Trades Hall offices until the beginning of February.

He thought of leaving South Africa after the strike but had no money. He was blacklisted 'because he had made 'himself offensive to the monopolists of the means of life . . . [who thought] to buy men's souls for bread'. But during the period of martial law he proved his worth to the labour movement and made many friends among party leaders. He grew particularly close to two lawyers, FAW Lucas and SP Bunting, who acted as legal advisers to the SALP.[1] In February he returned to his interrupted work as bookkeeper to the TMA, learning more about union activity. His friendship with Tom Matthews (of the TMA), already bonded by common Unitarian beliefs and the experience of two strikes, also deepened.

Later that month Jones moved to Germiston to act as agent for Colin Wade, a leading member of the SALP and a popular dentist in the town. The party fought 25 seats in the Transvaal provincial elections in February and won all but two, the 549 vote majority in Germiston being one of the biggest upsets experienced by the Unionists. Jones noted proudly in a letter of 1 March that: 'People do not know who to congratulate most, myself, or Colin Wade, the successful candidate.' Jones said that he was devoid of personal ambition and did not care for political honours, 'even were I ripe for it'. He had not sought election, though he did his 'share on the local platform in Germiston'. He had a 'delight at organization' and was being proposed for the general secretaryship of the SALP, previously held by Bob Waterston, one of the deportees, and then temporarily by Charles Clingman. Jones was concerned about working on the Rand, where he was more prone to asthmatic attacks 'although this does not incapacitate me for work when issues are keen'. Because the movement needed him, he said, he would 'make a virtue out of necessity' and remain.

Jones had changed perceptibly as a result of the strike and this was reflected in his new appraisal of socialism. At the beginning of August he was elected General Secretary of the SALP and, as he wrote, was immediately:

> swallowed up in the activities of a movement which [was] more than political, [was] indeed spiritual in its influence . . . For it must be remembered that the Labour movement out here is largely socialistic. Socialism of the large and glowing kind.

On 8 October 1914, with South Africa at war, he said the SALP was:

> the most militant and uncompromising of all Labour Parties . . . It is a party of emancipation, and is imbued with a spirit of brotherhood, having a greater number of lofty personalities than I ever expected to find gathered together in any association.

Jones had found a new satisfaction in his life, allowing him to use his administrative ability. Furthermore, he found new friends and deepened old attachments. Yet he spoke warmly only of three: Lucas, leader of the SALP in the Provincial Council who was anti-war[2] Bunting and Andrews, who were to play a prominent part in 1915 with Jones in launching the International Socialist League.

In May 1915 Jones wrote about Lucas's contemplated visit to Britain after a serious illness. He spoke of him as:

> the finest type of manhood and character that it has been my lot to meet, and represent[ing] the flower of colonial-born South Africans. He is an advocate of some considerable standing, not so

much for fluency of oratory as knowledge of Constitutional law. But, owing to the Russianised form of victimisation brought to bear by the highly organized capitalism of the Rand, his practice has dwindled to almost nil.[3]

Jones's warmest commendations were for SP Bunting, a comrade who was principled and dedicated, who showed such concern for him when he was unwell, tended for him and arranged for him to accompany the family on holiday. Jones first wrote about a troublesome cough on 20 October 1915. He was advised to holiday at the Cape — a trip which was beyond his pocket. He wrote again on 13 February 1916 to say that friends had taken him to the Cape at Christmas time and that he had tramped around Table Mountain. In January 1917 he wrote from Zululand about a particularly lengthy bout of illness and of his gratitude to his 'socialist friends' who showed such concern and kindness.

I was never without someone near by, and I was early in my illness removed from my private room to the house of a Socialist friend, and 'Comrade Bunting' (a man of 40 years, a solicitor, son of Sir Percival Bunting, late editor of the *Contemporary Review*, an accomplished musician, and an Oxford graduate, the mainstay with me of the Socialist movement here), proved a true friend, and spent his waking thoughts in taking up my work, and anticipating my needs.

Not until 19 August 1917 was Andrews mentioned. He was on his way to the Allied Socialist Conference in London, and Jones said he was a 'genial man, and would be glad of a pleasant jaunt in the real Wales, like friend Lucas had . . .' He was certain that Evans and Andrews would get on together and find common ground despite 'what you might consider the esoteric nature of his International Socialism'. There is little else in the letters about the friends he made in the socialist group. Despite their closeness and warmth he preferred, in his letters to Evans, to speak of impersonal matters. He seldom praised and he never wrote in anger — except when he mentioned the mine owners or mammon.

Travelling Far From Old World Conservatism

In 1914 the SALP was very different from the small group Jones had joined in 1911. The party won over Unionists and Nationalists in town and country, some because of the government's failure to solve the economic problems of the country, or to stem the widespread unemployment in the towns; and some repelled by the use of the armed forces against strikers on the Rand.[4] The Labour Party was at its peak and the provincial elections were an index of its strength but the euphoria generated by these successes concealed the tensions inside the party. The new members had taken a large step forward in joining the Labour movement — but they brought with them the conservatism and prejudices of the society in which they were nurtured. They claimed the right to the more highly paid jobs; or fought against being forced down to the level of the black wage earners. They found among the older members of the SALP many who agreed with them, and together they acted to keep the party firmly in its racist mould.

While the rank and file moved (or kept) the party to the right, Andrews, Bunting and Jones questioned old ideas and moved to the left. Their re-evaluation started during the miners' strike. Jones's former trust in Botha was shattered but that was only the beginning. Events in South Africa and abroad were moving fast and, to answer questions that had become pressing, Jones turned to the British labour press and the pamphlets they advertised. On 3 August 1914 (just after war was declared in Europe) he wrote to Evans thanking him for the papers he had sent, saying the Welsh papers were still most welcome, but:

> I must say that in the course of time one's reading changes, and one gets impatient of the purely 'palliative' persuasions of the old favourites. The *New Age, Labour Leader, Clarion, New Statesman*, and other organs proclaiming revolutionary changes, spiritual and social, for the ills of the time have supplanted old favourites.
>
> In this I fear I have travelled far from your old world conservatism. You cling to the past. A new pace is rising which will weave the best of that past into a future new and altogether glorious.

Responding to the offer of a newspaper subscription as a gift, he wrote from the Johannesburg office of the Labour Party on 8 October 1914, saying:

> I leave it to you. All I can say is that Revolutionary ideas on Society, Socialism, imply new ideas on art, on religion, on philosophy, on life . . . Periodicals which accept the revolution, whether in art, society, religion, or life in the whole are alone interesting now.

Evans was generous in his response. Jones received parcels of journals containing a heady mixture of radical politics and reforming arts, covering a wide spectrum of ideas: from Fabianism to Guild Socialism, syndicalism to parliamentarism, from the anti-militarism of the Independent Labour Party through parliamentary Labourism, Christian Socialism and, ultimately, radical pacifism and social patriotism.[5]

New Age, the vehicle of Guild Socialism (which also carried reviews of theatre, literature and the arts) denounced Marxism. Its variety of socialism deprecated calls for minimum wages, for recognition of trade unions, or support for co-operatives, because these all supported 'wagery' which was 'degrading and immoral'. On 1 January 1914, the paper called for a 'world of freedom' through a return to quality (instead of machined quantity), 'the move from the region of economics to essential religion', and so on. The next issue condemned 'the dead and decaying doctrines' of Marxism, Fabianism and Syndicalism and campaigned for 'the abolition of wagery and of building up a state out of a sense of citizenship, the flowering of economic freedom'. These ideas attracted the Johannesburg group — but the paper was discounted after the editors declared their support for the war on 6 August — because, they said, 'England above all countries in the world, is destined by Providence to form the nidus of the system that shall supplant the abominable wage system'.

All the journals gave prominence to the 1913-14 strikes in South Africa, to the deportations and to the reception accorded the deportees when they arrived in London. Their interpretations of what had happened were widely quoted. This opened or extended a dialogue between socialists across the ocean, particularly with the editors of *Clarion*, the vehicle for Robert Blatchford's ideas, *Labour Leader*, organ of the Independent Labour Party (ILP), *New Age* and *Forward*, organ of the radical left in Scotland and highly recommended by Jones. Also, the letter sent to the Colonial Office by Andrews, Bunting and others was printed in full by the *Clarion* on 20 February 1914. A Manifesto of the SALP on the railway strike, signed by Andrews, and indicating the stage reached by the future socialist leftwing in South Africa, was published with approval in *New Age* on 12 February, because it called for co-operation between the workers and the railway administration — in tune with the demands of Guild Socialism.

The *Labour Leader*, so warmly acclaimed by Jones (particularly after war was declared), compared South Africa to the conditions described by Jack London in *The Iron Heel*. It also reported that troops were parading in the streets of Cape Town and Durban and guarding railway stations with fixed bayonets during the general strike. Herbert Morrison declared in his weekly commentary on 15 January 1914 that: 'A grave is being dug by the South African government — a grave which will be large enough to hold itself and South African capitalism as well.' One week later Keir Hardie compared the events in South Africa with oppression in India and Egypt and was trenchant in his denunciation of the use of the armed forces: 'Militarism', he said, 'is the main stay of Capitalism . . . It is everywhere the foe to democracy, and is at all times the strongest bulwark of the ruling class.' In the same vein Fenner Brockway wrote about 'Military Despotism in South Africa', and described the siege of the Trades Hall. The British capitalist press was jubilant over the suppression of the strike, he wrote, and warned Labour everywhere that it would not achieve its emancipation until it gained control of the state.

Brockway wrote frequently in the *Labour Leader* on South Africa, attacking capitalism, the Liberals and Gladstone, their 'representative' in South Africa. He condemned the law prohibiting open air meetings, (used in 1913 to break the general strike), and noted that its promulgation by President Kruger in 1894 had been used by the British government as one of the excuses for intervention in the Transvaal.[6] Two weeks later he returned to the subject, comparing the repression on the Rand with 'an identical outrage in Dublin', and condemned the Liberal government for what had happened.

Colour and the Radical Press

On the crucial issue of colour, the British papers were silent or even retrogressive. Hardie had been pelted with tomatoes and eggs in South Africa in 1908 for his slogan 'equal pay for equal work regardless of colour or creed'. The *Labour Leader* had damned South African trade unionists for being anti-black,[7] yet, neither Hardie nor the paper said a word about this issue in 1914.[8] It was *Forward*, the most radical of the imported papers, which echoed the race prejudices of South African readers. I O'Connor Kessack filled the front page with 'The Case Against Lascars [Indian sailors] on British Ships'. He said that:

> Economic facts alone, putting all ethnological questions aside, [could] account for . . . [the growth of] prejudice against the black man . . . The Coloured man's life is low, his food simple and inexpensive, and his clothing so scanty as to be financially negligible. He costs the Capitalist a mere fraction compared to the white man. He is squeezing the white man out. This is the real Yellow Peril. The standard of life is in danger, and *the white man must either fight the evil influence or go under and carry white civilization with him*.
>
> This explains much of the African row. Capitalism has a great unquenchable thirst for cheap labour power and much profit. White men instinctively realise it, and we have just seen the preliminary skirmishes of the great battle which will determine whether African and Asiatic shall displace Whites.
>
> The man who talks of equality in this respect is not a Socialist; he is simply crazy and beyond hope.

The tirade continued, with statistics to show the seriousness of the problem (there being 47,211 Lascars and Asiatics on British registered ships in 1912), details of compensation (if any) for injury or death and so on.[9]

The tenor of the articles fitted comfortably with the thinking of white workers in South Africa and took no account of the nature of the society that could allow, and even nurture, this antagonism. Perhaps it was the conflict between socialist values and the contents of the article that led to an altered tone in an editorial in *Forward* on 2 May 1914, less than a month later. The social structure of South Africa was described, boldly — if not always accurately. The country, it said, consisted of:

> A Socialist working class in towns reinforced by officials, traders, etc. In the country an ultra-Conservative farming class, mostly Dutch.

[Outside of these an] international financial gang, without home, without roots, the perfectly unscrupulous economic man, with whom Botha was mad enough to ally himself.

[Beneath them all the blacks with a] large amount of Socialism in their tribal customs.

This characterisation of African 'communalism' was to become the *leit-motif* of 'African socialism' in the 1960s. But it was what followed that was important:

The white genius would be he who would give a new form and setting to what is after all the only permanent form of polity. Nothing will ever be done on the basis of exploitation and the 'natural' degradation of either class or race.

What Jones and his friends thought of the arrogant appeal to a 'white genius' is not known, but the implication was clear: black workers had to be organized.

Changing Values

Many of Jones's heroes and beliefs were challenged in the *Labour Leader*.. It reported the acccusations made at the British Labour Party, at its conference on 29 January 1914, that the Liberal government was the tool of the Armaments Trust — the body that dominated the world's arms trade. Lloyd George was scorned as the man who read Socialist pamphlets and converted them into Liberal speeches — before being turned into Conservative Bills. The journal included a report, on 4 June 1914, of Rev F Lewis Davidson's speech from the Chair of the Conference of the Church Socialist League, on 'The Church, Socialism, and Syndicalism'. Jones, rethinking his political philosophy, must have been presented with a further dilemma. Davidson's contention that socialism followed the 'teachings of Christ' came at a time when Jones was at odds with some Unitarians over the war. Did this influence him to write on 8 October 1914, that 'the question of Unitarianism versus Trinitarianism [had] became obsolete and futile' and that a religious revolution had to reflect itself in 'a complete change in the life of Society?'

In constructing a new world outlook, Jones found ideas on art, theatre and literature in *The New Statesman*. How he must have warmed to Bernard Shaw's assertion that 'vulgarity [had] complete possession of the cinema' (27 June 1914), an echo of his own criticism in the *East Rand Express* of the 'bioscope' in July 1911. He also discovered a new world of socialist and pacifist literature in the advertisements for books and pamphlets in the left-wing press. The *Socialist*, published by the Socialist Labour Party, advertised works by Marx and Engels, Kautsky, Lewis Morgan, Paul Lafargue and August Bebel and pamphlets on Industrial Unionism by De Leon. The *Labour Leader* sold books from the

National Labour Press on armaments and the War Trust, and works by Ramsay McDonald, HG Wells, Margaret McMillan and Leo Tolstoy.

Thomas Bell was to say in an obituary note in the *Communist Review* of July 1924, that Jones 'became known as an ardent student of Marxism' and was sent books from the Socialist Labour Party literature depot However, the major influence on Jones at the time was not yet Marx. He wrote to Evans from the offices of the International Socialist League on 20 October 1914 saying that: 'The war has brought out the revelation that the high postulations of Tolstoy, rightly understood, are the only effective foundation for the Labour movement.' Time would lead him to a more radical position but Tolstoy was a necessary half-way house.

South Africa at War

In 1911 the SALP had decided in principle to affiliate to the International Socialist Bureau — the Second International — and accepted the resolution on warpassed in Stuttgart, in 1907, which declared that:

[Socialists must] use every effort to prevent war by all the means which seem to them most appropriate . . . Should the war, nonetheless break out, their duty was to intervene to bring it promptly to an end . . . [and] to use the political and economic crisis created by the war to rouse the populace from its slumbers and to hasten the fall of capitalist domination.

It seemed increasingly likely in 1913-1914 that war would break out in Europe but it is not known whether the Stuttgart resolution was discussed in SALP brancher or whether the document was readily available to members. However, even if the resolution was known, it did not seem to carry much weight in the party. In statements made by party officials in early 1914 the possibility of war did not enter into their forecasts.

After the February elections members of the SALP were confidently predicting dramatic gains in the next general election and even a majority in parliament. In a letter to *Forward* on 25 April 1914, 'Red Flag' (Transvaal) predicted a hung parliament in 1915 and a Labour majority by 1920, and, in an up-beat message, Charles Clingman, secretary of the party, wrote to branch secretaries, on 28 June 1914, saying that the SALP could form the next government and their opponents granted that this was possible.

On 2 August 1914 a special meeting of the party's executive committee (as reported in the *Evening Chronicle*), met with some active party members. Obviously deeply influenced by the literature on the arms' trade they condemned the war which could:

only benefit the International Armament Manufacturers' Ring, and other enemies of the working class, and appeal[ed] to the workers of the world to organize and refrain from participating in an unjust war.

But these views were not supported by the majority of the party, entangled in the sea of patriotism that engulfed the country after the Legislative Assembly voted to declare war on Germany on 12 September 1914. The South African Industrial Federation reversed an initial anti-war stance and the *Evening Chronicle* on 15 September 1914 reported that at a Johannesburg District Committee meeting of the SALP 'a resolution approving the action of leaders of the party in supporting the government on the war was carried unanimously'. All Labour members of parliament voted with the government against the National Party on the war issue while Wilfred Wybergh, a close associate of Creswell and editor of the party paper, the *Worker*, wrote enthusiastically about the war, in defiance of the policy laid down by the Administrative Council.

Pacifists in the party, seeking to establish their own identity, formed the War on War League in September — employing a slogan used widely before the war, and which appeared as a headline in the *Labour Leader* on 6 August 1914 ('Labour's War on War/ Socialists Supreme Effort for Peace'). Although the League claimed to be an independent body, it included in its ranks a majority of the SALP executive with Colin Wade as chairman. It had a two line constitution: 'The members pledge themselves to oppose this or any other war at all times and at all costs.' The League's *War on War Gazette*, edited by Bunting,[10] carried news of local activity and items culled from papers abroad. A letter in *Forward* on 5 December 1914, expressing appreciation of the paper's attitude to the war, said 'Bunting has shamelessly cribbed your stuff, but it really is too good to be localised . . .'

When news arrived that the trade union deportees — previously the standard-bearers of class opposition — were expressing impatience at having to stay in Britain after war was declared, the anti-war group repudiated these men turned patriot. In Britain the *Forward* of 10 October 1914 said they were:

> so anxious to get back to fight for Smuts and the Botha government, [they] must have been taking our money and our sympathies under false pretences. We understood them to say that the government in South Africa was tyrannous, and required fighting *against*. Now it seems Smuts and Botha are the custodians of Liberty and Freedom in the temple of civilisation!

The deportees were sent back and were welcomed by the SALP.

The War-on-Warites were placed on the defensive. In a statement entitled '*Keeping the Red Flag Flying: An Address to the S.A. Labour Party*', (Johannesburg, March 1915), they felt obliged to explain their existence:

> The League was an inevitable reaction against the attitude of the militarist members of the Labour Party; a spontaneous protest

and corrective against their lapses and excesses. Had the Party stuck to its guns, there would have been no War on War League.

'All Africa, South of the Equator'

The war aims and expansionist ambitions of South Africa's leaders were formulated well before 1914. The incorporation of Southern Rhodesia and the three Protectorates had been discussed in 1910 at the time of Union — hopes of incorporating German South West Africa (SWA) and Mozambique came later. Botha informed Lloyd George at the Imperial Conference in 1911 of his plans to invade SWA when war was declared in Europe,[11] and he requested the transfer of Swaziland and Be-chuanaland in March 1913. Smuts, speaking at a banquet in Pretoria, was reported in the *Transvaal Leader*, on 23 October 1913, as drawing large applause for claiming that 'the day was not far distant when most, if not all of the country of Africa south of the Equator would be in the Union of South Africa'.

The Governor-General of Mozambique protested and Smuts retreated, stating, at Gladstone's suggestion, that he had only referred to other British territory, and that the news report had left out the words 'almost all'.[12] However, after the defeat of the German army in SWA, the government had no doubt about its future borders. Speaking at a victory celebration in 1915, Smuts declared:

> There is now the prospect of the Union becoming almost double its present area. If we continue on the road to union, our northern boundaries will not be where they now are, and we shall leave to our children a huge country, in which to develop a type for themselves, and form a people who will be a true civilising agency in this dark continent. That is the large view.

Later, as a member of the British War Cabinet, Smuts proposed that all, or part of, Mozambique be given to South Africa. In exchange Portugal would be given German East Africa (Tanganyika) and some financial compensation.[13]

In January 1919, Smuts speaking at the Council of Ten called for the annexation of SWA, claiming that the German administration had fomented the 1914 rebellion in South Africa and 'seduced officers of the defence force'.[14] This was absurd. Sections of the army had come close to mutiny during the general strike in 1914 and opposition to the war was widespread. National Party members of Parliament argued that the army was needed in South Africa to face the threat of a 'Native uprising'.[15] General De la Rey said before his death (reputedly by a ricochetting bullet when his car failed to stop at a road block set up to capture a criminal gang) that he did not believe a single life should be sacrificed for South West Africa, because the territory was 'bound to come into the melting pot at the end of the present war'.

Nor was the German administration innocent. It promised SG Maritz, one of the Boer rebels, that South Africa's independence would be guaranteed and that it would be allowed to annex Delgoa Bay, if he and his men fought for Germany and ceded Walfisch Bay.[16] In October 1914 Generals de Wet, Maritz, Beyers and others rose in rebellion. The government was informed of the disaffection in the army and was ready to stamp out the rebel forces.[17]

Stating that it was 'animated solely by a desire to avert civil war in the Union' the *War on War Gazette*, No 7, on 31 October said the League had made an offer of neutral mediation to Lord Buxton, the new Governor General. This was rejected and, on 1 November, Wade, its Chairman, moved at the Administrative Council of the SALP that the government be urged:

> to arrange an armistice and a conference with our disaffected
> fellow countrymen, with a view to securing the restoration of order
> and a peaceful understanding among the people.[18]

The motion was narrowly lost. The pro-war faction countered by proposing that three delegates be sent to General de Wet and his followers 'to prevail upon them to stop their rebellion'. Members of the War on War League rejected this formulation and, according to the Secretary, refused to join the proposed delegation.[19] The project was absurd and ultimately the mission had its credentials withdrawn because it approached the government and not the rebels.

In late 1914 an uneasy compromise on the war was accepted. The anti-war faction usually won in committee but members of the executive differed on the approach to the rebels, on attendance at an international conference on the war (which was aborted), on the convening of the SALP conference in 1914 and so on. Ultimately the annual conference was held in East London in December where party unity was maintained. The Executive Report to the Annual Conference said the choice of action was left to every individual.

Jones compiled the Report of the Executive. For this, he wrote to Evans on 13 January 1915, he was 'congratulated by members of the Conference'. There was an attack on the government's strike-breaking tactics and the arrest and deportation of trade union leaders and reports of the activities of Labour representatives in the national and provincial assemblies.

Furthermore, the 'Executive Report of South African Labour Party, Annual Conference, 28 December 1914', said that an elaborate system of passports was used to stop strikers communicating, and persons approaching public buildings could be shot on sight.

The war issue was not addressed, despite Jones's contention that the clash in the SALP over the war was welcomed because it had re-enthused several branches. The colour question hardly figured in the report, except for one brief item:

The Merriman motion, calculated to put the Labour Party in a cleft stick, and to further Corner House [the mine owners] schemes, namely, to abolish the Colour Bar on the Transvaal Mines, met with such puissant counter-attacks from our members that the sponsors of the scheme hurriedly dropped it.

The Evening Chronicle of 30 December 1914 reported that this was endorsed by conference:

Protests were made against the continued insidious attempts on the mines and elsewhere to employ coloured labour in the place of white men, for which the present war furnished an unrivalled excuse . . .

Little was achieved, nothing was altered. The opposing factions agreed to differ on the war and delegates put on a show of unity. Most of the out-going committee was returned, the majority being anti-war and Jones, writing to Evans on 13 January 1915, reported that he had been unanimously re-elected General Secretary. The initiative stayed with the anti-war faction and, on May Day, the resolution put to the assembled meeting in Johannesburg reflected their views. Drafted in the name of the SALP, it called for the unity of the working class of the world and appealed to fellow workers:

belligerent and neutral, henceforth to concentrate their entire energy to the building up of such effective International labour solidarity and organization as can alone overthrow Capitalism, Militarism, and Imperialism, secure universal peace and emancipate the world.

Although Jones did not join the War on War League, he said in his letters that he could write about little else than the war. He condemned journalists for whipping up war hysteria, and spoke of the 'colossal swindle in terms of religion and honour' that led to the mutual butchery of British and German workers in 'fratricidal strife'. He chastised Christians who endorsed this carnage and warned that 'a day of reckoning' was coming.

Writing to Evans of the rebellion in South Africa that had been squashed, he condemned Botha 'and his evil genius Smuts' who had made a 'holy mess of this country' and only governed through the magistrates courts. By way of contrast Ivon wrote of 'a well educated Kaffir parson' in East London who asked a Labour man in confidence whether he did not think that 'the war was an insult to civilization, and wondered what greater calamity justified the slaughtering of a million-odd men and its consequent suffering'.

Following the sinking of the *Lusitania* by U-Boats Jones wrote to Evans to condemn the anti-German riots of 12-15 May. He sent a copy of his pamphlet *Sorrow and Profits: War in Miniature*, in which he blamed Germany and Britain's 'scramble for spheres of influence and trade' for the war. In the subsequent holocaust common folk paid 'the awful blood penalty of their rulers' greed and pride'. Turning to the riots he said that in Johannesburg a Patriotic Traders and Consumers Alliance, together with a Petitioner's Committee, had failed to obtain a boycott of German traders, or to persuade the government to intern their competitors and sequestrate their property. While the press whipped up the public, they now used popular indignation to attack the traders and issued lists of premises to be demolished.

> For the men who fall in Flanders or go down with the *Lusitania* we can sorrow without despair, for they went down as men, with many touches of human affection and bravery.
>
> But for us and our people who remain, and are made by the Consumers' Alliance to stalk like wild beasts hunting down innocent citizens, our sorrow is unredeemed by hope.

Saying that humanity was in peril, Jones called on all 'reflecting people to contribute to save mankind from barbarism, and to lead men to the returning paths of reason, justice and fraternity'.

Nesbitt, in his reminiscences added weight to Jones's views on the riots saying that: 'The leading demonstrators carried in their hands lists of the local Germans and their addresses, and proceeded to visit them systematically.' They broke into homes and shops, offices and hotels and threw everything onto the streets.

> Chairs, tables, pictures, articles of clothing, pianos, clocks, carpets, every conceivable article of household or personal use, fell in showers from first, second, third and fourth story windows. Files of letters, bundles of papers and documents, cigars, cigarettes, ledgers and motor cars, all were flung or dragged forth.
>
> They were sprinkled with paraffin and then fired. There was some plunder, but usually the goods were just destroyed.[20]

The Administrative Council of the SALP met, according to David Ticktin in 'The War Issue' to discuss the sinking of the *Lusitania* and set up a vigilance committee to check the riots. However, it rejected Wade's resolution abhorring the riots, attributing them to 'trade interests working commercial ends on the justified indignation and sorrow of the people in the loss of the *Lusitania*'. Instead, the sinking was condemned and sympathy extended to the families of the drowned. There were also demands for state relief for those affected and a government enquiry into the riots.

Meanwhile Andrews and Jones, writing as chairman and secretary of the SALP, circulated a copy of a letter they had sent to the Rand press on 29 May but which had not been printed. In it they protested against the dismissal of men of German and Austrian origin who had been dismissed despite their having been 'British subjects of long standing'. They referred specifically to miners and employees of the Modderfontein Dynamite Factory. They also condemned workers who boycotted these men and added:

It is the opinion of the Labour Party Executive monstrous that
workers should so far forget the interest of their class as to hound
out of their jobs men with whom they have worked amicably for
years . . .

It is naturally the tactics of those who support the capitalist system of competition to trample on their competitors by every possible means. But the working class has nothing to hope from a line
of conduct which divides and causes bitterness in their ranks.

Despite this letter, the rejection of a more radical resolution on the
Lusitania riots was only one more indication of the split in the party. The
pro-war faction now demanded the revocation of the 'neutrality
resolution', and a special conference was summoned for August. Cres-
well (now a colonel) returned from SWA to mobilise the pro-war faction.
In a manifesto, entitled *See it Through*, he called for support of the war.
Jones (who now spoke out) and twenty prominent members of the party
including Andrews, Bunting, Gideon Botha, Clingman, Mason and
Wade responded on 20 July with *The Labour Party's Duty in the War: A
Reply to the "See it Through" Policy*.[21]

Socialist ideals, said Jones, implied:

the uplifting of the status of the working class by the application of
principles based on the economic researches of the foremost
thinkers of the industrial era. The iron law of competition is
supreme in Society. One class imposes its will upon and exploits
another class, which has to accept the moral but no less real
slavery of wages in lieu of starvation as the condition of existence.
This inexorable struggle cuts a dividing line across nations, with
the result that Labour follows Capital in becoming more and more
international.

Jones denied that white South Africans felt the ties of Empire. Imperialism, he declared, 'perpetuates racial [English/Dutch] dissention
within; and Imperialism, by rousing international jealousies, is largely
responsible for any menace that may exist from without'. He dismissed
Creswell's call to defend the Empire and claimed that Labour owed its
allegiance to the International working class movement. It was International Socialism that would 'triumphantly emerge . . . and emancipate
the world from the savagery of its military and capitalist institutions'.

Finally, Creswell's contention that Labour's task was to secure
economic concessions from capitalism while seeing the war through was
naïve. In the most forceful passage of the reply Jones said:

When war breaks out Labour cannot confine its attention to
economic evils, but must attack war itself as the concrete expression of them. Otherwise Labour is degraded to being made the
ambulance corps of militarism, content only to follow and pick up
its victims wherever it cares to ravage and despoil. Such an
auxiliary position, no matter what temporary political success it

may bring, must mean the extinction of the Labour movement as a force by lowering its status from being a movement of emancipation to that of a charitable organization.

The Declaration of Principles that was to be placed before the coming party conference called on all governments to end the suffering and distress caused by the war; to state the limits within which they would enter into peace negotiations; and called on the South African government not to send any contingents abroad. It also called for co-operation with the international labour movement in its efforts to restore peace, and for a policy of reconstruction after the war, with provisions for democratic control of foreign policy. But there was no call for workers' action to achieve these aims nor for the break up of Empire. The declaration only asked (in discussing post-war territorial changes) that the 'interests of the native and coloured populations' be adequately safeguarded.

One further document called for an anti-war position. The Report of the Rural Propaganda Committee, signed by Bunting on 5 August. It stated that, since the rebellion, support from Afrikaner workers had waned and had been further dampened by the *Lusitania* outrages. The change had been due to the 'increased violence of British imperialism on the part of prominent members of the Party'(*sic*). Even those who were members of the SALP could not be expected to remain if the 'party identified itself with imperialism'. The report concluded with the warning that there could be no hope of a Labour majority 'until a considerable portion of the country became more sympathetic to the gospel of Labour.' Yet faced with this task, the committee warned: 'At present the Party appeals to the Afrikander about as much as to the Kaffir.'

The special party conference met in Johannesburg on 22 August. The first move by the majority, led by Creswell, was to control the chair. To the accompaniment of 'roars of cheering and the singing of the *Red Flag*' or 'shouting, booing and cheering' Andrews, the party chairman, and JA Clark, the vice-chairman, were removed and replaced by pro-war delegates.[22] Many years later, Jones writing in the *International* of 19 January 1923, said that he remembered very well that evening of the debate when the horse racing fraternity, beholden to the party for 'favours' received from city councillors, attended:

Creswell used the racing element newly arrived in the Party to move the closure . . . [these] men, all jumping up to make the longest speech they were ever capable of: 'Move the question be now put'; and how they voiced their glee at the motion which put Andrews . . . out of the chair . . .

Thereafter, War on War members of the executive resigned and Jones followed the next day. If there was animosity between the factions, it was concealed. Tributes were paid at conference to those who resigned, and those who were leaving declared that they did not aim to

break the Labour Party. Despite the conduct of the pro-war majority
Andrews said he did not think their departure 'would inconvenience the
party' and assured conference (to applause) that 'it was in no fit of pique
that they had acted'. Jones was even more conciliatory. He said 'he was
at the disposal of the party to carry on the work until other arrangements
could be made'.[23]

The anti-warites formed an International League of the SALP and
stayed in the party to uphold the principles of socialism but this was
quixotic. The Creswell group, in control of the Administrative Council,
demanded that members standing for election pledge loyalty to the
government for the remainder of the war. This was too much. On 10
September, the *International*, a new paper with Jones as editor, announced the formation of the International Socialist League (ISL).

Jones delayed writing to Aberystwyth, partly because of ill health, but
also because he would have to explain his resignation as secretary. He
wrote on 20 October 1915 from the office of the ISL, saying that it was
unusually quiet because it was 'the date of the South African general
election'. He enclosed the latest copy of his 'little paper' and hoped that
it arrived. Censorship, he said, was 'idiotically strict, because it is a
censorship of opinion, not of fact, [and] one never knows what is going
to get through'.

By resigning from the party, because of the 'adoption of . . . a Jingo
policy', he had surrendered his paypacket and wrote on 20 October 1915
of 'prospects of plenty of southern breeze in my trouser pockets for
some years to come'.

I know that it will seem very strange to you and most of my old
friends, this opposition to the war. Well dear friend, it is a new
vision, which is implied in the Labour or Socialist movements.

Once again he tried to explain. 'Do you think', he sad,

there was no solution for the quarrels of diplomats by any other
means than the sacrifice of five million lives? Do you think it is any
revenge for the sufferings of unhappy Belgians to bereave some
more million unhappy German women? What a huge swindle is all
this washing of capitalist avarice and greed with the simple
idealism of the common people, adverse Bank Balances, International Credit, the demands of profits, the exhaustion of commerce.
These and not the Consummation of Justice, or the destruction of
Kultuur, will end the war, as they have made the war . . .

Although Ivon lectured his friend, he also knew that his hard line
offended. He said he had not heard from his brothers Tom and Jim for
a long time — and was afraid they were antagonised by his 'too virulent
enthusiasms'. He asked after old friends and wanted news of Miss
Evans, of Ty Tringad, and about George Eyre's work, especially as 'such
trifles as inspections of ancient Monuments [must be] retrenched by the
exigencies of war'. He was homesick and wanted to 'look at the lanes of

old Wales, once more', but had a presentiment, he said, that it would not be for a long time. 'The responsibility of carrying on this new movement rests heavily on my shoulders . . .' He ended this letter by speaking of the rout of 'human nobility and human credulity'. The *Inquirer*, he said, 'has disgraced itself by singing the same Song of Gore and hate as the war lords'.

Farewell, old Enthusiasms. Welcome new light, however weak and struggling.

Thus he greeted the Evanses in words that were to be his own motif in the coming years of isolation. He had travelled a long way in a short time, absorbing the lessons of wartime which, together with his experiences in two general strikes, had made him a socialist with strong convictions. His message was still eclectic but had been honed down to exclude many of the creeds he had picked up in his reading of the British radical and socialist press. He was too independent a thinker to accept all that he found. Rather, he absorbed and then threw out all that he rejected. What remained was moving him in the direction of the most radical socialism then known in the west.

10

THE INTERNATIONAL SOCIALISTS

The Break with the Labour Party

When the leaders of the South African Labour Party demanded that candidates for public office sign a pledge to support the war the anti-warites held a ballot on the question of secession. Expulsion and resignation coincided. On 24 September 1915 the minority launched the International Socialist League (ISL). Its objectives, printed the following week, were to propagate the principles of international socialism and anti-militarism, and to maintain and strengthen working class organization. Socialist societies in Cape Town, Durban, Pretoria and elsewhere were urged 'to link up in one International Socialist Organization for South Africa'.

The anti-war group broke reluctantly with the Labour Party. The years of work that had gone into building branches, winning recruits (among English and Afrikaans speaking workers) and fighting for their cause on Provincial Councils and the Legislative Assembly, were not lightly abandoned. Memories of the two strikes, in which they had all fought together, bound the labourites together. When Jones resigned his post as secretary, he still offered to serve the party and the War on Warites, ousted from the executive, did not leave the SALP. After the split became permanent they explained in the *International*, on 1 October, that they had stayed on in the hope that the SALP

might relent considerably in the application of its 'see it through' policy, and afford some prospect of winning it back to what the Internationals consider its native principles.

If severing connection with the SALP was difficult, the break with old ideas was even harder for many members of the League. The programme of the SALP had been their's, and, when the break came, League members claimed to be the inheritors of the SALP tradition because they had remained loyal to the resolution opposing war between capitalist states. After the conference the dividing line between the reconstructed SALP and the minority was the war issue and on this issue the gulf between the groups was unbridgeable. On all other matters the new League was as reformist as the parent body, and, at the time, there were no discernible differences over attitudes to segregation, to the organization of blacks or, methods by which socialist objectives should be pursued.

The future of the *International* was hardly assured. The ISL was small (and the number of writers even smaller), its news gathering capacity limited by its lack of contacts and the smallness of its budget and, even more important, it still had to demonstrate to its existing and potential supporters that it had something new to say. In so far as it succeeded, much of the credit must go to a few writers, including Jones, who carried the burden of seeing it to the press for the first two years, SP Bunting, who worked with Jones to alter the perception of socialism in South Africa and JM Gibson, who wrote an ideas column to help in the re-education of the membership. The demands on the writers were immense and Jones, denied the opportunity of writing to friends, had little time for rehearsing ideas before committing them to print. In a period of rapidly changing events speedy changes in copy for the printer was needed. Besides the major stories (and these were presumably edited), there were lead articles and the selection of documents and fillers to complete each issue. Precisely who assisted in the many tasks required for the production of a weekly is uncertain.

Many of the articles were written by Jones and these are now part of his story, as well as that the ISL. Many of the articles were unsigned and, although Jones's style can be traced, it is not certain whether they represent his own ideas, or whether he drafted collective articles. He wrote to Evans on 19 August 1917, saying 'I suppose you occasionally receive a copy of the *International*, which gives an inkling of my doings, although myself being the editor, the personal reference is kept under to the maximum.'

In the first issue he had announced the planting of the 'flag of the New International in South Africa'. The Internationalists, he said, were 'torn between their allegiance to the necessity for [white?] working class unity and to the fundamental working class interests which it violates', and this was grounds for the rift in the SALP. In the editorial he wrote almost exclusively about the war, linking international socialism with anti-militarism:

> In the conception of the Working Class International . . . there emerges to unawakened earth the trumpet of a prophecy. Even in the hour of its numerical supremacy we see the national sentiment fading before our eyes, and slowly reforming into the vaster constellation of International working class unity. This is now the only way to advance for Labour. The other way presents a vista of interminable despair with bayonets and cross-bones stacked on either side . . .

He included a quotation from Marx's *Eighteenth Brumaire* in the editorial, which contrasted middle class and working class struggles and, although it did not add significantly to what was said, it showed that new influences were at work. But the conversion to Marxism was slow. The literature offered for sale in the columns of the *International* (e.g on 12 November 1915), together with short extracts used as space fillers, indicate indicate the political philosophy prevalent in the League. There were books on militarism and military service, on the arms trust and on pacifism. The titles included: H N Brailsford, *The War of Steel and Gold*; ED Morel, *Ten Years of Secret Diplomacy*; Leo Tolstoy, *Patriotism and Christianity*; Newbold, *The War Trust Exposed*; Peter Kropotkin, *Wars and Capitalism* and Fenner Brockway, *Is Britain Blameless?*

Shortly before the split Jones wrote to the secretary of the British Section of the International Socialist Bureau, ito ntroduce the League, and say that the conference decision made a final split possible. The letter, reprinted in *International* on 17 September 1915, commended the anti-war stance both of the *Labour Leader* and *Forward*, and the anti-militarism of Karl Liebknecht and his 700 followers in Germany. He regretted that there was no evidence of attempts to enrol these anti-militarist minorities into a new international organization 'to replace the old one which must be admitted to have failed'. The British section was urged to contact the anti-war minorities of Germany, Austria, Russia, Italy and the USA, and to invite Liebknecht to assume the leadership. The existence of a new International would make it easier for many groups to secede from the pro-war social democratic parties and undoubtedly influence others, 'blinded by the call of patriotism, but nevertheless filled with that misgiving which no true Socialist can ever entirely suppress on the subject of war'.

The split from the SALP did lead to a revision of past policies but the process was painful. Many founding members fell away — some returning to the SALP, others confining themselves to trade union activity or abandoning politics. The *International*, largely under Jones's inspiration, widened the field of discussion. It concentrated over the years on two issues: the urgency of ending the war and the need for a new international, and the need to organize black workers — issues which separated it from all other journals.

A short piece entitled 'Let Saints on Earth in Concert Sing' earned Jones some renown and much calumny. Printed as a leaflet, it led to his arrest, for its publication and distribution, and of Andrews and Bunting for its distribution. Written to commemorate the second anniversary of the declaration of war it declared:

> No one is allowed to be neutral. Today it is either capitalism and war, or socialism and humanity. The Church has long ago succumbed to the worship of Moloch. Its parsons have every one gone helter-skelter to the side of the capitalist prostitutes of humanity. '*Let saints on earth in concert sing.*' This is one of the hymns we are enjoined to use on the day of celebration. Dance ye sanctimonious ones, at the cannibal feast on the blood of the workers. What matters it that more and more sons of the working class are required by the unappeasable monster of war, so long as he gives fat Contracts and Good Biz. Let there be no sackcloth and ashes, for today Trade and Casualty Lists boom together.

Jones condemned the Allied powers for being even more vicious than the Germans: violating small countries, suppressing justice and attacking trade unions. He pointed to the executions in Ireland, the violation of Greece, the imprisonment of Clydeside trade unionists and to atrocities in British barracks. He concluded with a call to the working class, without distinction of race, colour, or creed to destroy

the tyrant of modern society, its profit system, its Empire-building, its rattle of swords . . . a society in which you have nothing to lose but your chains . . .

The ISL was not slow in linking the war and economic gain. On 3 March 1916, after the conquest of South West Africa, the *International* quoted an open letter to Members of Parliament by George Hay ('the Don Quixote of Diamond Castles'), on the seizure of the diamond fields:

With the possession of Damaraland the Union controls 99 per cent of the world's diamond production. The bravery of our Citizen troops has ensured at least a 10 per cent advance in the price of diamonds, and, of course, a corresponding increase in the capital value of mines leased by us to company share-holders. The extinction of German ownership abolished competition and in diamonds we now have a 'full hand'.

The hostile reception to the anti-war message in Johannesburg was apparent. On 19 November 1915, at a public meeting, addressed by Jones, Bunting and Dunbar hecklers all but stopped the gathering, copies of the journal were snatched, torn and scattered and Jones and Bunting were attacked. At this juncture the police who were present arrested the three speakers, on a charge of 'publication of matter calculated to excite public feeling'. Bunting was found guilty in an initial trial, but all were discharged when the Attorney General refused to proceed.

The appeal to international workers' unity was only one short step away from an appeal for equality in South Africa. Yet racism was deeply rooted in the country and only the determination of Jones and Bunting, working in tandem, led to a call in the *International* on 1 October 1915 for 'The Parting of the Ways'. Referring to the final rupture with the SALP, Jones appealed to all socialist groups throughout South Africa to join with the new League. He then declared that:

An Internationalism which does not concede the fullest rights which the native working class is capable of claiming will be a sham. One of the justifications for our withdrawal from the Labour Party is that it gives untrammelled freedom to deal, regardless of political fortunes, with the great and fascinating problem of the native. If the League deal resolutely in consonance with Socialist principles with the native question, it will succeed in shaking South African Capitalism to its foundations. Then, and not till then, shall we be able to talk about the South African proletariat in our International relations. Not till we free the na-

tive can we hope to free the white. If militarism is to be destroyed,
capitalism to be chained, and the lust of conquest 'dragged captive
through the deep' by the immeasurably finer order of the Great
International that is to be, then

SOCIALISTS OF SOUTH AFRICA UNITE!

Despite this declaration, the manifesto issued by five members of the
ISL, when they stood for election to the Johannesburg Municipal council
in November 1915, showed no signs of advancement on the colour question. The five — JA Clark, AF Crisp, W Light, Bunting and Jones —
declared that they stood for clean administration, untrammelled by
policies designed to advance business interests. They wanted an improved environment for the city and an improvement in social services,
transport and amenities; a betterment of work conditions, with an eight
hour day, a minimum wage of 10s, paid holidays and the recognition of
trade unions. They also wanted a Rand County Council that would provide a unified administration for the area from Springs to Randfontein,
with the power to resist the Chamber of Mines and landed interests.

Despite demands that concerned blacks (which might have seemed
radical in 1915), such issues were still cast in the old racist mould of the
SALP and this was just another white persons' charter. The candidates
wanted: 'Strict supervision of White and Native housing, and the
development of Klipspruit [adjoining the sewage farm, and ten miles
from the centre of the town] as a Native township'.[1] Furthermore, the
Rand County Council would deal with compounds and Native townships. That is, there would be no alteration in the pattern of residential
segregation. On the matter of wages, it was also quite obvious that if the
minimum wage were accepted, almost all black labour would be driven
out of municipal employment.

That the ISL was still wearing the clothes of the SALP and this was
made apparent in the letter from PL Clark, printed the *International* on
12 November 1915. Written for the Durban Social Democratic Party in
answer to the call for unity on the left, Clark wanted clarity on two issues
— on 'Anti-Militarism' and the 'White Labour Policy' — before unity
could be considered. If the ISL upheld the latter policy, he said, it would
'be a great barrier' to unity between the two groups. Publishing the letter
was in line with editorial policy of directing attention to the black working class. On 7 January 1916, the *International* reported the strike on 21
December 1915 by some 3,000 Africans at the Van Ryn mines who had
protested over the 'loafer' ticket. This denied men a day's pay if a minimum of thirty-six inches of drilling was not completed. The miners were
acclaimed as men who 'did well for their race, but did better for the
working class. The spectacle of the white workers being locked out by
their black slaves is an unparalleled phenomena (*sic*).' The writer called
for an end to the indentured system, the abolition of compounds and of

passes, and concluded by saying 'as the first step to his safety the white worker must give the native a lift up to his own industrial status'.

The ISL position was still equivocal and showed that many issues had still to be worked out. The demands did not address the problem of the 'loafers' ticket — which worked to the advantage of the white miners, but called for measures of which (perhaps unwittingly) many white workers could approve: the pricing of blacks out of the labour market by ending the migrant labour system. Just two weeks later the ISL held its conference and the resolution on the race question, moved by Bunting, mirrored the line on the Van Ryn strike: that the League affirm the need to abolish indenture, compounds and passes and that black workers be lifted to the political and industrial status of the white. Many delegates expressed concern at this formulation and argued that blacks were biologically inferior. Consequently, a clause was added calling for measures to 'prevent the increase of the native wage workers and to assist the existing native wage workers to free themselves from the wage system'. This was the heritage of Labour Party policy and it would take much discussion, the departure of some racist hardliners and the recruitment of black workers into the ISL before real changes could be recorded.[2]

On the question of black attitudes to the war, the journal was strangely silent, although a reading of the English language press would have revealed much black disaffection. Yet it was only on 19 August 1917, that Jones commented in a letter to George Evans:

The German East [Africa] campaign has not affected South Africa much, and the presence of the Dutch section has kept the fever down, and the pressure of millions of natives who only talk of the war as a curious, if mighty, phenomenon in which they have no part or lot, except as wage earners in search of jobs, if they care to recruit so far. Otherwise in the ripening times of peace they are *'recruited'* for work, so that recruiting for war work brings no new terminology, no new [?] , but if anything greater opportunities of learning and advancing, which they are generally keen upon.

Nonetheless, it is doubtful whether the ISL had met with black workers during 1916 their contacts being mainly with leaders of the South African Native National Congress (SANNC), that is, part of a leadership that supported the government's war effort. Bunting noted in the *International* of 18 February 1916, that the Congress leadership had promised to suspend all campaigns against the government during the period of hostilities, despite deep antagonism over the 1913 Natives Land Act (limiting African land possession to 7.7 per cent of the country's total area). He said that the legislation on land could have led to war between blacks and whites if the war in Europe had not intervened but he drew no conclusions from this statement.

There was an exchange between Robert Grendon, editor of the African Congress paper, *Abantu-Batho* and Jones at a public meeting of the League. Grendon proposed a motion of condolence at the death of Kitchener, symbol for most socialists of the imperialist thrust by Britain. Jones explained from the chair:

> that whilst on common grounds of humanity they passed by his death with reverence, personally, they as socialists could not honour his memory, for in his calling he was the agent of the class who exploit both native and white working class and encompass the death of millions of our fellow workers.

The *International* of 6 June 1916 said this 'awkward little incident may have had its good effect on those present'. There the matter was allowed to drop. Yet further elaboration was needed to provide a socialist appraisal of widespread (and millenarian) hopes that Africans might gain their liberation while whites were locked in warfare.[3]

A statement on recruitment was reprinted in the paper on 14 April 1916., as a 'Manifesto against Economic Conscription'. A copy, sent to Aberystwyth had an explanatory note from Jones: this 'concerns "planned redundancy of workers to enforce conscription", as distinct from "privilege" of the officer class to volunteer'. The ISL had:

> hitherto studiously refrained from interfering with men who [had] sincerely and freely volunteered for military service. We have respected their courage though regarding it misplaced. We have instead endeavoured, in spite of manifold suppressions, to proclaim the international unity of the working class across all frontiers of race and country.

The ISL now felt it necessary to protest against the methods of the 'self-elected Recruiting Committee' which wanted employers '"to bring such pressure to bear upon their employees as will be best calculated to ensure their immediate enlistment", and to "refuse to employ single eligible men of military age after 30th April 1916."' This, said the ISL, would force young men to walk the streets hungry, or enlist. 'Enlisting for what?' the statement asked:

> What did the expenditure of £15,000,000 and considerable blood and tears in German South West [Africa] bring to the people of South Africa? Are mothers and widows of fallen soldiers to be consoled by the reflection that De Beers have gained control of German West diamond fields?
>
> And now economic conscription, brutal and unashamed, is being brought to bear on young men to compel them to take part in another business of butchery, at an expenditure of human life that is scandalous to contemplate. *Is this again for the expansion of the interests of the Corner House in German East Africa*?

The writer, (presumably Jones), did not need much prescience to interpret the government's war aims, for he was not far off the mark.:

> Kaffirs and Indians are fighting in the war 'for liberty and justice' (which the masters, *sub rosa*, pronounce 'markets and dividends').

What do these men get for it? Are they really honoured, for their sacrifices? They are subjected to the same indignities, the same restrictions, the same exploitation as before. So it will be with the white worker who have sacrificed themselves in this conflict.

In contrast to the sacrifices of the troops, the Manifesto continued, war profits were expanding, while workers on the home front had to work longer hours. Furthermore, freedom of speech was being suppressed and 'all publication of views distasteful to the government throttled'. The ISL protested against those who hoodwinked the people and 'clothed capitalist schemes in patriotic terms' — the press, the Christian Church, the Federation of Trades and the Labour Party. To those who sought deliverance:

> We again declare that it is the mission of the international working class, acting on its own authority, to free the world from the crimes of war and capitalism . . . [This] is the message of Socialism, based not alone on sentiment but on science, to the heavy-laden and the toilers today.

'Going it Too Fast"

Jones still pined for home but he now had an incentive to stay in Johannesburg, despite its effect on his health. On 13 February 1916 he wrote from Cape Town, where he accompanied Bunting on a much needed vacation.

> I should love to stay here for good, but circumstances won't allow. There is little industry here. Besides, the only thing that keeps me to South Africa is the organization with which I am connected. And I am determined to stick to it because I firmly believe that the principles for which it stands and which it will bring to fruition through the working class movement are of prime magnitude, and if we only be true, will form the only solution for the barbarism to which capitalism has brought the world.

The ISL was small and Jones was secretary, organizer and editor. He chaired the most important meetings or spoke from the platform, organized support for League candidates at elections for parliament and for provincial and municipal councils, maintained contacts in Europe and ensured that the *International* appeared regularly. But that was not all. Jones was a candidate in the Municipal elections in November 1915 and again in October 1916, was assaulted at a meeting and charged for publishing his anti-war leaflet.

It was just too much. As he had foreseen, he fell ill on several occasions and on each occasion he was unable to work. It seems that each time he was nursed back to health by his comrades, until ultimately, on 3 November 1916, the journal announced that:

our editor and secretary, overwrought by the strain of being a Municipal candidate and election agent as well, is confined to his bed by what we hope and believe is purely a passing indisposition. So concentrated in his hands has been the conduct of this paper and the administration of the League generally come to be that members, subscribers and readers are asked to bear meanwhile with the inevitable shortcomings, whether in contents or in circulation and office business, although as regards the latter it is hoped to make good before long.

The long periods of illness, during which time he was completely incapacitated, made it even more difficult for Jones to write. From July to December 1915 he had written only two letters to Evans and sent two sets of leaflets, cuttings, a short pamphlet and a card at Christmas. In 1916 he wrote even less: only two letters, a card and a momento from his stay in prison. Yet he remained close to his friends and copies of the *International* sent to Aberystwyth kept contact alive. Some of the journals were stopped by the censor but those that were received do not seem to have been kept. Perhaps they were too bulky to be stored even by so inveterate a collector as George Eyre Evans, or perhaps they were discarded because Evans could not agree with Jones. Was it this that evoked the response from Johannesburg on 20 October 1915?

> . . . whatever doubts you may have about the 'dangerous' and 'impolitic', and 'materialistic' nature of my strange creed, remember only that it has enough of the light that never was on land or sea to keep your ever idealist, and ethereal friend trustful in life, hopeful of man, and with a growing faith in the goodness some day to be realized of man's destiny which without that 'creed' he would not possess.

Theory and Practice

The writings of the American syndicalist, Daniel De Leon, were most readily available to the ISL and his ideas corresponded with their thinking. A proponent of industrial unionism (or one big union), his influence in South African left circles extended back to the days of the *Voice of Labour* edited by Archie Crawford and Mary Fitzgerald. A small group of De Leonists, grouped inside the South African SLP, collaborated with and wrote for the *Voice of Labour* and, after its demise, exerted an influence on some members of the Labour Party. When the ISL was formed John Campbell, Ralph Rabb, McLean and several others took their small SLP into the League. More recently the writings of De Leon had become available from the SLP in Britain and copies were made available through the ISL. The first ISL conference was pressed to adopt the SLP constitution by its local adherents and conference instructed the leadership to obtain copies of SLP literature. Jones accordingly wrote to the SLP of America, on 9 May 1916, requesting copies of their publications, constitution, 'platform, rules, etc'. He indicated that he approved of the step taken, saying:

I should pay one tribute to the marvellous influence that has been exercised be De Leon's works and SLP 'philosophy' generally here during the last year or so.

Jones ended his letter by saying that the ISL had

made Marx a name to be reverenced (*sic*), and the time is not distant when his true successor De Leon will be given his due place among the great ones of Socialism.

Jones wrote one more letter to the American SLP. On 9 July he asked them for copies of their catalogue and the possibility of getting the printing matrices of existing publications for production in South Africa. The ISL incorporated the objectives of the SLP at the Second Annual Conference in January 1917. These now read: 'To propagate the principles of international socialism, industrial unionism, and anti-militarism'.

Actually, the ISL had been pursuing this goal through most of the year, criticising the exclusiveness of white workers and urging the organization of black workers alongside whites. Headlines in the *International* through 1916 indicate the trend of thinking. On 17 March, the lead article headed 'Segregation Segregated' concluded 'Capitalism, even more than our socialism, compels us to seek for the application of the Internationalist principle to the native, or confess Internationalism bankrupt.' Two weeks later there was a 'Call to the Native Workers', the report of an address by George Mason (who had urged blacks to support the miners' strike in 1913) on 'Trade Unions and the Native Question'. Referring to the events at New Kleinfontein and the tailors' strike in December 1913, when Malay tailors joined white strikers, he said to acclamation from a mixed audience that the result of the strike in January 1914 would have been different if black and white workers had fought together.

On 30 June the the lead article ('White Man Wake Up') appeared in the *International* calling for the organization of black workers. It returned to the theme on 22 September, with a call for working class unity across the colour line, and scrapping the craft/semi-skilled divide. On 6 October the exclusiveness of white workers was criticised in a leaflet penned for the coming Rand municipal elections. Capitalism was called 'the great leveller', and it was said that the ruling class had 'long ago recognised that all workers are equal before great God Capital'. It continu*ed:*

The employing class, which exploits all labour without prejudice of colour whether it be white, black or yellow, so long as it is cheap, strives nevertheless to perpetuate that colour prejudice in the ranks of the workers themselves . . . .

[Therefore] It is for the white workers to stretch out the hand of industrial unity to the native workers, and enlist the enormous power they can wield from the side of the capitalist to the side of the working class and true civilization.

The white worker did not stretch out his hand and there were no signs of progress on these lines but the ISL did secure the attention of leading members of the SANNC who sometimes attended public meetings. This was an important development and it was followed by moves in mid-1917 to launch a black general workers union under ISL aegis. This was the first (albeit hesitant) step in placing the black working class at the centre of the struggle in South Africa.

Closing one Chapter and Opening the Next

On 22 August 1916 Jones informed Evans of his court appearance and enclosed his prison card ('the only place for a respectable man nowadays', he had written on 10 May). A furter card from Jones, written on 9 December, stated that he was on the border of Zululand 'recuperating from a breakdown'. He wrote nothing else that year — all personal life was submerged in his political activities and information on the latter has to be found in the columns of the *International.*

On 17 January Jones responded to a letter from George Eyre Evans which had expressed concern, by dispatching a telegraph from Gingindlovu, saying: 'Recovered, greetings.' He also sat down to write a lengthy letter: about his illness, and the farm on which he was staying, about Aberystwyth and about the war. It was a letter of great warmth that sought to bridge the gap between old and trusted friends. It was also a reaffirmation of positions previously taken and an exploration of ideas germinating inside the ISL. It was the end of his vacation on the farm and he apologised for not writing sooner. It had been hot and 'not conducive to mental exuberance' and, he said, he had never found writing mechanical. 'I must be "in the spirit of the Lord's day", as it were, or the pen refuses to inscribe.'

He said that he had collapsed because of the 'constant application to close office work, and arduous agitation', but was fortunate in having friends who had 'shown themselves exceedingly devoted throughout [his] illness'. There had always been someone nearby and early on, he had been removed to the house of '"Comrade Bunting" . . . the mainstay with me of the Socialist movement here . . . [who] proved a true friend, and spent his waking thoughts in taking up my work, and anticipating my needs'. Now he was on this farm owned by a fellow socialist, 'free of the cares of convention' and having the longest holiday he had ever had. He also added that the trip to Zululand cost him nothing, a theme to which he returned when he confessed himself to be penniless and unable to repay Joinson the money loaned to leave Wales in 1907.

The house, said Jones, was on the Zululand border. From its front he could see fields of sugar cane — the staple crop of the region and from the back he could see

a range of hills of a couple of thousand feet, being the escarpment which climbs up to the higher Veldland. The country is thickly studded with Kaffir Kraals, rising like toadstools in fairy rings direct from the soil. The Savanna Country — great parks of tall grass variegated with dark green copses of flowering mimosa, thorn, and more tropical plants in the creases of the hills — is beautiful and refreshing to the gaze.

The Zulu people, he said, had land to cultivate but still needed to work for the *Malungu* (white man) in alternate seasons of the year to augment the family income. 'So that really there is no part of Africa, unless perhaps Basutoland, where the native is not compelled to come into industrial contact with the white.' Why Basutoland was excluded, he did not say but the significance of this observation on 'industrial contact' was probably lost on Evans. The ISL had reached the stage where it was to turn to the black workers as the target of its organizational activity, convinced that here was the working class, even if many only came 'into industrial contact with the white' on a seasonal basis.

He could have said much more about the importance of the black working class — part migrant, part urbanised — in the economy of the country. These were the people to organize if a socialist movement was to sink its roots in South Africa — and this became Jones's priority when he returned to the Witwatersrand. But perhaps this was not the topic to pursue in remaking contact with Evans and he switched abruptly, first to ask about Aberystwyth, which he believed had 'undergone minimal changes during the past two years'. Then, in a change of mood, he spoke of the war and its effects on their friendship:

The last two years have been as momentous as many a hundred years in the history of man. Only the coming generation will be able to realize the prodigious Character of the Events, events incidental to the war, but more important than the war itself, through which we are passing. But I wonder how you are bearing through it all. We are getting very far apart, these stormy times, I fear. Our pursuits differ so, and the chasms of thought which the war is producing everywhere have not left us unscathed . . .

The people of Aberystwyth were not unscathed, neither in lives, as war took its toll, nor in principles, where conscientious objectors had faced tribunals and stood their ground. He expressed his pride in those who had fought for the right to dissent over fighting, even if he had no great sympathy with the conscientious objectors:

If the war is right then it is right to conscript. If there is such a thing as one people, all enjoying equal opportunity to bread and butter, then that people should be defended. My attitude concisely is that the division by *nations* is an effete one, arbitrarily kept up for the exploitation of labour. The real division cuts across national boundaries, that of International wage labourers versus International Capital.

The whole trend of the world is to bring this division inexorably to the fore, and all the economic agencies of the war have that effect. What the student of the future will read into the reports of the Military Tribunals is the victory of Top Capital, and the sweeping off the stage of the middle class, and the small trader class ...

This elimination of the middle class, he claimed, was an inevitable process which would concentrate the bulk of the population in the working class — and render them all a revolutionary force, able to overthrow capitalism. His tone had become hectoring and he stopped, with an apology: 'Excuse my dissertation! I always start a letter to you with a vow not to [write] on Socialism.'

He wrote of Aberystwyth, saying that the loss of the county's 'best young blood' made him sick at heart. He asked about his brothers with whom he had lost contact and his cousins who were in the milk trade. He wanted news of 'any old friends in Lampeter or Aber whom anything befalls or whom you happen to come across ... I was thinking today of that round faced lad with the humour and the cheerful heart, Tom James, my fellow worker at Lampeter, and wishing I could hear something of him. And many others who cross my mind in rare quietude.' However, the period of quiet for Jones was all but over:

I am returning to Jo[hannes]burg again for another year's grind. Having taken up what I consider the true side in this world conflict — the socialist side, I intend to give it my utmost, as thousands of men are giving their uttermost for the war god. So that it may not be said that I am shielding behind opinions to avoid doing the manly thing. I hope that if I had been able to see the rightness of this war, I should have been consistent enough to shoulder the rifle from the start.

On 7 March the first of two revolutions took place in Russia, leading to the overthrow of the Tsar and ultimately the victory of the Bolshevik party. Its significance lay in what was about to happen, both in Russia and in South Africa. Many individuals who had emigrated from eastern Europe were elated when they first heard the news but it was Jones who understood its significance for international socialism. In the months that followed the first revolution he was to chart the course of events in the columns of the *International* and he predicted long before most western commentators that the Russian revolution could not stop at the overthrow of the monarchy. The paths of capitalists and workers would diverge, he wrote, and give rise to new struggles in which the goal of the workers would be socialism.

His retirement to the farm marked off one chapter in his life and no one could have known in those weeks in which he fought to regain his health that even greater things were to be demanded of him. Jones was not to write to Aberystwyth again until August. The world was turned upside down in March and Jones 'gave his utmost' in defence of the revolution in Russia — exultant in its victories and calling for its support wherever he was, because this event gave new meaning to his all-too fragile body.

Jones did not know how close the revolution was when he wrote from Gingindlovu, but he could be excused: Lenin, who did shake the world, was saying in Switzerland that he did not know whether he would live to see the coming revolution in Russia. Both men saw that revolution, one as an actor, the other from afar — and their lives were to cross. Jones, who saw so brilliantly after the first revolution, that the process of change had still to be completed, was borne along by events and landed in Moscow to become a major publicist of Lenin's ideas in the English communist press. But in January 1917 that was a whole era away as Jones prepared to return to his 'year of grind in Joburg'.

The other matter to loom large in 1917 was the formation of the International Workers of Africa (IWA) by members of the ISL. Although this grouping was riddled with informers, had a short life time and was unable to build factory groups, it was the first known organization of black workers that met regularly. It is not altogether clear what role Jones played in the conduct of its affairs but the germ of the original idea can be found in the columns of the *International* — and Jones was involved in the writing of pamphlets directed at the workers.

The origins of the IWA can be found in the meetings called by the ISL to which members of the SANNC were invited. Their attendance was a novelty, and, after George Mason's meeting the *International* of 7 April 1916, announced that 'the usual monotone of white faces was broken by the presence of about a dozen dusky ones'. Those named as attending were Saul Msane (later Secretary-General of the SANNC), LT Mvabaza and DS Letanka — all of them prominent in Congress.

The number of Africans attracted by the ISL to its meetings was small and none was recruited to the League. In March 1917 a meeting was called to protest at the Native Affairs Administration Bill which allowed the Governor-General (or in effect the Minister of Native Affairs) to make what laws he liked by proclamation for the 'peace, order, and good government' of the Native Reserves. The *International,* of 16 March 1917 said that:

> a large sprinkling of Natives turned up . . . with a solid block of whites in full sympathy with the object of the meeting . . . It was gratifying to see how easily the whole audience caught up the spirit of forgetting for the time being there was such a thing as colour.

Jones outlined the salient features of the Bill from the chair and Msane, quoted as 'the veteran leader of the Rand Natives', was the main speaker. In his opening he said of the League members, 'I hail you as the conquerors of colour prejudice.' Horatio Bud-Mbelle, scion of a prominent family actively engaged in politics, also spoke and wrote an account of the meeting for the journal. He commended the League for the 'revelation of sincere sympathy' and the 'courageous step to combat race prejudice even against enormous odds'. He concluded by speaking of the 'Sisyphian task' before them in fighting against the laws of Parliament. The editor added a footnote:

> Truly a Sisyphian task if you look to Parliament only. The working class is still rolling up the stone of Parliamentary action and is periodically hurtled to despair by its disappointments. Today they are learning to back their ... [fight for] *political right* with *industrial might*. The self-reliance of industrial solidarity; every nerve answers to that iron spring.

Also tucked away in the main report of the meeting, was an intervention by a black speaker, RC Kupan. He apparently 'produced the Constitution and Rules" of a native trade union, started on the Rand, but suppressed'. Like so many other items in the journal, there was no elaboration and there is little information on Kupan, that union, or the nature of its suppression. But the message was not lost on members of the ISL. With the support they seemed to be getting from Congress leaders and their belief that industrial unionism would play an essential role in changing the country, the organization of a workers' group would not be long delayed.

The new chapter had been opened — and was to take the ISL into the post-war era with new perspectives. But this too was to be a task of Sisyphus. Most members of the ISL were still fettered by the ideas of the society they were trying to undermine and many mistakes would still be made. What is remarkable was the distance that some of these men and women had moved since they broke with the Labour Party. After an interval of only two years they were moving away from reformism, they were poised to open their ranks to Africans and they were about to start an African trade union. More than that, they had been prepared for the advent of revolution in Europe and the first concrete signs of the establishment of a state in which the ideals of socialism were raised aloft — and all this they had absorbed. They had got this far. Jones marched at their head.

11

THE APPROACH TO BOLSHEVISM

Solidarity with the Russian Revolution

On 23 February 1917, women in Petrograd celebrated International Woman's Day and used the opportunity to complain about the rationing system. They joined strikers from the Putilov engineering works who had been locked out: over the next two days, the demonstrations grew into a general strike that embraced the town. Within a week, power shifted to a Provisional government, the Tsar abdicated in favour of his brother, and a Soviet (or Council) of Workers, Peasants and Soldiers was established. On 3 March the Provisional Government broadcast news of the revolution. Eleven days later the Soviets appealed to the peoples of the world for peace without annexations and indemnities.

The revolution came as a surprise to most observers and the news that reached South Africa was both sparse and refracted through the columns of a conservative press. Even the journals from European socialists, which arrived three to four weeks after the event, were not particularly illuminating. Jones had to rely on his own appraisal of events in Russia and was unique in grasping the significance of what was happening. In the months that followed, he guided the members of the ISL through the confusing maze of events with an assured and deft hand. S P Bunting's obituary of Jones, in the *International* of 6 June 1924, entitled 'Ten Crowded Years of Glorious Life', was to sum up:

. . . from the time when the 'Red Light in Russia' first broke through a world of gloom, it was Jones in this country who first seized the full import and was least bewildered by the staggering events of 1917. At once he caught the scope of the Revolution which had been brewing in the Councils of the Zimmerwaldians (with whom he too had been maintaining contact), and when the Bolsheviks came to power he had already helped us to realise that this was no miracle but a great milestone on the march to human freedom in which the workers of South Africa, too, had been and were taking part.

There was no hyperbole in this praise, even if Jones over-estimated the gains of the proletariat in the first weeks of the revolution and misjudged the provisional government's control of the state machinery. On 23 March, under banner headlines, '170 Million Recruits', Jones wrote:

The Socialist International has become a far more tremendous thing by the Russian Revolution. It means that a people of 170 million has swung into line with the great proletariat of all

countries, on its march to the Revolution by the side of which all
previous ones are but 'shopkeeper's riots' in immensity.

Jones believed that the Russian workers were in the forefront of
revolutionary change, differing with his friends who said that the
workers were too weak to take the revolution further. Noting that the
capitalists and workers had common objectives in the conquest of political rights, he then cautioned:

> We see two streams in this, as in all previous revolutions. The
> Industrial Capitalist cry is now 'ORDER'. The proletarian driving
> power cries 'LIBERTY'. But the workers having won their
> 'Programme of the Day', and the Capitalists the control of the
> state, the two streams immediately disunite and the class war
> begins on the last lap to the Socialist Revolution. Now is the
> dangerous hour . . . 'order' . . . will be enforced at the cannon's
> mouth if necessary, 'tearing the side of the proletariat', as Marx
> once said, if the workers are not organised independently and
> strong to bear the shock of recoil.

He hailed the existence of a 'Council of Workmen' (and used the full
title, rather than Soviets, stressing the centrality of the working class in
the struggle). This Council, he wrote, was able to intervene to scotch
counter-revolution, even if not yet able to push forward to the Socialist
revolution:

> Only Russians can feel the thrill of the wonderful deliverance in-
> volved in a free press, free speech, and political liberty. Note,
> however, that the right to combine is won as a result of the workers
> combining . . .

And he concluded:

> This is a bourgeois revolution, but arriving when the night of
> capitalism is far spent. It cannot be a mere repetition of previous
> revolutions. It partakes infinitely more of a victory for the
> proletariat, as well as for the industrial capitalist. Now the two
> classes pursue their several ways; one 'to prosecute the war
> abroad', the other to pursue the class war at home and 'the
> Socialist Republic in all countries'. Let us look forward with great
> hope to the entry of the Russian elemental mass into the Interna-
> tional class struggle for human emancipation. The day of its com-
> ing seems immeasurably nearer by this awakening.

Besides the local *Star*, all papers were scrutinised for further information. These included the British socialist papers, the Italian *Avanti*,
the Frankfurt socialist *Volkstimme* and the *Cambridge Magazine* (which
carried an extract from the *Berliner Tageblatt*). Jones returned again and
again in the pages of the *International* to events in Russia, associating
the ISL with every forward move by the workers and acclaiming the
revolution as a complete vindication of Marx's ideas. An editorial on 11
May, bearing all the marks of Jones's writing, included the following:

The Russian workmen are simply wonderful. The joyful part of it is that there is going to be so many of them. To lead the world back from savagery seems to be their great mission. They are leaving capitalist government severely alone. The working class of Germany, France and England alone concerns them. And from their dominating position in the great Russian revolution — and every new report enhances its greatness — they are going out to reclaim the lost sheep of the Socialist International, bringing international working class action to bear for the confounding of the capitalist conspiracy to murder off the best sons of Europe. Hail the coming revolution, now within living sight.

On 15 June the journal printed a manifesto from the Berne International Socialist Commission (the Zimmerwaldian anti-war group) appealing for support of the Russian workers. In a foreword, Jones argued:

It should be noted that all the calls to revolutionary action on the part of the European Socialists is crystallised in the one of 'Down with the war! Long live the international action of the proletariat.' The war on war is becoming identical with the international class war.

Jones's comments were apposite. The Manifesto called on workers to 'fight the revolutionary fight, for bread, for freedom, and for peace', and had asked: 'Will the revolution kill the war, or will the war kill the revolution? The answer to this question depends on the attitude of the proletariat of Europe in these days of universal trial.' The International Socialist Commission had accepted the ISL's application for affiliation and their call for socialists to rally in support of the Russian revolution, against imperialism and for an immediate armistice persuaded the ISL to send a delegate to a peace conference convened for Stockholm. Jones had originally protested that the ISL did not have the resources to send a delegate, but he reversed his stand to show solidarity with the Russian workers who 'had applied a spark to the whole world-wide movement which cannot be smothered'.

Andrews was appointed as the ISL delegate, and, according to the *International* of 10 August, got a rousing send off from 200 socialists from across the country. New ground was broken again when BLE Sigamoney, secretary of the (Durban)Indian Workers Industrial Union, and RV Selope Thema, of the SANNC, spoke during the proceedings. Andrews sailed in August as representative of the groups that had been present at the meeting — the ISL, the Cape Social Democratic Federation, the SA Peace and Arbitration Society in Cape Town, the Indian Workers Union, the Kimberley Socialists and the Native Workers Union in Johannesburg, the precursor of the Industrial Workers of Africa.

The ISL also tried to stop a nomination meeting of the SALP adopting Creswell as the South African representative but they were unsuccessful. The Stockholm conference was abandoned due to official and unofficial pressures — including the blacking of British ships to delegates by Havelock Wilson, the seamen union's secretary. Andrews attended an Allied Socialist Conference in London but, allowed only observer status, he dismissed the proceedings as a farce. He stayed a year in Europe at the request of the ISL, speaking to British socialist groups and absorbing new ideas (particularly on the shop stewards' movement). He met Maxim Litvinoff, the Soviet representative in London, and served as a conduit for messages from the Russian revolutionaries to the ISL.[1]

The Bolsheviks opposed the Stockholm conference, saying that it would only detract from the revolutionary tasks that lay ahead but the ISL did not know this when they sent Andrews abroad. Jones spoke with hope of its possibilities in a letter to Evans on 19 August:

> Do you think the continuance of the present tremendous carnage is justified on any score of 'Liberty', Justice or Right? I suppose you have noticed however that the cumulative processes of war, driving society towards International Socialism, was foreshadowed in the vote of 184,600 British workmen to participate in the Stockholm Congress . . .
>
> Lloyd George, with his ruffian talk of knockout blows, still dominates Europe, and still, for the 'honour' and 'prestige' of statesmen, young men must go dumb driven to the slaughter. Tell me not they go gloriously. The kernel of the matter for which they fight, when stripped of fine words, is not glorious but sordid. The one ray of hope for the poor chaps in the trenches is the Stockholm Congress of European Workingmen.

The Rule of 'King Mob'

The ISL remained a tiny isolated group, unable to recruit among the whites, and not yet seeking to recruit blacks. The war situation added considerably to their problems. The English-speaking workers remained overwhelmingly loyal to the crown and the anti-war propaganda in the *International* only antagonised them. The Afrikaner workers, who might have been won on the war issue, were repelled by the appeals for unity with the black working class.

Individuals from the small Socialist Labour Party had joined the ISL soon after its formation and were initially very active, but many demurred when the ISL supported the Bolsheviks or were estranged by the League's participation in municipal or parliamentary elections. Others were antagonised when black workers were organised, and, together with some of the founders, left the League. It was only among sections of the Jewish community, (those who had 'danced in the streets of Johannesburg at the news of the fall of the Tsar'[2]) that recruits were won in the wake of the Russian Revolution. To accommodate them, a

Yiddish speaking branch was formed in August 1917. However, after the victory of the Bolsheviks, the support from this section also withered, and only a minority committed to revolutionary change stayed in the League.[3]

There were also other pressures. Open air meetings called by the ISL were often broken up by soldiers, some orchestrated by recruiting sergeants, while the police stood by. One particularly nasty episode was reported on 4 May 1917 in the *International* under the headline 'Mob Law on May Day'. In a leaflet announcing the May Day celebration, the ISL called upon workers to end the war and re-establish the working class international. Among the speakers billed was Horatio Bud-Mbelle. A hostile crowd gathered in front of the Town Hall. After scuffles in which several socialists were beaten up, the meeting was abandoned. Soldiers 'arrested' Bunting and Jones and marched them to the Town Hall 'to give an account of themselves'. Fortunately they were rescued, and released by an army captain. The police were hostile and would not offer protection to League members, standing by when the social evening that was to follow the meeting was also broken up.

Worse was to follow. Under the heading 'King Mob', the *International* on 19 October, reported an increase in attacks on League speakers at the regular Sunday evening meetings since 7 September, culminating in attacks on the previous Sunday. Once again the police kept away until the fight was practically over. Men and women were beaten up — League members giving as good as they got — and Sam Barlin (who was to join Jones as a delegate at the third conference of the Communist International in 1921) was threatened with lynching.

The League was isolated. Some opponents declared that they broke up meetings not because of the ISL's anti-war position but because it was organising blacks. Meanwhile, the police arrested Barlin and H Barendregt and said that they could not interfere to preserve law and order! The Chief Magistrate hinted at dire penalties if the ISL 'persist[ed] in defending [themselves] against violence caused through "exciting public feeling"'. The Trades Hall Society, already determined to punish the ISL for inviting blacks to their meetings, banned all its gatherings and ordered the League to vacate its office in the building.

Then, in January 1917, Colin Wade secured only 32 votes at a Parliamentary by-election for Troyeville, Johannesburg — against Creswell, who won with over 800 votes. This, said Jones, on 2 February in the *International*, was because the SALP had won the small property holders and craft unionists and 'came immediately after the League gained working class rock-bottom at its annual Conference'. The 'great mass of the proletariat, which was only represented by 32 votes in the Troyeville contest, happens in South Africa to be *black*, and therefore disfranchised and socially outcast'. The ISL could not look to 'Labour Party constituents . . . for any large backing' — its task was 'to awaken the native wage-earner, and . . . his white prototype . . .' within industrial unionism. This was a change of focus in ISL thinking and was mentioned by Jones in his letter of 24 November 1917:

> Our work is tending more and more in the direction of lifting up the masses of the native workers. But we are deficient in knowledge of the native languages, and it is part of my next years' scheme to acquire a 'book' knowledge of their 'tongues' if I can get relieved [of official duties].
>
> Our anti-war agitation I may say has taken quite a second place to this, the awakening of the native wage earners to a sense of their historic mission of human emancipation.

'Wake Up, White Workers'

In all that Jones and his comrades wrote, either in letters or in the *International*, there was little reference to the changing face of industry in South Africa. In his *Report on Communism in South Africa*, written in 1921 when he was in France, Jones was to devote a short passage to 'Industries', saying that:

> In a country of a million square miles, agriculture is of necessity a staple industry, though the old Boer farmers' methods are obsolete, and there are vast tracts of land held up idle by the licensed syndicates in combination with the mining houses.
>
> The Gold Industry of the Transvaal, with its Witwatersrand gold reef sixty miles long, is a world-renowned phenomenon. The Reef, with the town of Johannesburg at its centre, provides the economic stimulus for the whole country. The diamond mining industry of Kimberley and Pretoria, the coalfields of the Transvaal and Natal, the Sugar Estates of Natal, sum up such industries as affect the world market. The Railways are owned by the State.

Statistics were not easily accessible and this undoubtedly accounted for the sparse description which gave neither indication of the economic development of the country nor information on the growth of the Afrikaner or the black proletariat.

The number of black workers on the mines stayed constant at 180,000 during the war years but in manufacture it is estimated that the number of establishments and employees nearly tripled between 1911 and the early 1920s. Furthermore between 1915/16 and 1918/19 the number of firms increased from 4,000 to 6,000, the number of white workers employed in manufacture rose from 39,500 to 53,600 and of black and Coloured workers from 61,600 to 89,500. Wages paid to black workers over the war years were pegged, or rose only slightly, but retail prices rose by an estimated 31-39 per cent. Consequently, workers clamoured for higher wages and were responsive to calls for organisation.

Andrew Dunbar, writing on the working class in the *International*, on 1 December 1916, referred to an article in *Abantu-Batho* on the conditions of black workers — a change, he wrote, from that paper's

Native Contingent [the army's labour corps] flagwagging, aping of Europeans, adulation of pro-native-landlord protests against Land Acts, old-fashioned bookish aspirations for the vote as the be-all and end-all, and snobbish cravings by an educated few for social recognition by an educated few . . .

The article was redolent of the anarchist philosophy which carried some weight in the ISL at the time, but its significance lay in Dunbar's conclusion that the Congress paper 'sounds at last the initial rumblings of a spontaneous, indigenous class-conscious industrial movement in South Africa'. He then quoted from the article, portions of which provided information to League members on the conditions of the working class:

The unskilled labour and all kinds of drudgery, both on the mines and in urban areas, are done by the native people . . . They form the major population of the country and they belong to the working class . . . They are the mainstay of the country's industries and the backbone of the land's prosperity . . . And they are the hardest worked and the least paid . . .

Native servants, at business places, private offices and private homes, are extremely overworked. In laundry work especially, which is done mostly by women, there is a regular sweating-system of a most shameful character. Bundles of washing of extra-ordinary quantities of clothing are required to be done within a certain time at quite a low wage — a bundle that takes the whole day to wash being paid for with one or two shillings. Some steam laundries, we are told, do not give time even for meals, a woman starting to iron at seven in the morning on to six at night without a break . . . The same kind of overwork obtains at some big offices in town where natives commence duties at quite early hours and are not allowed a single hour for preparing and taking their meals till late at night.

The usual rate of pay [in all work] is from 7s 6d to 15s a week. Out of this a man is expected to pay his rent, feed his family and himself, pay taxes, provide for doctor's bills, dress decently with his dependents, and do a thousand-and-one other things. It is impossible! He must be driven to do extreme things in order to get a livelihood or meet domestic requirements. Talk of crimes of theft, illicit liquor dealing or even violence!

The time was ripe for trade union organisation — and if white trade unionists would not allow blacks into existing bodies, a separate black union had to be started. In an article entitled 'Wake Up, White

Workers', on 24 August 1917, Jones quoted from a recent conference of the South African National Union at which it was stated that the blacks were becoming the real working class, with the whites tending to become an 'overseer class'. This completely vindicated ISL calls for the solidarity of all labour, he said. The ISL had not been premature in its stand, but had leeway to make up.

> The choice is even now being offered to the white workers of becoming police boys for the capitalists or of standing shoulder to shoulder with the Native proletariat in its emancipating march.

The only hope for the white workers to prevent their degradation into 'a police boy class', he concluded, was the coming Conference of Industrial Workers, which could give rise to a rank and file movement cutting across race or colour.

The white workers did not respond, and the ISL went ahead with the formation of a black worker's union. However, except for one intervention, Jones played no direct role in this. On 29 June the *International* announced that he 'had overtaxed his powers' in assisting Andrews, the candidate in the Benoni constituency, for the Provincial Council. Jones wrote of this to GE Evans on 19 August:

> I have been kept to the house for 4 or 5 weeks, with another breakdown, although I was able to do a little writing for the paper in the latter half of that. I have to go much more carefully than I used to, as the strenuous life of the last three years in the labour movement, mainly in my secretarial capacity, has robbed me of my old stamina and strength. Through the kindness of friend Bunting, however, I have not been at a loss where to lay my head, and have had a chance to recuperate.

When Jones returned, he did not embark on any new activities, He was still the secretary of the League and editor of the journal, still wrote and spoke at some meetings — but so far as can be ascertained, he attended only one meeting of the new union and his one direct involvement was the writing of a propaganda leaflet for the IWA. This alone was an effort that placed Jones politically at the very centre of the League's attempts at organizing the black workers. The effects of the leaflet exceeded expectations, but when he wrote on 24 November and mentioned the move to organise black workers, this was as yet unknown:

> The year that draws to a close marks a period in my plans. It has been a very chequered one for me, with sickness for two months. Next year I wish to be relieved of the secretaryship and editorship of the *International* and have notified my committee accordingly. But so far there is no one to take my place, and if no arrangements can be made I shall have to stick to the plough to the end of another furrow. But I am making a big bid for release and a chance to get my health back to its 'pre-war' state. I have brought the little

paper through 111 numbers, beyond our wildest hopes when we started.

The Industrial Workers of Africa

The *International* of 5 August 1917 reported that Gordon Lee of the ISL had started an Indian Workers Industrial Union in March with about twenty workers in Durban on the lines of the IWW. BLE Sigamoney became the secretary and represented the union at the ISL meeting of 5 August, when Andrews was chosen to go to Stockholm. The union was not given an easy passage. Its members were subjected to harassment, their employers threatened them with dismissal and their meetings were broken up by soldiers. It continued for a few years but it did not thrive.

Intervention by Rueban Kupan (who sold patent medicines in the mine compounds) at the ISL meeting in March 1917 suggest that others had tried unsuccessfully to form unions. Finally the Native Workers Union (NWU), was formed in Johannesburg on 5 August 1917. From its inception it was riddled with police informers, who were elected to its committee and sent in detailed reports on the organisation. Because they kept the minutes there now exists a record in the Department of Justice files of attendance, of speakers and of the subject matter of these meetings — or at least what was understood by the policemen of what was said.[4] On several occasions the policemen recorded statements about the need to keep spies out of the organisation although it was these men who were ultimately responsible for translating union propaganda into the vernacular!

The first meeting reported in the files took place seventeen days before the official launch, at the shop owned by Jacob Neppe in Fordsburg (at the western end of the town centre). There were ten whites, all from the ISL, and 20 Africans, including two police spies dressed as miners. The group met weekly, with attendance fluctuating between a dozen and over fifty. Besides the whites, who came from the ISL, most of the audience were Africans and this included members of the SANNC (Herbert Msane, Bud-Mbelle) and Talbot Williams, Mr Adams and George Crowe, members of the Transvaal APO which had been revived in April.[5] Horatio Bud-Mbelle was secretary in the early stages of the organisation but he seems to have resigned this office and his place was taken by a policeman.[6] The members included T William Thibedi (who was to rise to prominence in the Communist Party as an organiser), R Kupan (who lived in Troyeville — the scene of the ISL's electoral disaster), A Cetyiwa and H Kraai. Cetyiwa and Kraai later left for Cape Town and organised the dock workers before Clements Kadalie arrived to start his Industrial and Commercial Workers Union of Africa — or ICU.

Dunbar spoke at the early gatherings and his message was couched in syndicalist terms. On 19 July he was reported by the police as saying 'that if mineworkers strike and are prepared to go to gaol and continue striking, the government will have to talk'. At the next meeting the report was to the effect that:

the only thing they want us to do is to come in Union with all the white workers and be organised together and strike . . . all the workers, white and black, should come together and make meetings . . . and fight against the capitalists and take them down from their ruling place.

He was also reported as saying that white workers are also ill-treated by the capitalists. Africans had first 'to strike for the abolition of the Pass Laws, and they should do it this way: the Natives should come together and at the end of the month they should refuse to go to the Pass Office to register their passes . . . he was sure the Native Affairs [Department] cannot arrest the whole lot of them, it can only arrest a few'. Once the pass laws were abolished it would be possible to organise with the whites and strike. 'We can gain what we want, if we strike for everything, we can get everything.' The phrase 'We want everything' was later to become the slogan in many campaigns.

The talk was not always of trade unionism. On 16 August, Bunting argued that the SANNC was too middle class and was not interested in the working class struggle. In a series of questions, he elicited from an African at the meeting that Congress consisted of 'Exempted natives [those not required to possess a pass], shareholders and a couple of lawyers'. Bunting summed up by saying:

So they organise themselves, so as not to have their lands and exemption certificates taken away from them. They don't want to get their race free from slavery.

On several occasions questions were asked at NWU meetings about the presence of whites and, on 20 September, an exclusively black gathering was requested and convened. There the role of whites was challenged and, in particular, it was asked whether the socialists were leading them astray. Ultimately the meeting decided to accept whites, so that members could learn from 'the white men socialists'. Apparently the members of the NWU were satisfied after this meeting (although it is not clear where the police now stood: were some being won over, as one report in the Justice Department files suggests?). It moved the following week to form the group into a socialist workers' group — not as a political organisation but as an industrial body. It was to be known as the Industrial Workers of Africa (IWA).[7] Office bearers were elected and it was decided to publish a leaflet in Zulu and Sotho.

The minutes of meetings record that Ivon Jones and 'Barron Wright' (seemingly a mishearing of the name Barendregt) were asked to write the text and co-operate with a publication committee that included

Msane and the acting chairman, Hosea Phooko, who were to translate it. Jones wrote the leaflet but when Msane and Phooko failed to do the translating, two policemen on the IWA committee undertook the task, and followed Jones's version closely.[8] The *International* printed Jones' original version on 15 February 1918:

OF THE BANTU RACE! Why do you live in slavery? Why are you not free? Why are you kicked and spat upon by your masters? Why must you carry a pass before you can move anywhere? And if you are found without one, why are you thrown into prison? Why do you toil hard for little money? And again thrown into prison if you refuse to work. Why do they herd you like cattle into compounds, WHY?

Because you are the toilers of the earth. Because the masters want you to labour for their profit. Because they pay the Government and the Police to keep you as slaves to toil for them.

If it were not for the money that they make from your labour, you would not be oppressed.

But mark! You are the mainstay of the country. You do all the work, you are the means of their living.

That is why you are robbed of the fruits of your labour and robbed of your liberty as well.

There is only one way of deliverance for you, Bantu workers. Unite as workers, unite! Forget the things that divide you. Let there be no longer talk of Basuto, Zulu, or Shangaan. You are all labourers. Let Labour be your common bond.

Wake up! And open your ears. The sun has arisen, the day is breaking. For a long time you were asleep when the great mill of the rich man was grinding and breaking the sweat from your work for nothing. You are strongly urged to come to the meeting of the workers and fight for your rights. Come and listen to the good news and deliver yourself from the chains of the Capitalists. Unity is strength. The fight is great against the many pass laws that persecute you, and the low wages and the misery of existence.

WORKERS OF ALL LANDS UNITE. YOU HAVE NOTHING TO LOSE BUT YOUR CHAINS. YOU HAVE A WORLD TO WIN.

Ten thousand copies were printed, and, at an IWA meeting of 25 October, Jones advised those who undertook its distribution to proceed secretly and with caution. It was later reported that bundles were given to friends and distributed in Pretoria, Rustenberg, in the mine compounds and across the Witwatersrand. The leaflet was well received by the SANNC, members of the APO and by individual workers who were attracted to IWA meetings. On 9 November two members of the APO (Talbot Williams, newly appointed organizer for the APO in the Transvaal and Crowe) who had attended a meeting of the IWA At

Williams' invitation nine members of the IWA were elected to attend an APO meeting to speak to its members.

The *Abantu-Batho* response was enthusiastic, if surprising. In an earlier exchange the Congress paper had warned workers to 'Beware of Labour Cranks'. The *International* of 19 October 1917 had responded by attacking the paper as the mouthpiece of the Chamber of Mines and called on Africans to organize industrially and fight for themselves. This was now forgotten and the SANNC urged workers to support the IWA, to struggle for higher wages and to 'arrange hours of work and all the rights of the workers'. A forthcoming meeting between APO and IWA members was announced in the *International* on 30 November 1917 and support given for amalgamating African and Coloured workers in one organisation.

Among the responses was one from a newcomer on 6 December. According to a police report he said he had been given the leaflet and:

he found the contents to be very useful to him as it read about what had been a trouble to him for some time. So he thought to come to the meeting and hear what was said there . . . since he came in he found they were talking of fighting for our rights and the increasing of our wages, liberty, etc. The natives were hard working men and only received 1s 8d per day, out of which he has to support his wife and children, he has no place to live in and must live anyhow. We should surely fight for our freedom and kick everything out of our way and fight for what we want.

Representatives of the Transvaal National Congress, the APO and the IWA, met on 21 and again on 28 December, to consider joint industrial action by African and Coloured workers. Williams provided the lead, and it was decided to appoint a committee from the three organisations to co-ordinate industrial action.[9] The committee, if it met, was overtaken by events.

The IWA leaflet spread everywhere. In January 1918 the *Rand Daily Mail* reported that it had been distributed in the mine compounds. Industrial action by black workers commenced in February 1918 with the boycott of all the concession stores on the Van Rijn, Kleinfontein, Modderfontein, Modder Deep, Geduld and other mines by African workers. This action spread rapidly across the Witwatersrand and at one stage 15 mines were affected. The workers, who found that money had depreciated during the war by fifty per cent or more, complained that prices were too high and thay rejected statements of white officials that the increases were due to the war and that whites were also affected. Reporting from Benoni, one detective said:

At first it was thought that only east coast Natives were involved, but all tribes were involved, *and each tribe had its own system of picketing.* (emphasis added)

Indeed, on the mines, although there were few signs of discord between ethnic groups, there is evidence of ethnic leaders organizing and
leading their compatriots. Thus a copy of a 'Notice to Natives', found in
the Department of Justice files in 1918, reads:

> I beg of you people of Gaza [east coasters] that a person seen
> going to the Jew stores [that is, the mine concession stores] on
> Tuesday must be thrashed and the articles that they bought taken
> away from them and if a purse it must be thrown away and if a
> blanket it must be torn.
> If one of a tribe goes and buys the whole tribe will be included

> I finish here.

The nature of the boycott varied from mine to mine. Africans confined to the compounds tried, in some cases, to break out and attack the
stores. They were driven back by police. In Springs a large number of
women marched on the store and threatened to break it up. Once again
the police intervened to stop the destruction. And in Brakpan 600 Shan-
gane workers marched to the Charge Office to demand their release
[from their contracts]. They were driven back by mounted police.

The boycott was not a success, even if a few prices were lowered.
Within a few weeks it was all over, some men were jailed, and conditions
on the mines remained as before.[10]

The publicity given to the leaflet by the press meant that the ISL had
a scoop in its hands, but it did not, in its first response, claim credit for
what was happening. Besides being concerned with a possible brush
with the law, there were other problems to be resolved. The black
workers, it was thought, were not yet capable of confronting the mine
managers and there were reservations about the use of the boycott.

The ISL countered the *Mail's* story by saying that prices in the mine
stores had doubled, although wages had remained stationary. Yet, although the boycott had been 'marvellously unanimous' it was misguided.
The worker was not robbed as a consumer but at the point of production:

> The boycott is mis-directed, the solidarity displayed is the sig-
> nificant thing. It ought to make white Trade Unionists pause in
> admiration, and reconsider their relation towards this mass of
> unskilled labour which they today spurn . . .

The *Mail* misquoted the leaflet, including statements like 'All
workers should come together to fight for their rights and reconquer the
country.' Ivon, tongue in cheek, said: 'Being a Socialist organisation, we
also have seen the leaflet referred to. If it is the same one, our English
version of it, rendered by a most capable interpreter, is very different
from the *Mail* one.' He then printed the original copy as written by
himself![11]

Perhaps the full significance of the leaflet was not (at the time) realised by the leaders of the ISL. Its publication obviously did not, and could not, create a boycott; that action was rooted in the intolerable conditions in which the miners found themselves and the increased store prices had become intolerable. The leaflet touched a nerve and it was the unexpected initiative of IWA members that helped precipitate the action. In an incident reported by a policeman, Rueben Kupan was seen reading from the leaflet in a compound room and explaining its contents. It was also reported that on 15 March a member claimed at an IWA meeting that the leaflet had helped cause the boycott and urged that more be printed

There were innumerable small strikes in 1918 often involving a small number of workers. Then, in the middle of the year, following a successful strike by white municipal workers, the 'bucket boys' or night soil workers (also municipal workers) came out on strike on 6 June, demanding that their wages be increased from 1s 8d to 2s 6d per day. Fifty workers came out initially, and 35 were arrested and sentenced. Thereafter another 152 came out. All were arrested and Magistrate TG MacFie sentenced them to two months imprisonment for breach of contract, with orders that they be returned to work as convicts without pay. Those refusing to work would be flogged, those trying to escape would be shot. This was too much. The clamour for their release forced the hand of the prime minister and they were freed.

Rejecting talk in the press of ISL influence on the workers, the *International* of 5 July 1918 poured scorn on the notion that white agitators were behind the action. It cited ISL representatives at SANNC meetings, who had opposed strike action to support the bucket boys, because the workers were unorganized. The talk from Congress platforms had been empty, precisely because there had been no preparation of the workers:

Of course we are not apologising. A great 'forward movement' of the native and white proletariat is inevitable in the near future, and we have done and are doing all we know to help it on. Perhaps, after all, it is a pity that a general strike was not allowed to mature. It will come anyhow one day ...

Nevertheless, Bunting, TP Tinker and HC Hanscombe of the ISL, J Ngojo, H Kraai, and A Cetyiwa of the IWA, and DS Letanka and LT Mvabasa of the Transvaal Congress were charged with commissioning public violence. The case collapsed when Luke Massina, who had been sent into the IWA by the Native Affairs Department but had informed ISL members of his role, told the court that the crown case had been fabricated. The agitation over the bucket workers led to a demand by the SANNC for an overall increase of wages by 1s per day, to be enforced, if necessary, by a general strike from 1 July. The response was overwhelming. Selope Thema, a Congress leader, writing about the event a decade later, said that at the time all the Transvaal African population was seething with dissatisfaction and a general uprising was feared. Saul

Msane, Secretary-General of the SANNC who condemned the call for a
strike, was stigmatised as *Isita wa Bantu* (enemy of the people).[12]

It appears that Talbot Williams was probably involved in the organization of the strikes. If this was indeed the case, the police inside the
IWA would have informed the authorities and this would explain the
remarkable story, that in June, Williams 'got cold feet'. Being assured of
protection, he made a signed confession to a magistrate and promised
to do all in his power to stop the strike. Williams left the Transvaal and,
moving to the Cape, was employed as an agent of the National Party. He
justified his departure by saying that 'one must live'. This was reported
in the *International* of 8 November 1918, when his death in the influenza
epidemic was announced.

Early the following year, on 1 March, the *International* returned to
the subject to answer attacks in the press, in particular the *Natal Mer-
cury*, which accused the 'Industrial Workers of the World, notoriously
financed by Germany', of inciting African miners to boycott the stores.
The socialists it said, 'permeate the natives with the pernicious doctrine
that they are slaves, and so on . . .' and for this 'there would be trouble'.
Once again Jones criticised the boycott, which tackled the branch rather
than the root, but he also said that a number of blacks had been meeting
under the name of the IWA, 'to learn, carry out, and organise upon the
principles of the Labour Movement'. The ISL was assisting and had
collaborated in producing the leaflet:

> For years we have preached the solidarity of Labour irrespective
> of race, colour, or grade — preached it on the Town Hall steps till
> the audience got tired of it, preached it at meetings, on leaflets and
> in this paper, as the vital basis of Labour Union . . .

Jones's account of the leaflet in his *Report on Communism* of 1921
tended, if anything, to understate its effect:

> This leaflet reached a still wider mass of native workers, and was
> introduced and read to the illiterate labourers in the mine com-
> pounds . . . In 1918 the propaganda of the IWA, and the pressure
> of the rising cost of living, produced a formidable strike movement
> among the native municipal workers, and a general movement for
> the tearing up of passports . . . The ISL was charged with inciting
> to native revolt; but the chief native witness for the Crown broke
> down . . . The moving spirits of the IWA were driven out of Johan-
> nesburg by the police, some to find their way to Cape Town, where
> a more permanent movement of native organisation has since
> been formed.[13]

'The Call of the Bolsheviks'

On 24 November 1917, two weeks after the Bolsheviks took power,
Jones wrote about the revolution to George Eyre Evans. He started with

a phrase adapted from Marx ('Force is the midwife of Revolution')[14] resorting as he had not done for a long time, to the language of the bible, hoping to convince his friend of the new found truth:

> The world is going through great changes, the greatest in the history of human society . . . [T]he light that is breaking forth from Russia will illuminate the dark places of the Earth. The Russian autocracy was the shadow across the world, but the Russian revolution is the light of the world. The . . . Russian Cossack terrorised all European movements for liberty into submission, far beyond the borders of Russia. But today, the revolutionary spirit, that is, the spirit of emancipation is animating the peoples of France, Italy and even Germany.
>
> In England it is not absent. But today the British Army is the weapon that the Cossack was yesterday, the instrument in the hands of Capitalist governments which cows all the revolutionary movements of the Continent into quiescence . . . But a couple of years will see tremendous developments.
>
> The press of England will become hysterical and tear out its hair in desperation. But don't be disheartened by it. The extension of the liberation movement from Russia in the East to the countries of the West is inevitable. When it comes, even now, while the newspapers paint it in letters of dire calamity, possess your soul in sweetness, good friend, and be assured that it is good to be alive to see it, and to be young is very reason. In the alchemy of progress the old names of democracy and justice and freedom of small nationalities becomes the repositories of the new tyrannies. And the new liberty comes in gusts, unknown to the prophets of liberty who preached to the old world.
>
> And the people walked in great darkness, saw a great light. But the light is pictured as a great terror by the paid charlatans of the press and the pulpit. And it shall come to pass again as of yore that the message of liberty shall go forth, not from the scribes and pharisees of the capitalist temple who repeat the words democracy, justice and equality, but from the unknown fishermen of the unpaid working people.
>
> Look out for the new dawn. Its crucifiers will be Asquith, Lloyd George, and other scribes and pharisees. They whitewash the [?] of the prophets of liberty, and persecute the children of the prophets.[15]

Jones wrote in more measured terms for the *International* on 16 November, explaining the conflict between Kerensky and the Bolsheviks, the working class character of the Soviets, the need for peace, and the bloodless character of the October Revolution. The proletariat, he said, was generous and humane. But, he warned, if the Bolsheviks should fail then, as in the Paris Commune (of 1871), 'we can expect the most bloody massacre of the workingmen of Petrograd that history has ever recorded'. He included some of the sentiments from his letter, but in a different idiom and in more sober terms, writing for example, about 'the abuse and filth of Capitalist journalism . . . being poured without restraint on Lenin and his party'.

The Russian Revolution, and the threat to it, made it even more urgent that the war be brought to a close. The ISL could do nothing to stop hostilities but the point could be stressed in the *International* and Jones wrote about it to Aberystwyth. In his letter of 24 November 1917 he spoke again about the war, 'because I suppose it dominates all the world. I have very little else to talk about'. He was pained by the portraits of 'young men who fell in Flanders,': that were printed in the *Welsh Gazette* and contrasted them with those 'whose every utterance is besmirched with the profit and emoluments and rewards flowing everywhere from this slaughter: '"Patriotism" is a word forever damned in this war. Think over yourself, of all those who exhort the people to continue the slaughter, how many of them derive their position and profit from its continuance . . .'

He condemned those who 'exhorted the people to continue', and those who 'dare not advise to the contrary for fear of losing trade or position' and concluded: 'I only ask you not to heed their lies, and not swell the misguided applause they receive, for your own souls sake in the days that are to come.'

In the last edition of the *International* he edited before leaving Johannesburg, Jones was defiant. On the war, the Russian revolution and the IWA, he flung down the challenge to workers to achieve unity and to pursue the struggle against the ruling class. In the ISL manifesto, 'The Call of the Bolsheviks' (printed in the *International* of 1 March 1918), he called for solidarity with the workers of Russia.

> The bourgeoisie are opposing the workers by force, wherever there is a hope of saving their precious private interests from being captured by Labour for the common weal.

Capital, he said, thrived on war, but alongside this, there was a war of international capital against the working class:

> What can we do? It is our part as workers to denounce these capitalist slanderers of the Russian proletariat. It is our part to help in the great class struggle of the toilers of all lands that is now beginning. The humbug of national war is being exposed. Behind it all the exploitation of the workers of all lands stands out as their chief aim, their dearest treasure.

Jones attacked the mob law used by the police as 'the only law on their side so far'.

> The most avowed opponents of 'Bolshevism' just now are in Europe, the German Junkers, and in Africa, the Union Govern-

ment. We wish them joy of each others partnership but for our part we are right up against the enemies of Labour, white or black, whether they be German, British, or anything else.

Jones was exhausted. Finding a replacement proved difficult and he was released as editor only after he had completed the edition of 1 March 1918, which announced that he was leaving Johannesburg for an indefinite stay on the coast. His place as secretary would be filled by TP Tinker, and as editor, by SP Bunting. Appeals were made for other members to help in the office.

One more chapter had closed for the ISL, but Jones had other tasks ahead of him and even 400 miles away, on the east coast, the Johannesburg group would still need his assistance.

Scene from 1922 general strike: Whites and Blacks gathered around the banner 'Workers of the World Fight and Unite for a White South Africa'

12

'THE BOLSHEVIKS ARE COMING'

'Pro-Working Class, not Pro-Colour'

During its short existence the *International* had taken a stand against the colour bar. From the pens of its main contributors came a string of articles informed by contact with Africans. Some had been involved in the wave of African working-class action across the Witwatersrand in 1918 and were members of the Industrial Workers of Africa, others were leading members of the Transvaal National Congress who came to ISL meetings. From this followed several interventions in debates on general grievances; the land question, class demands, and so on.

Despite claims in recent literature that the early communists erred in stressing class rather than colour in their analyses, Jones and his comrades were far closer to an understanding of the central problems of the country than many of those who followed. They made mistakes, some of them serious, but they were clear on the need to build black working class organizations. In so doing they faced criticism from within the League and hostility from without. On 22 February 1918, under the heading 'Pro-Working Class, not Pro-Colour' the journal answered its critics:

> We give increasing attention to the native workers not because they are natives but because they are workers. Correspondents who send us notes on coloured and native grievances . . . should note this. We are not concerned with the civil disabilities of Indian storekeepers or native lawyers or coloured middle men. For us they all belong to the parasitic class. Our concern with the natives and our faith in them is our concern in them as workers, as potentially the revolutionary proletariat.

> We are pro-working class, not pro-native. Constituting as they do the big majority of those who do the work of the country, we want the native workers to realise that it is their historic mission to bring about the emancipation of Labour. Everything is marking time for them. We also want the white worker to realise this . . .

> . . . colour is only an incident, one of the difficulties, one of the barriers. Our propaganda does not aim at emphasising colour lines. It aims at showing that colour lines do not exist for Labour. The class struggle cuts across nations, creeds, and demarcations of colour.

Doubts had been expressed about the possibility of taking a socialist message to Africans who were non-industrialised, many of them 'small herdsmen and farmers'. The *International* of 8 February stressed that the ISL was aware that only the development of large scale industry would resolve the problem, and that only the town proletariat could provide the lead for the vast mass of the peasantry.

[Nonetheless] no distinct line can be drawn between the native on the soil and the native in the town industries. There is constant intermigration. The natives in the reserves are themselves right up against the wage system. Nearly all the natives in the Natal reserves work intermittently for the sugar farmers and further afield. Though many may be comfortably off, in the mass they are never far from want and misery. This is the object of the reserves in the Capitalist order of things, a cheap sponge to take in and squeeze out the reserve unemployed as required.

The problems encountered in white worker's action came to the fore in a polemic in the *International* in April 1919, after a strike by tramway men and power station engineers for higher wages in Johannesburg. According to the account in Cope's biography of WH Andrews, *Comrade Bill* the men on strike left the town without lights or public transport for two days. Andrews proposed to them that they take control of the public utilities and run them for the local inhabitants. The strikers set up a Board of Control (dubbed a 'Soviet') and restored the lights and trams. The authorities capitulated and once the workers' demands were granted, the 'soviet' was disbanded. Cope included a brief note on the controversy in the ISL over the issue and a comment from Andrews that he and Bunting had 'little in common in character or temperament, but were bound together by a "working agreement for the cause"'. But there was more to the story than recorded by Cope and what happened is still crucial for events today.[1]

The first months of 1919 were marked by widespread strikes, pass burnings and riots by African workers. In Bloemfontein a strike for a minimum daily wage of 4s 6d, centred in the black township, failed, but led to the formation of the first of two bodies known as the Industrial and Commercial Workers Union (ICU). In March the Transvaal Native Congress resolved to campaign against the pass laws and renewed the demand for higher wages. Action followed almost immediately. On Sunday, 30 March, after addressing a meeting at Vrededorp, Johannesburg, Congress leaders collected passes from those present. On the Monday several hundred men gathered at the main Johannesburg pass office, where passes were collected and destroyed. Those who would not comply had their documents taken, were instructed not to carry them again and told to demand more pay. Groups of 20-30 men and women then scoured the town, collecting passes and telling the men to demand higher wages. The police, together with a Civil Guard organised to assist them, tried to round up the groups and succeeded in retrieving hundreds of passes. Those arrested all gave their names as 'Congress'. The campaign escalated on Tuesday when a meeting in Vrededorp resolved to pull working men out of the workshops and to pay special attention to the Municipal Compounds and the mines. Delegates at the meeting came from several Transvaal towns and they too were instructed to collect passes in their own towns and to get the men to leave work. As a measure of intimidation the government brought the South African Mounted Riflemen (SAMR) from Pretoria to Johannesburg. They were used outside the courts on the Thursday when the crowd tried to release those who had been arrested.

The campaign could not succeed, and Congress leaders stayed away from rallies after the arrests. Nonetheless the defiant spirit remained and was to fuel further struggles, particularly on the mines. There are too few available accounts of the responses to the campaign among the people involved. The one account left in police reports is redolent of the women portrayed in Aristophanes' play *Lysistrata*. A Miss Kekane, speaking on 29 April, after having been released from jail because of her participation in the anti-pass campaign, urged her listeners to carry on the fight, saying that the women would help the men. She ended by declaring 'If any man comes to me and says he loves me and I find that he has a pass I shall kill him stone dead as I don't want this pass.' The response of men who might have 'loved her' is not recorded.

It was suggested at the time that the SANNC was using the strike of the white tramway men and power station engineers to further their own aims. Yet the decision to launch the anti-pass campaign preceded the strike and there was little sympathy for the black workers from either the Board of Control or from the white strikers. Many black passers-by in Johannesburg were assaulted by the whites who had met to cheer their 'Soviet' in the Town Hall.

The struggle however was far from over. The clamour in the countryside rose in intensity as drought gripped South Africa and Mozambique. The country had experienced a cycle of droughts and heavy rainfall (which washed away the crops) since 1912 and the situation had been worsened by cattle disease and then by the post-war influenza epidemic. Men on the mines and in the towns received more urgent requests for money from their families. Yet, despite the inflation, there had been no increase in wages. Mineworkers, house servants, shop workers, dockers and clerks all clamoured for increased wages, and many linked their misfortunes to the notorious pass laws.

There were strikes in several towns but the storm centre remained the Witwatersrand. In rapid succession black miners, sanitary workers, house servants and others came out on strike, and almost always faced opposition from white workers, which led at times to open conflict in the streets.

The black miners, whose strike was by far the most important, saw their white counterparts win an increase of 8s a day for white worker after merely threatening to strike. Africans were given an increase of 3d per shift. This was derisory and the workers were incensed. After the price of cigarettes increased by 3d to 8d per packet, African miners boycotted the concession stores. This continued for several days and was accompanied in some cases by rioting. The following day (11 February) the first strike took place. On Friday 20 February the *Rand Daily Mail* noted that there was a marked degree of cohesion among the workers who had a 'system of picketing which has been sufficiently complete to prevent numerous peaceably inclined and satisfied Natives from going to work'. By Saturday the 21st eleven mines were out involving 42,000 men. On Sunday the SANNC called a meeting at which 2,500 were present, with a few representatives from the mines. The meeting expressed its solidarity with the miners' demand for higher wages and urged the workers to avoid violence. This was one of the few occasions in which Congress leaders called for solidarity: otherwise they had little effect on the course of events.

The miners, confined to the compounds, faced constant provocation from the police who searched the men for weapons and arrested strike leaders. Generally the workers kept the peace although, at the Village Deep mine, there was a scuffle which led to shooting and a bayonet charge: three Africans were killed, and forty-seven injured, twelve of them whites. But as the strike continued, bringing out a total of about 80,000 (with a maximum of about 40,000 on any one day), men were forced down the shafts with rifle butts and sometimes with fixed bayonets.

The white miners did not strike, nor did they stay neutral. Their union recommended to their members 'that they carry on operations on the mines as usual . . . provided it is the wish of the management' [and furthermore] that . . . they uphold the maintenance of the colour bar as at present constituted, and deprecate any attempt made to imperil it; and recommend the strongest possible measure to combat any such attempt.

As it was the wish, the white miners went underground and, when necessary, did the unskilled work to get the gold ore out with the rock. The tension between white and black workers grew as the strike crumbled. At the beginning of March black workers at the Spring Mines offered to work for a week without the help of the whites, and guaranteed to double production. It is not certain whether this offer was repeated elsewhere, but it marked a turning point in the campaign by African workers for a more responsible and permanent position in the productive process. If the challenge had been accepted by the mine managers the status of Africans in the mines would have been altered irrevocably and a permanent work force would have taken over from migrant labour. The offer was spurned despite repeated efforts by the mine owners to reduce the number of white workers. Either it was felt inexpedient to antagonise the white workers, or the management felt that a response to the black workers during a period of industrial action, would be used as a lever to win further concessions. The white workers responded angrily and it was reported that there was an increase of violence and assaults underground.

Only the ISL issued leaflets calling on white workers not to scab, but to no avail. The appeal was ignored and, without support or centralised organization, the great strike crumbled.

In June Magistrate MacFie (of the 'bucket-boy' trial) called on the South African Industrial Federation to join the Defence Force to deal with 'native unrest'. The SAIF, represented by Archie Crawford (one time syndicalist) and J Forrester Brown (former war-on-warite and member of the ISL) declared that they were prepared to raise Labour Battalions for use in case of a rising or rebellion, providing they were not employed against white strikers. They were prepared 'to prevent outrages on white women and children' they said, and although they added that Africans were entitled to organize to protect their positions they made no representation on their behalf. Such, said the *International* on 5 July 'is the corrupting influence of false labour organization, of labour-fakirdom, of miseducation, of capitalist flattery and bribery, of sectional and colour pride and prejudice'.

The government having anticipated some of the reactions to post-war discontent, took steps to contain any disturbances and, through the Governor-General, Lord Buxton, kept Lord Milner at the Colonial Office informed of strikes and disturbances. In March and April 1919 Buxton sent details of widespread strikes by whites in the building trade on the Rand and Pretoria and of the 'soviet' in Johannesburg. There was also mention of strikes, or threats of strikes, on some mines, among hairdressers, bank clerks and others. The dispatches were routine, but there was a note of urgency after Buxton received a request from the Minister of Native Affairs, FS Malan, on 3 April for aeroplanes, bombs, explosives and flares for use against Africans if the situation got out of hand.

A telegram from Buxton, received in London on 5 April, was more explicit. He said that the government wanted one Lt Gearing and his aeroplane (then on show in South Africa) to be made available for demonstration and moral purpose on Africans if they got out of hand. This was because the South African Defence Force had no planes and no pilots. Buxton had agreed, if the Minister asked for it:

on the clear understanding that it will not be used except in connection with serious disturbances among natives, and that its use is not required or requested in connection with any European disturbances, that its main object of utilising its services is the moral effect on the natives . . .

He also added that Lt Gearing could only use bombs or guns under stringent conditions, and in 'extreme necessity . . .' Lord Milner gave his approval two days later. The South African government did not require the aeroplanes on this occasion and made no request for the services of Lt Gearing or his plane. In March 1922, just three years later however, Smuts was to use the South African Air Force's aeroplanes to bomb white strikers into submission.

Apart from the SANNC, the only group that gave its support to the strikes or was sympathetic to African demands was the ISL. Its full involvement was concealed to avoid legal action and the *International* denied involvement in the events of 1918-20. This was not corrected in subsequent publications although Jones, in his 1921 report on *Communism in South Africa* said that

> In 1918 the propaganda of the IWA . . . and the pressure of the rising cost of living, produced a considerable strike movement among the native municipal workers, and a general movement for the tearing up of passports. Hundreds of natives who had burned up their passes were jailed every day, and the prisons were full to bursting. Gatherings of native men and women were clubbed down by the mounted police.
>
> . . . But the most portentous event so far in the awakening of the native workers was the great strike of mine workers on the Rand in March 1920 . . . For the time being all the old tribal feuds were forgotten, and Zulu and Shangaan came out on strike together irrespective of tribal distinction to the number of 80,000. Without leaders, without organisation, hemmed in their compounds by the armed police, the flame of revolt died down, not without one or two bloody incidents in which the armed thugs of the law distinguished themselves for their savagery.
>
> The mining industry has been wobbling in its attitude towards the educational and civil advancement of the natives. Hindered by political organizations, and the Frankenstein of race prejudice which it has itself conjured up, the Chamber of Mines hesitated in its desire to reduce working costs by opening the higher industrial employments to native and coloured men. In the last few years the *Star*, the Chamber of Mines' daily, has incessantly declared in favour of the civil advancement of the natives, vigorously attacking the white unions for the denial of opportunity to the native worker. These appeals, made in the interest of lower working costs, are nevertheless unanswerable in logic from the Labour point of view. The native does not care what the motive may be. He sees in his economic exploiters the champions of his civil rights. Now that the capitalist parties are safely seated in the government saddle we may look forward to steps being taken to realise the programme.

The role of the ISL in the miner's strikes and the anti-pass campaign was only revealed by Jones, but details have remained obscure. Bunting's role was never in doubt. He had defended many Africans in the magistrates court and was perceived as sympathising with their cause which led on one occassion to his being frog-marched and severely manhandled by whites when he left the court. He lambasted the Board of Control and the strikers in the *International* on 4 April. In an editorial entitled 'A"White Soviet" and the Red Herring', he noted first that it was a big advance to move from 'old-fashioned strikes' to the control of industry and public institutions in the interests of the working class but thereafter he condemned the Board on two counts. Firstly, they negated the whole idea of a Workers' Council (even for whites) by excluding workers in industry, by not seeking to extend the Council outside Johannesburg and by announcing that they were only a temporary institution. Secondly, and of greater importance, they had not sought to include the black municipal workers and generally ignored or excluded 'the vast mass of the workers of this country, the most flagrantly oppressed victims of the most glaring form of capitalist exploitation, the exploitation of the black races and their labour by white capital . . .'

It is humiliating to have to keep on emphasising that the essence of the Labour movement is Solidarity, without which it cannot win. The outstanding characteristic of the capitalist system in South Africa being its Native labour, the outstanding movement of the country must clearly be the movement of its Native labourers. . .

Bunting was still groping for a socialist answer to the problem of ethnicity and reverted to the Labour Party 'solution', saying that under socialism the 'Native problem' would be solved by restoring the land to the Africans and providing them with the facilities to develop their agriculture. This would remove the cheap labour basis of industry and the white man's fear of being undercut.

Jones saw more clearly that the black proletariat was at the very centre of the South African struggle — although he too was to provide a bizarre solution. Writing as Cincinnatus in the *International* of 14 February 1919, about Hertzog's appearance at the peace conference in Versailles, he feared the Americans might favour the Nationalists and grant them state power in the northern regions, where they would use their poor white following 'to crush the revolutionists and slaughter the native workers', and this made it imperative that the white workers be won over to the side of socialism.

Jones's rebuttal of Bunting, in his article of 11 April, was based on a comparison of South Africa and Russia, with their backward proletariat and his belief that the white workers had to be won over. He said that ISL policy was directed towards class solidarity and it was pernicious to divide the working class, even if white and black workers were sharply separated in function by the colour line. It was wrong to look only at the mines, where whites were generally gangers (that is 'contractors' who had their own gang of black workers and were paid according to the quantity of rock removed). In all other occupations blacks were labourers or hodmen and this placed whites in a strong position, in that blacks had few skills and could not be used as scabs against them. Only white workers were 'as yet politically articulate', and the functional gap between white and black workers made the former 'masters of the political situation' and they could establish the dictatorship of the proletariat by themselves. Then, in his own construction of the theory of 'uninterrupted (or permanent) revolution', Jones continued: '. . . as has been well said, *unless within twenty-four hours after the revolution the whole proletariat experiences the joyousness of freedom* (even though hungry), the revolution fails'.

To get the economy working (after this 'revolution'), the white worker would be wholly dependent on his black fellow-worker, and 'the working class becomes one, knowing no demarcation of colour'. He then argued that the white workers were not themselves exploiters despite their supervisory duties. That was why there were no workers' political parties expressing an exploitative relationship:

> The only way to account for this is by the assumption that the white proletariat is a revolutionary factor, it is the engine of revolution in South Africa, just as the comparatively small industrial proletariat of Russia steered the big mass of the Russian people into the Soviet Republic.

Conceding that the black workers were 'ultimately the true revolutionaries, with potentialities undeveloped, and that the clarity of the class struggle here is really due to their mass psychology', he continued:

> Be it so. The working class is interdependent . . . [W]hile not abating our cry for unity of the proletariat, white and black, let us not slide into the false idea of Unity which ignores or sneers at either section of the proletariat. For that is to be anti-proletarian again in the below-zero direction.

Jones and those closest to him, unable to resolve the problem of colour within class, try as they might, left behind a legacy that socialists would not easily overcome.

A Spell of Fever

Jones left Johannesburg for Durban in March 1918 and there he linked up with LHH Green and others who had been largely inactive. By mid-March the *International* announced that the Durban branch had resumed activity and that several Coloured and Indian comrades had met. Yet, inevitably, Ivon's main contribution came through the pen. His contributions in the *International* were concerned mainly with the defence of the Russian revolution against the counter-revolution.but his writings also dwelt on the need for schools for African workers; on Jack London's foreshadowing of fascism in *The Iron Heel* rejecting the novel as being too pessimistic; and on a new topic for the paper, the recruitment of labour for the mines from Mozambique.

The League had not been able to pay Jones for some time before he left Johannesburg[2] and once again he wrote to Aberystwyth to say he could not repay the loans to Joinson and Evans. He needed money and, at the invitation of SM Pettersen, a leading member of the ISL in Durban, he had moved to Linga Linga in Mozambique.[3] There he managed a team of three whites and about fifty Africans, dismantling equipment for the Grindrod Whaling Company and dispatching it to Durban.[4]

Jones said that Linga Linga was 'a day's journey by sea, or more, north of Delagoa Bay . . . situated on the inside point of·land which makes a large inland bay on the far end of which is Inhambane, the nearest town'. The whites in Linga were Portuguese and Jones felt triply isolated: by language, by the strangeness of his new occupation, and by being generally ostracised because of his political position. He even felt neglected by friends and complained of not having heard from Aberystwyth for a year. In a wave of remorse he wrote from his lonely outpost: 'I deserve to be neglected, for thus have I conducted myself, in my correspondential duties'. It was Sunday and he concluded with 'that matchless hymn' of 'Hellas' by Shelley — the copy of which he had opened after 'long estrangement':

The world's great age begins anew
The golden years return.
The earth doth like a snake renew
Her winter weeds outworn;
Heaven smiles; and faiths and Empires gleam
Like wrecks of a dissolving dream.

Jones had been moved by these words and he continued

Oh write no more the tale of Troy
of Earth Deaths, Scroll must be,
Nor mix with Lucian rage the joy,
That dawns upon the free . . ..

Although George Evans noted on the letter that he replied two days after receipt, Jones wrote again on 6 October to say that he had received cables and responded immediately, but no letters had arrived. Perhaps, he said, there was some mistake in forwarding his letters. However, there is another possibility. From letters found in the South African government archives, it is apparent that Jones had been under constant surveillance from the outset, undoubtedly based on information from the South African police. Also, the Portuguese authorities were most concerned about the presence of a 'revolutionary' in their colony and Jones's mail was undoubtedly intercepted.

The authorities concern about Jones would have been intensified when his article, 'The Land of Linga Linga', appeared in the *International* of 19 April 1918. He described conditions ironically in this 'apparent paradise'. The blacks, he said, carried no passes and were free to come or go as they pleased. The blacks owned the land they squatted on and had few wants aside from 'simple food and a figleaf' and 'his only ambition, women and wine'. The Africans, who did not carry passes, he continued, found fish for themselves in the bay.

As for the effete Portuguese settler class, they 'were not after invention and enterprise'. They travelled at a leisurely pace, and would hold up the train at stations in order to take a drink. This did not extend to invitations to black passengers — the colour bar being maintained outside the bed. And just around the corner there were the recruiters of the Witwatersrand Native Labour Association (WNLA), 'far away from trouble makers . . . where there were no shopkeepers and farmers jealous of the competing mine magnate in the grab for native labour . . . Furthermore, with the average daily pay of 300 reis (that is, nine pence) and with hut and wife taxes to pay, the WNLA recruiter had the only answer.

Jones later wrote two articles for the *International*, on 13, 27 September entitled 'Why do Mozambique Natives Come to Johannesburg?'. He reviewed the work of WNLA and dismissed stories of recruiter atrocities: these were men only doing their job, obtaining labour for capital. The colony, he said, was an anomaly: politically dependent on Portugal but an economic dependency of South Africa. Administrators were paid in sterling and the money for this came from the hut tax, paid by mine labourers via Johannesburg. He despaired of anything happening in 'this abode of bureaucratic petty bourgeoisdom' with its 'low existence of primitive squatting'.

In his second article Jones described the conditions of east African labour, pressganged into service in Nyasaland for military and commercial reasons. For them there was no way out. If a man was sent north he probably died, a 'physical wreck from fever and privation' and the punishment for attempting to escape was death. Many Africans sought out the 'Componi', as they called the WNLA, as a refuge from the terrors of the pressgang and it was only when they came to Johannesburg that they became proletarians.

Jones saw little possibility of development in the colony. The one hope, he said (repeating a theme used by many leftists), lay in capital investment destroying the existing structure, thereby bringing the country into the arena of the class struggle and opening up the prospect of socialism for the African. Meanwhile, with the high rate of mortality on the mines, the choice for the men of Mozambique was 'the frying-pan of Johannesburg, and the hell fire of Nyasaland'.

Other forms of hell fire were at work inside Jones. He wrote on 6 October to say he had been smitten by malaria soon after arrival:

> I have been through a spell of fever again which has laid me up for several weeks, not of the virulent kind, but the aftermath inter-mittence of the first acute attack in April. A low fever which weakens me dreadfully and makes life miserable.

This miserableness was echoed in his feeling that the war had opened a chasm between himself and his former friends. He had still not heard from Aberystwyth and noted that it was over a year since he had a letter. He had been rummaging in his cabin trunk, 'the same I left Aber with', had found the pile of weekly postcards sent by Evans to New Zealand and was reminded of 'happier days — when the heart was young':

Not to say that I am old yet. But I am one of those who age in spirit, before their time. I still have to battle with the malady I left home with; it is never absent, and the fever on top of it is a test of ones hold on these glimpses of the moon. When you see me again, which let us hope will be ere long, do not expect the smiling fresh youth of Lampeter days, but an old young man, with an incipient baldness, a more cynical view of life, and bereft of those long, long thoughts which made the [?] barrenness of Aber yet roseate hued in spirit. Still I trust for what is lost, something is gained.

It is getting on twelve years since I left Aber. How they have slipped by as of stealth and look back on me with a Mephistophelian grin! Well, if I can keep up, Aber shall see me yet and that at a not very distant date ...

I cannot imagine what Aber looks like now. I expect it has changed as much as 50 years of normal development. So has the world in general since 1914 squeezed in 50 years into the 4 short ones that have elapsed since then in normal advance.

Jones was no longer coping with the physical demands being made on him, but he nevertheless spoke of staying as long as possible despite the heat, because the pay was good — '£20 a month all found' — allowing him to save and thus repay his loans, as soon as he could 'get back to civilization, and facilities for remitting English money'. But his real desire was to get back to the Wales he knew — or perhaps feared he no longer knew. He sent regards to JD Stephens ('him with the voice, the hearty friend, one of those it is my devout wish to see again, and revive old memories'), but he noted that there would be few kindred topics now and that 'it is only a heart to heart talk that can restore the old enthusiastic bond of friendship'. He felt more certain of renewing bonds with George Eyre, because

... you, I know, ask no questions, make no demands, only that 'to yourself be true', so it follows as the night the day, one cannot be false to any man. On this at least I can meet [you] squarely again, only that the working out of the principle has led us along divergent paths.

Then he proclaimed:

But there is a bright morning to come. A grand reconciliation of antagonisms in a higher unity that will transcend not only the clash of rights, but will also surpass all our imaginings. Truly the lion shall lay down with the lamb, the wilderness shall blossom with the

rose, the mountains shall dance with joy and the trees of the field
will clap their hands. For we are on the eve of what all the prophets
have yearned for, although we recognise not, nor even welcome
the strange garb in which their poetry becomes flesh. The people
walking in darkness saw a great light. But the light dazzled them
into antagonism at first owing to their long accustom to the dark.
But the full day brings joy and common understanding . . .

Jones was still at Linga on 29 November when he wrote again. The
armistice had been signed and he was obviously more cheerful than
previously. But he was tired — a factor he ascribed to the heat — and he
had just written to Stephens in Welsh, the effort of which did not allow
him to write again at great length that day. He said that he was resigning
from the whaling company, but would stay till January to allow for a
replacement to be found. He planned to stay a month or so in Johannesburg, to fix passport and other matters, after which he would be returning home. The news from Europe was stirring but they could talk about
that when they met again.

He also wrote to Bunting on 10 December, saying he would not be at
the coming ISL conference. Referring to Tinker's resignation as
secretary in November he said he could not take the post again. He
needed 'a change without hard work to get the malaria out of the system,
and various incidentals such as bad teeth'. He also spoke of his 'growing
desire to go to Wales. New scenes with the old gospel ever new may
revive enthusiasm, especially with the stirring events brewing'⁵

However, Jones's return home had to be postponed. He visited
Johannesburg early in January but arrived after the conference. Then
back in Linga, too ill to continue working, he was taken to the Sweet-
waters Sanatorium in Pietermaritzburg (*International,* 24 January). His
plans were quite upset and had to be made anew, he wrote from his
sick-bed on 20 February 1919. But the letter was mainly written because
he had just read of Kitty Evans' death. 'I was on the point of writing to
you when the *Ymofynydd* [the Unitarian journal] came with the sad and
so unexpected news', he said. It was a letter of condolence dispatched
immediately, with promises of a longer letter the following week.

That too was not to be and it was not until 8 May that he wrote again
— this time with startling news. He had been arrested, tried, and found
guilty of 'inciting to public violence after drafting and circulating a
leaflet . He had spent four days in jail after sentencing and pending bail
was now out, awaiting an appeal. 'Don't worry', he wrote,

I like His Majesty's Sanatorium, what I saw of it, and we have
fought the good fight in any case. 'Follow the gleam' you told me
once. It makes no difference if you can't follow me after my gleam.

His health had improved, having been very bad after Linga Linga,
and that had left him with 'a few legacies'. Now he was fitter, and with

'natural methods of healing, feeling more bright and hopeful than for many, many months'.

'The Bolsheviks are Coming!'

In March 1919 he had drafted a leaflet, together with LHH Greene, directed 'to the workers of South Africa — Black as well as White', calling for a united struggle against capital. This appeal was made against a background of strikes in and around Durban, and particularly militant strikes in the docks. Entitled 'The Bolsheviks are Coming' the leaflet was printed in English, Zulu and Sotho.[6]

A spectre is haunting Europe — the spectre of Bolshevism!

What is this Bolshevism that the ruling class is so much afraid of?

Have they not had enough killing? Or is it a thirst for righteousness that makes them pack Tommy Atkins off to freeze in the snows of Archangel ?

The Czar massacred half a million nomads in Southern Russia in one swoop. They did not send an army against him.

Why are they so scared of Bolshevism? Why do they turn pale at its shadow as at the ghosts of murdered men? Why?

We will tell you why!

The Great War of Nations is over, and the Class War against Labour has openly begun.

Bolshevism means the rule of the working class! [where] . . . the Capitalists cannot carry on their Robber System any more.

After condemning the capitalist press for lying about events in Russia, the authors continued:

The workers of Russia and Germany are forming themselves into Soviets — that is: Councils of Workmen.

They are taking over control of the country into their own hands . . .

This means the end of the Profiteering System . . .

Why have the workers of Russia and Germany to shed their blood?

Because the Capitalist Class of all countries will sooner tear the people to pieces with their cannons rather than let the people rule.

The workers are the people.

Remember the massacre of the workers of Johannesburg in 1913 and in Bloemfontein last February![7]

Down with British militarism! It is a weapon to crush the workers.

Down with Allied intervention in Russia!

Down with the Capitalist Class in all countries!!!

The hope of the workers is coming from Bolshevism. The free commonwealth of labour is an actual fact in Russia today.

Bolshevism means the victory of the wage-earners. It will soon spread to Britain, France, America and throughout the world.

Get ready for the World-wide Republic of Labour,

The way to get ready is to combine in the workshops. Combine as workers, no matter what colour.

Remember that an injury to one is an injury to all, be he black or white.

While the black worker is oppressed, the white worker cannot be free.

Before Labour can emancipate itself, black workers as well as white must combine in one organization of Labour, irrespective of craft, colour or creed.

This is Bolshevism: the solidarity of Labour.

WORKERS OF THE WORLD UNITE!
You have nothing to lose but your Chains.
You have a world to Win.

The authorities were furious said the *International*, on 11 April 1919, and the local press carried lurid stories of 'the circular being placed "surreptitiously" under the doors of many city residences' . The two authors were charged with contravening the Moratorium (war-measure) Act and the Riotous Assembly Act, 'calculated to create alarm or excite public feeling, and exciting public violence' through the distribution of the leaflet.[9] Greene lost his job and his wife was turned out of the cafe she kept. Jones was ordered to leave the sanatorium.

At the subsequent trial a succession of witnesses, white and black, was produced to tell the court either that the leaflet excited disgust or dismay, and would either rouse Africans to riot and bloodshed, or was frightening to Africans.[8] Josiah (James) Gumede, secretary of the Natal Native Congress, even said the African's position under Bolshevism would be akin to slavery.[9] An Indian who appeared said he was afraid of the news that the Bolsheviks were coming, but he didn't really believe they would come. (*International*, 16 May 1919.)

A statement for the defence, handed to the court by Greene and endorsed by Jones,[10] included the following:

[W]e appeal to all proletarians to unite in fields, factories and workshops, in order that their voice may be articulate politically. But this working class unity which we ask for is not the unity of a section. One section of the workers can never alone appropriate the fruits of their labour, or the control of their particular industry.

The Communists hold that the emancipation of the working class must be the task of the working class itself . . .

Revolution does not mean 'murder, anarchy and sudden death'. Revolution means a radical change in the government of the country . . . Not merely a revolution giving votes to all, but a revolution giving bread to all.

The defendants then described what had happened in Russia and quoted accounts from western journalists, politicians and government envoys:

[T]he Bolshevik idea is the socialist idea, and has nothing to do with the crimes charged against it . . . [It] is a political creed, a matter of public opinion which we have a right to discuss in common with the newspapers which so violently oppose it.

The native worker has an inalienable right to pursue his aspirations and make them heard in the political life of the country. We claim the right to declare Labour as one and indivisible by colour demarcations . . . We do not regard the disenfranchisement of the native people as disqualifying them from making and receiving political appeals.

The statement referred to the trial of John Muir in Britain in 1793 for advocating parliamentary reform. He was sentenced to fourteen years transportation. Thirty years later, a juror asked to account for the verdict said they had all been mad. In less than thirty years, said Greene, optimistically, that will also be the opinion of those who now exclude Africans from political and civil rights.

Jones, under cross-examination, said he had never been in a township or a native reserve. He was not addressing African peasants but sought only to organize the working class, black and white. He answered allegations of incitement to violence, and claimed that the method of combination proposed in the leaflet were the opposite of mob action. 'We decry mob action as futile, and point the way to that silent and ordered action of labour in the workshops at the point of production as the way of peace.' He continued:

We claim that our programme leads away from violence. We claim that the native workers, left to themselves, blindly groping in conditions that are increasingly trying, are liable to follow the mistakes of all inexperienced workers by relying on crowds for strength instead of upon their labour. We maintain that such a policy of 'let things rip' is a dangerous one for South Africa in the presence of a large Boer population whose traditional way with the native is that of the rifle and who still live in the past, ignorant of the modern development of labour. To avoid in the industrial field the territorial strife of the pioneer and tribal days, that is our aim. When we ask all workers, Dutch, English and native to combine in the workshop on matters affecting their labour, those who object to this can only do so because the property interest is dearer to them than the welfare of the people.[11]

The magistrate ignored most of the points made and, reviewing past trials in which Jones had been involved, decided that these dangerous revolutionaries should be punished. They were each sentenced to a fine of £75 and four months imprisonment, plus £10 or one month.

Jones was preoccupied with the trial and did not write again until June from Durban. He said that bail had been set at £100, and that the appeal was due in August. The magistrate's judgment, he wrote, was considered 'such a flagrant violation of constitutional liberty as to demand an appeal to a higher court':

> This is all being done by the organization, but the case occupied so much of the prosecution's activities, so many witnesses, etc., that the documents for the court of appeal take a lot of preparing, hence the delay. My little 'nest egg' is tied up in the bail, and the intervening months since the unrest have taken a good slice of my savings. In fact I can hardly realise that six months have flown since January, when I was invalided back from Mozambique with fever. It took me three months to convalesce from that; and then my incorrigible propaganda proclivities; then arrest, and since 2 April a long drawn out hearing, and now waiting for appeal.

The *International* reported, on 29 August, that on appeal tthe Supreme Court quashed the sentence. After five months of waiting the threat had been lifted He returned to Johannesburg and was once again editor of the *International*. However when he wrote to George Eyre on 1 December he said that he found the work too much for his strength:

> I gather that my system is beginning to feel the long struggle against the tuberculosis enemy; and that unless some radical change of occupation and life helps, I have not the physical resources to carry on the fight much longer. However I view either alternative with calmness, only regretting, in looking back on one's life, the many broken threads of friendship and love, the unful-filled promises, my inconstancies. I was looking last night, again through Ben [Morris's?] 'Smorgion Aberdar', and again the memory of that dear comrade of ours moved me to grief that he is gone, grief and regret, increasing with the fleeting years. What can we do to embalm the memory of that choicest of souls? Oh what treasures we played with long ago without knowing their price!

He wrote with a deep nostalgia and resignation. He was hurrying to catch the Christmas mail 'to send you word of what cheer the world can give on the occasion'. He complained again that he had not heard since the death of Miss Evans ('your good sister and my dear friend'). 'The intervening silence leaves a greyness over what used to be Aberystwyth. I hear nothing of it now'. He wrote about the loneliness that must now be the lot of George Eyre, and said he gathered that he was expected home any moment and this was the reason he had not heard.

He also said that 'the notoriety given by my arrest' made it difficult to get employment. He had little money after paying sanatorium expenses and the need for care in the coming months. The long spell of weakness after malaria left him without funds to return home. Once again he had to defer payment of the loans and might have to return to Linga to earn more money. The company there was 'anxious' for his services but this had to wait for the appeal. He was contemplating working as a motor mechanic and trying to learn something about it: mechanic's work being 'the only one where the powers that be cannot victimize an agitator very easily'.

Also, in view of the coming winter, the state of his chest made it impossible to travel home. He was disconsolate over his inability to see old faces or 'the face of dear old Wales'. 'I am sorry', he wrote, 'that the stirring character of the times breaks our plans. Nothing certain stands nowadays, and none can live above the ferment of the times except by fossilization.'

And he concluded: 'If I am going to stop here, I intend to settle on a farm. It may be only a passing whim. Write me a few lines.'

The Newlands Red Commando

Miners and their wives throwing stones at the police in 1913

4

THE DELEGATE FOR AFRICA

13

THE ROAD TO MOSCOW

Last Duties in South Africa

Since the trial and his returning to edit the *International* Jones's position had, if anything, hardened. In a typical editorial, written on 28 November 1919, after attending a conference called by the Labour Party, he condemned it for its reformism and insipid economic demands. In particular, and in light of events to come in 1922, he was scathing in his condemnation of Waterston's 'horror' at the thought of revolution to secure change in South Africa. In his report Jones said there was 'No talk of the abolition of the wage system; or the working class as the regenerative power; no hint of the emancipation of Labour.' As a criticism of the Labour Party this was unexceptional: the SALP had never called for a radical alteration of the class structure of South Africa. Yet despite Jones's militant tone, there was no criticism of the most crucial of all questions: the role of the black workers in changing the country.

The ISL always walked along a knife-edge in its discussion of ethnicity and colour. It had claimed that it was not pro-colour, but pro-class; it had further come out against any racism in the struggle, and had been alone in calling on the white workers not to scab when the African workers were on strike. In all this it was in advance of any other group in the country. However, when it was necessary to insist that the struggle for 'the emancipation of labour' was not possible without full African co-operation, the ISL leaders failed to speak out consistently.

It is not certain how long Jones continued as editor — but failing health led to his relinquishing the post again. Yet, in May 1920, he organized the League's most successful ever May Day celebrations in Johannesburg — although he does not seem to have spoken at the meeting. He then departed for Natal, where the weather was kinder and, having made his preparations for departure, he set sail for Europe in the first week of November. In an article written before he left he said: 'if I have lived rapidly I have LIVED, for it is the Socialist movement that brought the zest into life for me.'

After a painfully slow journey of 58 days in a ship that stopped at every port on the East Coast of Africa, Jones landed at Marseilles. The journey had left him prostrate and, as he was to explain to GE Evans, only the kindness of two elderly Unitarians, who took him into their home in Nice, allowed him to recuperate. On 8 January 1921, one week after he landed in France, Jones sent Evans a full account. He said that he had been ill in South Africa, and decided the time had come to make the journey. The passage through the tropics had brought on a malaria attack, and he had not recovered until passing Port Said. On landing in Marseilles he was 'little more than a skeleton'. Mrs Evans, the Unitarian with whom he had been in contact had met the ship and had brought him back to her house, the Villa Vittoria, in Nice. Good food and weather that was crisp but tolerable, had allowed him to regain his strength. His hostess had urged him to stay a few months before deciding on earning his livelihood, and he was fortunate in having good friends to fall back upon. He hoped to get to Wales when the weather warmed, but he had to solve the bread and butter problem. Of his general condition he said:

The chest is always with me, and I congratulate myself on having kept it at bay so well for fourteen years. Hence I do not feel a bit discomfited that I have not been a 'success' in the sense of making a fortune. I know that if I had wished to pursue that worldly goal I could have been in a good flourishing position, fit to return to Aber as the successful emigrant. But I am thus constituted George, and ever was, that I cannot go into the big pew to gain trade. Not physically combative, I have retained the non-conforming spirit of my unitarian days, even in SA and this has once led me to jail. You once gave me a written motto:

Follow the gleam lad, come what may
Whatever the world and folks may say.

I forget the rest. This may have led me to paths far from Unitarianism.

Jones also wrote to his comrades in the ISL and some extracts were printed in the *International*. His first note contained information on his trip and his state of health and there was a note on Marcel Cachin, veteran French socialist 'who was converted to Bolshevism after his visit to Russia last year.' Jones continued:

His speech in Parliament on behalf of Clara Zetkin [who had visited France] was a magnificent example of how the class war can be fought in bourgeois parliaments. And the tigerish conduct of his opponents, snarling at him at almost every sentence, betraying the capitalist ferocity behind or breaking through all legal forms, was a portent of the coming storms . . .

He is the most satisfying case to me of all the visitors to Moscow of one coming back with a vision splendid, of a Moses on Mount Pisgah having perceived the promised land, of a Galahad having found the Grail — in his greying years he is consumed with the fire of a new gospel.

On 4 February an article by Jones appeared in the *International* on the devaluation of European money, on the rarity of metal coins and on the daily depreciation of money. Entitled 'The Destruction of Money' he said that almost all money in circulation in France consisted of poorly printed paper notes, down to the 50 centimes piece, much of the printing illegible or smudged from constant handling. Over and above the printing of money by the government, big towns like Marseilles and Nice printed their own notes — retrievable only in the towns of origin. When he arrived at customs everyone was excited at the vision of the coins he carried. He saw in this 'The destruction of money . . . bringing about the destruction of the capitalist system — just as soon as the proletariat are ready to grasp the hollow thing and bring it headlong to the ground.'

Jones wrote four more letters to Evans from the Villa Vittoria, sending the last on 20 April, when he stated that he was about to leave, go through Paris and on to Britain. It was a period in which he recuperated and was at least physically comfortable: having a troublesome cough in the night and early morning, but not much during the day. On 27 February he said that he had been to the doctor about his chest and believed that if he exercised care, he could arrest the malady. The bacteriological examination was satisfactory. He had a good chance of getting rid of the bacilli, although the lesions of old attacks remained:

> only a moderate number of tuberculous germs and a complete absence of all the associated germs usually found. The rest of my constitution he found perfectly normal, in spite of malaria, liver and spleen being unaffected . . . Only my heart he found weakened by persistent coughing, but very regular . . .

Jones received the *Welsh Gazette* from Evans and he commented (as of old), on the names of acquaintances and the local politics in the paper. He wrote slightingly now of Independent Liberalism and said that it was only in an economic backwater like Cardiganshire that it could give 'a dying flash or two in the embers'. He also wrote about the many objects he had carried with him through his travels: his watch and wallet, both given to him by George Eyre Evans, the latter inscribed with Jones's name, and 'Secretary of the New Street Meeting House'. On this he commented that he had 'since been secretary of other and very different organizations'. He would return these, safe and sound, when he arrived at Aberystwyth.

On 31 March he wrote that the hospitality of Mrs Evans and Mrs Griffiths (her servant and then companion for 25 years) was undoubted and they pressed him to stay. But, he said,

> I am captured body and soul by the Communist movement, and that is the burning interest of my life now. I hesitate to inflict myself on friends who are either antagonistic to the idea or are at least indifferent. Nay, perhaps, the indifference I do not mind if we have other points of contact.

But his ideas were anathema to the residents of Villa Vittoria, and he had an aversion to their preoccupation with spiritualism. He had warmed to the French and 'made the acquaintance of a young lady who gives conversational lessons', and he added 'now I hope to get on better!!'. He was also pottering round the garden, pruning the vine and

orange trees. He found the weather perfect — and that left him un-
decided about moving. He thought he would like to be on a farm,
'ploughing and hay making for a few months', perhaps in the Lampeter
district. The charm of the Teifi still drew him, 'but he was afraid of the
pain of disillusionment. Old friends had gone but nonetheless 'the old
Welsh spirit is always the same'. Nostalgia had obviously taken a grip,
and he spoke of his desire to attend the Meeting House,

> and hear some good Welsh sermons again, purely from the love of
> the language, and the euphony of its sounds — for indeed of all
> languages Welsh, I find after many wanderings, to be the most
> musical. Of course that does not say that I have conscientious
> objections to the Meeting House — of course not. I shall even be
> prepared to give a discourse — if you are prepared to listen to it
> — I should try to keep out points that would shock, but I am afraid
> it would no longer be prayerful . . .
> . . . the watchwords of emancipation of ten years ago, today
> become the slogans of reaction. Unitarianism once was alive, not
> afraid to be in the world, had a clue to the ills of the world — is it
> so today — has it a way out other than death for the chaos of the
> world? Unitarians and greater than Unitarianism — they love
> truth . . .

It was the old order that was bankrupt, said Jones, and the old ideals
of pacifism had no place in a world in which tyranny was raising its head
and the poor getting poorer. He envisaged fresh wars, more hatreds,
and impending catastrophe . . .

> if all our idealism is not to suffer wreck, where is the clue to it all.?
> Hence I am a Communist, and a follower of Karl Marx — in very
> self-preservation!!

He said in the letter of 27 February that he had no plans for the
future, and would like to stay in Nice awhile, if only he could get a job.
On 31 March he repeated that he had no immediate plans. Again he said
he must either get a job here soon or come to Wales and find something
to do. In his last letter from Nice on 20 April he still said he had no
definite plans. He was going to Paris for a day, and then to London for
a few days. He wanted to get to Britain soon, before the seamen's strike
stopped him — and it was convenient to leave Nice within a week,
before Mrs Evans' friends arrived on 1 May. The letters give no intimation of plans to go to Russia nor any indication that he might be expected
there in June, and there was no sense of urgency in his movements.
Events seemed to be moving slowly, with Jones content to bide his time,
Yet, Roux states that Jones met Karl Radek in Nice, they became very
friendly and Radek invited him to attend the coming conference of the
Communist International.[2] If he knew that he was expected in Moscow,
he was being very discreet. Alternatively, when he got to Paris these
plans may have been discussed.

There was one early indication that Jones might have had some plans which were to take him on the road to Moscow. Writing on 1 February, he said that he had made contact with the local branch of the socialists. He was not taking part in their activities but had been busy 'writing for them an *exposé* of the political history of South Africa within the last 10 years'. The document, *Report on Communism in South Africa*,[3] was completed on 29 March 1921, but whether it was presented to the group in Nice (or indeed to Radek) and sent to Moscow, or whether it was sent to South Africa and then forwarded to Moscow, is uncertain. It certainly found its way to the Executive Committee of the Communist International and formed the basis of the South African report to the third congress of the Comintern in June.

Settling Accounts with the Past

The report provided an account of the ideas and activities of the small group of comrades who had launched the International Socialist League, and were about to become the core of the Communist Party of South Africa. None was more able to draft this document than Jones and it was published as a pamphlet in South Africa, both as a history of the movement and as a set of principles to guide the members in the future. It was also a vehicle within which Jones could continue the revision of his own ideas in the light of his growing understanding of social change. That is, it was 'a settling of accounts' with the past for Jones, and an attempt to charter a course for the future. Inevitably there were serious flaws in his account. He had still to find a formula that would elucidate the problems of ethnicity within class, and for this he would find it necessary to incorporate the ideas of the Russian Marxists. He also had to distance himself from the parochialism of the South African group and the narrowness of their grasp of colour issues.

Jones had adopted a new world (and even universal) outlook, but had come to it piecemeal. As a result, although old truths were replaced with new — and none were too small (or too large) to be confronted — Jones did not resolve some issues until much later. Consequently his discussion of the role of Africans in the working class movement covered a patch-work of problems, ranging from the history of conquest through the contemporary situation in South Africa. The report even set out Jones's new understanding of Dingaan's (Dingane's) Day — first told to the Evanses in his letter of 16 December 1911, and repeating at the time the conqueror's account of what had occurred. Under the heading 'Dutch Nationalism and the Native', Jones now wrote:

The great festival of the Dutch Afrikander people and of the Nationalists in particular is Dingaan's Day. This day is made the occasion of political appeals on present issues, as well as a com-

memoration of December 16th, 1838, when the Dutch Voortrekkers crushed the power of the Zulus in a bloody battle fought on
the Blood River, Weenen. On this festival the dual oppression
bearing on the small Dutch farmer are inveighed against: justifi-
able hate of British imperialism and of the British Chauvinists on
the one hand, and hatred of the progeny of Dingaan on the other,
his own hewers of wood and drawers of water. 'Presbyter is only
Priest writ large.' More glaring than in most Nationalist movements the freedom demanded from British rule is almost avowed-
ly freedom to more fully exploit the native.

Jones retained his disdain of rural Afrikaners and condemned the
parochialism and narrowness of a people who paraded on Dingane's
day and invoked 'the rifle and the sjambok . . . as the appropriate remedy
for native grievances'. He recalled the events of 1914 when 60,000 burghers were brought into the Witwatersrand to break the strike and the
trade union movement and he now noted that there was no white labour
movement in the rural districts. Furthermore, he condemned Afrikaans
as a 'crude patois' that was being 'tortured into requisition as a literary
medium' replacing the historical and literary treasures of 'the mother
Dutch'. However, he thought that the young Afrikaner intellectual
would not long endure 'such a self-imposed sentence of solitary confine-
ment . . .' Yet, he said, it was the Afrikaners who held out the hand of
conciliation to the British, and it was the latter who spurned the hand of
friendship. Furthermore, when Jones referred to the Afrikaner workers
he relented. They had become 'good trade unionists and loyal agitators
for their class . . . [but] always of course within the limits of their colour'.

Jones had been among the first to call for the organization of African
workers and his understanding was in advance of the thinking of his
time. Yet, in 1921 he still combined the crudest stereotyping with sharp
insights. After saying that 'the natives in their tribal land live very close
to the soil, they and their habitations seem part of it, elemental in their
simplicity of life', he changed tone, and exposed the real nature of the
African Reserves:

the function of the native territories [is] to serve as cheap breeding
grounds for black labour, the repositories of the reserve army of
native labour − sucking it in or letting it out according to the
demand of industry. By means of these territories Capital is
relieved of the obligation of paying wages to cover the cost to the
labourer of reproducing his kind.

The African, he said in the report, had no vote and no political rights
and a breach of contract at work [such as a strike] was a penal offence.
Mine workers worked on a system of indenture and were housed in
compounds. In the towns their dwellings were not fit for cattle and all
were subject to innumerable pass laws. Most had been in jail at one time
or another for contravention of these laws.

Unlike most other commentators Jones distinguished between the trade unions formed by African workers, and by the Congress, 'composed of chiefs, native lawyers, native clergymen, and others who eke out a living as agents among their compatriots.' African workers were able to grasp the difference between their union and the Congress and, he claimed,

the growing class organizations of the natives will soon dominate or displace the 'Congress'. The national and class interests of the natives cannot be distinguished the one from the other. Here is a revolutionary nationalist movement in the fullest meaning of Lenin's term.

He gave an account of the Industrial Workers of Africa and the Industrial and Commercial Workers of Africa, of the 'bucket strike' and of the shooting in Port Elizabeth, when Masabalala, the trade union leader was imprisoned. He spoke with pride of the strike of 80,000 black miners, 'without leaders, without organization, hemmed in their compounds by the armed police . . .' The ISL had called on white miners to show solidarity in leaflets headed 'Don't Scab'. The appeal had been ignored and:

The Mineworkers' Union Executive called upon its members to side with the masters and endeavour to run the mines, and publicly condemned our propaganda. But such is the division of labour in South Africa that whereas either black labour or white labour can stop industry, neither can properly start the wheels going again without the other.

The logic of the situation demanded a completely new approach. The white workers would not, or could not, accept the African workers as allies. The ISL could not win the white worker and yet 'was denied the support and inspiration of the great mass of propertyless proletariat on which the European parties are able to draw.' Appealing for assistance from the Comintern ('A few missionaries, revolutionists who need a spell of sunshine, would be very welcome'), Jones had to say:

The revolutionary movement depends almost entirely on a few advanced spirits drawn from the thin upper crust of Labour aristocracy. Owing to the heavy social disabilities and political backwardness the natives are not able to supply any active militants to the Communist movement. The immediate needs of white trade unionism, in which a number of our members are actively engaged, tends to throw the more difficult task of native emancipation into the background. The white movement dominates our attention, because the native workers' movement moves only spasmodically and is neglected. It needs a special department, with native linguists and newspapers. All of which require large funds, which are not available.

Herein lay the problem — and it was beyond the capability of the group of communists to find a solution. By January 1922 — less than a year away — they were to flounder on this very issue and crumble. Despite Jones's insights, many of the same errors can be detected in his report. But meanwhile it was time to move on and Jones left Nice on his way to Aberystwyth, where he planned to stay for some time.

He said in his letter of 31 March that if his friend was not in when he arrived, it would not matter. He would ensconce himself in his chair, until George Eyre returned, and then might go to south Wales for a day or two, or perhaps Aberdare, where he had a comrade who had been in South Africa a few years back. He would bring his books with him — but said that he had jettisoned a lot when he left South Africa. After leaving Nice, Jones went to Paris where he must have decided on a change of plan. On 20 April, he wrote again, this time to say that he would be visiting his brother Jim in London from where he would write. He did go to London where he stayed for a week with his brother.

Jones arrived at Ty Tingrad (the Evans's house) and finding George Eyre away, visited old friends, his aunt Jane Evans and spent the evening with JD Stephens. He stayed only one night The trip to Britain had to be curtailed, because a strike of Norwegian sailors was expected and he had to catch the early train next morning for Newcastle where he boarded a boat for Norway.

Black miners on strike in 1913 being rounded up by the police and driven back to work

14

DELEGATE TO THE
COMMUNIST INTERNATIONAL

Famine in Russia

From Norway, where his ship was bound, Jones went on to Stockholm and, writing to Evans on 22 May, he said Europe was a small country and he would have more time when he came back. He travelled on to Riga and then Moscow — entering a new spell of activity that was quite unforseen. From some accounts Jones came to Aberystwyth accompanied by a friend and there is mention of a 'princess'. Perhaps there was someone but this remains in doubt and he certainly had no close companion in Moscow from where he wrote on 21 August. In a previous note referred to, seemingly lost, he said 'we shall tell all about Russia on my return', adding parenthetically, 'editorial "we"'. Now he wrote that he had seen too little of Wales, 'just a dash through'. However,

> To me the world has become very small now, and a run over to Russia looks no more than a trip to Pontrehydfendigaid used to be in the old days!! Except that in the former case to have to watch the police! I did not know if I could get across until I got to Newcastle, and from there, if sent forward, the Norwegian Party were to tell me further. Hence I could not give much [account] of my goings, and left JDS to tell you privately.

It was warm in Moscow, as warm as in South Africa, and he hoped to be away before winter came. Having 'in some measure' fulfilled his mission in Moscow, he would be back in Wales soon and stay a few days at least. He sent greeting to his friends whom he hoped to see when he returned and spoke of his hope that he would be able to tramp through Cardiganshire and said that his health was fairly good — though not yet quite satisfactory. He made light of his illness insisting that they were well looked after, 'and not allowed to share in the privations of the poor Russian people' but, he remarked, the food was 'not exactly constituted for a chest complaint'. There was more than nostalgia in the words with which he closed the letter: 'I still remember that afternoon tea with eggs and nice bread and butter!!'

Jones wrote about conditions in Russia, of the famine, and the fortitude of its people. Perhaps, he said, the *Welsh Gazette* would publish a few articles 'if they were not too communistic in flavour'. He would send one or two and see. The people of Moscow suffered from lack of food, but they were not in the worst affected areas although the conditions were serious indeed, and the 'Moscow workers sacrifice a quarter of their daily rations, which is already small, to the relief of the famine areas':

> The result is that after the privations of seven years of war and civil war, and the blockade, and now the drought and failure of crops, the people are beginning to show that lack of stamina and mental vigour which I feel after only two months with specially favoured food. What wonder that they have to appeal for outside aid! They have done wonderfully, performed epics of martyrdom. And will do it again.

Sending regards to Stephens, he said 'Will write to him later, unless I return first!' He did not return. He was needed in Russia and, selflessly, despite the rigours of the weather, he stayed to serve as a publicist for the revolution, for Lenin and for the Third International. He wrote thousands of words that were published in the communist press in Britain and South Africa, but the letters he sent to Aberystwyth were not received — only a note in November 1922 to Evans, from his brother Jim in London, saying that Ivon had asked him to write because he was ill, and would write soon. It was not until 25 January 1924 that George Eyre Evans heard from him directly but, by the time a reply was delivered, Ivon had died. The letters that were sent from Russia to George Eyre, providing descriptions of events inside Russia, were lost in the turmoil of the time. What remains are the articles but what was lost were the more personal letters that were posted, if not received. What was lost, however, were the personal details that would have been priceless cameos, detailing conditions of life in revolutionary Russia.

Delegate to the Communist International

The Third International was formally inaugurated in Moscow in March 1919. Delegates came from both former war camps but the number that arrived was abysmally low. There were 51 delegates: 35 with decisive votes representing 17 countries. In South Africa the ISL gave immediate support to the new international and accepted the 21 conditions for affiliation. This was the realization of Jones's call in 1915 for a new international and his acclaim for the Russian revolution.

Intellectuals and workers in Europe, inspired by events in Russia, and despairing of the socialist parties, came to the defense of the first workers' state in history. Some visited Russia, arriving via Scandinavia and crossing the Finnish frontier into Petrograd. They came by stealth, breaking through the European blockade as part of a two-way traffic, for others left Russia because they opposed the Bolsheviks or found living in the turmoil of Russia intolerable. Many had been caught in the crossfire between reds and whites or were the victims of pogroms and they quit this inhospitable country. The two streams crossed, each unnoticed by or unconcerned about the other.

Poets, painters and writers came to Russia, some to support the government, others critical or curious about the new society being built. Journalists and writers interviewed the country's leaders and diplomats arrived to argue, bargain and intrigue. Isodora Duncan arrived to dance in the theatres, John Dewey, Walter Citrine and HG Wells (and many others) came to see what was happening or to press upon the new Commissars their own ideas for rebuilding Russia.

Some brought ideas that acted as a leaven in a country eager to effect change — but there was also a ferment inside Russia where people believed that a socialism was in the process of being built. Victor Serge, revolutionary and supporter of the regime, writing about 'Intellectual Life in Russia' said.

At this time, in spite of civil war, in spite of great privations, and in spite of the paper shortage and the enormous difficulty of accomplishing any great intellectual work in the face of the cold, the famine, the uncertainty of the morrow and the physical and nervous exhaustion of the whole world, there are nevertheless, in Petrograd and in Moscow, centres of intense intellectual efforts, and nearly everything that left the nationalized press was interesting, powerful, imbued with the intense, raw and violent life of the hour.[1]

Serge spoke of 'impassioned research, a certain grandeur, an effort wrapped in social transformation', of surging intellectual life and of Russia serving as a model for other countries.

Few visitors could be described as communists. Even delegates to conferences in Moscow knew little about Bolshevism and brought with them ideas imbibed from the IWW, the syndicalist or social democratic movements. Speaking about delegates to the Second Conference of the Comintern (July/August 1920) Serge was scathing in his characterization of the persons drawn to Moscow:

To tell the truth, outside Russia and perhaps Bulgaria, there were no real Communists anywhere in the world. The old schools of revolution, and the younger generation that had emerged from the war, were both at an infinite distance from the Bolshevik mentality. The bulk of these men were symptomatic of obsolete movements which had been quite outrun by events, combining an abundance of good intentions with a scarcity of talent . . .[2]

The situation did not alter in 1921 and Jones was closer to the Bolshevik ideal than many others who attended. Yet he too was profoundly ignorant of Russian revolutionary literature, knew little of the writings of the older generation of social democrats in Europe and had only a fragmentary knowledge of the works of Marx and Engels. His enthusiasm was invaluable and his industry welcomed by functionaries responsible for the daily work of the International. Jones learnt fast but, like many of his contemporaries, agreed uncritically with much of what was undertaken in Russia and his adulation of the leadership is transparent in the articles he wrote.

Jones travelled extensively in Russia, learnt Russian and read the local press (which he translated for English speaking delegates to Moscow). He wrote for the communist press in Britain and South Africa about the transformation taking place in Russia, reported on party and other conferences and discussed the contributions of the main speakers. He was also working on a series of articles on Lenin's writings for the British Communist Party just before his death.

Report to the Comintern

The road that took David Ivon Jones to Moscow was paved with hope. Not to find a release from the disease that had taken him from his beloved Aberystwyth — but the possibility of restructuring society in which he believed so fervently. This was, at least in metaphorical terms, the 'new Jerusalem' and he had entered it.

An edited (and mistranslated) version of his report on 'Communism in South Africa', written afresh by Jones appeared in the newspaper *Moscow*.[3] This provided notes for delegates who would have known little about the country and presented his (and the majority) view on the position of the white worker. Jones began with an apology:

The South African delegates [Sam Barlin — a tailor and trade union secretary — and Jones] were introduced to the bare footed, 12 year old delegate from the Novgorod Young Communist the other day. The first thing he asked us was 'Why aren't you black!'

Coming from South Africa, we feel quite apologetic about our colour. An African delegation should at least include Negroes. This will be remedied in time; but it would be a mistake to think that in future there should be no white South African delegates. The African revolution will be led by white workers. In Africa there are 150 million natives, it is true, and a few hundred thousand white workers. But the industrialised and semi-proletarianised native workers moving in and around modern industry do not number more than a couple of million. These are mainly found in the Union of South Africa . . . Here is the entry to the African Continent.[4]

He described the country, the provincial divisions, the railway that stretched from Cape Town to Elizabethville in the Congo and wrote of the Witwatersrand which produced half the world's gold.

This is the economic university of Southern Africa and of territories to the north. Here natives and whites are exploited side by side under two sharply distinct standards of life. Here you have the proportions of native [to] white skilled very much the same as those obtaining on the world scale: namely, a European factory proletariat, viz-a-viz the mass of Asiatic and African cheap labour. South Africa is thus unique in presenting a replica of the world problem revolving [sic] a solution for it.[5]

We are in the habit of calling these white skilled workers the aristocrats of labour. But they are not ordinary labour aristocrats. The white workers . . . had some very militant fights. [He described the strikes of 1913 and 1914, the massacre, and the deportation of nine union leaders].

It was in the 1913 strike that it first occurred to some of the most militant white workers that the native workers are also a factor in the labour movement. And from that time . . . a growing minority of the white workers . . . realise that the emancipation of the white can only be achieved by solidarity with the native, and . . . laugh derisively at the superficial socialism which ignores the native working masses.

Since then the white workers of South Africa have participated in the general enthusiasms from [for] trade union organization. But there has been a decline in general militancy although hardly a union . . . escaped conflict with the masters during the last few years. The general tendency . . . in the policy of the South African Industrial Federation is one of collaboration with the masters on Joint Boards, etc. The master class has realised that the white workers have to be humoured as a protection against the native masses, and as a means of keeping white and black workers apart.

He discussed the problems experienced in organising black workers:

Progress is slow! but that is due no less to the lack of resources in the Communist movement than to the backwardness of the native himself. For it is the peculiar task of the Communist movement to shake the native from his age old sleep. The Communist movement is almost a purely white workers' movement so far, and has its work cut out to keep the revolution before [them]. But it is . . . solidarity with the native workers, that distinguishes [it] . . . from all other sections of the labour movement in South Africa. The 'left' anarchist joins with the Labour politicians in branding us a 'kaffir party'. The native worker is the touchstone of [the] revolution. He can only [He alone can] organize the revolution. The 'kaffir stock market' [gold shares] in London rests on his cheap labour. It depends on his remaining illiterate and backward, and content with his pig-level of existence.

The very idea of native trade unions sends the master class into hysterics. Another shilling or two in their daily pay would create a panic on the market. But the native worker is not very worried about the problems of his boss. He is a typical proletarian. He is a lovable sort. We cannot listen to his loud uproarious laughter without being reminded of Marx's conception of a proletarian.

Jones spoke of black workers in struggle: of 80,000 unorganized mine workers who struck work for higher pay in 1920 and before that of the protest by Africans (in 1918) against the passes. Hundreds were marched off to gaol. Then came the strike by municipal workers which 'so alarmed the authorities that several members of the communist movement were arrested, and a grand charge of incitement to revolt brought against them'. He told of Luke Messina, usually described as a police informer, who actually played a very different role. It corrects earlier accounts, including his brief reference in 'Communism in South Africa':

The chief witness for the government was a native named Luke Messina, a member of the Industrial Workers of Africa ... He had been sent into the union as a spy by the Native Affairs Department, and informed us of the fact. After reading to the court the elaborate affidavit placed in his hands by the authorities, he told the court the affidavit was false in every particular, and the whole case broke down amid great sensation.

Our concern ... is not to emphasise the native movement to the exclusion of the white, nor the white to the exclusion of the native. Our message to the white is 'solidarity with the native workers'. In the white political field we have a fine opportunity of forcing the issue on the attention of the white workers with immunity from the police. And the echo of this propaganda reaches the native workers as well ...

The [white] Trade Union movement ... was naturally reflected by a fairly vigorous Labour Party, with a social democratic structure, to which the trade unions affiliated ... It had a right wing led by Creswell, a mine manager; and a left or more class conscious element, led by Andrews, a mechanic, who today is the secretary of the Communist Party of South Africa.

Jones explained the split in 1915 on the war issue and the formation of the ISL. Two candidates stood in the general election 'as a demonstration of its position and, as expected, got heavily defeated'. When the League then 'declared for a revolutionary platform regarding the native workers', most members 'slunk back' to the Labour Party.

What part will Africa play in the world revolution? Our Indian comrades are fond of that clause which says that European labour cannot emancipate itself without Africa and India; while the British comrades regard it as a moot point. This one thing is certain: the native workers of Africa feed by their labour a large battalion of White Guards in the West End of London.

He wrote of the Industrial and Commercial Workers Union of Africa (ICU); and said there was a group of blacks in the CPSA. 'And it is [now] evident that the black battalions of the proletariat of Africa and India must first be on the march before world capitalism can be brought to the ground'.

Barlin brought a 5,000 word 'official' report from Johannesburg. similar to Jones's longer report but lacking his punch. It too described the development of the (white) labour movement since 1910, the strikes of 1913-14, the break over the war and the emergence of the ISL. There were reports on the move to organize black workers, the anti-pass campaign (which it claimed, was organized by the IWA in conjunction with the SANNC), the strikes of black municipal workers [the bucket 'boys'] and miners (involving 40,000 workers daily) broken up by the police and 'white mobs of hooligans', and the formation of the ICU.[6]

The report said that Andrews had introduced the shop steward movement to South Africa after the British model, but this had not developed because the white workers had ignored the blacks and the shop stewards were bound to the Federation of Trades. There was also an account of the municipal 'Soviets' in Johannesburg and Durban.[7] the pattern in both was the same, with the blacks being excluded. But, ignoring the controversy in the pages of the *International* in 1919, the 'Soviets' were blessed with a new interpretation:

> The strategy was excellent in both cases. They wisely reckoned that as a permanent institution under capitalism the Soviet was impossible. After giving the rank and file a taste of their power, and the unconditional surrender of both councils, the Boards of Control or Soviets withdrew. Such experiments can only be successful by forcing the whole proletariat to capture control first of political power.

Quite what the delegates to the Congress made of this muddled thinking is unknown. There are no known reports of discussions on the documents but perhaps the delegates were too absorbed in what was happening in their own countries or in Russia and too ignorant of events in South Africa to offer any significant comment.

There could have been few delegates who did not follow with anguish the course of events in Russia. Although the civil war was effectively over, entire regions of the country were devastated by famine — leaving an indelible impression on all who witnessed it. Although the worst effects were passing by July 1921, its impact would still be discussed in the months to come. Serge, quoting from letters from the famine-stricken regions, said on 8 November 1921 that:

> Men and horses eat grass — it nourishes a little. Or else earth — one dies of it, but with a little less suffering. In order not to see them succumb they abandon their children. Samara is the centre of the devastated area ...
>
> Samara is a dead city. Children in the streets, lying on the sidewalks, thin and mangy dogs, coffins — rags, filth, stench, The horror. These children are abandoned. With their little fingers they search in the dung of horses for the remains of badly digested hay ...[9]

Against this situation other problems paled into insignificance and the New Economic Policy (NEP) was introduced, opening the market to farm produce. The Bolsheviks believed that, with NEP, the peasants would bring food into the cities again, but Lenin spoke of the return to market forces as a giant step backwards.

Serge said of the Third Congress that it started with 509 delegates representing 48 countries — 291 with votes, 218 consultative. Later, as more delegates reached Russia, the number increased to 603. But he was critical of the proceedings and said the atmosphere was:

> much the same as the previous Congress, except that the attendance was larger and the proceedings were more relaxed. With the coming of the NEP, the famine was getting a little less severe, and people anxiously expected a policy of appeasement to follow. The foreign delegates showed no interest in the tragedy of Kronstadt and, except for a few, deliberately closed their minds to any understanding of it. They sat in commission to condemn the Workers' Opposition; this they did with enthusiasm without giving it a hearing. They considered NEP amenably enough, to be (as one of the French delegates put it to me) 'an inspired turn to the Right' that had saved the Revolution. It was hardly inspiration to yield to a famine after the situation had become quite insupportable. But the majesty of the Russian Revolution disarmed its supporters of all critical sense; they seemed to believe that approval of it entailed the abdication of the right to think.[10]

It was a period in which the revolution was retreating and Alfred Rosmer in his memoir was less poetic than Serge, but equally damning

> in these delegations there were journalists, teachers and writers, some of whom said openly that they were not communists and they had come only to study some particular branch of Soviet activity. The differences which had emerged over tactics, the serious failures in Poland, Italy and Germany, encouraged among them a sort of dilettantish attitude . . . This helped to create an atmosphere of easy-going scepticism. These people carried no risk of being carried away by revolutionary passion.[11]

There was little or no criticism from these delegates of what was happening in Russia — nor could there be. As Serge had said (above) *'the majesty of the Russian Revolution disarmed its supporters of all critical sense; they seemed to believe that approval of it entailed the abdication of the right to think.* (my emphasis.)

Proceedings at the Congress were dominated by the Russian leaders, and a few of the more prominent delegates. The atmosphere was set by Trotsky's opening address. He spoke of defeats and disappointments and of mistaken actions and of a delay in the European revolution that had once been expected in months. Lenin was no more reassuring in his address:

It is plain at a glance that after the conclusion of the peace, however bad that was, we did not succeed in provoking a revolution in the other capitalist countries, though the revolutionary symptoms were, as we know, significant and abundant.[12]

Other delegates had a time and place to speak, but unlike the leaders they received little attention. Jones's contribution was mentioned briefly in *Moscow* on 15 July. He urged that the problem of the Negro which was centred in South Africa be considered by the Comintern, and moved that the Executive Committee of the Communist International (ECCI) devote serious attention to the blacks, and the workers' movement among the blacks, as an important part of the Eastern [that is, colonial] question.[13] Although accepted, nothing was done, and only when US blacks arrived in 1922 did ECCI act on this issue.

Jones wrote two reports on the conference. Firstly in *Moscow*,:

The Indian and African movements do not count for much in the great struggle now pending. But in the Indian and African masses? There for the first time Africa and India can say 'I know that my redeemer liveth' . . .

[The Comintern] brings in all toiling humanity, and says to the white worker, not only of South Africa, but of all lands, solidarity with the black working masses is the first step to emancipation.[14]

He concluded with a statement on the Indian and African people:

Their ancient weapons of spears and assegais were broken in their hands by the machine of capitalist industry, and the future offered nothing but the prospect of slavery in perpetuity. But the cry of the Petrograd workmen in 1917 was 'Long live the Socialist Republic in all countries!' and the cry is still travelling to the uttermost ends of the earth, to the lowest layer of the toiling people. And they are moving in response to the call.

He also described his contribution in the *International* of 16 September:

I was asked to speak, not so much for South Africa, but on the Negro question in general, the centre of which question, however, is South Africa. Most of my 'co-orientals' were dark or olive, and a murmur of surprise ran through the tables when they saw that the South African delegate was white! My remarks were directed to emphasising the importance of the whole question to the international movement, and to point out that in South Africa is being evolved a solution for the problem, the most aggravating form of which is found in America.

Jones impressed many with his devotion and seriousness and he was elected to the ECCI with a 'consultative voice'[15]. He returned to the Negro question in *Communist Review* in 1922. He had made friends among the Americans and used his newly found knowledge to write on 'American Imperialism and the Negro'. He said the US had extended its control of Haiti because of its concern over the strategic control of Panama and had come to dominate Liberia through indebtedness. He described US black organizations and condemned Marcus Garvey for condoning Imperialism by welcoming the 'intrusion of Yankee money' in Africa but commended the African Black Brotherhood which looked to Russia for 'guidance and inspiration in the struggle' and joined with class-conscious white workers in seeking proletarian emancipation.

The question of colour was to become a central issue in the general strike that shook the Witwatersrand in 1922. Jones reverted to the position he had adopted in the argument over the Johannesburg 'soviet' in 1919. He expended a vast amount of energy writing about the strike (corresponding particularly with members of the CPSA on policy)[16] and, at one stage in 1922, he contemplated a visit to Britain to raise support for the workers. Jones's belief that the white workers were central to socialist transformation in South Africa was wrong in 1922, as he had been wrong in 1919, but the ruthlessness of Smuts and the South African government and the news of the bombardment of working class areas were issues that he alone could raise from an international platform.

In July 1923 he wrote again on the 'Negro question', this time on behalf of a Comintern committee. The strike in South Africa had made him rethink some of his ideas and there was a shift in emphasis. It is also most probable that he sought the advice of his American friends. It seems more appropriate, therefore, to review that article after tracing the history of the general strike in Chapter 15.

A Publicist At Large

When Jones arrived in Russia he had only two years to live and for much of that time he was an incumbent of a sanatorium for tuberculosis in the Crimea. Yet, in the time available to him, he travelled extensively in Russia, took a keen interest in events in Russia and abroad, intervened in debates in the CPSA, and obviously sought to win support for the (white) workers' struggle through 1922. Although he made a lasting impression on the men (and women?) visiting Moscow, few have left notes of their contact with him.

He wrote two articles for the *International* from the Crimea on the need to apply the 'United Front' tactic in South Africa. These were a reply to an article by Manuel Lopes rejecting this course for South Africa. Jones's articles maintained that the CPSA would only find its way out of isolation if it secured a united front with the Labour Party. He called for the application of Lenin's tactic to win the support of workers who still considered the SALP as the party of socialism. Noting that the trade unions were no longer affiliated to the SALP, he said that the first step was to ensure that they returned to and controlled that party. He also directed attention to the communists' need to organize the black workers, and quite unrealistically proposed that the United Front use as its slogan, 'the abolition of indentured labour'. No one could be averse to this, he said. It would be accepted by white miners, it was a plank taken from Creswell's programme and it would demonstrate to the black workers that the communists' championed their cause.

Jones wrote to instruct the party members. Besides discussing local issues, he wrote either about events in Russia or about socialist theory. These were sent to Britain as well as South Africa. In writing about Russia — many articles appearing under the title 'Russia Day by Day' — he described the countryside and its people. Although these can be read as 'propaganda' (and that would not have been in conflict with his intentions) this was no departure from his style of writing — as is demonstrated by a reading of his letters to Evans.

'Re-Baptised With The Revolutionary Faith'

The most pressing problem in Russia in 1922-23 was the state of the economy. The debate raged on the significance of the NEP: was it working, was this a fatal retreat or an inevitable transitional period in the revolution? In June and July 1923 Jones wrote about the problem in the *Communist Review* — first as an essay on the significance of the policy for Russia, and secondly on proletarian reaction to the change.[17]

The June issue carried his article on 'The New Economic Policy'. His purpose was not only to explain what was happening, but also to reassure workers in the west that if there had been a retreat it was in order to strengthen the socialist state. In any case he argued, the Russian proletariat did not think it was a retreat: 'it was simultaneously a retreat and an advance'. He explained that in previous presentations of the case for the Russian revolution there had been an impatience to show that the Russian worker 'was already better off than the workers in the west'. This had been too optimistic and there had to be a reassessment of what was happening. Industry was languishing and, quoting from Lenin and Trotsky, he said that like any good army, the party had to know how to retreat and maintain good order.

The period of War Communism had created 'the illusion that the proletarian revolution involved the immediate socialising of every form of production and distribution down to the village shoemaker', but:

> Much of the Communism of the Civil War period differed very little in form from the 'War Socialism' of the Imperialist States, except that the one was in the interest of the workers, and the other in the interests of the capitalists, which, of course, makes all the difference in substance. But both were war necessities.

The proletariat had to capture power 'to protect its very interest', and to develop its own mode of production and distribution. But is was not yet able to do this on the morrow of revolution:

Without large industry there can be no proletariat. Without a proletariat there can be no revolution. Without all these there can be no Communism. Under 'War Communism' large industry languished, the proletarians were getting declassed, scattering in all directions . . . The Communism we strive for can only come from superabundance. The first task of the Proletarian State therefore is to produce superabundantly.

Jones ranged far and wide in discussing the problem, quoting extracts from Soviet leaders to make his points. 'It is not Communism that introduces the machine', he said, 'It is the machine that will introduce Communism. Lloyd George said that Bolshevism can't make locomotives. More wonderful things happen: locomotives can make Bolsheviks'. However, Russia contained a vast population not yet affected by industrialization, and NEP (said Lenin) 'arose from the need for an effective economic link between the peasants and the town proletariat'. He continued:

The petty bourgeoisie cannot be separated as persons from the petty bourgeois mode of production. Capitalist industry is easy to capture because the capitalists take no part in production. But the petty producers are a tangible economic mass which cannot be ignored as individuals. Unlike the capitalist class they represent an economic problem even when we have swept away their mode of production, and in Russia this mass is huge.

Nonetheless, Jones was optimistic. Hadn't Trotsky said that by 'holding the state power, the proletariat has the scissors with which it can at any time clip off private trade. . .' Jones also quoted extensively from Lenin: on his description of the Russian economy as 'State Capitalism' or 'controlled Capitalism'; on the need for 'strict accounting and control'; on the need for capital to build industry and on his warning that whole sections of the state apparatus, inherited from the old regime, were sabotaging the building of industry. Jones believed that the Russian proletariat would provide the impetus for transforming society and he ended the first article by citing the devotion of the Don Bas miners who, 'starving and cold, stuck to their machines to save the mines from being flooded . . .'

His second article was about 'The Industrial Heroes of "Don Bas"'. Written after a trip to the Donetz Basin in the Ukraine, he spoke about the organization of work in the locomotive works in Kharkov (which provided the answer to Lloyd George's sneers) and of mines in Kadivka, Pavlovka and Briansk. It was from this area that men had been mobilized to defeat the White-Guard general Denikin during the civil war. It was these miners who, during the occupation of the Ukraine after Brest Litovsk, demanded that the Germans pay Russia for the coal they removed. They paid,'and deported 300 of the agitators to Soviet Russia'.

The region was becoming an organic unity in which metal and chemical works and mines were interconnected, and all were fed by farms organized for the purpose. Here was 'a self-supporting unit, a Republic of its own, although the workers are anything but parochial in their outlook'. Jones, as he concluded in his inimitable style said, here was an example that deserved to be known everywhere: 'Anyone who wishes to be re-baptized with the revolutionary faith, let him go to Donetz Basin!'

The Church, The State and Famine Relief

Soon after Jones arrived in Moscow, Lunacharsky, the Commissar for Education, issued a decree (13 June 1921) forbidding the teaching of religion to any person under 18 years, except at home. This followed an uneasy period in which confrontation between the state and church had alternated between persecution and public debate on the role of religion in the country. The new Patriarch, Tikhon, who had been chosen by the church in November 1917, declared that the church was not concerned with political parties and accepted any government 'that came from God' — but because the Bolsheviks were professed atheists, he excommunicated the government. The Bolsheviks tried to establish a new church hierarchy under the more compliant Bishop Antonin but the power lay with Tikhon and for some time there was an uneasy truce.

The government also met opposition from the Catholic clergy and in Easter 1923 they were arraigned (as was the orthodox church) on charges of refusing to surrender church vessels to famine relief. The government also demanded an acceptance of the decree forbidding the teaching of religion. Catholic clergymen were tried for counter-revolutionary activities and one received a prison sentence. A second was executed in March 1923, leading to widespread condemnation in Britain and elsewhere. Tikhon was deposed, but the state backed away from bringing him to trial.

Jones had long since discarded his beliefs in Unitarianism but he does not seem to have written any account of his 'conversion' to atheism. The radicalization that followed his involvement in the strikes of 1913-14 followed by the war, had moved him onto a trajectory in which religion played no part. That had been enough and there had apparently been no need for a searching philosophical investigation of his religious past. But now, with the state confronting the church, he wrote several report on the trials and declared his own rejection of religion. His articles appeared in *Inprecor* and (more fully) in the *Communist Review*.[16] They aimed to explain the government's approach to religion and to the church — linking the new confrontation with the plight of famine-bound Russia. However, in using the articles to state his own acceptance of atheism (if that is what was intended), what he said sat uneasily with his own life-story. His account of attitudes in Russia, in which only a partial picture was presented, was in any case very different to that of his native Wales. Religion in Wales had played a radical role, so that generalisations from events as they unfolded in revolutionary Russia were not always valid.

The communists, said Jones, refrained from frontal attacks on religion. They knew that religion had two sides: it was both 'a reflection of the primitive outlook of the peasant' and it was also 'created by the exploiters who organize these native beliefs in the interest of reaction'. The communist state could not impose on the toilers a philosophy that was appropriate to a more advanced society but had to use the human side of religious belief to draw out the revolutionary conclusions, as in fact the 15th century reformers had inspired the revolt of the serfs. The backward classes, he said, could have free access to the Christian gospel, while at the same time religious superstition was combatted 'by the lessons of science'. Shifting the time sequence, he said:

The early Christians did not destroy the heathen temples, but took possession of them. This is the historical method adopted by the Russian Communists towards the Church.

But this was a dubious comparison. Were the Bolsheviks then to be conceived of as building a new religion? Or had Jones not seen where that kind of argument was taking him?

The immediate problem had arisen in 1922 because the Russian church possessed considerable movable wealth and, with the coming of NEP and forms of credit and exchange in the economic life, this wealth could be used for counter-revolutionary ends. Then came the great Volga famine and, as it became more harrowing, the state came into conflict with the church over the possession of this wealth — and ordered the appropriation of all valuables not essential to church rituals. Tikhon denounced the decree and, supported by enemies of the Soviets, urged resistance. The decree had been promulgated as an essential move to save millions from starvation and, in its enforcement, it was found that many of the most precious jewels, listed at the time of the revolution, had been sold for counter-revolutionary purposes. Subsequently, a meeting of the church synod called for the unfrocking of Tikhon and abolished the office of Patriarch.

The affair had been settled by the synod and, with that, Jones was satisfied. In fact he had tried to explain too much in too restricted an article. He had not really examined the basis of religion in Russia or elsewhere, had over-generalized from the Russian example and had linked the problem of the church to the famine, which would not necessarily have convinced any but the 'converted' in Britain or South Africa.

15

THE GENERAL STRIKE OF 1922

The Red International of Labour Unions

One of the bodies established by the Communist International was the Red International of Labour Unions (RILU) or Profintern. Its objective was to win the workers and their organizations away from the Amsterdam based International Federation of Trade Unions and build a revolutionary base from which to carry through the fight against capitalism. The first gathering, planned for 1 May 1921, was postponed until July to accommodate delegates attending the Third Conference of the Comintern.[1] There were 380 delegates present, 336 with voting rights. From the outset the syndicalists present, clashed with Comintern leaders on the status of the RILU. They demanded a complete break with existing trade unions and independence from the Comintern.

Alfred Rosmer, a member of the Executive Committee of the Communist International and a founder of the RILU, opened the conference. He had the unenviable task of having to press the Comintern demand for an 'organic link' between the trade unions and itself. He had been a revolutionary syndicalist in France before joining the Communist Party and would have preferred a more conciliatory approach than his official position allowed. He believed that the opposing opinions were not all that divergent and that delegates 'equally devoted to the Revolution, and to communism' could be contained in the same organization.

The anarcho-syndicalists, and particularly the French delegation, claimed that the position of the trade unions had been decided by the Charter of Amiens, which established the autonomy of the unions from political parties. Some of these 'pure syndicalists' had withdrawn from the Comintern conference and, when they spoke of the 'true principles of trade union action', they were greeted with angry shouts: 'You're always talking about the general strike, but you never make it. It's us who do that'.[2] The divide between syndicalists and communists at the conference was exacerbated by the confrontations between the two sides inside Russia. There was the seamen's revolt at Kronstadt, the emergent forces under Makhno in the Ukraine and the break with the left Social Revolutionaries, leading to arrests and, in some cases, arbitrary shootings. Delegates demanded the release of all those held by the police and there were angry exchanges when the conference closed.

Jones was present and, accepting fully the Bolshevik government's position on the anarchists, attacked them trenchantly in November 1921 in the *Communist Review*, journal of the British Communist Party.[3] He displayed a bitterness that is not often found in his writings, saying that what Plekhanov wrote about the 'propaganda of the deed' was amply demonstrated by the armed bands of Makhno and the bomb throwers whose release was being demanded. He scorned anarcho-syndicalists who opposed relations with Communist Parties or the Comintern and 'evaded reference to the Soviet Republic and the Dictatorship of the Proletariat' but could not demonstrate how they would 'pull down and keep down the bourgeois state power [nor] how they will build up a proletarian state upon its ruins'.

Jones accused the anarcho-syndicalists of petty bourgeois utopianism, of claiming that they wanted to keep the movement purely proletarian yet ignoring the overwhelming power of the bourgeois press which 'gave bourgeois minds to common proletarians'. They wanted to break up the capitalist state but were unable to build another in its place. Finally he maintained in his article that

> Anarcho-syndicalism in the hour of revolution would halt the proletariat at the stage of immediate demands, at the stage of disrupting the capitalist state power in the interests of the petty bourgeoisie, without going forward for the formation of a proletarian state power in the interests of the proletariat. We are here speaking of class motives, class designs of an instinctive character imposed upon workers by petty bourgeois anarchism. In actual effect, of course, the conditions for the most effective struggle for the immediate needs of the proletariat are also, in the revolutionary crisis, the condition for the attainment of the ultimate objective. The means and the end become one. The dualism of the peaceful era of capitalism vanishes.

Jones attacked anarchism and other currents that posed as socialist. The Guild Socialism that had attracted him before the war was condemned because it 'long[ed] for a state of consumers' and his reformist pacifism of 1914-6 was finally discarded. Such positions, he said, were futile, childish and harmful and their counter-revolutionary potential was realised in Kronstadt and the camps of the White Guard. 'Forward' he thundered 'to the Communist International, not back to the Charter of Amiens, is the test of true revolutionary policy today'.

This was an article written at a historical moment in the development of events in Russia, antagonistic to those who prevaricated in the face of counter-revolution but avoiding discussion of the fault-lines that were opening up in the Soviet Union, whether in Kronstadt, the Ukraine or elsewhere.

Just two months after the syndicalists demanded a general strike at the RILU, it seemed to became a reality in Johannesburg. This was an event that few parties in the Third International understood and Jones offered an analysis. He was now speaking on a world platform, but his message was also directed specifically to his comrades in South Africa.

He wrote on the strike while it was in progress and provided an analysis of the event in his (long forgotten) 'The Workers Revolt in South Africa'.[4] Jones was well informed of events and his article contained some penetrating insights but he still harked back to his polemic with Bunting at the time of the Johannesburg 'soviet' in 1919, and repeated in his report on *Communism in South Africa*.

The Origin of the Strike of 1922[5]

The general strike of 1922 was one of the most traumatic events in the struggles of the mainly white working class against their employers and the South African state. Although it started as a dispute against wage cuts on the mines, the strike developed into a revolt and ended with the aerial bombardment of portions of Johannesburg and the Witwatersrand. The workers were pounded into defeat, leaders of the strike were killed (or ostensibly committed suicide) and three men died on the gallows.

It was a pitiless struggle, leaving the organizations that had been actively engaged in the strike severely weakened. The trade union movement entered a period of dormancy and the white miner's organization, almost destroyed as a result of the strike, was effectively incorporated into the state machinery. The Communist Party suffered a decline that left it ineffective over many years. The strike also had a profound effect on the political future of South Africa. The incumbent government of General Smuts was defeated at the polls by a coalition of the National and the Labour Parties in 1924 — leaving the way open for National Party hegemony, until it merged with the South African Party (led by Smuts) in 1934.

Employers in South Africa, caught in the post-war depression, had called for the replacement of white workers by blacks. In July 1921, EJ Way, president of the Institute of Engineers, spoke for many when he called for the removal of half the white workers and the employment of skilled black labour. He said the ending of the 'sentimental colour bar' would save over £1m per year: £419,000 in wages and £600,000 for paying the recruiters of black labour. If labour costs were lowered, low grade gold mines could be reworked and other areas, idle for want of capital, would also be opened.

In his *Report on Communism in South Africa* Jones offered his explanation of the urgent need felt by the employers to replace the white workers. He said then that

> During the war, the capitalists, urged by the necessity of keeping up gold production, discovered that it paid them to regard the white workers as an unofficial garrison over the far larger mass of black labour, and that it was not bad business to keep the two sections politically apart by paying liberally the white out of the

miserably underpaid labour of the black . . . The premium on the
mint price of gold enabled the Chamber of Mines to keep up this
policy of economic bribery till the end of last year. Now it seems
as if it had come to an end. The bribe fund has petered out. The
premium on the mint price of gold is being reduced and under the
threat of closing down the non-paying mines the white miners are
compelled to accept lower pay. During the last few months there
have been unofficial strikes [at the Simmer Deep last year] . . . The
mines have withdrawn the 'stop-order' system . . . [This made] the
Union an adjunct of the Chamber of Mines. Now this 'privilege'
has been withdrawn as a measure to weaken the none too pliant
membership. . .

In December 1921 the mines, the electrical power stations (the VFP)
and the engineering companies announced wage cuts and an end to both
piecework and underground contracts for white workers from January.
It was also widely held that the colour bar, which guaranteed white
workers their jobs on the mines, would be scrapped. All attempts by the
Mine Worker's Union and the South African Industrial Federation
(SAIF) to secure arbitration was rejected by the Chamber of Mines. The
workers resolved on strike action. On 31 December they set up an Augmented [strike] Executive, consisting of the executive of the SAIF and
representatives from forty affiliated unions, under the chairmanship of
Joe Thompson, The white coal miners came out on 2 January and, short-
sightedly, they told the blacks to stay out of the struggle. There was no
call for solidarity action. Supervised by officials, the black workers supplied the country's coal without any difficulty.

On 3 January the Chamber announced plans to axe 2,000 white
miners and it was rumoured that larger numbers would be made redundant. On the 9th over 20,000 men answered the strike call, closing mines,
some private engineering firms and all VFP stations, except Rosherville
— which supplied power only for pumping and lighting in the mines.
Despite some regional defections, most stayed out throughout the
strike. Negotiations to end the strike, which extended from 15-27
January, failed to reach any agreement.

Old themes resurfaced. Bunting reported that at many strike meetings there was talk of phthisis. Men said: 'We have but a few years to live
in any case; we may as well stop a bullet as linger in mortal disease'. The
memory of 1913-14 was ever-present: at a funeral procession in
Boksburg for two men shot dead a banner stated 'Remember 1913' and
a SAIF banner read 'Remember our Comrades murdered in 1913'.

The strikers of 1922 were bitter. From the beginning they declared
this to be no 'ordinary strike'. It is a strike 'for the future of South Africa,
a strike in which all selfishness has been cast aside', said Thompson.
Creswell, leader of the Labour Party, declared in mid-February that the
strikers were fighting 'that the industries of South Africa should be

conducted on lines contributing to the mass of the people . . . they should
from all classes receive the fullest support and financial help'.[6]

On 5 February 1922 the *Sunday Times* reported an address to strikers
by Jack Cowan, Mayor of Springs and a former trade unionist, in the
Johannesburg city hall. He was even more emphatic.

> Rather than go down in the struggle we are prepared as a last
> weapon to have a revolution . . . There have been two wars in my
> lifetime, and I have fought in both . . . If it comes to fighting, and
> God forgive that it should, I am going to do a bit of fighting for
> myself this time. I have done enough for the other side. I have
> always recognised and supported governments, but when govern-
> ments want to down you and your children, and when Smuts, the
> Prime Minister, is backing the Chamber of Mines to put the white
> standard of South Africa in the background and the Black stand-
> ard in the foreground, it is time for every man to put his thinking
> cap on . . . if we have to fight . . . some of us will go down, but what
> is the difference . . . in a year or two, half the people in this hall will
> go down with phthisis. What is the difference between having to go
> down a hole to die or having to die fighting for a chance for your
> kiddies.[7]

The trade union movement was in financial difficulties when the
strike began. The SAIF and the South African Mine Workers Union were
penniless and, although some unions, including the Boilermakers,
Reduction workers, Woodworkers and Engine drivers were better
placed, most were unable to provide strike pay. Consequently a central
fund was set up for the alleviation of distress among miners who were in
need of food. Street collections, plays, dances and horse races were
organized to raise funds. Contribution came from sections of the white
middle class and, more importantly, from farmers who sent provisions
over several weeks, alleviating the conditions under which the miners
lived.[8]

The Augmented Executive was large and unwieldy and there was
little consensus on the strike or its progress. Only a few of the affiliated
unions came out on strike and only a small number agreed to come out
if called upon. The National Union of Railways and Harbour Servants
did not join the strike and the trains carried troops from coastal towns
to the Witwatersrand without hindrance. Despite sympathy for the
miners and resentment over pay and working hours, strikes on the railways were illegal and those that came out would lose their privileges as
civil servants.[9] The Typographers also continued work, printing anti-
strike commentaries in the newspapers. There was no popular paper
providing strike news and support for the strike until the *Transvaal Post*
appeared on 13 February. The paper claimed to be 'The Champion of
an economically free South Africa' and declared that it was fighting for
'the supremacy of the White Race'.[10]

In protest against the use of scabs, public amenities were cut off: power workers walked out in Johannesburg plunging the city into darkness until volunteers got the machines working again.[11] By the end of February trams had stopped running in Johannesburg; squads of commandos marched around the town, watched by police who kept them moving. Seven hundred special police, paid and armed, were used to protect mine property and there were reports of attempted train wrecking, of train derailments and of power pylons being dynamited.

Headlines in the press proclaimed: 'An Organized Revolution', 'Red Regime Atrocities', 'Unadulterated Bolshevism', 'Lenin's Last Desperate Attempt'. A journalist writing on the strike said:

> Today Johannesburg is only dimly beginning to know that it has escaped from the foul conspiracy which seized on the strike as a means of Bolshevism . . . As an individual who witnessed the growth of violence, who has seen the attitude of Bolshevists, who has seen the mob defiance of the police, who has witnessed the attacks on Natives . . . and who has day by day wondered at this plague of unredeemed brutality of men and women, I say there was a calculated design to repeat on the Rand the unnatural outbreak of crime in Russia that horrified the entire world.[12]

Support from the white middle class did not last. Inconvenienced by the stoppages, the average Johannesburg citizen joined the special constable force to protect persons and property, and to reduce the effectiveness of scab hunters. The farmers, who sent food to the strikers also grew impatient. Drained of resources they sent less and less to the strikers and some warned that they would (and subsequently did) answer Smuts' call to join with the armed forces to end the strike.[13]

On 13 February, Smuts, represening the government, met a deputation but refused their moderate requests to end the strike. He insisted that the miners go back and accept the best terms available to them, pending a parliamentary settlement.[14]

The Commandos

In mid-January, when the trade union leadership was obviously faltering, strikers, organised on semi-military lines, and known as commandos, were growing in strength and in influence. Present in districts, sub-districts, and in every town on the Witwatersrand (but lacking arms in most cases)they elected commandants, generals, and captains. Some were formed by trade unions and athough they kept in touch with the local strike committees they acted autonomously. Some were peaceable, others wanted to use force. Initially they were straggly bands of men, but former officers with war-time experience soon instilled discipline.

As soon as commandos had learnt to march in columns, they eagerly showed their smartness to the public, and to other commandos. Soon they were marching through public streets to mass demonstrations, each commando headed by buglers, a mounted section on horses, and then the 'infantry' on column of route. After the infantry came the cycle and motor cycle section, which formed the dispatch riding, scouting, and later, in some cases the dynamite laying section of the commandos.[15]

The first commando, composed of smallholders at Putfontein on the East Rand, were all republicans. On the night of 18 January they disarmed and imprisoned two policemen guarding a pump house near Modder East mine and, after merging with another armed commando, resolved to attack police camps on the East Rand. This was vetoed by union leaders who ordered the policemen's guns restored. Yet, at the end of January, 500 men paraded in military formation at Fordsburg (Johannesburg). The commandos said that they proposed to preserve the peace and good order, stop scabbing, protect property, and defend white society against black marauders. The men were trained to unseat horsemen and taught how to make bombs but, initially, they remained friendly with the police. Their fight, they said, was against the magnates, not the authority of the state. This changed after 4 February when there were reports of widespread scabbing in several coal fields. When the SAIF called meetings across the Rand to get workers to stand fast, General Smuts gave his assurance that adequate protection would be afforded scabs to restart the mines. He brought in the police and it was this that led to a regimentation of the commandos.

The government had been preparing for a show down even before the strike began. The Defence Committee of Trade Unions, composed of trade unionists reporting on the strike, said in their findings that: 'The 1914 Martial Law proclamation was carefully revised and printed as early as the 30th January 1922'. The Minister of Defence, not to be outdone, boasted on 8 April that he 'had been prepared for this affair from the 1st of January not only (sic) from the 30th'. The state consequently moved to stop the commandos. A proclamation of 7 February, signed by Colonel T G Truter, the Commissioner of Police, stated.

The use of bodies of men such as commandos to pull out officials working on essential services constitutes a crime of public violence, and every person who forms a unit of such body or commando, or who counsels, instigates or incites to the commission of such act is guilty of the crime of public violence, and would, if convicted by the courts, be subject to heavy punishment. The police have been instructed to take action in all such cases.[16]

From 8 February men on several gold mines expressed the desire to return to work. The police were ready. Pickets were arrested and by mid-February picketing had almost stopped. On a few occasions there were clashes with police and, where the police fired on the crowd, a number of strikers were killed.

The leader writer of the *International*, writing on 10 February (before this proclamation was published), had no doubt about the importance of the commandos, even if they did make mistakes.

The Red Flag commandos of the Rand are a real contribution to working class weapons and one for which, as far as we recall, there is no precedent in the industrial history of the English-speaking working class at any rate.

... We salute you Red Guards of the Rand! You are better men on 'commandos' then you ever were in the stopes and shops. It is fit and proper that you should appropriate the military formation and discipline hitherto monopolised in your master's cause, for your own. You are learning to discard what masters and pastors had taught you, the lies that soldiering must mean soldiering for the bosses and their pirate flags. You are teaching yourselves and your fellow-workers of the world that there is only one army worth joining, the Red Army, and only one cause worth living and dying for, the cause of the Red Flag, which alone can ennoble war and bloodshed.

In Moscow Jones concurred. He said that the commandos were 'in open preparation for an armed conflict . . .' They intimidated and arrested scabs and had them tried at the Trades Hall and they set up Red Cross sections in preparation for battle. Woman's commando were set up and one of them tried to get the operators out of the central telephone exchange.[17] After skirmishes with government troops, he said, commandos took possession of some white working class suburbs, but, he added, the strike committee was split: some wished to limit the action, others prepared for the expected bloody conflict.

Meanwhile Smuts defended his approach in Parliament. When National Party leaders said on 17 February that the strikers' aim was to prevent a curtailment of the whites' sphere of work he claimed that most workers opposed the strike. The mines were being worked out and increased costs required cuts. To maintain a white South Africa (on which he agreed with the opposition), a lower scale of living was needed:

White South Africa would be immediately more helped by the maintenance of the low-grade mines in full force, and the whole of the gold mining industry at work, rather than by the retention of the *status quo* agreement [namely, the ratio of whites to blacks employed underground].[18]

Revolt . . . For a White South Africa

The revolt on the Rand was confined exclusively to whites. Despite the presence of Africans at some of the rallies they were not involved in the strikes or in the revolt that followed. Nor was there any appeal to black workers to join the strike, although some white miners condemned

African workers for scabbing. Unsurprisingly there was no support from any black organization and the leaders of the SANNC, except for one letter from the Transvaal section appealing for an increase in wages for the workers, stood aloof from the struggle. There is no statement on the strike in documents of the SANNC available to me. Only some African chiefs and headmen, summoned by the Native Recruiting Corporation, toured compounds to quiten down the workers.

Dr Abdurhaman, the leader of the African Peoples Organisation condemned the strike and the crimes of white labour. The white workers were only interested in preserving their privileged position in industry and had been content before their own wages had been cut. They had done nothing to improve the wage packet of black workers on the mines.[19] The ICU, not yet organized in the Transvaal, could only speak from afar. At a meeting in Cape Town (no date given), Kadalie 'condemned the attacks on non-Europeans' and called on the government to protect the people. He also 'blamed the colour bar for the trouble on the Rand, and demanded its abolition'. When there were calls from the strikers for an armed revolt,

> the ICU called on non-whites to be loyal to the government, King, and country. On its side the government assured the country that the Africans had done nothing to cause trouble.[20]

This assurance would not prevent Smuts from proceeding with discriminatory legislation against the Africans after the white workers were dealt with. But for the duration of the strike the government was assured of black support and the white workers, contemptuous of the blacks, seemed oblivious of the consequences of their policies and actions.

The slogan 'For a White Africa' appeared everywhere during the strike and, in retrospect, this stamps the events of 1922 as racist. For many of the strikers the slogan was undoubtedly racist but the issue, as seen in 1922, was more complex. The interpretation given to this slogan by many trade unionists, and by the CPSA, was related to the prevailing standard of living of whites and the contrasting conditions under which blacks lived. With white miners earning seven to ten times more than blacks, their replacement would increase the mines' profitability considerably. It would lower wage levels and reduce all standards of living. The *International* stated in an editorial on Friday 27 January 1922

> Natives at starvation wages, that is the thing to attack: that is what ruins the white standard. Well, then, if you want 'White South Africa', your campaign . . . must be rather in the direction of encouraging native labour to become 'unpayable expensive'. . .
>
> The white workers are under a very real and proper fear of competition from this cheap labour: in fact, except for a few skilled trades and the protection of the colour bar, they cannot compete with it under capitalism, and in fighting for the colour bar, they are at best fighting only a rearguard action . . .

Fellow workers, ask yourself, am I really for the whites as whites — landlords, magnates, profiteers, exploiters and all — or am I rather for the workers as workers, white, brown, yellow, black and all — and against the capitalists as capitalists — THE ONLY REAL BLACK MAN?

It is not in the spirit of the Voortrekkers who conquered Dingaan . . . that you will achieve a White South Africa. It is in the spirit of the humble but very determined industrial proletariat of Russia, who overthrew the master class and made work, for the common good, the one condition of 'status'. There is no remedy for the situation, there is no future for the white workers, under capitalism. Communism alone can make South Africa a white man's country, in the sense that Communism alone can secure to every worker — whatever his colour — the full product of his labour. Only when that is secured will a White man be safe: only then can you begin to talk of a 'White South Africa'.[21]

By using the slogan of the day, the writer of the editorial endorsed the worst aspects of white supremacy. The argument against the capitalists ('the only real black man"!) used the race prejudices that afflicted white society. Despite appeals to revolutionary events in Russia and rational arguments against trying to hold onto an unreal status quo the party's definition of a 'white South Africa' was fatally flawed.

Jones argued differently. In his one article on the strike in 1922 he condemned the British press, either for its silence, or its reports justifying the massacre of workers. 'International finance', he said, 'looks after its own'. The strike, which continued for eight weeks, presented 'lessons of great importance' for the international working class, because:

(1) It presents us with the problem of colour prejudice within the ranks of the workers in its acutest form, there, where the conditions for its solution are already maturing.

(2) It is the first great armed revolt of the workers on any scale in the British Empire.

(3) It presents one of the most striking examples of the use of the aeroplane as the supreme capitalist weapon against the workers, and suggests serious problems for the military mechanics of revolution.

(4) It is a victory for imperialist capital, on the one hand extending its tenure of life by expansion, on the other performing a revolutionary role by drawing in still wider masses of the backward peoples into the world movement.

Yet Jones's analysis proceeded on the premise that the white workers stood at the forefront of the South African revolution, an argument that dominated policy in 1922. These white workers, and in particular the miners, had now 'revolted' against the Chamber of Mines, the embodiment of capital in South Africa. Jones explained:

The Johannesburg gold mines produce more than half the gold of the world. They are concentrated in a single management, with the ultimate control in London ...

The gold mining industry of the Rand has been described as the fulcrum of world capital. Twenty years ago the old Boer republics became an obstacle to the Chamber of Mines, and the whole British army was requisitioned to blow them out of existence ... After the job was done the Rand magnates got leave to import fifty thousand Chinese workers under indenture.

These were repatriated, said Jones, because the mine magnates had discovered that 'the Chinaman was too much of a revolutionary to be profitable'. Their departure had raised anew the question of recruiting black workers for the mines. There were 200,000 black, and 25,000 whites on the mines. 'Herein lies the root of the conflict. The white miners are a block to native progress'. This repeated what he had said in his *Communism in South Africa*. That is, that the class consciousness of the white worker was 'so far, fitful and easily lost. He is used to lord it over the unskilled native as his social inferior'. Moreover, black labour was little more than the assistant to white labour:

As workers whose functions are wholly different in the industrial world, there is hardly any competition involved; indeed, the white miner is as much interested as the Chamber of Mines in a plentiful supply of native labour, without which he cannot start work. They are therefore annoyed at any strikes of natives, and are prone to assist the masters in their repressive methods, although in the case of white strikes they are not behind-hand in appealing to the natives not to go down the shafts ...

If Jones had stopped at that point his understanding of events in 1922 might have been very different. But, he continued, ' ... natives as a rule are unwilling to go without the white miners'. Contrary to what he would say a year later, he spoke of the African's use of the word 'boss' in addressing white workers as a convention like 'sir', and animated by 'respect for the white worker as his industrial educator'.

One of the white miner's nightmares, he said, was the loss of his monopoly over blasting underground. This he took up again in his article on the strike, where he said

Their legal privileges are an anachronism. *Yet no Communist can withhold support of their resistance to the capitalist offensive.* (my emphasis)

Since the repatriation of the Chinese repeated attempts have been made to open up the skilled positions to the natives, and to break down the legal [job] monopoly of the white miners ... The question became acute at the end of 1921. The low exchange value of the pound sterling had for two or three years enabled the mining industry to sell gold at a premium. With the improved position of the pound sterling as against the dollar, the premium is disappearing, and the mining industry is compelled to work on the bare mint price of four pounds five shillings.

The employers, needing capital to open up the undeveloped portions of the Reef, wanted more than 'a mere drop of wages': they required a drastic reduction in the number of white skilled workers and a more intensive exploitation of black labour.

Industrial black labour, said Jones, consisted of men in the engineering and other industries who were becoming proletarianised, and the mine labourers who greatly outnumbered the whites but could not take decisive action. He dismissed them summarily and unfairly as:

> the lowest possible form of cheap, unskilled labour drawn from one of the most primitive peoples in the world, politically passive and industrially unorganized, recruited on indenture from the tribal reserves, and housed round the mines in closed compounds under strict police supervision, with hardly a vestige of civil rights.

The situation was explosive, but problems created by the division of workers on grounds of race seemed insoluble. Jones explained:

> The white workers . . . yield a power quite out of proportion to their numbers. They can stop industry. But this passive native mass is a constant menace (*sic*) to them, and is used against them by the capitalists, whereas the white workers fail to take the surest means of securing their position by common organization with the natives, as advocated by the Communist Party.
>
> The condition of affairs accounts for the state of armed conflict into which the general strike developed. At the last it was a conflict for the control of the industry, for the abolition of the Chamber of Mines, and for ousting Smuts from power.

Side by side with this analysis Jones descended to crude populism. Gold mining capital, he declared,

> rules directly by the bayonet and the policeman's baton. It brutalises whole masses of the backward peoples. Their noble naivete (*sic*) can only be preserved for humanity if the working class movement is able to snatch them from the grip of capital without too great a loss of time.

Discussing the social forces in South Africa, Jones said the Afrikaner nationalists had nothing to do with the rising. Initially they supported the strike [and at that stage farmers gave strikers cattle as gifts or on deferred terms and shopkeepers gave generous credit terms]. They then repudiated the strike and contingents of white farmers joined with Britishers in suppressing the strikers. Yet Jones declared that this was not a colour issue:

> It was not a conflict of whites against blacks, but a pure class struggle between the politically conscious workers, who happened

to be white, and the capitalist class . . . The international offensive of capitalism spreads to the colonies . . . In South Africa it takes the form of a demand on the part of the Chamber of Mines that the mining regulations be altered to allow cheap native labour into more skilled positions. This means larger gangs of natives working under fewer skilled whites . . . a demand for the general reduction of wages [and] a reduction of one fifth in the number of white workers . . . Hence it was for the white workers a question of very existence.

For the communists it was also a question of 'very existence'. Believing the white miners to be 'politically conscious workers' they backed them, underestimating the impact of racial antagonisms opened up by the strike.

The Defence Committee started from a different position but employed similar arguments. It said wages were never mentioned and the struggle focused 'on the question of the Colour Bar, including the Status Quo Agreement'.

[The] dominant principle for which these men fought was the old principle vital to the welfare, if not indeed to the existence, of every civilised community, for which men have always fought and will always fight as long as they are men and not emasculated parasites, and that is that free men will not tamely submit to be ousted from work and they and their descendants degraded into pauperism by the substitution of slave labour.[22]

African labourers were described in terms similar to that of Jones. Their conditions, they said, were akin to chattel slavery; they lived in closely guarded and policed compounds and were paid starvation wages. This would not be tolerated by a white 'unless he were a convict'.

With such a system of labour the European cannot compete, and would not if he could since it must in the end degrade all labour to that level, unless a clear line of demarcation can be drawn and maintained.

[The ending of the Status Quo Agreement would] extend that form of Negro slave labour to all the occupations which had hitherto been free labour occupations and . . . oust the dearer Europeans from them.

They said the mine owners and their political supporters deceived the world in claiming that the colour bar 'was an irrational and immoral attempt to keep black labour in subjection for the benefit of white workers'. And here, they too descended to the ubiquitous racism of South African whites.

We do not deny that there is some, although very little, truth in that. The aversion of all white races to living and working on a basis of equality with the Negro no doubt enters into the matter; but a part of even that aversion is due to a sound instinct to

preserve the purity of the race and part is due to an instinctive
perception of the fact that the European worker who accepts
equality with the Negro tends to become in the end . . . a Negro
ceasing to live up to the standards, traditions and inspirations of
the great White race, which can be the heritage of them alone. The
mere fact that the Negro submits (*sic*) to be compounded is, in
itself, sufficient to make it impossible for him ever to be an associate on equal terms of White men, whose ancestors have fought
their way to freedom . . .

[The dominant reason for supporting the colour bar was] a deep
seated and righteous objection to the extension of the slave labour
system which is known as compounded Native labour.[23]

The Defence Committee said that workers held two points of view:
one which claimed that low grade mines could only be worked at a profit
by unskilled black labour, which they could accept because gold mining
was a temporary phase and not a permanent part of national life. The
other view was that these mines could be worked profitably by whites
who were paid adequate wages.

But all of us are agreed that the slave labour system, existing as it
does only by virtue of special legislation, must be kept by legislation within the narrowest possible limits.[24]

The Committee's position was absurd as was Jones in failing to see
what was clear to some members of the CPSA. Frank Glass, secretary of
the Cape Town branch, where the strike had little support, stated in the
International on 17 February, that the white workers were too backward,
their trade unions too weak and the party's forces too insignificant to
make a revolution — and part of the reason lay in the racism of the white
workers which disqualified them as leaders of a united working class.[25]

Call for a Republic

Early in February the General Strike Committee instructed workers to
'see that all scabs from Roodepoort to Geldenhuis Deep [mines] are
withdrawn immediately . . .' The miners were both frustrated and angry.
It was at this stage that Tielman Roos, the leader of the Transvaal National Party, called a conference of Nationalist and Labour MLAs. On
the eve of the conference, Bob Waterston, now leader of the Brakpan
commando, moved at a Johannesburg meeting that:

This mass meeting of citizens is of the opinion that the time has
arrived when the domination of the Chamber of Mines and other
financiers in South Africa should cease, and to that end we ask the
members of Parliament assembled in Pretoria tomorrow to
proclaim a South African republic, and immediately to form a
provisional government for this country.

Waterston elaborated:

We realised that this was the last step and not the first. But . . . when the provisional government is formed in Pretoria, as tomorrow we hope it will be, it will be a constitutional step, and it will lie with the other side to attack this provisional government and put it out by force.[26]

Nationalist and Labour MLAs were horrified. Tielman Roos denounced the idea of revolution and one Nationalist said that Labourites had fought the 1914 rebels — let them wait till the next election before talking about a republic. Labour MLAs were also opposed to the proposal and spoke of treason. They said people would be shot on the streets of Johannesburg. There was no support for Waterston despite his claim that 90 per cent of workers were prepared for any step rather than go down without a fight. Within days he withdrew his proposals and blamed others for having suggested the plan to him. There was also no support for Percy Fisher (who spoke for the strike committee) when he proposed that a provisional government would be formed that afternoon to take over the mines. Finally a conference committee advised constitutional methods to secure a change of government.

Racist Attacks?

There was never any picketing of blacks working on the mines. Jones, in trying to explain, had to repeat the racists' arguments

No violence had been made against them on the part of the white workers — only against the skilled workers who blacklegged. Natives were not regarded as scabs, their whole outlook and mode of life being too primitive (*sic*) for the conscious workers to attribute any responsibility to them.

He also commented on a photograph, which he said, appeared in a 'capitalist journal' of a crowd of strikers bearing a banner — the banner that has haunted socialists in South Africa ever since:

WORKERS OF THE WORLD, UNITE AND FIGHT
FOR A WHITE SOUTH AFRICA.

'In the crowd', he said, 'several black workers were to be seen. Till the fifth week of the strike this slogan did not betoken any race enmity. That dastardly evil was left for Smuts to do'.[27]

The commandos responded to rumours of black rebellion and over the course of a few days there were ugly clashes between whites and Africans in Brixton, Vrededorp, Ferrairastown, Sophiatown [all working class suburbs or black townships of Johannesburg] and the new Primrose mine near Germiston where African workers attacked a procession of strikers with assegais, revolvers and pickhandles. According to Herd, blacks were attacked by the crowd and many had to be rescued by the police: several were killed, and more than 20 injured. The police claimed that this fighting was a ploy to embarrass the authorities and intimidate citizens. Strike leaders claimed that the region was inflamed and that blacks were arming and anxious to attack whites, but, they said, it was mainly non-striking hooligans who attacked blacks.[28]

Jones explained, using material he had received from South Africa, how, once again::

> The cry of native rebellion, with its mythical horrors of rape and massacre, always conjured up to confuse the class issue, was again set going; and it diverted many of the strikers for two or three days from the real issue.

The Communist Party maintained that the blacks were armed by mine officials and used as mine guards. The fact that fighting started simultaneously all along the Reef pointed to a concerted and organized plan and news of the clashes surprised at least some of the strike leaders. Fisher and others of the Committee of Action threw themselves between excited whites and blacks to stop the fighting. The CPSA intervened by printing thousands of leaflets that read:[29]

LEAVE THE KAFFIR ALONE!
WORKERS, HANDS OFF THE BLACK WORKERS!

It is not they who are your enemies, but the Chamber of Mines which exploits both them and you.

Keep your attention fixed on defeating the Chamber: that is your only job in this strike.

The Chamber's agents and CID [police] provocateurs have repeatedly tried to foment trouble between whites and blacks in order to divert your attention from your only job in this strike. Remember that they tried on the same game when the Municipal Board of Control was established in 1919, and they succeeded then.

DON'T FALL INTO THIS TRAP AGAIN

The natives will not fight unless someone goads or incites them to do so. See that you do not play that part, and treat whoever does as the worst of scabs. Beware of police frame-ups.

LEAVE THE KAFFIR ALONE!

The Defence Committee claimed that whites only attacked Africans on three occasions. Firstly, on 7 March, when blacks stoned a procession of strikers outside New Primrose mine, the men together with whites who came to their assistance retaliated by attacking mine officials and Africans. In the fighting two whites and two blacks were killed and twenty blacks wounded. The other cases involved whites who were not strikers. They attacked the Municipal Compounds in Marshallstown and in Ferrairastown: five Africans were killed and eighteen (including three whites) were wounded. They also claimed that Africans killed four whites in Sophiatown and rioted and threw stones at whites in the vicinity of Fordsburg and Apex railway stations. The trouble said the Committee 'was confined to an area of not more than two square miles out of the 150 square miles affected by the strike . . . where Negroes and Europeans live cheek by jowl in slums and in extreme poverty . . .' In these fights between poor whites and blacks, a white man and an Indian woman were killed and an African wounded in Brixton. The Committee added that the blacks on the Rand were afraid and justifiably armed themselves with knives, etc, but the feared Native uprising never took place and the blacks were well behaved (*sic*).[30] The evidence suggests that the confrontations were exaggerated. Hessian, who was biased against the strike and the strikers, nonetheless said in his dissertation that:

> There were a few occasions in which commandos attacked Africans, but these were ascribed by strikers, by the Transvaal Native Congress and the government to older workers (sometimes described as 'hooligans') who came from the poorer areas.[31]

The Move to Martial Law

In late February the level of violence rose. Strikers assaulted white scabs and 'police spies' and placed them on 'trial', paraded provocatively, and so on, while the police arrested strikers and commando members. Finally the police fired at strikers who gathered at the Boksburg jail to serenade their imprisoned comrades with the *Red Flag*. Three were killed and several wounded. It was said later that the shooting was pre-planned, ostensibly to establish police authority.

An approach by the strikers' leaders, now in an enlarged or Augmented Executive, to meet with the Chamber of Mines on the 3 March, when the strike was crumbling, was rejected and, in a provocative letter, the mineowners informed the SAIF that they would not be recognized in future.[32]

A move by the Augmented Executive to end the strike was rejected by the strikers and a Committee of Action, backed by the Commandos, was set up, consisting of Andrews, H Spendiff, George Mason, Percy Fisher, J Wordingham and E Shaw. On Sunday 5 March this committee met with delegates of strike committees from across the Reef and called a general strike. At this point the 'more temperate strike leaders faded out of the picture'. The response was confined to the Rand. Some unions called their workers out, some did not, and others, like the railwaymen only came out after their families were threatened by strikers.

Smuts watched and waited. On 31 March he said that as early as the 17th of February he and his colleagues, feared that for a couple of days they might lose control of the Rand, but they had decided to give the country an object lesson with reference to the subterranean, menacing dangers even at the risk of a couple of days revolution in Johannesburg.[33]

Answering a call from the Committee of Action, thousand of men from the commandos came into Johannesburg. They patrolled the streets, recruited workers and pulled shop assistants out of stores; they commandeered rifles and revolvers; wielded bicycle chains attached to sticks, old swords and bayonets, spears, assegais and poles barbed with spikes or hooks.[34] The police were reinforced by the South African Mounted Rifles and the Civic Guard, bringing their strength up to 8,000 men. There was shooting between strikers and scabs and clashes between strikers and blacks. The government, refusing to negotiate with the strike leaders, responded with force and used aircraft to disperse gatherings. The preparations of 1918 to use an aeroplane had become a reality, not against black demonstrators, but against the whites on strike. On Thursday 9 March the Active Citizen Force and 26 burger commandos were called up and martial law declared by the Friday. This heralded the end of the general strike, but at the same time brought a crowd estimated at 90,000 onto the streets of Johannesburg. That morning armed revolt broke out.[35]

It transpired from court cases and the official Martial Law Enquiry of 1925 that Commandant General AA Sandham, a miner, had ordered commandos to gather at selected spots armed with rifle and revolvers, bombs, sticks and stones. But no one body was in control of events and several commandos, who were not contacted, played no part in what followed. Many prominent strike leaders knew nothing about the mobilization and few of those who did parade knew what the assemblage was about. When questioned during the subsequent court cases or the official Enquiry, members of the commandos gave diverse reasons for their involvement. Some had been told there was a 'Native rising' and they were to rescue the women and children, others heard that there was to be a drive against scabs. There were those who had been told that they would overthrow the government and the capitalist class, and if only they could take the police stations and hold out for 24 hours, thousands of men in the OFS would swarm across the border with arms to help the revolt. There were even stories about Americans who would be coming to assist.[36]

Early on the morning of the 10th the commandos attacked railway property and police posts. For several days banks, shops and offices were closed by order of the local strike committees; restaurants, cafes and hotels got permits to open at meal times; produce was commandeered and butcher shops emptied of all meat; newspaper vendors were chased off the streets. Some telegraphic communications south of the Rand were disrupted and some train lines blown up, but the post offices opened under police guard.[37] Householders foraged for food and, with menfolk away, women set up elaborate warning systems for self-protection. Snipers were active in the southern suburbs of Johannesburg and typographers who refused to strike at the *Star* were armed to protect themselves and the premises. Jones provided a graphic account of events in his article on the strike:

The outlying mining towns of Benoni and Brakpan were already dominated by the armed strikers. In a few hours aeroplanes were hovering over the scenes where commandos were mobilizing. Boer commandos were soon on their way to fight for the government . . . An aeroplane dropped a bomb on the Benoni Workers' Hall, and blew the whole building full of executives and strikers to atoms.

[In] Johannesburg, the workers' commandos took possession of the working class suburbs of Fordsburg and Jeppe . . . They also entrenched on the neighbouring low hills overlooking the military camping ground. Here half a dozen aeroplanes operated on these positions with deadly effect . . . Artillery bombardment proceeded at the same time, but the position was stubbornly defended, and only given up after terrible losses. Here where no bourgeois property was endangered, the aeroplanes could operate with impunity.

Fordsburg was different, said Jones. From there the centre of Johannesburg could be controlled and air attacks would have led to destruction of valuable property. Then, after all other resistance had fallen, Smuts threatened a general ground bombardment and the Boer commandos and the regular troops massed for the final assault:

Here, in those few tragic hours, the brave victims of capitalist ferocity atoned many times over in blood and tears, and deeds of heroism that move the proletarian heart, for the anti-native outrages committed in their name a week before. Here the red forces were directed by Fisher and Spendiff, two miners' leaders followers of the Communists, and while ardent strike militants, most fervent partisans of the negro workers at the same time.

The bombardment was expected to last ten minutes. It went on for seventy minutes . . . It was only a question of time, and the issue was never in doubt, for Smuts only directs final assaults for political reclaim when the issue is absolutely safe.

Fisher and Spendiff were killed, said Jones: 'On Spendiff was found his membership card of the Communist Party. Thousands of prisoners were taken, and the militants weeded out for the court martials'. Jones was not to know that a month after the article appeared four men would go to the gallows and that another fourteen had death sentences commuted. He concluded with the claim that the revolt on the Rand had inspired workers in Australia — and that 'the deed of indictment against capitalism [was] filling up from every land and every clime; and the roll of honour of proletarian heroism [was] growing from Africa, Australia and India . . . '

In its response the Comintern condemned the imprisonments and killings and said the mine magnates' aim was to reduce the living standards of white workers to that of blacks. However, its analysis of the struggle could only lead to further confusion among its adherents. It said that the strikers were mainly Afrikaners, while the capitalist side was almost exclusively represented by British subjects. Eventually, Afrikaner nationalism and the class struggle of Afrikaner workers would be linked. The task was to break down the race prejudice of the South African white workers and link them to the Negro and other coloured proletarians in a common fight which would be both national and social.

But the tide had turned in South Africa and the labour movement surrendered its class aims for a minority stake in the government. The SALP joined with the National Party to defeat Smuts in the general election of 1924. The CPSA gave its support to the electoral pact and then, drawing back, urged Labour not to join a coalition government. Hopes for uniting black and white workers receded and the CPSA went into decline as its members either deserted or were ostracised by the trade unions. Acutely aware of the difficulties, Jones stated in his letter of April 1924, just before his death, that:

> As a matter of fact, there is no room for a CP in white South Africa *except* as the watchdog of the native, as the promoters of rapprochement, watching *within* the broader organizations, for every opportunity to switch the white movement on right lines on this question and scotching every conspiracy to rouse race hatred and strike breaking of race against race.

The pain that Jones must have felt when the revolt failed is revealed in the letter. His work in South Africa (1910-1921) had been devoted to building a socialist movement in the country. However the 'white movement' was not switched 'on the right lines' and there was no 'rapprochement' inside the labour movement. With few exceptions white and black workers were not brought together in struggle because the social forces holding them apart were greater than any conceived common interests. That was a dilemma with which socialists in South Africa would have to grapple in the decades to come.

It must remain a moot question whether they were successful.

16

FOLLOWING THE GLEAM

Lenin and World Revolution

There were few occasions in which Ivon Jones did not refer to, or quote from, Lenin when he wrote about events in Russia. He saw him as the architect of all that was precious in the building of the new society and the inspirer of world revolution. The adulation found in Jones's articles was not very different from that of other adherents of the Comintern.

Jones had come to Moscow without any reservations. He had been an admirer of Lenin since 1917 and under his editorship, or guidance, Lenin's name had appeared again and again on the pages of the *International*, as the leader of the Bolsheviks and the architect of the October Revolution; as the leader of the new state and inspirer of world revolution; the proponent of industrialization and the man who switched the economy along new tracks to rescue it from collapse. Then came news that Lenin had been shot. Jones wrote from Moscow on 14 April 1923 to say that Lenin was recovering after something approaching a stroke, but the bulletins indicated that he would never be the same again:

> If he can only be kept alive, even if he does not work, his name and his word are such a power in Russia, as to become a legend — but all through mentally he is unimpaired. Trotsky at the Ukrainian Party conference moved a touching resolution of greeting to Lenin. Trotsky is taking more and more active part in the apparatus of the industrial administration.

Jones added in the *International* of 18 May that Lenin's last public pronouncement concerned the establishment of a Control Commission to stop a counter-revolutionary move by non-party members. He did not question this measure and was unable to foreshadow the way in which it could be mis-used to remove or destroy all the old Bolsheviks and ultimately to place all power in the hands of one man..

Trotsky was revered alongside Lenin in the International Socialist League as architect and co-leader of the revolution. Writing from Russia, Jones linked the two names, quoting from both their speeches to explain what was happening. Now that Lenin was ill, Trotsky's name appeared even more frequently — as if party members were being prepared for a new leader of the revolutionary movement. Trotsky was proclaimed as the Red Army leader, as economist and as industrial manager, and Trotsky was quoted on the NEP and on the peasants.

On 1 June 1923 the *International* printed an article by Jones, written on 22 April. The first topic was Lenin's health. He had been forced to

miss the Communist Party conference for the first time since 1917, when
he had been in hiding from the forces of reaction in revolutionary Russia, 'But Lenin dominates this Congress nonetheless. The issues discussed are raised by him'. It was Lenin who had warned 'of the danger
of the state machine running away from the control of the proletariat
and its directing organ, the Communist Party'. The principal aim for the
coming year, as formulated by Trotsky, was the closer alliance between
the peasants and the proletariat, under the hegemony of the latter.
Under the heading 'Trotsky as Industrialist', Jones wrote:

> It is significant that Trotsky wrote the thesis and delivered the
> report on Industries. It is assumed that he will take over the direc-
> tion of the Supreme Council of National Economy. I was told by a
> comrade that the 'specs' (bourgeois specialists) in that depart-
> ment are shaking in their shoes . . . The army is the one great
> department where punctuality is combined with courtesy . . .

> By the way, Trotsky is learning English in his spare time and
> everyone is anxious to help, so that he will be able to address the
> Comintern Congress in four languages instead of a paltry three!
> Whatever position he takes in the direction of industry, it is as-
> sumed he will remain the head of the army.

The *International* reported the following week on the two main items
of the Congress: Trotsky's speech on industries, 'a masterpiece of
penetrating analysis', that demonstrated the centrality of state industries
for the dictatorship of the proletariat and the tribute paid to Lenin when
hundreds of non-party delegates visited the congress bearing 'presenta-
tion flags for the party and for its leader'.

During the coming months Lenin seldom appeared in public. He was
fighting for his life and striving to save his party from the degeneration
that was to overtake it so soon after his death. The struggle within the
ranks of the Bolshevik party received little or no publicity and it was
Lenin's life that was the talking point among most party members. On
21 January 1924 Lenin died and on 2 February Jones wrote the first of
his commemorative articles: 'Lenin the Immortal'. The essay appeared
in the *International* on 14 March and was devoted to a discussion of
Lenin's break with the Mensheviks on the question of party organization. Jones had been studying the pamphlet *What Is To Be Done?* and the
polemics surrounding the split in the Social Democratic organization. In
his opinion, the new direction given to party structure was central to the
success of the October revolution and, because the work was not known
to English speaking readers he had decided to devote his article to it.

A second article, entitled 'Lenin's Death and After' appeared on 4
April. In another glowing tribute to the man and the leader Jones said:

> How great a personality was this, when everybody, a whole nation
> leaned upon him as upon an everlasting rock, as the great
> 'tovarisch' [comrade], whose friendliness seemed to permeate a

whole people. And yet he spread this all-pervading friendliness without seeking to. He was ever concerned about the nuts and screws of the machine of emancipation.

Jones spoke of the recruitment of tens of thousands of workers into the party. Like others he interpreted this entry of politically unsophisticated members as a tribute to Lenin and Lenin's party. He continued:

Lenin never preached on matters of personal conduct or morals. But it may safely be said that no saint or preacher ever had such an influence on people as the very character of Lenin's, his crystal simplicity of mind; his simple manner of living, though all the luxuries of Russia could be at his command. This is the unprecedented fact in Lenin which has captured the heart of the people. For the first time in history they see a man striving for an ideal, achieve great power, and still strive on, simply, serenely, combining great power with a great ideal.

In seeking to demonstrate the advance of socialism Jones found no issue too small or too trivial. He discussed the minting of small coins and the advancement at the Yalta sanatorium where Bolshevik-trained doctors and administrative staff were replacing the old Czarist officials. He also returned to the question of the Central Control Commission which he described as an instrument for controlling bureaucratism and for building socialism. There was an irony in this article that would only become apparent later. Both the Control Commission (led by Stalin — although his name never appeared in the articles), and the inflow of untried workers into the ranks of the party, were to be used to subvert the Soviet state. But that was an issue for the future. At this point Jones saw in these events the strengthening of the new state and its protection from the very men who were about to take control. Then, almost as if it was an afterthought, the article came to an abrupt end that seems to have been overlooked, or been ignored, in the years to come:

If my letter seems, as usual, inordinately optimistic, that is not because I wish to convey that everything in the garden is lovely. No! but what is unlovely is not significant of the trend of things — an indisputably disappearing factor which the revolution is sweeping away. Russia is only interesting to me as the vanguard of Communism. And one must write about those things which show that it is leading on to victory.

There were no further articles (or 'letters') in the *International* and no disclosure of what was 'unlovely'. But it is doubtful whether Jones, isolated in the Yalta sanatorium — and grateful for the attention he was given, would have disclosed his doubts in 1924. For him it was a necessity that he write only *'about those things which show that it is leading to victory'*. This blind faith was to become one of the great obstacles to those who tried to reappraise the nature of the Soviet Union in the years to come. Trotsky and Serge stood in the forefront of those who wrote to warn of the degeneration of the Soviet state and it is doubtful whether Jones would have remained silent had he lived. This must remain in the realm of speculation because David Ivon Jones did not live beyond 1924. Unfortunately the vast majority of party faithful did remain silent.

Lenin's First Writings

In May 1924 the British journal, *Communist Review*, printed Jones's article on 'Lenin's First Book' and he was asked to write a series of articles for the British party on Lenin and his contribution to socialist thought. He wrote only one piece: 'Lenin's First Newspaper: A Spark that Grew into a Great Flame' and this appeared in the July issue of the *Communist Review* with an editorial note stating:

> This article . . . was one of the first to explain for English-speaking readers the outstanding role played by VI Lenin in establishing the Bolshevik Party, of his newspaper *Iskra*, and of his famous work *What is to be Done?* — not at that time available in English.

Almost all of what Jones wrote in his two articles was new to his readers, few of whom had seen (or heard of) the newspaper *Iskra* (*Spark*), or read Lenin's writings. In his articles, Jones was historian, socialist propagandist and revolutionary instructor. He was also, in the spirit of the time, adulatory and uncritical. Whatever Lenin had written was sacrosanct and essential for the training of young revolutionaries. The author believed, furthermore, that it was not enough to discuss the books that Lenin had written. The reader had to know the background of the people against whom Lenin was polemicising and the movements in which they appeared. Lenin's message had to be spelt out for an audience that did not have a background in Marxism. In 'Lenin's First Book', there was a short history of the Narod movement (that is, of the Narodniki — or 'populists'), an account of their move to assassination, and their claim that Russia did not have to pass through the 'stage of capitalism'. Lenin disagreed profoundly with the Narod philosophy and took issue with their leaders — claiming that capitalist relations already existed in the country. Instead of leading the students along the false path of 'peasant [that is petty bourgeois] socialism' they had to be directed to revolutionary Marxism.

Jones had read, in the original Russian, Lenin's writings on the Narod movement, and quoted from them — not only to demolish the populist arguments, but also to explain Lenin's contention that the urban proletariat stood at the centre of the revolutionary struggle.

> Subjected to the same bourgeois exploitation that in substance is the exploitation of the whole of the labouring population of Russia, this class ['the factory worker, the city proletariat'] is placed however, in specially favourable conditions for its emancipation: it is altogether divorced from the old society, a society wholly based

on exploitation; the very surroundings of its life organise it, compel it to think, and give it a means to enter into political conflict'. Lenin called upon the revolutionary intelligentsia to join the class in its struggle.

The Narodniki, said Jones, had 'passed into history', but Lenin had said that the social-democrats would take up the democratic demands, 'sharpen them, and make them more profound'. The workers had to build up their own movement, which could then enter into alliances with other parties on 'concrete issues', but the spirit of the book was against the degeneration of such alliances 'into wholesale promiscuity'.

This article ends with Jones's own translation of the last paragraph of the book, calling on socialists to devote their entire attention to the proletariat. When this class had 'imbibe[d] the idea of scientific socialism, the present isolated economic conflicts would be transformed into a conscious class struggle. Jones concluded on the note:

One is at a loss which to marvel at most: Lenin's great faith in the proletariat, or the proletariat that vindicated that faith. Lenin and the Russian proletariat 'climb the hill together' from the very foot.

'Lenin's First Newspaper' was written as a commemorative essay and the tone was accordingly exhortatory. The concluding words rang out in messianic tones: 'And his deathless name shall still lead us on from strength to strength; and revolution after revolution shall be monuments to his memory'. This was more than sentiment: Jones had accepted Lenin's ideas on party organization completely, and he used the occasion to sketch the historical background to Lenin's call for a party of professional revolutionaries, maintaining that this alone had led to the Bolshevik victory in 1917.

Jones's article provided the first account available to many Social Democrats of the early history of the Russian party: of the organization in exile of the Emancipation of Labour group in Geneva and of the formation of the League of Struggle for the Emancipation of the Working Class in St Petersburg, led by Lenin. Then followed arrest and exile and, while Lenin was in Siberia, the emergence of Social Democratic groups in all the large Russian cities, but they lacked experience and were broken up by the police. What was needed, said Lenin, was a party in which group activities were directed from a central body.

It was not only a matter of organizational form. The young Social Democrats spoke incorrectly of the worker's economic struggle as paramount, and dismissed political struggle as the task of the liberal bourgeoisie. They wanted concrete results and decried ideological discussion and theory. 'How familiar all this is to any party worker', wrote Jones, 'no matter in what part of the world he may be!' The liberal bourgeoisie and the petty bourgeoisie both wanted revolution, of a sort, and they saw in the working class a force to be exploited politically'. But the question was:

Whose revolution it was going to be, whether the proletariat should be a tool in the service of the bourgeoisie, or whether it should retain the lead in the revolution [and this] depended on the correct proletarian tactics and the correct methods of organization in these critical days.

Recalling the debates of the first social democrats of Russia, Jones said that Plekhanov had corrected the intelligentsia who said that the proletariat were necessary for the revolution by saying: 'No, on the contrary, *the revolution is necessary for the proletariat*'. (his emphasis)

After serving his sentence Lenin stayed briefly in Russia before going abroad to organise, with other exiles, the newspaper *Iskra*. Lenin's ideas on party organization, sketched in its columns, were reformulated in his book *What is to be Done?* Jones concentrated on a few topics from the book, choosing those which he thought were relevant to the young communist parties of 1924. He outlined Lenin's contention that the workers on their own could not advance beyond 'trade union consciousness' and Lenin's attack on the 'economist' theory that the workers were only interested in material issues. The elemental movements of the masses, said Lenin, imposed on Marxists the duty of forming an efficient organization of revolutionaries. Only when so directed would it become 'a real class struggle'.

Jones then highlighted the issue of democracy in the revolutionary movement. Lenin demanded a centralised party, based not on democracy 'but on the mutual faith of comrades'. 'Vulgar democratic tendencies in the Party reflect bourgeois party tendencies' said Lenin and Jones concurred. Jones noted that when the Duma had functioned temporarily before the war, the party had had greater freedom of action and there were elections in the party organization. Only when Tsarist Russia reverted to its old despotic ways had the party returned underground – and it was only now, after the conclusion of the civil war, that 'workers' democracy' could apply inside the Russian Communist Party.

Jones quoted Lenin as saying that the workers 'respond to every case of oppression, violence and abuse, no matter to what class they are applied'. Only then would they stop being the 'rearguard of bourgeois democracy'. Given this programme, Lenin had declared, the Russian proletariat could clear away the buttress of European and Asiatic reaction and 'make the Russian proletariat the advance guard of the international revolutionary proletariat'. This said Jones, had come to pass. 'Whatever Lenin set himself to do he achieved'.

Once Again, The Negro Question

Jones was never free from the effects of tuberculosis and the rigours of Moscow were not conducive to any respite. He had expended a vast amount of energy over the strike in 1922 on the Witwatersrand and this proved almost too much for his health. He had kept at his work for too long and had ignored new symptoms. When examined it was found that he needed an operation because of a 'TB growth'. Although the operation was slight, it had been almost too much for him. He had survived but had to move to the Crimea in order to recuperate. On 17 November 1922 he wrote to Johannesburg from the Crimea to say that in August his comrades in Moscow had ordered him 'down South over the damp Autumn months'. The letter, printed in the *International* on 10 February 1923, painted a picture of the Crimea in glowing colours and was yet another advertisement of the glories of the Soviet state.

> On the way down to Simiferopol . . . the landscape in late August was an ever changing feast of green freshness here, and golden ripeness there, and brown earth further on, where no sooner is the harvest garnered when the plough begins anew for the sowing of the winter wheat.

His fellow passengers spoke of the novelty of having the trains run on time after the turmoil of the civil war. The area had not yet been cleared of White Guards but that would be achieved soon. Jones could see no wrong: the officer he met was 'a fine type of proletarian commander, little given to talk, no bookworm, but a proof that the working class has the elements that can rise to grapple with any situation'.

He stayed for some months in Yalta and then, impatient at being away from the centre, he returned to Moscow.

.When however the Communist International met again in December 1922, Jones was still receiving treatment in the Crimea. He did not even meet with Bunting (who was the South African delegate) and was unable to participate in the pre-conference discussions. Warren K. Billings from the US reported on the Negro question (printed in the *International*, 2 March 1923) and although he started his report by speaking about the colonial question, most of his address was devoted to the position of blacks in the US. He ended by presenting a 'thesis' on the negro question. This was probably drawn up by a Comintern committee — and seems to have been based more on hope than substantive fact. Billings said that there had been a movement of revolt among the colonial people against imperialism after the war and it was recognised by the colonial powers (and by US magnates) that the further accumulation of capital depended on more intensive colonisation of regions inhabited by the black races. He then moved a resolution couched more in terms of ethnicity than of class, calling on the Comintern to support 'every form of negro movement which tends to undermine or weaken capitalism or imperialism'; to organize negroes everywhere and form a united front 'when negro and white working masses coexist'. The resolution also called for work among negroes to be carried out by negroes and asked that immediate steps should be taken to hold a negro congress in Moscow.

When Jones returned to Moscow he presented his own 'thesis' in an article (in the *International* on 13 July 1923) entitled 'Africa's Awakening: For a World Negro Congress'. It called on 'Party organs in Britain, America, Belgium, etc., . . . [to] devote special attention to the negro question and to the preliminary work necessary for the calling of a World Negro Congress under the banner of the Comintern'.

Jones had thought afresh on the problem since the general strike and this was reflected in his new writing. In a passage that foreshadowed the writings of CLR James and Eric Williams on the relationship between slavery and capitalism,. he said:

[The Negro] is the greatest living accuser of capitalist civilization. The wealth of England and America is built upon his bones. The slave ships of Bristol and New York, with good Quaker prayers to speed them, founded the fortunes of many a Christian home. Every capitalist government is drenched with the blood of the Negro. British capitalism in South Africa, the French in the Cameroons, Belgium in the Congo, and the German Empire in Damaraland — they all constitute the blackest record in human history of mass slaughters and human violation of every primitive human right continued up to the present day. Even the liberation of the American slave was only an incident of a civil war between two factions of property holders engaged in a quarrel over the forms of exploitation, and was not the aim of the war as is commonly supposed. And as an aftermath of that war there was created a social attitude towards the Negro race which leaves the one time chattel slaves still degraded outcasts among the peoples of the earth.

Racial animosity, he said, was 'artificially generated'. It pervaded all Anglo-Saxon society and had also infected the working class.

The African Negro is the hewer of wood and the drawer of water even for the white workers of Europe. The workers of England are trained from childhood to regard the Zulu and Matabele wars as heroic exploits, rather than foul pages in English history. Hence the apathy and social prejudice towards the Negro race, for we hate most what we have injured most. But this period is passing, just as the days of the Second International are passing. The workers of Europe are no longer sharing the profits of their masters. The Communist International has appeared, and calls into the one great proletarian family the Negroes of Africa, as well as the peoples of the East, along with the revolutionary proletariat of the capitalist countries.

He condemned previous congresses 'composed of . . . the very thin layer of negro intelligentsia, who placed vain hopes in professions of loyalty to their oppressors . . . [and] greeted the recruitment of negroes into the French army as a mark of citizenship', as well as those called by

Garvey 'who has captured the imagination of the Negro masses in America, and whose slogan "Back to Africa" and "Africa for the Africans", are even spreading into Africa itself'. It was the Comintern which offered the 'first ray of hope for the Negroes throughout the centuries of their oppression' and blacks at the Fourth Congress of the International favoured a World Congress of Negroes. He continued:

The proletarian character of the Negro mass is not so distinct in America as for instance, in South Africa ... [where] the Negroes form a race of labourers, without any shopkeeping or small tenant element. Probably the small property psychology of the tenant farmers and the small trader element in America reflecting on the purely labouring Negro masses has a lot to do with what is now notoriously known as 'Garveyism', a charlatan exploitation of awakening race consciousness which, in so far as it takes anti-white forms, is secretly encouraged by the capitalist class both in America and in South Africa. The number of Negro farmers, mostly with very small holdings, according to the last American census, was 949,889, which with their families, represents a big proportion of the Negro population in America.

But awakening race consciousness in Africa tends to have a positive side among the large industrial masses, namely, the outliving of old tribal sectionalism. What the South African bourgeoisie calls a native hooligan is one who, having worked some time in the towns, no longer recognises the authority of his tribal chief. Race consciousness, in the case of the Negro in Africa, is a step towards class consciousness, because his race is a race of labourers. The coming World Congress will have to decide the question, how far the movement towards race consciousness can be directed into proletarian forms.

Opposing the Garvey movement, said Jones, was 'the foremost leader of the negro intelligentsia in America, Burghardt du Bois, a graduate of Harvard', whose books contained 'a glimmering apprehension of the truth that negro emancipation can only come through proletarian emancipation ... Undoubtedly, America will supply the leaders of negro emancipation'. But negro emancipation was not an American question;

... it is a question of Africa, as our American comrades themselves have declared. Who is to get this great Africa, the capitalist class or the Comintern? And when is the European proletariat going to stretch out the hand of brotherhood to the masses of Africa, and wipe out centuries of capitalist wrong? The status of the American negro cannot be raised without the awakening of Africa. But it is no less true that the European proletariat cannot obtain a real link with Africa except through the more advanced negroes of America.

In South Africa, he said, (reversing his standpoint in the report of 1921) blacks saw every white as an oppressor, a master or boss.

Even the oppressed among the whites appears to the black the
most violent curser of the Negro. And therefore it is no wonder
that news of class emancipation in Europe must appear to him a
purely domestic affair of the whites. A few young industrial
workers are beginning to hear news of the Communist Party and
of its actions on behalf of the blacks, and these are beginning to
spread the idea. They see Communists gaoled for declaring the
solidarity of black and white workers. But a more imposing gesture is needed to convince the Negro masses that a new dawn is
breaking, that 'white man' and 'oppressor' are not one and the
same thing, that there is an army of liberation coming to aid him,
the revolutionary proletariat. Time is pressing, the Negro armies
of Imperialism [that is, black US troops], are already on the
Rhine. Only the Communist International can reconcile the
Negro and the white races, and only through proletarian solidarity
can this reconciliation be achieved.

Jones was touching on the most sensitive nerve of all: the tension and
hostility between white and black workers — most particularly in South
Africa. He called for working class solidarity and, to achieve this, he put
his faith in the Comintern to 'reconcile . . . the races'. This, however, was
all that Ivon Jones could do or say. At the insistence of Bill Andrews
(who had been in Moscow for the previous nine months as a member of
the Executive Committee of the Comintern) he had to return to Yalta
for the last time. Whatever his plans for the future, and his letters show
that he wished to travel again — he was not to leave the sanatorium alive.
Yet, mentally alert, he would continue writing — both for the press and
to friends. His letters to Andrews and to Evans (the only ones found)
were significant and their contents round off a remarkable ten years of
revolutionary striving.

Jones's Last Letters

On 14 March 1924 the *International* printed a letter from Andrews to
Jones on conditions in South Africa. This was a report on the state of the
party and the working class. The major section dealt with the white trade
unions, the desertion of the struggle by the SAIF, the need for Labour
Councils to bypass the old union federation, the Nationalist-Labour
Party pact and the communists, continued pressure for a 'United Front'.
In a short reference, Andrews claimed that the 'relationship between
white and non-white worker is becoming rapidly a burning one' because
the issue was discussed and voted upon in some of the unions — so far
with negative results — but the fact that it was being discussed was a sign
that circumstances were changing. Andrews mentioned activities in
which the CPSA was active: the German Famine Relief Committee, the
agitation to have the strike prisoners released and support for Labour

Party candidates in elections. There were large meetings to hear his report back on conditions in Russia and the Young Communist League was growing.

Jones's reply, although critical of Andrews' theoretical understanding of history, endorsed his friend's standpoint. Yet, acutely aware that he did not have long to live, his letter pointed in a different direction. Except for details on the weather, the mail, fiscal reform and greetings to friends, Jones's letter is printed in full as an appendix to this chapter.

Jones was acutely aware that the Communist Party was small and had little contact with the workers. The party would have to learn to combine the struggle for reforms with the revolutionary struggle or, as he put it, how to make the struggle for reforms revolutionary. In losing the trade unionists, the party was not unique. It illustrated the 'difficulty of forming a real mass organization'. He quoted from Lenin's *What is to be Done?* which said 'that the political struggle of the working class is not exclusively a struggle for the economic betterment of the workers, but also a struggle in which the party of the workers enters in defence of every oppressed section, even non-worker sections, of society'.

To overcome the isolation, said Jones, the CPSA had to think in terms of forming a united front with Labour during elections. He also referred to his previous suggestions for improving the party's paper and the need to establish a party-funded bookshop.

Jones said there was no room for a CP in white South Africa *except* as the watchdog of the African. The party had to promote rapprochement, watching, *within* the broader organizations, for every opportunity to switch the white movement on right lines and to scotch every conspiracy to rouse race hatred and strike-breaking.

It was the party's 'stand for Bolshevism' since 1917 that was their vindication, 'and in all minds Bolshevism stands for the native worker'. Now they could even 'dissolve temporarily except for a nucleus for the paper', to give comrades like Bunting a breathing space, and 'to get in through the proposed Trades Councils, Trade Unions, etc . . . and even into the electoral machine. It would be a great asset to have the govt pay our organizing and travelling expenses'.

He then chided his friend for having little grasp of historical processes. To make this concrete he discussed the Cromwellian and French revolutions and then extended his example to include Ramsey MacDonald's attitude to India, which he found disgusting.

A 'Political Testament'

A few weeks before he died, Jones dictated a 'Political Testament' in Russian, signed it and had it witnessed. In it he urged his comrades:

1. To maintain solidarity with the Russian Communist Party (Bolsheviks).
2. To carry out the great revolutionary mission imposed on colonies in general and South Africa in particular with revolutionary devotion and dignity, concentrating their efforts on shaking the foundations of world capitalism and British imperialism.

As his third point he wrote: .I beg pardon of Russia and the Russian Communist Party (Bolsheviks), whose guest I was and whom I loved and with whom I became one, for my inability, due to ill-health, to give the energy, intelligence and strength which the cause deserved.

He died on 29 May in Yalta on the Crimea and was embalmed and buried on 14 June in the Nova-Dyevitchi Monastery in Moscow. The Head Matron of the sanatorium, S Dondorskaya, [T Bell speaks of Nurse Davidovskia] wrote to his brother in Canada to say: 'Your brother had an international reputation and was highly appreciated by all who knew him. He is a great loss to the movement he worked and died for'.

There were many tributes to David Ivon Jones: in the pages of the *International* and of the international communist press; in the *Welsh Gazette*, and elsewhere. Yet Jones might well have been most amused and gratified by a 'tribute' that pre-dated his death. On 3 November 1923 an editorial in *Umteteli wa Bantu*, a publication financed by the Chamber of Mines, said

The Native peoples are shortly to have another white Bolshevik to torment them. Mr Ivon Jones ... is charged by the High Priests of Muscovite iniquity to 'take direct initiative in the direction of awakening the African masses as a necessary step to the world revolution' ... Before he left for Russia in 1920 Mr Ivon Jones worked hard for Native converts to his Communistic ideals ... The Natives have gone away unimpressed, and the Native Communist is rare. But one cannot trifle with pitch and escape ultimate defilement, and if the Native peoples would preserve their well-being they must give Mr Ivon Jones and his kind a wide berth. It will be serviceable to remember that the Ivon Joneses are Bolsheviks, and that the Bolsheviks revile God and make a mockery of Christian faith and practice ...

Your Gleam You Have Followed

On 28 January 1924 Ivon Jones had written to George Eyre Evans from the Tuberculosis Institute in Yalta. He said he had written from the same clinic the previous year. Since then he had gone back to Moscow but had a serious relapse and had to return. Unfortunately the continual relapses meant that he had had to resign himself to a quiet existence over the next few years — not many of which were left for him. The weather had been severe and in Moscow there had been 20 degrees of frost. Every window and door had been puttied up, and without ventilation the houses were most unhealthy. In Yalta the temperature was around freezing point and here too the rooms were kept sealed. He often mused over Ty Tringad and thought how nice it would be to sit 'by the fire in that library'. But he feared there had been an estrangement. He had not realized that communism made such a vast difference and made friendship between people with opposite views on the Russian revolution an impossibility. He had continued,

> One could wish that a person's personal belongings might not mar the serenity of his or her views as the ultimate good in society nor distort his judgment as to what is best for the majority, nor blind his vision to the substance of slavery all around him.

He had accepted that it was the case and 'was prepared for rebuffs without too much lamentations. Life after all is a stern affair, unless we like to turn our backs upon it':

> I remember how you once sent me a card. I was then at Lampeter — 'Follow the gleam lad, come what may', and I did not think, nor do I now, that you made any reservations, even if this gleam led one to paths which then would have shocked us both at the very mention thereof.

Jones had written about the death of Lenin, 'the greatest figure of this century, and indeed of centuries'

> Such a man, whether seen from near or from far, appears rarely. Such a sense of world responsibility, such monolithic sincerity in word and action, such a love of the oppressed in all lands, combined with a science of action for their deliverance.
>
> But I must not bore you, although I am at present under the immediate sense of a great loss.

Jones had not known what his immediate plans were — although he had occasionally been doubtful about prospects. He would have left Russia in 1923 but was stopped by the relapse. But he had to leave and would have to return to Britain or go back to sunny South Africa. In any case he had intended finishing his visit to Aberystwyth — 'if you have an invitation'. In his reminiscing he said that Aber had painful memories. Lampeter was more attractive:

> it is free from the associations of snob pauperdom of one's early life which meet one in ghost form at every corner in Aber. Ah, the beautiful Teifi, the trout, the trees, the jovial people there, the touch of pagan humanism which respectful Aber has not.
>
> Perhaps I may yet taste it! What say you? (That is a GEE query). Well old fellow wayfarer of long ago, I hail thee once more.
>
> David

George Eyre replied on receipt of the letter on 18 June. It had taken months for the letter to arrive and Ivon was already died. Evans's letter was returned unopened and arrived back on 2 July. Were the previous delays, and the failures of delivery, due to interference by British intelligence? Or were they the result of post-war chaos? Whatever, it seems unlikely that the letters that Jones received from Aberystwyth over the years will ever be found. The only one we have is the last that Evans sent and this too was deposited with Jones's letters in the National Library of Wales. Such testimony of the warm bond between the two men makes it the more regrettable that no others have been found. It started without any formal address, brimful of affection:

> At last! At last! dear old Dai comes a letter from you to my home: the *first* to reach me since one dated *Moscow, 19 August 1921* and to which it was obvious I could make no reply seeing that you gave no definite address — since then old man I can definitely say you've never been out of my thoughts . . . but I am glad to hear from you — no Dai, no, be your opinions what they may — no holding of such is to separate me from you. Your gleam you have followed — yea — I told you I made no reservations. I make none now. This door is as open to you today as it ever was . . . What more can I say? 'Tis the man, not his opinions, so come along as jolly soon as ever you can. I've failed to find Yalta on any map! 'Tis somewhere and you are therein and I abide and wait — No matter to me what be your thoughts . . .

The biographer can only regret that David Ivon Jones, or Dai, did not live to read the welcoming letter. Yet, had it been delivered, we might never have had direct evidence of the spirited warmth of this collector of antiquities and gatherer of earnest young men. The collection of letters at the National Library in Wales is a tribute to George Eyre Evans, to David Ivon Jones and to that gleam perceived by Dai Jones during his sojourn in South Africa.

APPENDIX

The last letter sent by Ivon Jones to Bill Andrews, in Johgannesburg, in April 1924. We have not seen the original and this version ic taken from portions printed by Cope, from a retranslation from the Russian as quoted by AD Davidson, and a version found in the Simons' papers.

Dear Comrade Bill,

I was pleased to receive your long (at any rate long for you!) letter. I didn't know whether you had already left England or not. But now you are home, and your account does not make me feel particularly glad. In reality, there is no sign of success as yet which might cause us to feel glad. I have started a letter to Bunting on that very theme — that the stratum of workers in the party is small in number, and because of this we are cut off from the masses. From references to it in the **International** I realized that they had received one of my letters. But I've written several of them, including two articles — I allowed myself this since you had already left. However, your letter is the first I have received from South Africa. Perhaps I have adopted the wrong tone in my writings, have been too bombastic or shown some other errors?

Raithaus wrote to me from Sevast where he has a niece or someone. He apologised for not having called in at Yalta, blaming it on the timetable of boats departing for Odessa and Constantinople. He is hoping to come here again, as a party delegate to the Fifth Congress [of the Communist International]. I think it would be a mistake to elect him as a delegate, only because he can afford such a trip. He is a typical representative of those elements in the party which are its financial support, and at the same time, the cause of its weakness. He is a sympathizing petty-bourgeois. If we can't send an active party worker, it's better not to send anyone at all. A short advance notice of the congress clearly indicates that now that the foundation of the Comintern has been laid, representatives from the parties of distant colonial countries should not necessarily be expected to attend every time. And since we now have to admit our lack of success (excluding young people) there is no reason for us to send a delegate. We need to concentrate on the future, when we will be able to send Edward Roux from the YCL and together with him a genuinely class conscious Negro worker. We must set ourselves this goal and within two years create the conditions for sending such a delegation.

Up till now the party has spent a lot of time campaigning for assistance so any saving from the delegates' and other funds will be timely. **Young Worker** has devoted itself to the question of pupils in a businesslike way. What a long chalk this is from the old Socialist Labour Party's hatred of all 'reform', although, of course, if the situation ceases to be revolutionary, our struggle for 'reforms' must inevitably become reformist, yet we are learning how to combine the struggle for reforms with the revolutionary struggle, or rather how to make the struggle for reforms revolutionary. I have just been reading one of Lenin's early brochures of 1902, where he declares that the political struggle of the working class is not exclusively a struggle for the economic betterment of the workers, but also a struggle in which the party of the workers enters in defence of every oppressed section, even non-worker sections, of society. For example, he cited the call to the workers to demonstrate against the Czar drafting students into the army. A positive attitude on every issue!

It is a pity you did not include just a few newspaper cuttings in your letter — interviews and other material. I receive individual copies of the **International,** probably even most of them. I see the lay out has changed again. I like the new title drawing, it's just a pity that the hammer and sickle are missing. But overall it is a definite improvement. Now a big question: what will Bunting live on — will he have to return to his old job? I am sure that the perspectives outlined, if not his own, then in any case your perspective, as well as those of the party as a whole, are not to his liking. I expressed the opinion to Bunting that even if we had to return to the idea of a Johannesburg committee with an unpaid secretary, it would be worth doing in order to guarantee ourselves a point of support in the working class. We have lost the trade unionists, but I doubt if that is anything peculiar to us; it is a general South African, if not a British trait, the difficulty of forming a real mass organization. How many active branches has the Labour Party got? Apart from the special excitement of electioneering, which the name 'Labour' gives it, it has no more organizational cohesion than the CP.

Our trouble is isolation. [We allowed them to keep the name in 1915]. The point is how to get a foot in again. Now it will be very hard. There may be a chance during the elections to put you up as United Front candidate with the LP somewhere. The CP would be justified in a little manoeuvring to get this. The CP as an affiliated section, with members in SALP branches, would be the thing of course.

As a cold matter of fact, there is no room for a CP in white South Africa except as the watchdog of the native, as the promoters of rapprochement, watching, within the broader organizations, for every opportunity to switch the white movement on right lines on this question and scotching every conspiracy to rouse race hatred and strike breaking of race against race. We have done something on this question since 1914, even if the damage is great. But history does not count damages, organizational damages, in order to shift forward a peg. And this peg could not have been shifted forward as it has been without the tremendous sacrifices, the wanderings in the wilderness of the last nine years. We must be humble and satisfied, satisfied that we did our best. And I hope that Bunting, with all his wonderful devotion and self-sacrifice of the last nine years, will not feel that his labours have been in vain. We have made our protest. We have insisted on certain questions. We stand for Bolshevism, which since 1917 has come to our vindication, and in all minds Bolshevism stands for the native worker. Now we can safely review tactics, if necessary even dissolve temporarily except for a nucleus for the paper, in order to give comrades like Bunting a breathing space, and use this in order to get in through the proposed Trades Councils, Trade Unions, etc, into the Labour Party machine, and even into the electoral machine. It would be a great asset to have the govt. pay our organizing and travelling expenses.

14 April 1924

Excuse the poor paper and ink. As always, I am writing this lying in bed. Spring came late and the cold, damp winter had a bad effect on my health. Up till 1 December I was well on the way to recovery and began to walk, but during the winter months I again took to my bed. Just when the weather began to improve and I could count on continuing the treatment, I started getting terrible neurological pains in my lower back and legs, especially in the knees. These lasted until last week. I've become totally helpless; I can't move around or even cross the room without assistance. I feel especially weak in the knees. The doctors evidently don't fully understand what is happening to me, let alone the general exhaustion of the organism and the deterioration of my condition during the winter. The disease of my lungs is no worse than in December, but other ailments have started tormenting me. The pain has been so acute that I couldn't get to sleep without morphine. Hence I am pretty well resigning from my claim to 'futures', and preparing to close my accounts as they stand, with all the mistakes and 'damn foolishness' thrown in! The next few weeks will show what my prospects are, and if it appears that the trouble is chronic, I shall put in my checks. I don't know but that I have been a burden too long. After all, it is an egoism not compatible with Communism to lie bedridden indefinitely, waited upon by people who might do useful work. The time will come when it will be considered a piece of obsolete individualism, or even superstition, to wait and wait until the last breath heaves out. Just as a midwife's function is to help people in, so a doctor's should be to help people out once it is clear they are no longer any use. But it is hard to get the truth from doctors. That's the situation I am in. I don't know what will become of me, but I feel I have little chance of recovering and leaving Russia. Still, we'll see. But meanwhile let's talk about something more cheerful.

You may be interested to learn that your letter, written on the 9th March, and bearing the Johannesburg postmark of the 10th reached me in my room on the 11th April, bearing the Moscow postmark April 6th. I think this is very quick travelling! Consider the number of re-sortings it has to go through — Cape Town, presumably England, Moscow, Sebastopol. In 1921 a letter from Odessa to Moscow took more than the present letter from South Africa. So we are getting on!

Today I read about MacDonald's defeat on the housing question. But he is still holding on to his post. He is the most unprincipled and despicable time-server of all those who have been in the post. Baldwin and Lloyd George occasionally showed they knew how to put up a fight, but MacDonald's only wish is, apparently, to show the capitalists what a good boy he is. The position he has adopted on India is disgusting. It's interesting that Menshevism has the same features everywhere and is repeating itself in England, despite your 'reading of history'. Equally, the same basic features of revolution must reveal themselves everywhere — if not in form, then in substance. Your 'reading of history', dear William, smacks of the petty-bourgeoisie, and always has done. But your understanding of the present is quite correct. For you haven't learnt to read history from a class point of view. And if England didn't follow the example of France in 1792, then a reading of history from a class point of view reveals the reason for this: (1) By the time the bourgeoisie had already, to a significant extent gained hold of power, the feudal system had largely gone into decline and the industrial revolution was maturing. (2) Cromwell had already accomplished everything that was necessary in the previous century and the French, basically, just followed the example of the English. The revolution led by Cromwell did not go beyond the bounds of legality and logic. It introduced sufficient revolutionary changes. Like the French revolution, it moved from a petty-bourgeois platform (yeomen) to a strictly bourgeois platform (the class of entrepreneurs). You are accustomed for several years now to consider England as a country doomed to compromises. But the Chartists had no respect for law and order. Only recently the British workers acquired such respect. I am convinced that once the masses realise that government and capitalists are one and the same thing, whatever ministers are in power, there will be unrest in the country and the workers will not stop at the abolition of the constitution. It is quite possible that an explosion will occur as a result of the people defending the constitution, which will have to be thrown overboard in the very process of its defence. In America the CP now has a flourishing daily paper. The movement for the creation of a worker's party, in which the CP is taking the lead, is spreading despite the opposition of Gompers. Once such a party has been created, it will adopt positions further to the left than Gompers' supporters. The USA is somewhat exceptional, but Britain will soon find itself drawn into the flow of current events. Even in complete calm one must always be prepared for a sudden squall.

15.4.24

I have had to break off. Much writing tires, and the pains interrupt. The spring is late, but we have not yet got regular sunshine; although for most people it is already nice enough weather if somewhat cloudy, owing to the tendency of the mountain range to gather mists, so long as snow lies in Russia. Since you left we have had a currency reform, so far successful, silver coinage, but this place has not yet received any, as an enormous quantity is required, but what remains of the Soviet rouble is stabilized, because the government has announced a firm price, 500 (000,000) to 1 kopek. So now everybody counts in kopeks and roubles as pre-war. I have seen specimens of the new silver coins, very beautiful, and in full go in the large centres. Meanwhile the government has to observe most stringent economies to avoid revenue escape.

How is Tyler? I had plans to write to half a dozen comrades, but in present state I must postpone. And Rabb and Ada Rabb? I started by writing to Haynes, thinking he was fully active in the party, his 'Para' being then in the paper. I hope that my suggestions for improving [the paper] were not used as a pretext for a diversion. There are now some very expensive books in your catalogue, with a marked tendency to make book-selling take priority over the propagation of communist principles, with the aid of spiritual fare. There are some really unlikely books in the catalogue, while some propagandistic publications which have long established themselves are missing. Why for example do we no longer find John Reed's **Ten Days That Shook the World** — the best communistic reporting in all literature? I propose that Ralph think of opening a bookshop with a neutral sign, such as 'Books for Workers', which would be under the control of the CP and act in co-operation with the party. The shop should, of course, have a stationary section. The most suitable person for organizing such a venture is RB as he loves books, loves propaganda through books, loves seeing books on shelves and stroking them lovingly. He could combine his new duties with other types of his economic activity if he were given a girl as an assistant who was trustworthy and capable of running the shop while he was out. This would be extremely valuable for the entire labour movement. At the same time the existing press could be turned into the press of the 'Books for Workers' society, its activities should be expanded to those of a fully-fledged publishing house. Gradually Ralph would concentrate entirely on working in such a publishing-house. It should be opened in the centre and not in some side street. Everyone agreed? Resolution passed! Next business!! Of course my regards to Ralph, I often think of him and the other comrades, and wish I could grasp them by the hand once more. I see from papers that Sam Barlin has left Johannesburg. any news of John Campbell? Whenever you happen to be in Natal give my regards to Lawrie Green. I suppose SMC is clean out of it now. His creditors will demand it of him, and the clearing up of the point re Free Masons in the Communist International puts him before an irksome dilemma. Well, we exploited SM ruthlessly, some of us must allow. I have not written to him for a long time. I gather that Kathleen and Willie are well and hearty. Have you seen Mr and Mrs Newbury yet? Give them my regards and also to Isabel Schikling. And of course the Chapmans, although I do not agree with Jessie Chapman as a candidate, but one can object to a friend's nomination! Chapman is very faithful to the cause. Where has Dan Bekker gone to? By the way you should ask Alper to give you the letter from the Association of assistance to Jews in Russia, which I sent to him in 1922 from the Jewish Relief Association. From this letter it is clear that not a single penny from the thousands of pounds which were collected by Jews in South Africa has arrived in Russia. But Russia has the burden of 300,000 orphans who were victims of the Jewish pogroms.

Now dear Andrews, I must finish this letter. When I can I'll write again. Give my warmest love to everyone. No doubt I shall think of others as well. Where is Parky? And Mrs Hockley, etc.

Your old friend and Comrade

Ivon

(Tell Bunting to write).

In a PS Jones compared the words of the **Internationale** as sung in South Africa with the version used in Britain and Russia and urged that a new version be used.

REFERENCES

The George Eyre Evans material relating to Jones in Wales and New Zealand are all NLW No: 7979A (Jones's day-book), 7950B (Lampeter); immediately relevant are, 7949B, 13384A, 13391A (diaries of Evans), 13368B (George Eyre Evans' life register), 13367C and miscellaneous, 13628C, 13370A, 13367C, 13435B. See also 13561C, 13562C, 13330A, 13437C, 13564E, 13580C. Specialist references in Chapters 7-16 are noted below

Chapter 7

1. Union was proclaimed on 31 May 1910. The Governor-General, Lord Gladstone, arved in South Africa on 19 May and on the 21st invited Louis Botha, Prime Minister of the Transvaal, to form a ministry. The first general election was held on 15 September and the Legislative Assembly convened for 4 November.
2. The accuracy of these figures has since been criticised: the African population being undoubtedly greater than shown.
3. Until 1930, only men had the vote, subject to property or income qualifications. Some Africans, Indians and Coloureds were on the voters roll in the Cape. In 1930, white women over 21 years were enfranchised, and in 1931 the qualifications for white men lifted. The number of white voters more than doubled; that of the other ethnic groups decreased slightly.
4. Cape Times, 5 March 1913
5. Before the war of 1899-1902, the Cape and Natal were self-governing colonies; the Orange Free State and South African Republic, independent states. After 1902 they all became self-governing colonies, and then Provinces under the 1910 constitution.
6. The populations of Kroonstad and Heilbron were about 8,000, and 2,000 respectively; half of each were white, the rest black. Riviera and Oosthuizen were tiny villages.
7. Described in a letter from Boksburg, on 16 July 1911, as white tenants who rented a few acres on the larger farms in exchange for seasonal labour. Mostly impoverished, they provided the pool from which the unskilled 'poor whites' of the towns were drawn.
8. Blacks were called Kaffirs, from the Arabic Khafir (infidel) and Jones used the word unselfconsciously. In time Kaffirs became 'Natives' and then 'Bantu'. The communists introduced 'Africans' in the 1930s, but 'blacks' was favoured in the 1970s.
9. A name meaning 'great man in retirement who could be called upon in a crisis' and once ascribed to Washington.
10. 11 July 1911.
11. The article appeared under four headings: Thinking Loudly/ Native Associations Unite/Powerful Organisation/Question of Polygamy.
12. 28 July 1911.
13. Commenting on the exchange Jones said: 'There is nothing more amusing than a Jingo paper like the Star tumbling over itself in disclaiming any defection from the Jingo faith and the least suspicion of humanitarian sentiments.'
14 When he moved he paid £2 for a bedroom 'plus usual cleaning and a morning cup of coffee from the black houseboy', £5 for board, and '10s extra for washing'.
15. There were 36,268 males and 7,309 females in Boksburg (1911 census). Of these 7,122 males and 4,515 females were white. Most Africans worked on the mines, the rest were mainly in domestic service.
16. Thereafter, the journal carried letters from local Indian leaders and Mr Bhyat; extracts from Indian Opinion; and attacks on Indians by SALP leaders.
17. Those calling on the goverment to remove Indian traders and workers on the mines, included R B Waterston, trade unionist and town councillor of Boksburg, secretary of the SALP in 1913, a strike leader in 1913-14, and one of those deported by Smuts in January 1914 and Dr McNeil, with W H Andrews and Dan Simons, at a SALP meeting in Boksburg. (East Rand Express, 11, 18 November 1911)

18.Thanks to Lou Haysom for permission to use material from her unpublished biography of Mary Fitzgerald.

19. **Voice of Labour**, 5 January 1912.

20. **Gold Fever**, Cape, London, 1936. The extracts quoted in this section are from pp 30-33 and pp 80-81. Thanks to Miriam Basner for this reference.

21. Reynold's Newspaper, under the headline 'City of Dreadful Death' carried reports of the concern over phthisis.

22. Nesbitt, all quotations from pp 29--35.

23. See **International**, 19 January 1923.

Chapter 8

1. Employers objected to contributing 3d weekly; workers, to the 4d deducted from wages, its administration by friendly societies and insurance companies and its failure to get to the roots of poverty.

2. He sent a cutting to Aberystwith (an unknown newspaper of 11 September 1912) in his letter of 22 September.

3. Cope, pp 126-28.

4. Written c/o Colin Wade, a SALP Provincial Councillor, Germiston.

5. See Hirson, et al, 1987.

6. Gladstone to Colonial Office, 22 January 1914, CO 4990. On 31 January he gave the total number of white workers as 92,000.

7. On 31 January 1914, Gladstone said miners earned £20-£40 a month, CO 5950.

8. **Manchester Guardian**, 9 July 1913.

9. Katz, pp 326-29; Cope, p 126.

10. **Evening Chronicle**, July 1913, passim, carried a series of articles on the July days, under this headline.

11. Letter from F D P Chaplin, joint general manager of Consolidated Gold Fields to J X Merriman, 15 July 1913, quoted in Katz, p 382.

12. This account is compiled from newspapers , Cope, pp 130-34 and Katz, Ch 9.

13. R Outhwaite, **Reynold's Newspaper**, 6 July 1913. He also wrote of trade unions being 'a matter of life and death for the workers if they are to prevent the spread of phthisis'.

14. **Cape Times**, 21 July 1913, from a letter sent by a clergyman to Rev Balmsworth, and read at a protest meeting (see below).

15. Extracts were also printed in **Labour Leader**, London, 7 August. Similar letters from 'A Scotchman' and A S Purchase, appeared on 10, 11 July in the **Evening Chronicle**.

16. A correspondent of the **Daily Chronicle** (7 July 1913) likened the events to the Paris Commune, but that was obviously an exaggeration.

17. **Daily Chronicle**, 4 July 1913; **Transvaal Leader**, 8 July 1913.

18. Reported in Britain by one of the deported trade unionists (see below). There were several variations of the story, told by different men — none of them confirmed by the main actors of the day.

19. **Evening Chronicle**, 21 October 1913, quoting wage rates from the secretary of the Braamfontein branch of the ASRHS. Union recognition was held up by ASRHS refusal to concede the administration's right to alter the union's rules 'if deemed necessary'.

20. O'Quigley.

21. Official sources listed thirty eight instances of explosions on tracks, trains or railway property, or interference with points, and so on, CO 7843; **Manchester Guardian**, 10 January 1914.

22. Cope, p 148, says 'he played a leading and exceedingly suspicious role ...' See also pp 150-52 on the position in the union.

23.. Cope, p 150. For the proclamation terms, see **Transvaal Leader**, 14 January 1914.

24. Letter of 21 January 1914, sent surreptitiously to the Colonial Office, after previous communications had been blocked. CO 5258. **The Clarion** printed a copy that had been sent to the editor.

25. O'Quigley; Cope, pp 154-55, describes the measures (and brutalities) of the armed forces. The **Transvaal Leader**, 13 January 1914, ('Free State an Armed Camp'), said streets in Bloemfontein recalled war days, but strikers were 'orderly and peaceful'.

26. Written by a syndicalist stone mason, Bob Bower, it was first published by Jim Larkin's **Irish Worker** in July 1911, and reprinted in **The Syndicalist** whose publisher included Mann, in January 1912. (See Bob Holton, p 114). The Johannesburg leaflet ascribed it to Tom Mann.

27. **Trekking On**, 1933, pp 63-5.

28. Letter to his sister, Ada Nield Chew, reprinted in **Labour Leader**, 18 June 1914, and **Socialist** (Glasgow, July 1914).

29. The deportation was forecast in the letter to the Colonial Office of 21 January (above); and by the conservative **South Africa**, ten days before the event (quoted by Cope, p 158).

30. Report by 'Our own Correspondent', **Transvaal Leader**, 28 July 1913. The cutting sent to Aberystwyth, signed by Ivon, indicates that he was the author.

31. See **Transvaal Leader** reports of 10, 12 November 1913, when the magistrate met the Volksrust Vigilance Committee; and 18 January 1914, when the Minister of Justice, N J de Wet, 'acknowledged the valuable support given to the Government ... in resisting the Indian invasion'. See also Hirson, et al, 1987.

32. Letter to E Carpenter, quoted in **Labour Leader**, 28 August 1913. There is no copy in the Carpenter collection at Sheffield.

33. Brian Willan, p 163, states: Plaatje 'personally drafted a resolution "dissociating the Natives from the [white miners'] strike movement" after the idea had been put forward.'

34. But see **Transvaal Leader**, 10 January 1914, 'Indians want to Help Strikers'.

35. FHP Creswell, speaking on the Indians, and W H Andrews on the Land Act, both in the Legislative Assembly, quoted in **Rand Daily Mail**, 13, 16 May 1913.

Chapter 9

1. Roux, 1944, p 20.

2. Lucas was to become a protagonist of Henry George's 'single tax' theory.

3. There were two letters. One on 25 May 1915, the second undated.

4. Ticktin. See also records of SALP.

5. I found copies of these journals at the British Library. Given the fare available in Johannesburg these must have made exciting reading.

6. In the second of a series of articles on 'The Failure of Liberalism' on 1 January 1914, h

7. Katz, p 271; **Labour Leader**, 16 July 1909, quoted in Simons, p 115. The slogan was revived in the **International**, of 25 August 1916, by L H Greene, as 'Equal Pay for Equal Work — Black and White Alike'.

8. 'Puff', in **Clarion**, 6, 13 February 1914, mentioned the Indian workers' strike, but satirically. However he did say that a small minority of white worker's leaders supported them.

9. 11 April 1914. A second, similar, article appeared on the 18th.

10. The censors forced it to close in November 1914.

11. Lloyd George's memoirs, quoted in Swanson, p 634.

12. Public Records Office, Kew, CO 40707.

13. Louis, pp 18, 108.

14. Lord Hankey (secretary, Imperial War Cabinet, and to British Empire delegation at the Peace Conference), p 57.

15. See Mr Grobelaar, **Evening Chronicle**, 11 September 1914.

16. Walker, p 557.

17. The extent of government preparedness is unknown, but if Botha and Smuts were forewarned, accounts of the 'accidental death' of de la Ray needs reinvestigation.

18. The Secretary's Report to Branches, including accounts of the SALP Administrative Council meetings, signed by Jones, were sent to Evans.

19. Report to Branches, with an account of the meeting of the Administrative Council, 15 November 1914.

20. **Gold Fever**, p 102.

21. The English version was sent to Evans, the first section, outlining the anti-war position, signed by Ivon. A Declaration of Principles, completed the pamphlet. The 'Reply' was also published in Dutch.

22. Cope, pp 172-73.

23. In a cutting from the **Rand Daily Mail**, 25 August 1915, sent to Evans.

Chapter 10

1. This site, which was designated a 'Native area', is now incorporated in Soweto.
2. There can be no certainty on which factors influenced the delegates. At one stage Jones and his friends were influenced by the attack on 'wagery' in the journal New Age, and it is this that might have influenced the delegates.
3. See Grundlingh,
4. A phrase, used by Jones in his letter of 17 January 1917, to explain his physical collapse.

Chapter 11

1. Cope, p 192.
2. Sachs, p 132.
3. B Bunting, p 56.
4. An account based largely on these files is in F A Johnstone. The files, on microfilm, are available in London.
5. The Star, 11 April, reported that a conference of all branches in the Transvaal and OFS had reorganised the northern section.
6. At some stage Mbelle went to Port Elizabeth. I have found little further information on his activities, except for his election to the New Brighton (township) Advisory Board in 1929-30.
7. Initially it was called the Society of the Industrial Workers of the World. One week later the name was altered to IWA.
8. The texts, as translated into Zulu and Sotho (and retranslated into English), are in the Department of Justice files. They are printed in Johnstone's article as an appendix.
9. International, 4 January 1918; Reports of two Native Constables, December 1917.
10. R Cope, Notebooks. A copy, on film, is available at the Borthwick Institute, York. It contains notes made by Cope in his writing of the biography of Andrews. There are no references but obviously much of the information was obtained through interviews with Andrews.
11. Also reprinted in B Bunting, pp 33-34. In an editorial note Bunting states, incorrectly, that the leaflet was: a) distributed by the ISL, and b) distributed during the boycott. Nothing is said about ISL criticism of the boycott of stores.
12. Umteteli wa Bantu, 21 September 1929. See aos Bonner for a more detailed account of the leadership of the SANNC and the events of 1918-20.
13. The reference to the 'chief native witness' also concealed a story that was not disclosed until told by Jones in the journal Moscow. The story of Luke Messina is told below in Chapter 15.
14. Marx's phrase was: 'Force is the midwife of every old society pregnant with a new one', Capital, Vol 1, Chapter 31
15. The use of biblical images was not a return to the faith, but probably an adaptation from Wordsworth (The Prelude, book xi). In his enthusiasm for the French Revolution the poet wrote: 'Bliss was it in that dawn to be alive,/But to be young was very Heaven! (thanks to Paul Trewhela for this reference). In the very next sentence Jones wrote that 'the wreck of the war has carried with it the flotsam and jetsam of liberalism, Christianity, and every idealism'.

Chapter12

1. See Cope, pp 202-204. What followis is compiled from Roux (1944), pp 40-44, and the International, 4 April 1919.
2. The International, 4 October 1919, reported that Ivon had 'repudiated, somewhat indignantly even . . . all his alleged claims against it for arrears ;alary, etc . . . returning a cheque recently sent him in respect of same.'
3. Many years later Petterson reappeared as a National Party senator.
4. Letter dated 23 June 1918, received by Evans on 16 August.
5. Two copies (now in the state archives) were sent: to Bunting and to C B Tyler (in case the first was stopped). Both were intercepted and forwarded to Defence Headquarters, Pretoria.

6. Brian Bunting, p 38, states that the leaflet was circulated at the end of 1918 and early 1919. At the trial it was disclosed that the order to the printers was made on 27 March 1919. 10,000 copies were printed.

7. Witnesses for the crown argued that there had been no massacres in Bloemfontein in February 1918. Jones had got it wrong, but there was a strike that paralysed the location, there was rioting, and the police fired — reportedly in the air.

8. Copies of trial transcripts, letters, the pamphlet concerned, and some press cuttings are lodged at the Rhodes University Library, Grahamstown. These were found by Dave Evaret who kindly copied them for me. Fuller versions of what was said by the two accused were printed in the International.

9. Gumede appeared at a later date as the radical president of the ANC (after visiting Berlin and Moscow in 1927-28).

10. Jones, who answered questions under cross-examination, could not submit a written statement. Greene, who did not appear as a witness, was able to present a background paper which gave a synoptic history of Marxism and the workers' struggles for socialism.

11. A printed copy of the statement sent to Aberystwyth was signed, 'Here is the Dreamer, DIJ'. The statement and cross-examination were printed in the International, 16 May 1919.

Chapter 13

1. Printed in the International, 3 December 1920 and quoted in Simons, p 263.

2. See Roux, 1944, pp 48-49. Mrs Rebecca Bunting, who read the manuscript to Roux's book critically, corrected the spelling of 'Radek', but did not comment on its accuracy.

3. Also reprinted in B Bunting, pp 41-56.

Chapter 14

1. Inprecor, 12 August 1922, Vol 2, No 68.

2. Memoirs, p 104.

3. Vol 1, No 14, 9 June 1921. Moscow was the organ of the Third Congress of the Communist International.

4. Moscow, which appeared in several languages simultaneously, was poorly edited, and the text is garbled. In quoting, alternative wording is provided in square brackets.

5. But compare the passage in 'Communism in South Africa' where he said, 'South Africa ... is an epitome of the class struggle throughout the world. Here Imperial Capital exploits a white skilled proletariat side by side with a large native proletariat. Nowhere else in the proportions obtaining on the world scale do the white skilled and dark unskilled meet together in one social milieu as they do in South Africa. And nowhere are the problems so acute of two streams of the working class with vastly unequal standards of life jostling side by side, and the resultant race prejudices and animosities interfering and mixing with the class struggle.'

6. Printed in Communist International, Vol 3, Nos 16-17.

7. A Board set up in January 1920 by municipal workers in Durban during a strike. following the victimization of a trade unionist. In composition and function it was similar to the Johannesburg 'Soviet'.

8. Rosmer, p 134.

9. Inprecor, Vol 1, No 6.

10. Memoirs, pp 137-8.

11. Rosmer.

12. Quoted in Carr, p 383. See also Rosmer, p 129-33, for a discussion of these two contributions.

13. Quoted in Sheridan Johns.

14. Reprinted in International, 20 August 1921.

15. Communist Review, No 5, September 1921.

16. Extracts from letters, opened by the censors, appeared in the Report of the Martial Law Judicial Committee. Jones was to say that they were quoted out of context.

17. The articles overlap and I quote from either in what follows.

18. Inprecor, No 29; Communist Review 3(4), June 1923. See also his 'May Day in Moscow', International 15 June 1923, much of it concerned with the case of Patriarch Tikhon.

Chapter 15

1. Carr, pp 395-97. Carr states incorrectly that Zinoviev, who actually withdrew from the conference, was in the chair. Rosmer addressed the opening session of the RILU and I have consequently used his version of events.
2. Rosmer, p 137.
3. Vol 1, No 7, November 1921.
4. **Communist International**, October 1922
5. For discussion of the strike see Herd, Hessian, Diamond, Simons and Simons, Cope, Johnstone, S P Bunting, Glanville, Defence Committee of Trade Unions on the Witwatersrand. A review article on the post war disturbances in South Africa, including much of this section, appears in Hirson, 1993.
6. Hessian, pp 71-72. Although this work was antagonistic to the strikers, Hessian scoured the local press and found material that is not easily available.
7. Quoted in ibid, p 132.
8. Ibid, p 64.
9. Ibid, pp 68-69.
10. **Workers Dreadnought**, viii, 52, 11 March 1922. This British paper, with reports from and sold in South Africa by syndicalists, ignored the **International** in their report.
11. Herd, pp 40-3.
12. Glanville.
13. Hessian, pp 77-79.
14. Ibid, p 80. The deputation consisted only of National representatives. Labour delegates who were to have attended, arrived too late to participate.
15. Hessian, pp 144-49.
16. Reprinted in **Workers Dreadnought**, viii, 52.
17. This commando, noted by Jones, was led by Eva Green, a member of the CPSA, and subsequently one of the first woman trade union organizers. (Information from Eva Green's daughter)
18. Defence Committee, p 26.
19. Report of a meeting of the CPSA in Cape Town to hear a report from a miner's representative, **Cape Times**, 2 February 1922. See also Simons, p 297.
20. Sheridan Johns III, notes in Karis and Carter, Vol 1, p 146.
21. **International**, 27 January 1922..
22. Defence Committee, pp 5-6.
23. Ibid, p 7.
24. Ibid, p 7.
25. Glass changed his mind at some point and praised the miners for their action.
26. Quoted in Defence Committee, p 12.
27. In this he was correct and, although there is no obvious explanation for their presence, it does seem that many Africans had no disagreement with the strikers. However, there were other photographs in which white women paraded with placards, bearing the same slogan, and obviously intent on calling for racial separation.
28. Herd, p 48.
29. **International**, 10 February 1923, following a trial of one of those accused of involvement in the riots of March 1922. The leaflet was also reproduced in the article.
30. Defence Committee pp 15-18.
31. Hessian, pp 83, 69.
32. Ibid, p 82.
33. Herd, pp 45-6.
34. Ibid, p 49.
35. Hessian, p 137.
36. Ibid, p 171.
37. Herd, pp 57-58.

BIBLIOGRAPHY

Primary Sources

Department of Justice Files, South Africa. — Microfilm at the School of Oriental and African Studies, London.
Dispatches drom the Governor-General of South Africa to the Colonial Office, London. Public Records Office, Kew, London.
Letters and Diaries of Ivon Jones, Welsh National Library, Aberystwyth.

A film based on the life of David Ivon Jones, entitled The African from Aberystwyth, made b-Teliesyn Helwick House, 19 David Street, Cardiff CF1 2EH, and directed by Colin Thomas, was transmitted in Welsh on Sinnel Pedwar Cymru and in English on BBC Wales in 1986. Gwyn A Williams was the narrator.

Secondary Sources

Phil Bonner (1979), 'The 1920 Black Mineworkers' Strike. A Preliminary Account', in Bozolli.
------ (1982), The Transvaal Native Congress, 1917-1920. The radicalisation of the black petty bourgeoisie on the Rand, in Marks and Rathbone.
Belinda Bozzoli (ed) (1979), Labour, Townships and Protest: Studies in the Social History of the Witwatersrand, Ravan.
Brian Bunting (ed) (1981), South African Communists Speak, 1915-80, Inkululeko Publications.
SP Bunting (1922), Red Revolt: The Rand Strike, January-March 1922, CPSA, Johannesburg.
EH Carr (1973), The Bolshevik Revolution, Vol 3, Penguin.
RK Cope (c 1944), Comrade Bill: The Life and Times of W H Andrews, Workers' Leader, Stewart Printing, Cape Town, c1944
R K Cope (nd), Notebooks. A copy on film is in the Borthwick Institute, York.
Dictionary of Welsh Biography
John Davies (1993), A History of Wales, Allen Lane
AB Davidson (1972), South Africa: The Birth of Protest, 1870-1924, Moscow.
Defence Committee of Trade Unions on the Witwatersrand (1924), The Story of a Crime: being The Vindication of the Defence Committee in connection with the Trial by Special Criminal Courts without Juries of 195 man and 6 women, arising out of the strike on the Witwatersrand in 1922, published by the Committee.
Charles R Diamond (1969), 'African labour problems on the South African gold mines with special reference to the strike of 1946', MA thesis, University of Cape Town.
PGifford and Wm R Louis (eds) (1967), Britain and Germany in Africa, Yale University Press.
Ernest Glanville (1922), Through the Red Revolt on the Rand, Argus Printing.
AGrundlingh (1987), Fighting their own War: South African Blacks and the First World War, Ravan.
N Herd (1966), 1922: The Revolt on the Rand, Blue Crane, Johannesburg.
Lord Hankey (1963), The Supreme Control at the Paris Peace Conference, 1919, Allen and Unwin.
Bernard Hessian (1957), 'An Investigation into the Causes of the Labour Agitation on the Witwatersrand, January to March 1922', University of the Witwatersrand MA dissertation.
Baruch Hirson, Julia Wells, and Judie Jancovich (1987), 'Whatever did happen at Jagersfontein? or Diamonds are Forever - but Gold is for Now!', The Societies of Southern Africa in the 19th and 20th Centuries, Vol 13, Institute of Commonwealth Studies, London.
Baruch Hirson (1993), 'The General Strike of 1922', Searchlight South Africa, No 11.
Bob Holton (1976), British Syndicalism, 1900-14, Pluto.
Sheridan Johns (1975), 'The Comintern, South Africa and the Black Diaspora', The Review of Politics, Vol 37, No 2.

FA Johnstone (1976), **Class, Race and Gold: A Study of Class Relations and Social Discrimination in South Africa**, Routledge and Kegan Paul, London
----- (1979), 'The IWA on the Rand: Socialist Organising among Black Workers on the Rand, 1917-18', in Bozzoli.
D Ivon Jones (1921), **Report on Communism in South Africa**, International Socialist League, Johannesburg.
----- (1922), 'The Workers Revolt in South Africa', **Communist International**, October.
Thomas Karis and Gwendolen M Carter (1972), **From Protest to Challenge, A Documentary History of African Politics in South Africa, 1882-1964**, Vol 1, Hoover Institute Press, Stanford.
Elaine Katz (1976), **A Trade Union Aristocracy: A History of White Workers in the Transvaal and the General Strike of 1913**, African Studies Institute, University of the Witwatersrand.
Phyllis Lewsen (ed) (1969), **Selections from the Correspondence of John X Merriman, 1905-1924**, van Ribeeck Society, Cape Town .
Wm R Louis (1967), **Great Britain and Germany's Lost Colonies, 1914-1919**, Clarendon.
Shula Marks and Richard Rathbone (eds) (1982), **Industrialisation and Social Change in South Africa: African Class Formation, Culture, and Consciousness, 1870-1930**, Longman, London.
Islwyn Ap Nicholas (1978), **The Unfurled Banner: The Story of David Ivon Jones**, typescript.
Ann O'Quigley (1981), 'The 1914 Strike', **The Societies of Southern Africa in the 19th and 20th Centuries**, Vol 11, Institute of Commonwealth Studies.
Denys Reitz (1933), **Trekking On**, Faber.
Alfred Rosmer (1971), **Lenin's Moscow**, Pluto.
Edward Roux (1944), **S P Bunting: A Political Biography**, African Bookman, Cape Town.
----- (1947), **Time Longer than Rope**, Gollancz, London.
Bernard Sachs (1949), **Multitude of Dreams**, Johannesburg, 1949
Victor Serge (1930), **Year One of the Russian Revolution**, Paris
----- (1976), **Memoirs of a Revolutionary**, Oxford University Press.
J H and R E Simons (1969), **Class and Colour in South Africa: 1850-1950**, Penguin.
M W Swanson (1967), 'South West Africa in Trust, 1915-1939', in Gifford and Louis.
David Ticktin (1969), 'The War Issue and the Collapse of the South African Labour Party, 1914-15', **South African Historical Journal**, No 1, November.
Eric Walker (1946), **A History of South Africa**, Longman, Green.
Brian Willan (1984), **Sol Plaatje: South African Nationalist 1876-1932**,Heinemann.
Gwyn A Williams (1991), **What is Wales?** Penguin.

Newspapers and Journals

Cape Times, Clarion, Communist International, Communist Review, Daily Chronicle, Daily News and Leader, East Rand Express, Evening Chronicle, Financier and Bullionist, Forward, Inprecor, International, Labour Leader, Manchester Guardian, Moscow, New Age, New Statesman and Nation, Nation, Rand Daily Mail, Reynold's Newspaper, Round Table, Socialist, South Africa, Transvaal Leader, Star, Umteteli wa Bantu, Voice of Labour, Welsh Gazette, War on War Gazette, Workers Dreadnought.

INDEX

INDEX271

Price, Dr Richard, 47
Price, W T, 43, 48
Pryse (of Gogerddan), 9, 11
Pugsley, Alfred S, 45, 47-48, 53, 55

Rabb, Ralph, 156
Rabbiting, 72, 77-78, 79, 82-83
Radek, Karl, 202
Rebecca Riots, 4, 16
Rand Daily Mail, 174, 104, 189
Randlords, 102, 111, 116, 117, 126
Red International of Labour Unions, 221-222
Rees, Geronwyn, 14-15
Rees, Harry, 30, 33
Reitz, Denys, 125
Reform Act of 1867, 5
Reform Act of 1884, 6
Report on Communism in South Africa, 203, 223ff
Rhyd-y-Bont, Hannah, 26
Rhyfel y Sais Bach, 16
Richards, E M, 11-12
Richard, Henry, 10
Riviera, 91, 95, 99
Roberts, Evan, 50
Roberts, William M, 70, 71-72, 78-80, 83, 88
Roos, Tielman, 234-235
Rosmer, Alfred, 214, 222
Rowlans, W Bowen, 12
Ruskin, 82, 110, 224
Russia, 207ff (see also Russian Revolution), famine, 207-208, 213, New Economic Policy, 214, 217, need for industry, 217-218, Patriarch Tikhon and religion, 219-220, Russian revolution, 160-162, 163ff, Central Control Commission, 241-243
Russian revolutionaries (1905), 65-66

St David's University College, 24, 29
Salem chapel, 20, 41
Sampson, HW, 122
Samuel, David, 18, 19-20, 42
Sandham, AA, 238
Schreiner, Olive, 128
Scotch Cattle, 16
Serge, Victor, 209, 213, 214, 243
Sharpe, Coverdale, 54, 100, Liberal church, 107-108, 111
Shaw, E, 237
Sheep shearing, 73
Shepstone, T, 98
Shiloh chapel, 19-20, 21
Sigamoney, BLE, 165, 171
Simons, Dan, ('Kaffir brethren'), 130
Slavery and capitalism, 248
Smuts, General J, 89, 90, 113, 120, 125-126, deportations, 125, war aims, 140, 1922 strike, 186, 226ff, 237-238, 249

Socialist, 137
Socialist Labour Party, 137-138, 156, 166
Sotho people, 91, language, 92
South Africa, compared to New Zealand, 96, economy of, 89-90, Ivon Jones attitude to, 94
South African economy, 90, 168, 219
South African Industrial Federation, 139, 211, 237
South African Labour Party, 45, 93, 101-102, 109, 113-114, 126, 199, 212, Ivon Jones joins, 98, 110-112, call for complete segregation, 98, 100, 102, 126, 142, intervention of horse-racing fraternity, 107-108, expectations of electoral success, 113, 1914 srike, 123-124, first world war, 138ff, resignation of anti-warites, 145-146, 148, win parliamentary by-election, 167, pact government, 240, South African legislative assembly, Flag and language question, 90, budget and defence force, 90, declares war on Germany, 139
South African Manufacturers' Association, 89
South African National Party, 89, 139, 140, 203 = 204, 234-36, pact government, 240
South African National Union, 170
South African Native National Congress, P ka I Seme announces its foundation, 98, Ivon Jones response to formation, 98, at ISL meetings, 158, 161, article on African labour conditions, 169, Bunting's criticisms of SANNC, 172, IWA leaflet well received, 173-174, solidarity with miners, 184,
South African Party, 112,
South African war aims, 140ff
South Wales Miners' Federation, 8
South West Africa, 140, 151
Soviets (Russia), 154, 178
'Soviets' in South Africa, 182, 187, 213
Spendiff, H, 237, 239
Staffordshire Regiment, 130
Star, 118, 186
Stephens, JD, 47, 52, 86, 191-192, 207-208
Strikes
1913, New Kleinfontein, 105, 115-116, 118, phthisis as cause of strike, 117, racist overtones, 118, fears of British financial papers, 118, spread of strike, 119, troops break up meetings, 119, riots and arson in Johannesburg and Benoni, 110, shooting by Dragoons, 119-120, Labuschagne shot, 120, looting of Indian shops, 120, Smuts and Botha agree terms, 120, Smuts prepares for next strike, 120, miners kept under control, 121, Ivon Jones sums up, 121, black diamond field strikes, 128, black miners strike, 129-130, Malay tailors join strike, 157, Brockway on strike, 135-136
1914, 121ff, 204, Creswell's appeal, 122, Letter to the Colonial Office, 122ff, Repressive measures, 122-24, deportations, 124, army's provocation, 125, strike defeated, 122, 125,